The Postmodern God

BLACKWELL
READINGS IN
MODERN THEOLOGY

General Editors: L. Gregory Jones and James J. Buckley
Duke University, North Carolina; Loyola College, Maryland

Blackwell Readings in Modern Theology is a series of constructive anthologies on important topics in modern theology. Each volume brings together both classic and newly commissioned essays on a particular theme. These essays will provide students and teachers in colleges, universities, and seminaries with a critical entry to key debates.

Published works

The Theological Interpretation of Scripture
Classic and Contemporary Readings
Edited by Stephen E. Fowl

The Postmodern God
A Theological Reader
Edited by Graham Ward

Inquiring After God
Classic and Contemporary Readings
Edited by Ellen T. Charry

Theology After Liberalism
A Reader
Edited by John Webster and George Schner

Theology and Sexuality
Classic and Contemporary Readings
Edited by Eugene F. Rogers, Jr.

The Postmodern God

A Theological Reader

Edited by
Graham Ward

Blackwell
Publishing

BLACKWELL PUBLISHING
350 Main Street, Malden, MA 02148-5020, USA
108 Cowley Road, Oxford OX4 1JF, UK
550 Swanston Street, Carlton, Victoria 3053, Australia

First published 1997
First published in the USA 1998
Reprinted 1998, 2000, 2001, 2002, 2004, 2005

Library of Congress Cataloging-in-Publication Data

The Postmodern God: a theological reader / edited by Graham Ward.
    p. cm.— (Blackwell readings in modern theology)
Includes bibliographical references and index.
ISBN 0–631–20140–8 (hbk : alk. paper). — ISBN 0–631–20141–6
(pbk : alk.paper)
    1. Religion—Philosophy. 2. Postmodernsim—Religious aspects.
3. God. I. Ward, Graham. II. Series.
BD573.P67   1997
210—dc21   97–8620
                                                CIP

A catalogue record for this title is available from the British Library.

Set in 10½ on 12 pt Ehrhardt
by Ace Filmsetting Ltd, Frome, Somerset

The publisher's policy is to use permanent paper from mills that operate a sustainable forestry policy, and which has been manufactured from pulp processed using acid-free and elementary chlorine-free practices. Furthermore, the publisher ensures that the text paper and cover board used have met acceptable environmental accreditation standards.

For further information on
Blackwell Publishing, visit our website:
www.blackwellpublishing.com

This book is dedicated to the memory of
Michael Jackson, Priest, 1925–1995
"Serve the Lord with gladness"

Contents

Contents ───

Part II Selected Essays

Notes on Contributors

Pamela Sue Anderson
Senior Lecturer in Philosophy at the University of Sunderland. She is the author of *Ricoeur and Kant: Philosophy of the Will* (Atlanta, GA: Scholars Press, 1993) and A *Feminist Philosophy of Religion: The Rationality and Myths of Religious Belief* (Blackwell, 1997).

Frederick Christian Bauerschmidt
Assistant Professor at Loyola University, Baltimore, where he teaches theology. His essays have appeared in several journals including *Modern Theology* and *New Blackfriars*.

Rebecca S. Chopp
Professor in Theology and Dean of Faculty and Academic Affairs at the Chandler School of Theology, Emory University, Atlanta, Georgia. Her books include *The Praxis of Suffering: An Interpretation of Liberation and Political Theologies* (New York: Crossroad Publishing, 1986), *The Power to Speak: Feminism, Language, and God* (Crossroad, 1989), and *Saving Work: Feminist Practices of Theological Education* (Louisville, KY: Westminster John Knox Press, 1995).

Valentine Cunningham
Professor of English Literature at Oxford University and a Fellow of Corpus Christi College. His books include *British Writers in the Thirties* (Oxford University Press, 1989) and, more recently, *In the Reading Gaol: Postmodernity, Text, and History* (Blackwell, 1994).

Susan J. Dunlap
Assistant Professor of Pastoral Theology at Duke Divinity School, Durham, North Carolina. She has written about pastoral care and the counseling of depressed women, using Foucault's analysis of power. She is a minister in the Presbyterian Church.

Mary McClintock Fulkerson
Teaches contemporary philosophy at Duke Divinity School. In her recent book, *Changing the Subject: Women's Discourses and Feminist Theology* (Minneapolis: Fortress Press, 1994), she uses Foucault's account of bio-power to temper the dominant feminist mode of gender, power, and language.

Robert Gibbs
Teaches philosophy at the University of Toronto. He is the author of *Correlations in Rosenzweig and Levinas* (Princeton University Press, 1992) and various essays on Jewish philosophy and contemporary Continental philosophy. He is currently finishing a book entitled *Why Ethics? Signs of Responsibilities.*

Kevin Hart
Professor of Modern Languages at Monash University, Clayton, Victoria. He writes poetry and translates as well as being interested in theology. His book on Derrida and negative theology, *The Trespass of the Sign: Deconstruction, Theology and Philosophy*, was published by Cambridge University Press in 1989.

Craig James
A doctoral student at the University of Cambridge, where he is working on the concept of sovereignty in Sade, Nietzsche, and Bataille. He is a contributor to the journal *Modern Believing*.

Grace M. Jantzen
John Rylands Professor at the University of Manchester. She has published many books including *Julian of Norwich* (SPCK, 1984) and *God's World, God's Body* (SPCK, 1984). Her most recent book is *Power, Gender, and Christian Mysticism* (Cambridge University Press, 1995).

Cleo McNelly Kearns
Teaches at Rutgers University, New Jersey, and the New Brunswick Theological Seminary. She is the author of *T.S. Eliot and Indic Traditions: A Study of Poetry and Belief* (Cambridge University Press, 1987) and edits the Cultural Criticism series for the American Academy of Religion.

Jean-Yves Lacoste
To date, none of his work has been translated into English, other than the excerpt from his book *Expérience et Absolu* (Paris: Presses Universitaires de

France, 1994) which is included here. His first book, *Notes sur le temps*, was issued by the same publisher in 1990.

Gerard Loughlin
Teaches Christian theology, ethics, and philosophy of religion at the University of Newcastle upon Tyne. Besides contributing to a number of leading journals, including *New Blackfriars* and *Modern Theology*, he has recently published his first book, *Telling God's Story: Bible, Church, and Narrative Theology* (Cambridge University Press, 1995).

Jean-Luc Marion
Professor and Director of the Department of Philosophy at the University of Paris X Nanterre. As yet, only one of his books has been translated: *God Without Being*, translated by Thomas A. Carlson (University of Chicago Press, 1991). There are plans for the Northwestern University Press to publish a translation of his *Réduction et donation: Recherches sur Husserl, Heidegger et la phénoménologie* (Paris: Presses Universitaires de France, 1989). Other significant work of his has been translated into Spanish and Italian. For an introduction to his work in English see "Jean-Luc Marion's *God Without Being*," *New Blackfriars*, 76 (July/August, 1995).

John Milbank
Reader in the Faculty of Divinity, Cambridge University, and a Fellow of Peterhouse. He is also one of the editors of *Modern Theology*. His books include *Theology and Social Theory: Beyond Secular Reason* (Blackwell, 1990) and *The Word Made Strange: Theology, Language, Culture* (Blackwell, 1996).

Catherine Pickstock
Research Fellow of Emmanuel College, Cambridge, where she teaches theology and philosophy. She has published articles in *Modern Theology*, *Theology*, and *Literature and Theology*, and her book *After Writing: Language, Death, and Liturgy* is published by Blackwell (1997).

Gillian Rose
At the time of her death in 1995, Professor of Social and Political Thought in the Department of Sociology at the University of Warwick. Her books include *The Melancholy Science: An Introduction to the Thought of Theodor W. Adorno* (London: Macmillan, 1978), *Hegel Contra Sociology* (London: Athlone Press, 1981), *The Dialectic of Nihilism: Post-Structuralism and Law* (Blackwell, 1984), *Judaism and Modernity: Philosophical Essays* (Blackwell, 1993), *Love's Work* (London: Chatto and Windus, 1995), and *Mourning Becomes the Law* (Cambridge University Press, 1996).

Graham Ward
Dean of Peterhouse at Cambridge, where he teaches modern theology, literary

theory, and philosophy of religion. He is the author of two books, *Barth, Derrida and the Language of Theology* (Cambridge University Press, 1995) and *Theology and Contemporary Critical Theory* (London: Macmillan, 1996), and is also senior editor of the journal *Literature and Theology*.

Edith Wyschogrod
Professor of Philosophy at Queens College, City University of New York. Her books include *Spirit in Ashes: Hegel, Heidegger, and Man-made Mass Death* (Yale University Press, 1985) and *Saints and Postmodernism: Revisioning Moral Philosophy* (University of Chicago Press, 1990), and she edited *Lacan and Theological Discourse* (Albany: State University of New York, 1989).

Acknowledgments

There can never be an end to our debts. As human beings, we are always profoundly indebted; it is the mark of our dependency. Therefore I skim the surface here and omit (or even forget) a multitude. I am deeply grateful for the conversations I have had here at Cambridge with my fellow theologians – John Milbank, Catherine Pickstock, and Janet Soskice. I owe special thanks to my students, both undergraduate and postgraduate. Teaching clarifies, and the opportunity to teach English, philosophy, and theology to some of the finest contemporary minds has enriched my work immeasurably. Phillip Blond, Conor Cunningham, David Grosier, Laurence Hemmings, and Craig James have each left a watermark of their presence in my thinking. Throughout I have been loved, supported, consoled, and cajoled by my wife Mary, and the delight of Rachel and David. The book itself I have dedicated to Mary's father, Michael, who taught me lessons in courage and integrity I am still trying to learn.

I would also like to thank Rachel Lee and Sandra Raphael at Blackwell Publishers, whose experience and organizational skills have made the production of this book possible.

Graham Ward
Peterhouse
The Feast of St Peter 1997

The publishers are grateful to the following holders of copyrights for their permission to reprint the material included in this book:
Georges Bataille, *Theory of Religion*, trans. Robert Hurley (New York: Zone Books, 1989), pp. 43–61. Copyright © 1989 by Urzone Inc.

Jacques Lacan, "The Death of God," in *The Seminars of Jacques Lacan*. Book VII. *The Ethics of Psychoanalysis 1959–1960*, trans. Dennis Porter (New York: W. W. Norton and London: Routledge, 1992), pp. 167–78. Copyright © 1986 by Les Éditions du Seuil. English translation copyright © 1992 by W. W. Norton and Company Inc.

Roland Barthes, "Struggle with the Angel," in *IMAGES/MUSIC/TEXT*, trans, Stephen Heath (New York: Hill and Wang, and London: Fontana Press, 1977), pp. 125–41. Copyright © Roland Barthes; English translation copyright © Stephen Heath. Reprinted by permission of Hill and Wang, a division of Farrar, Straus and Giroux Inc. and HarperCollins Publishers Ltd.

René Girard, *Job: The Victim of his People*, trans. Yvonne Freccero (London: Athlone Press, 1987), pp. 154–68. Reprinted by permission of Athlone Press and Stanford University Press.

Michel Foucault, *The History of Sexuality*, vol. 1, trans. Robert Hurley (Harmondsworth: Penguin Books, 1979), pp. 57–73. Copyright © 1975 by Éditions Gallimard. English translation copyright © 1978 by Random House Inc. Reprinted by permission of Georges Borchardt Inc.

Michel de Certeau, "How is Christianity Thinkable Today?" *Theology Digest*, 19 (1971), pp. 334–45, and *Heterologies: Discourse on the Other*, trans. Brian Massumi (Minneapolis: University of Minnesota Press, 1986), pp. 80–100. Copyright © by University of Minnesota Press.

Jacques Derrida, "How to Avoid Speaking: Denials," trans. Ken Frieden in *Languages of the Unsayable*, ed. Sanford Budick and Wolfgang Iser (New York: Columbia University Press, 1989), pp. 39–62. Copyright © 1989 by Columbia University Press.

Luce Irigaray, "Equal to Whom?" trans. Robert L. Mazzola in *differences: A Journal of Feminist Cultural Studies*, 1/2 (1989), pp. 59–76. Copyright © 1989 by *differences*.

Julia Kristeva, *In the Beginning was Love*, trans. Arthur Goldhammer (New York: Columbia University Press, 1988), pp. 23–44. Copyright © 1988 by Columbia University Press.

Rebecca S. Chopp, "From Patriarchy into Freedom," from *Transfigurations*, ed. Susan M. Simonaitis, Susan M. St Ville, and C. W. Maggie Kim (Minneapolis: Augsburg Fortress, 1993), pp. 31–48. Copyright © 1993 by Augsburg Fortress.

Jean-Yves Lacoste, *Expérience et absolu* (Paris: Presses Universitaires de France, 1994), pp. 213–33. Translated by permission of the publisher.

Gillian Rose, "New Jerusalem, Old Athens," from Rose, *The Broken Middle* (Oxford: Blackwell Publishers, 1992). Reprinted by permission of the Gillian Rose Estate.

Edith Wyschogrod, *Saints and Postmodernism* (Chicago: University of Chicago Press, 1990), pp. 243–6 and 251–7. Reprinted by permission of the publisher.

Introduction, or, A Guide to Theological Thinking in Cyberspace

Graham Ward

Surfing the net is the ultimate postmodern experience. Facing your SGVA display – low radiation/anti-static – poised over the multimedia controls, you launch into new forms of spatiality created by flows of electronic information. In Disneyland colours you download texts, pictures, video clips, voices from anywhere in the world, regardless of time zones. Electric libraries in São Paolo, chat-lines in Florida, info sites in Sydney, data banks in Vancouver, on-line shopping in Paris, audiovisual tours with 3-D graphics of the Vatican, the White House, the Kremlin, the Taj Mahal – are all available at your fingertips, twenty-four hours a day. Time and space as conceived by empiricists collapse into omnipresence and multilocality. And the ride is continuous, for the electronic tide maintains you on the crest of impending satisfaction, far above any ocean floor, fast forwarding toward endless pleasures yet to be located and book-marked. Time disappears, boredom is deflated. The drug of the ever new, instant access to a vast sea of endless desire which circulates globally; browsing through hours without commitment on any theme imaginable; dwelling voyeuristically in one location until the pull of other possibilities reasserts the essentially nomadic lifestyle of the net-surfer: these are the characteristic experiences of living in cyberspace. Cyberspace is an undefined spatiality, like the contours of a perfume, and you are an adventurer, a navigator in uncharted waters, discovering the hero inside yourself. You act anonymously, simply as the unnamed, unidentifiable viewpoint of so many interactive network games, and where an identity is needed, you can construct one. Reality is soft, malleable, permeable, and available only through the constant discharge of electronic energy signaling across the cosmos. Discourse is energized, sexualized. It issues from nowhere and sheers off toward a thousand synthetic horizons, all presented like so many Hollywood sunsets and sunrises. In this land of fantasy and ceaseless journeying, this experience of tasting, sampling, and passing on, truth, knowledge, and facts are all only dots of light on a screen, evanescent, consumable. This is the ultimate in the secularization of the divine, for here is a God who sees and knows all things, existing in pure activity and realized presence, in perpetuity. Divinization as the dissolution of subjectivity within the immanent, amniotic satisfaction, is the final goal and object of postmodernity. Cyberspace is the realization of a metaphor used repeatedly by Derrida, Irigaray, and Kristeva – the Khora, the plenitudinous womb, dark, motile, and unformed, from which all things issue.

But this God is only available, and this religion can only be accessed, by those with sufficient financial backing. The postmodern condition is indissolubly associated with "a shift in the way in which capitalism is working these days."[1] David Harvey, whose book *The Postmodern Condition* considerably deepens and renders more subtle the thesis linking postmodernism to late capitalism propounded by Fredric Jameson,[2] points out how the culture of postmodernism both reflects and promotes the shift to advanced market-driven economies, economies defined by "deregulation" and "diversification." The book argues that the move from modernism to postmodernism is implicated in the socio-economic shift from a capitalist logic based upon Fordist production and Keynesian state regulation to a capitalist logic based upon "flexible accumulation." Harvey emphasizes – in a way that might restrain those who proclaim postmodernism itself is *passé* – that this historical transition is still far from complete. Cyberspace will deepen. Information technologies and telecommunication will expand and become ever more complex. And cyberspace is yours only at a price; for cyberspace is constituted by countless stall-holders purveying their wares to those who have international credit-card facilities and telephone links. Information costs. The costs begin with purchasing the computer and its software, and they accumulate as time itself is bought from an internet server who mediates access. (The names of the various servers in themselves tell a story – Magellan, Excite, Lykos [from the Greek for greedy, rapacious?].) The costs are extended by every purchase made, club joined, and PIN number obtained. Capitalism, advanced technology, the acquisition of goods, and the meltdown of the real all coincide with the developments of cyberspace. And not having access to this announces poverty, intellectual and material. Having access is like possessing a porthole in an old Spanish galleon which gazes out beyond the maps at those *terrae incognitae*, those worlds beyond the lip of the Western European horizon which awaited discovery, brave hearts, and annexation, at the birth of the modern in the fourteenth and fifteenth centuries.[3] But in cyberspace the journeying is imaginary. In cyberspace nothing is produced, though everything is marketed. Cyberspace *is* now the marketplace, though its reality is virtual, for such is the nature of the real.

The thesis proposed here, on the basis of an analysis of cyberspace as a cultural metaphor for postmodernism, is that modernism is linked to specific conceptions of time, space, and substance, and that postmodernism explodes the myths and ideologies constructing these conceptions. Fredric Jameson, examining the new spatial experience of postmodernism – the illusion of depth, the drive for immediate, theatrical impact so that the spatial order dominates the temporal – coined the word "hyperspace." In 1984 he wrote that "We do not yet possess the perceptual equipment to match this new kind of hyperspace, in part because our perceptual habits were formed in that older kind of space I have called the space of high modernism."[4] In 1991 he modified his estimation of what we "do not yet have" – cyberspace is developing rapidly, and the I who perceives high modern spaces is disappearing into it. He notes that hyperspace "has finally succeeded in transcending the capacities of the individual human body to locate itself, to organize its immediate surroundings perceptually, and cognitively to map its position in a mappable external world."[5] If we wish to apprehend the postmodern God, we have, then, to investigate the project of modernity with reference to the shapes it gave to time, space, and bodies. For these shapes portrayed the face of modernity's god – the god whom Nietzsche (following a suggestion by Hegel) pronounced dead.

Of Time, Space, and Bodies

There are ideologies of space and time and the nature of the entities which construct or fill them. In fact, there are only ideologies of these things, for our experience of spatiality, temporality, and corporeality is caught up with conceptual notions which prescribe an understanding, a nature, to space, time, and bodies. Look at the relationship of people to buildings and the rather wayward depiction of exteriors in early mediaeval art – on the Bayeux Tapestry, for example, or even later, in the fifteenth century, with the paintings of Apollonio di Giovanni. Compare these with the sixteenth-century paintings of Paolo Veronese and Jacopo Tintoretto, who were partly inspired by the unprecedented development in civic architecture which took place in Venice throughout the Renaissance.[6] It is not simply that perspective has been discovered and now true proportionality can be executed. Changes in the understanding of time, space, and the orders of creation have taken place. A language is needed to speak about and represent relations and practices within the space–time continuum, but these discourses are historically and socially embedded. It was only late in the mediaeval period that "space" denoted linear distance between two or more points or objects. The championing of Euclid only began with figures like Robert Grosseteste in the thirteenth century. It was Dr John Dee who gave the first ever lectures on Euclid's *Elements* to a crowded lecture hall in Paris on July 20, 1550. The date is enshrined because of the sensation the lectures caused. It is with a foundational discussion of Euclidean geometry that Descartes begins his *Discourse on Method* and, as Stephen Toulmin has recently observed, the natural philosophy which sought new epistemological foundations for a re-envisaging of the cosmos in the seventeenth century had to be rebuilt upon these geometrical analyses.[7] Furthermore, it was only in the seventeenth century that space came to denote a continuous, unbounded extension, void of matter – following the work of Copernicus, Kepler, and Galileo. A shift is evident from the high Middle Ages to the Enlightenment in which space, once seen as symbolically designed and allegorically interpreted, becomes that which is mathematically determined, empirically perceived and calibrated. The shift is perhaps best made plain in the way the two foremost commentators on Euclid at this time – John Dee and René Descartes – are viewed. Dee died in 1608, when Descartes was already twelve years old, but Dee is known as an Elizabethan magus, an alchemist, a magician,[8] while Descartes – whose work profoundly influenced Newton – is understood to be one of the fathers of modern scientific method.

Time too did not stand still; nor did its meaning. The time of candles, sand-glasses, and water-clocks may not have changed very much, but time's availability and precise calibration did change with the discovery of the spring (which made pocket watches possible from around 1500) and the regularity of the pendulum's swing (which made pendulum clocks the most precise form of time-keeping in the mid-seventeenth century). Calendarial, liturgical, theological, and existential time changed the most, and likewise, so did the relationships between these various modes of time. By liturgical time I mean the annual Church cycle from Christmas to Advent; by theological time I mean the position of the present as it is viewed in relation to the eschatological coming of the future kingdom and the inauguration of salvation in Christ at the incarnation; by existential time I mean the experience of the times and temporality within which any human being exists. Time began to fragment from the Reformation on. Hamlet's apocalyptic cry, "The time is out of joint," was felt by many.

Calendar time changed, and not uniformly over this period. In March 1582 Pope Gregory XIII decreed a new calendar and to facilitate its operation suppressed the days October 6 to October 14 that year. This time had no existence. Spain, Portugal, and parts of Italy followed suit immediately. France adopted the new calendar from December that year. But the Catholic states of Germany still employed the ancient Julian calendar until late in the following year. It was not until 1700 that the Protestant states of Germany agreed to Gregorian dating, and in that year Denmark and Sweden also fell in line.

England maintained its own use of the ancient calendar until 1750. This meant that for the first time in many centuries the celebration of Church festivals did not unite all Europe. The spatial fragmentation into nation-states had its temporal forms, but worse was to happen concerning the liturgical calendar in this period.

The Reformation and the spread of Protestantism unpicked the ecclesial weave of the annual cycle. Before the Protestant break, time bore a sacred inscription through the liturgical round from Christmas to Advent. A round of feasts and festivals regulated the working lives of all people. But with the turn to Reformed religion certain devotions and practices were perceived as superstitious (a powerful, desacralizing word at this time) and financially unprofitable (there were holidays in August and September, when the harvests were being gathered). As the Cambridge historian Eamon Duffy has recently pointed out about the Acts passed regulating the involvement in the liturgical year in England, "the Crown decimated the ritual year, not only wiping out a multitude of local festivals, but removing many major landmarks from the Sarum calendar."[9] The secularization of time, its precise measurement and financial value developed throughout the sixteenth century. This is reflected in the writing of history. For Francis Bacon writing the *History of Henry VII* in 1621, events were to be traced back to causes – "the characters of the several regions and people, their natural dispositions etc."[10] By the early seventeenth century, history as founded upon and understood in relation to Scripture was collapsing under the strain of discoveries in natural history. "[T]he expanding time-scale of geology and zoology [gave] historians a new freedom to manoeuvre and speculate," Stephen Toulmin writes.[11] Time no longer had a beginning, purpose, and conclusion. Time now was also divorced from space, as scientists in the tracks of Descartes sought for eternal truths. Only with Einstein was time returned to space, and then it became an aspect of space, a fourth dimension – with important theological consequences.[12]

Shifts in the understanding of space and time effect shifts, as they are affected by shifts, in the understanding of bodies, matter, or substance. For the mediaeval and Renaissance alchemists bodies were permeable; nothing existed in and for itself; its existence and meaning issued from its contextual position within the chain of being. Sir Philip Sidney, Elizabethan poet and courtier, called his famous sonnet sequence *Astrophel and Stella* because the flower the astrophel, being star-like in form, was thought to draw something of its beauty and power from the celestial stars themselves. *Stella* is Latin for star and became the pseudonym of his beloved for he, as Astrophel, drew the powers to live and love from being correlated with her. Allegory did not arise as a process of interpretation; it arose out of a doctrine of creation. All was gifted and given; corporeality had to be understood theologically. God is not only the creator and external to creation, God is the sustainer and maintainer of creation, operating through the incarnate Spirit of His Son (the Logos who spoke the worlds into being) within the created orders. The physical body of any person was mapped onto the social body and the social body was part of the ecclesial body fed by the sacramental body of Christ – and this comprised the *corpus mysticum*. The use of "body" in each of these several contexts was not deemed a metaphorical extension of the literal, that is, of the physical body. The separation of literal from metaphorical according to an either/or logic came much later and can be discerned in the debate concerning the eucharist as it engaged the Catholics, Luther, Zwingli, and Calvin. For Aquinas the historical sense could not be divorced from the allegorical and spiritual senses. The human body, because created immediately by God (rather than instrumentally through angels or natural processes) bore spiritual properties or potential.[13] And though heavenly bodies were distinct from earthly bodies, all was made from nothing by God, and analogies made possible some knowledge of the impassible and formless.[14] But a shift is effected in which bodies come to be understood as discrete entities, objects for a possessive perception.[15] Galileo bears witness to the shift when he writes: "I think that in discussing natural problems we should not begin from the authority of scriptural passages, but from sensory experiences and necessary demonstrations."[16] The created order takes on an autonomy, governed by mathematical configurations and geometrical relations. It becomes a timeless construct, a machine to be interpreted according to the laws of mechanics. The world is not gifted and given, but an accumulation of entities owned or waiting to be owned, property to be arranged, labelled, evaluated (according to the market and demand) and exchanged. The emergence of science is concomitant with the emergence of capitalism. Increasingly through-out the seventeenth century, this autonomy of the world (and the autonomy of human observation and reasoning which creates and reflects it) had no need of spiritual properties; it was a self-sustaining, self-defining, immanent system. The secular was divorced from the sacred. Only as such could the world become an object of human knowledge – rather than a God–given mystery to be lived in and respected – subject to investigations into the causal nexus of laws which determined and maintained its existence.[17] If Galileo and Descartes clung firmly, if somewhat schizophrenically, to their Catholic allegiances, the road to atheism (atheism as concomitant with the logic of secularism) was being paved and some, like Spinoza, were not afraid of proceeding along it.[18]

The reorganization of spatiality, temporality, and corporeality in early modernity is paralleled by a shift with respect to the relationship in language between rhetoric and logic. For Aristotle the logic of one's argument was inseparable from the argument's power to persuade and the discipline shown by the writer or speaker with regard to the appropriateness of style to content. In early modernity the weave of logic and rhetoric starts to come apart. Where, for Aquinas, the spiritual and the literal interpretation of scriptural language were coextensive, Luther and Calvin express a concern to locate meaning in the literal sense of the words, eschewing the allegorical and metaphorical. Nevertheless, throughout the sixteenth century Wisdom was inseparable from Eloquence – hence Luther's own highly rhetorical style and Sir Philip Sidney's Protestant defence of poetic imitation in *An Apology for Poetry* (composed in the 1580s). But with the increased attention to literal meaning (and the blurring of any distinction between the literal and the historical) there grew up a perception that texts contained meaning, meaning that could be extracted, separated, and made independent of its context. The concern with the expunging of rhetoric (or the policing of the rhetorical so that "rhetoric" comes to be synonymous with "ornamentation" and therefore unnecessary, even indulgent) so that clear, lucid ideas can become self-evident, begins here. In his book *Essay Towards a Real Character*, Bishop John Wilkins insists that "names as such express their natures" and therefore we need to rid ourselves of obscurities which occur through the employment of metaphors, synonyms, and phrasal verbs, for "like other affected ornaments, they prejudice the natural simplicity . . . and contribute to the disguising of it with false appearance."[19] This is a moral task. In fact, Wilkins believed by expunging language of such "affected phrases" religious tolerance would become possible, since many differences in religion, he felt, were the result of wild errors disguised through rhetoric. The end result is a form of discourse in which the objectivity sought by scientific research into Nature can be constructed: the prescriptions on style set out by Thomas Spratt at the inception of the Royal Society; the attempt by Bishop Wilkins to create a language in which names referred directly and clearly to the objects being named; the speculations throughout the seventeenth century on the nature of the *Ursprache*, the primal language. The fetishization of the literal, the unacknowledged presupposition that language refers to things that are pre-linguistic, that words correspond to objects, that discourse is concerned primarily with reference, with responding to and describing the objective nature of the world outside its system – this ideology of language has constructed, borne, and affirmed the project of modernity.

The reorganization of spatiality, temporality, corporeality, and language reflects a change in social relations and the practices which inscribe them: the secularization of those relations in which religious associations were expunged from the public realm (where they had been the source of far too much contention and internecine warfare). The privatization of the religious led to the erasure of God-talk from the public arena – privately one could believe what one wished, but these beliefs had no "street value." Secular ethics and politics flourished in the wake of a flagrant humanism.

I wish to argue that with postmodernism God emerges from the white-out nihilism of modern atheism and from behind the patriarchal masks imposed by modernity's secular theology. The emergence of the postmodern has fostered post-secular thinking – thinking about other, alternative worlds. In the postmodern cultural climate, the theological voice can once more be heard. It has been noted that "something vital has happened to our experience of space and time since the 1970s so as to provoke the turn to postmodernism."[20] I have described the nature of that experience in terms of the development of cyberspace – a spatiality which is only virtually real and within which time and materiality (as conceived by the project of modernity) disappear. In such a reorganization of space, time, and bodies, theology can engage with postmodern debates. It is significant, then, that the work of several of the philosophers represented in Part I of this *Reader* draws upon concepts, metaphors, and texts culled from before the onset of modernity. Levinas clearly proceeds with reference to the God of the Jews and the Torah, Barthes's Protestant sensibilities are made manifest in Valentine Cunningham's introduction, Foucault recalls the liturgical practice of confession in the Middle Ages, Girard investigates the Old and New Testaments, Derrida is interested in the writings of Meister Eckhart, Irigaray defines her own project in terms of incarnation, and Kristeva returns to John's Gospel and the Christian economy of salvation in the move from the Cross to the Resurrection. Several of the essays in Part II reveal theology both responding to the new cultural conditions and revisiting premodern theological figures in their own reaction against the secular modes of space, time, and bodies, ushered in and fostered by the project of modernity. John Milbank returns to Augustine, Jean-Yves Lacoste draws inspiration from the writings of Francis of Assisi and Aquinas, Jean-Luc Marion also looks to the work of Aquinas, along with the mystical theology of Pseudo-Dionysius and the work of the Cappadocian Fathers. Several of the writers in this section root themselves in a long and complex historical tradition – Lacoste and Marion in the ecclesial traditions of the Catholic Church, Milbank and Pickstock with the ecclesial traditions of the Anglican Church, Gillian Rose within the traditions of Jewish philosophy. Their thinking does not take place outside time and space in an objectivity, a vacuum, a view from nowhere created by modernity to replace God's omnipresence and omniscience. Their work does not aspire to the decontextualization of modernity's project; it takes its standpoint and the historical embeddedness of that standpoint seriously. And yet, postmodernism is not antimodernism – as we shall see.

The Anthropological Turn

Various dates or landmark events have been suggested for the inception of both the modern and the postmodern. The modern has been dated from 1436 and the establishment of the Gutenberg press, 1520 and Luther's split from the

Roman Catholic Church, 1648 and the end of the Thirty Years' War, among others. Stephen Toulmin has suggested a complex interweave in which modernity issues from the humanism of the sixteenth century and the development of science in the seventeenth.[21] Similarly, for postmodernity, dates have ranged from the late 1930s when Arnold Toynbee first coined the term, the publication of Robert Venturi's architectural manifesto in 1966, the student riots in Paris of May 1968, to July 15, 1972, when a Le Corbusier-inspired housing development in St Louis was demolished on the grounds that it was uninhabitable. All of these dates relate to cultural expressions independent of a theological conception of the created orders. I wish to suggest, in accordance with the shifts in the conceptions of time, space, matter, and language sketched above, a different genealogy and location for the modern and the postmodern. This genealogy and positioning will be crucial to an appreciation of what I understand by the emergence of the postmodern God, that is, the current postmodern climate within which theological discourse is once more culturally significant.

The shift toward the autonomy of human reasoning, the basis of secularism, came much earlier than humanism. The anthropological turn, so famously summed up in Pico della Mirandola's encomium on the condition of man (*De hominis dignitate*, composed in the 1480s), was founded upon philosophical trends already circulating in the thirteenth century. Pico della Mirandola was himself considerably influenced by the work of the Islamic philosopher Averroës,[22] whose work had its first major impact upon Western culture among the Parisian scholars from about 1250. By 1270 Averroism was being condemned by clerical authorities and refuted by Aquinas. But, as the Swiss theologian Hans Urs von Balthasar has noted, the origins of the modern period lie hereabouts, with the early struggles between secular philosophers and Christian theologians, and the birth of Neoscholasticism:

> What is characteristic here is that in Neoscholasticism, when the feeling for the glory of God was lost – that glory which pervades the Revelation as a whole but which is not perceived by conceptual rationalism . . . – there perished also the sensorium for the glory of Creation (as "aesthetics") which shone through the whole theology of the Fathers and/or the Early and High Middle Ages . . . For Suarez, as for Scotus, the word "real" denotes that which is compossible, realisable . . . because the essence of the "real" within comprehensive Being has already been thoroughly individualised . . . It is a short step from here to Descartes and Kant . . . viz., the turning from Being to mental concepts, from things (and God) existing *in themselves* to things existing "for me" and "from me" . . . This *res extensa* is the pure quantitative element, the unlimited empire of numbers, and it is here that the metaphysical origins lie for the ideal of mastering the whole of the external world through numerical calculation.[23]

With Averroës (or, rather, the mediaeval Christianization of Averroism)[24] Being is equated with reason and hence the world is comprehensible in its own right (a right given to it by the minds of men). The dignity of the human – humanism, widely conceived – begins to swell: "there was a rising emphasis on sovereign man – on man the maker, inventor, rule, sage, and beautiful being."[25] Man becomes interpreter, measurer of his world – a world streched out around him, like Keats's Cortez standing on a peak in Darien with the Atlantic on one side and the Pacific on the other, buoyed up by the adulation of his fellow conquistadors. Metaphysics as the rational science of Being, in which being is composed of individual bodies existing in ontological relationship with each other, was given exemplary and influential expression by the Spanish Jesuit Francisco Suarez in his *Disputationes metaphysicae* (1597). It was this work on the analogy of being, the great Chain of Being – in which God is conceived as the most real, the cause, end, and summation of Being – which gave rise to the struggles of Descartes, the monadology of Leibniz, and the cosmology of Wolff.[26] Metaphysics, as such, makes possible the projects of modernity founded upon the autonomy of human reason. Here lies the origins of the onto-theology which Martin Heidegger, in the twentieth century, will see as receiving its final formulation in the work of Hegel: the onto-theology, the metaphysics, which Heidegger sought to overthrow. With the overthrow of such metaphysics – which is also the overthrow of secularity – the project of postmodernism, I wish to argue, is announced.

It is time now to introduce and develop what is understood by the two nouns "postmodernism" and "postmodernity." I take the first to denote a critical stance to modernism, though not necessarily an iconoclastic stance (which is the way the American architect and art historian Charles Jencks describes it when he views the destruction of the Le Corbusier-inspired building in St Louis as the symbolic end of modernism and the symbolic beginning of postmodernism).[27] I take the second to name a description of certain cultural conditions pertaining to developed countries in the 1970s and 1980s. The first, then, names a philosophical position, the second a period concept. This is important for the argument which follows, not least because in describing "postmodern" as a philosophical concept I am defining its application with reference to certain forms of philosophizing. This stands not in opposition to, but in some tension with, the way "postmodern" is more frequently employed as an aesthetic concept with reference to architecture, painting, literature, and film.[28] As such it names certain forms of what Jean-François Lyotard has termed trans-avantgardism – movements beyond the modernism of the Bauhaus or Malevich, with their aspirations toward purity and presence in favour of *bricolage*, irony, pastiche of aesthetic depth, *kitsch*. I would allow that the two applications of "postmodern" (philosophical and aesthetic) and the sociological notion of postmodernity do become interchangeable at the point where the postmodern critical position *vis-à-vis the* project of modernity comes to dominate and eclipse the cultural conditions within which modernity lived and breathed. To clarify further: there were major philosophical critiques of the anthropological turn, the scientism of knowledge, and the Enlightenment rationalism that arose within the project of modernity and did not shake its foundations. The corpuscularianism of the Irish theologian George Berkeley, the language mysticism of the eighteenth-century German thinker Johann George Hamann, the skepticism of David Hume, the critiques of Hegel by Schelling and Kierkegaard, the nihilistic rhetoric of Nietzsche are all such examples. These voices, nevertheless, were dominated by what Jean-François Lyotard has called the "grand narratives" of the eighteenth and nineteenth centuries, "such as the dialectics of Spirit, the hermeneutics of meaning, the emancipation of the rational or working subject, or the creation of wealth."[29] When Lyotard goes on to define "postmodern" as "incredulity towards metanarratives,"[30] then postmodern as such would characterize the thinking of the philosophical critiques I have listed, which worked within and upon the modern. This is not to give equal emphasis to each of these critiques – some (like Kierkegaard's and Nietzsche's) were more radical than others. But when the incredulity toward metanarratives becomes a pervasive cultural skepticism, when the worldview of modernity no longer becomes believable, then the postmodern characterizes a sociohistorical and economic period which we can call "postmodernity." I emphasize this because I understand postmodernism as always with us, whereas there are indications which suggest "postmodernity" as a particular cultural emphasis is over.

This is to say nothing more and nothing less than what Lyotard himself has gone on to say concerning postmodernism, although he uses "postmodernity" to name the event of the postmodern. But for him the postmodern is a site for the questioning and rethinking of the modern, it "is not a new age, it is the rewriting of some features modernity had tried or pretended to gain . . . But such a rewriting, as has already been said, was for a long time active within modernity itself."[31] Elsewhere, he makes the point that to see the modern being superseded by the postmodern would itself be a modern conception, allied as the modern is to notions of linear development and the new. "[T]he 'post' of 'postmodern' does not signify a movement of *comeback, flashback,* or *feedback* – that is, not a movement of repetition but a procedure in 'ana-': a procedure of analysis, anamnesis, anagogy, and anamorphosis that elaborates an 'initial forgetting'."[32] In Greek, the prefix *ana-* has the sense of "going beyond" or "an upwards movement," as well as "going back" or "repetition." If Lyotard explicitly counters the suggestion that postmodernism is concerned with repetition, he relates the "post" (which means "after" or "futural") to a going beyond the modern in a way which is also a return to what was forgotten in the establishment of the modern. Hence he can also speak of the postmodern as the condition of possibility for the modern. The postmodern is both future and past, or, as he puts it: "to be understood according to the paradox of the future (*post*) anterior (*modo*)."[33] In this sense, the postmodern, rather like Freudian psychoanalysis, is concerned with the repressed other scene – what is forgotten so that modernity can forge its own origins. The project of modernity was obsessed with determining origins – of the world, of time, of knowledge, of the human animal, of language. It was obsessed with grounding, finding grounds for, with legitimation and endorsing various modes of legislation. Postmodernism is, then, a movement at the end of such grounding, following the fall of the legislators.[34] This returns us to our inability to ground, our inability to determine origins. Postmodernism reminds us we are already too determined ourselves; we can never exhaustively account for the conditions which make the world, time, knowledge, the human animal, language, possible. At the origin we find we have always already begun, we already inhabit a difference. As Irigaray puts it, playing with the singular and the plural, "On the first day, the first days, the gods, God, make a world by separating the elements."[35] In the beginning there is always a doubling, at least, because the origin issues from difference. Postmodernism, as a philosophical concept, has concerned itself with the forgetting of that doubling, the forgetting of difference.

Thinking Through Difference

I have suggested so far two tasks that postmodern philosophical thinking undertakes. First is the overcoming of metaphysics as conceived in modernity as the correlation of Being and reasoning (the thinking through and therefore intelligibility of all that is). Second is the thinking of difference – that which is repressed in order that the modern might be constituted as the new, the novel. Postmodernism reminds modernity of its own constructed nature; the arbitrariness and instability of its constructions. I have also suggested the close relation between the projects of modernity and secularism, or ideologies of immanence. The word "secular" comes from the Christian Latin word for the world, *secularis*. Unlike the older Latin word *mundus*, *secularis* denotes the world as opposed to the Church, the world regulated according to its own internal logics. Where these two tasks of overcoming metaphysics and re-examining difference come together is in the work of Martin Heidegger. But Heidegger (who deeply challenges the historicism of the nineteenth century, which thought in terms of evolution and progress) is aware he builds already upon a tradition. He announces a line of thinking only available to be thought after Hegel and after Nietzsche. Moreover, it is with these two earlier figures that he suggests the philosophical problem of difference first asserts itself.

Put briefly, the philosophy of difference examines the problem of the other – both the other person (in French *autrui*) and the other in general (in French *autre*). It raises, once more, the question of transcendence. Within the immanent logic of modernity's secular worldview, difference announces itself clearly when Kant, in developing his account of transcendental reasoning, draws a distinction between two realms, the noumenal and the phenomenal. The phenomenal realm is the realm in which intuitions, worked upon as they are by the twelve categories of the understanding, are transformed into concepts, pictures of what the world and our experience of it is, and then into ideas regulated by the transcendental ideals of pure reason: God, freedom, and immortality. The noumenal is the realm about which we cannot know anything. It is the exterior in which things are in themselves. We can know nothing of this realm because it lies outside the operation of the transcendental reasoning. The noumenal cannot become the object of our experience and yet things as they are provide the condition for any experience at all.

Kant's division between the noumenal and phenomenal is not dualistic – there are things out there and their being out there makes possible any thinking of which I am capable. Nevertheless, these categories produce antinomies, tensions, paradoxes. With Hegel they are translated into the realms of the subject and the object, but the realms are now even less distinct. The structure of the subjective consciousness – which is both *in itself* and *for itself* – internalizes the difference which is engaged in a continual dialectic. The subjective *Geist* ("spirit" or "mind") appropriates, through negation, the objective *Geist* in a movement toward the absolute realization of *Geist* in which the two positions become integrated. The integration is possible, and likewise the movement toward it, because the *in itself* and the *for itself* belong, ultimately, together. The final synthesis (whether Hegel conceives its possibility is a matter of considerable debate) is a victory for the immanent – for the other, the outside, is seen to belong fundamentally to the inside. The positive work of negation, then, leads to wholeness; the many belong to the One: *Geist* ("spirit" or "mind") knows itself. In coming to this knowledge that which is other is overcome and so difference is recognized as illusory: "In this [absolute] knowing, then, Spirit has concluded the movement in which it has shaped itself, in so far as this shaping was burdened with the difference of consciousness, a difference now overcome."[36]

Nietzsche

The placing and overcoming of difference within the consciousness can be seen at the final exaltation of the human condition, which Balthasar noted was the mark of modernity's project. For Hegel, consciousness is much larger than any individual human consciousness. Nevertheless, since human consciousness is a correlative part of consciousness as a whole, then Heidegger is correct in viewing Hegel's work as the last move it is possible to make in the game of metaphysics. Furthermore, it is significant that when Nietzsche's madman, confronting the crowd in the marketplace "who do not believe in God" proclaims that God is dead ("We have killed him – you and I"), the madman goes on to ask "Is not the greatness of this deed too great for us? Must not we ourselves become gods simply to seem worthy of it? There has never been a greater deed – and whosoever shall be born after us, for the sake of this deed he shall be part of a higher humanity than all history."[37] Man the measure of all things has now become god, as Feuerbach understood.[38]

The death of God makes possible the future race of the *Übermensch* or the genius – those who will affirm life in its pluralism and unending difference. With this death is the death of humanism also, of the human as the meaningful center of creation. Following the madman's pronouncements there is only silence – his silence and the silence of everything else around him. It is the silence of what Levinas will later term the anonymity of the *il y a*: "a place where the bottom has dropped out of everything, an atmospheric density, a plenitude of void, or the murmur of silence."[39]

The significance of Nietzsche's work for postmodern thinkers, and the centrality of his proclamation of the death of God for postmodern theologians who name themselves as such, requires that we understand exactly what Nietzsche is saying here and the shift his work announces with respect to a thinking of difference. When Nietzsche makes the claim that "God is dead" we have to ask what kind of claim he is making. It is not a theological claim, as it is in Hegel where the death of God is the death of Jesus Christ, the Son of God and the second person of the Trinity. For Hegel, Christ's death is God's absolute deliverance of His transcendent being to the immanent movement of history and community. This is not Nietzsche's claim. Neither is Nietzsche making the claim that "God does not exist" – an onto-theological claim made by an atheist. "God" in Nietzsche's assertion is used metonymically. That is, it is a name which substitutes for and sums up a way of doing philosophy in which a highest principle is sought that grounds the possibility of all things. As "the White House" is a name substituting for and summing up the American government under its presidential head of state, so "God" is a metonymy for "absolute Truth," "absolute Goodness," "absolute reality," "absolute reason," the origin and measure of all things (Being in modernity's understanding of metaphysics). When the madman and Zarathustra announce that God is dead, they are proclaiming what Nietzsche states in other places in his work:

> What therefore is truth? A mobile army of metaphors, metonymies, anthro-pomorphisms: in short a sum of human relations which became poetically and rhetorically intensified, metamorphosed, adorned, and after long usage seem

to a nation fixed, canonic, binding: truths are illusions of which one has forgotten that they *are* illusions.[40]

All things that live long are gradually saturated with reason that their origin in unreason thereby becomes improbable. Does not almost every precise history of an origination impress our feelings as paradoxical and wantonly offensive?[41]

[M]orality itself [i]s a symptom of decadence.[42]

[F]acts are precisely what there is not, only interpretations.[43]

Nietzsche announces the death of modernity's god. In doing this his work expresses both the final working out of modernity's project and a postmodernism that will gather pace to become, finally, a culturally dominant force – the postmodernity of the seventies, eighties, and early nineties of the twentieth century. Heidegger pictures Nietzsche's work as the consummation of metaphysics;[44] Habermas portrays Nietzsche's work as the entry into postmodernity.[45] With the death of God Nietzsche announces the overcoming of metaphysics, for he announces that there is no foundation, no ground, no origin that ultimately is not governed by a perspective, i.e., we, as human beings, desire and require it. We cannot think or have knowledge at all without radically selecting from a multiplicity of sense data what we are to think and know. In an act of Titanic iconoclasm he announces a nihilism in which there is no truth, goodness, reality, reason, origin which is not contingent, ephemeral, and the effect of the human will. "Man projected his three 'inner facts', that in which he believed more firmly than in anything else, will, spirit, ego, outside himself – he derived the concept 'being' only from the concept 'ego', he posited 'things' as possessing being according to his own image, according to his concept of the ego as cause. No wonder he later always discovered in things only *that which he had put into them!*"[46]

What is also significant is that the proclamation that "God is dead," that the considered structures of reality are man-made, is a historical claim. Heidegger's work on Nietzsche considerably amplifies this. Nietzsche is announcing the end of a certain epoch – a metaphysical epoch that no longers holds. We live now – and Nietzsche insists that we ourselves recognize deep down that this is so – in a time when we understand that all the building blocks of our systems have been anthropomorphized idols, and the idols are passing away with the onset of night. Insofar as Christianity (frequently lampooned by Nietzsche for its slave ethic) once had a purpose in giving power to the lowly, its purpose is now over. Rather than energizing, now it enervates. The madman announces the death of God to those "who did not believe": "we *have* killed him" in the past, over the years when the Christian currency was gradually being devalued. What remains, for Nietzsche, is rhetoric itself – a mobile army – and what he calls in *Genealogy of Morals* the "will to truth": "in us the will to truth becomes conscious of itself as a *problem*."[47] This will to truth, later termed the will to power, is the will to create artistically, the will to enhance life through drawing Dionysian intoxication into Apollonian form: "The aesthetic state possesses a superabundance of means of communication, together with an extreme receptivity for stimuli and signs. It constitutes the high point of communication and transmission between living creatures."[48] But this will is not an individual's – not Nietzsche's nor Zarathustra's – it is the anonymous will of life itself. As one recent Nietzsche scholar has pointed out: "Nietzsche's model for the world, for objects, and for people turns out to be the literary text."[49] The world as text is a body of metaphors laced with and empowered by a "libidinal narcissistic energy."[50]

The influence of Nietzsche's work on the thinkers represented in Part I cannot be overestimated. It was bequeathed to a generation of French thinkers through its influence on Sartre's existentialism. Nietzsche's philosophy makes marketeers of us all, for we are forced to face the radical selectivity involved in all our opinions. No position is without its ideology; every position requires a genealogy in order to understand the perspective it is coming from, the will to power that it represents. Foucault's own social analyses are rooted in this thinking. The indeterminate identity of the sign, the resultant instability of meaning or semiosis, so important to Derrida's notion of *différance*, is also rooted here. When Michel de Certeau died in 1986 he was working on a book concerned with the anthropology of believing. One of the abiding questions Certeau wrestled with was what makes belief believable. His work frequently charted the changes in Christian belief structure, and in doing so was working with Nietzsche's observation that "belief in the Christian God has become unbelievable."[51] Bataille, Derrida, and Irigaray have all written books on Nietzsche. The work of Lacan, Barthes, Girard, and Kristeva all betrays the influence of this figure. But for several it is an influence directed also by close readings of Heidegger's philosophy of difference. For although Nietszche breaks up the part-and-whole metaphysics of modernity, espousing the plurality of differences, a monism remains – the chaotic flux of life itself in which everything is interrelated. It is a flux without shape or destiny, a flux in which all differences are of equal value. Nietzsche's nihilism, his life-affirming nihilism, collapses all differentials into an infinite indifference. This makes all talk of interrelations metaphorical – for only things which are already distinct can have relations. Relations between appearances in a world of appearances cannot be relations at all. The other is rescued from Hegel's omnivorous dialectic of Spirit, but it has no value as such because it can be given no identity. It is only another interpretation, a necessary fiction, a "dreaming in order not to be destroyed."[52] As Nietzsche states quite clearly in a series of passages in *Will to Power* (556–60), the world is not out there, ready-made. There is no essence or essential nature of a thing. There is only our perspective on it, constructing it. Outside interpretation and subjectivity nothing has existence, the Kantian "thing-in-itself" (the basis of difference for Kant) is not there. Transcendence and the transcendent are equally impossible.

Among postmodern thinkers Gilles Deleuze has taken up and developed this line of Nietzschean thinking, this monistic vision, in his own account of difference. But Heidegger's project announces, right from *Being and Time*, that it is concerned with establishing and examining the nature of the Kantian difference, the thing-in-itself. He wishes to move beyond the subjectivity and interpretations of being there (*Dasein* and its phenomenological hermeneutics) toward an analysis of Being itself. An exteriority announces itself here; beyond the perspectivalism and indifference of Nietzsche's thinking, Heidegger announces another overcoming of metaphysics through an examination of ontological difference. Like Nietzsche, Heidegger recognizes that all seeing is seeing *as*, but in Heidegger it is Being which gives beings to be seen. Truth as *a-lētheia*, as revealing a Being-true out of a hiddenness, can once more be spoken of.

Heidegger

For Heidegger ontological difference – the difference between Being and beings – makes possible the metaphysical project, but the metaphysical project itself demonstrates and requires the forgetting of this difference. Whereas I have argued throughout this introduction for a close association between metaphysics and modernity, Heidegger wishes to see the establishment of the metaphysical concern with identity as wholeness, and Being as the ground of that identity and wholeness, as the project of philosophy post Parmenides. Insofar as this ontological metaphysics then conceived this Being as self-determining, *causa sui* as *causa prima* and *ultima ratio*, God was conflated with Being as such. "If science must begin with God, then it is the science of God: theology."[53] Metaphysics is then an onto-theological project; although Heidegger takes pains to explain that by theology here he means statements of representational thinking about God, mythopoetic utterance – he does not refer to the God of faith, there is "no reference to any creed or ecclesiastical doctrine."[54] I would want to suggest that Heidegger is stamping a Cartesian and Leibnizian program onto a tradition which is much more heterogeneous. Witness: Plato's Good beyond Being, Aristotle's ambivalence concerning the relation of God to paronomous being, Gregory of Nyssa's *diastēma* between God and creaturely existence, Anselm's distinction between the nature of God's Being and our own. The theological and the philosophical are neither synthesized nor synonymous in these projects. Nevertheless, Heidegger does emphasize that German Idealism crystallized a metaphysics of identity and synthesis[55] of which Hegel's onto-theology – where theism has become a philosophical question – was the ultimate working out. He then suggests his own thinking leaps beyond this.

Heidegger wishes to think this fundamental difference *as* difference. This difference is unthought in the metaphysical tradition because it conceals itself as we begin to think. Heidegger refers to this concealment by its Greek term *lethē*, because *lethē* (concealment) is at the heart of the Greek word for truth, *alētheia*. When we begin, then, difference is forgotten and truth concealed. Heidegger is aware that his project is always attempting the impossible – to step back beyond thinking within the path thinking opens up into the future, that is, to think the heterogeneous origin. This is important, both for evaluating Heidegger's project with respect to the end of modernity and his influence on those later seekers of a nonfoundational origin (Levinas, Derrida, and Kristeva). As Heidegger writes: "The step back thus moves out of metaphysics into the essential nature of metaphysics."[56] But then Heidegger's project, in leaping beyond metaphysics, has no place to rest its head.

Like Nietzsche, Heidegger conceives the claims he is making as relative to a specific time. The move beyond onto-theology is made necessary by the epoch of the death of God announced by Nietzsche. Therefore it is not that Hegel was wrong to think as he thought, for Hegel brought to consummation the thought of Being then possible. But the times have changed and the thinking of Being has moved on. Since, for Heidegger, science is "the absolute, self-knowing knowledge,"[57] which can only proceed on the principle of identity – that A *is* A – and can never ask the question concerning the nature of that *is*, the all-embracing rationalism of metaphysics makes possible technology in all its forms. He names advanced functionalization, systematic improvement, automation, bureaucratization, communications, the atomic age as identifiable traits of modernity. His philosophical step back is, therefore, a move beyond modernity's obsession with the technological. With Heidegger the end of modernity is announced. Announced but not accomplished, for the place Heidegger moves to is the "between."

The between issues from the differentiation of Being as an unconcealment which overwhelms and beings which arrive in and through that unconcealment but which conceal their event of arrival. As Heidegger puts it, "The difference of Being and beings, as the differentiation of overwhelming and arrival, is the perdurance (*Austrag*) of the two in *unconcealing keeping in concealment*. Within this perdurance there prevails a clearing of what veils and closes itself off."[58] The clearing is created from a differential tension. A certain interval or space is opened by this tension which manifests the difference between Being and beings. But we must not allow the spatial metaphor to confuse us. This clearing is not just spatial. It is a temporal clearing, a clearing which shifts constantly as time shifts. That is why the clearing is also named perdurance. The Being which gives itself in unconcealed overwhelming cannot be represented as such. We can think the difference, but we can only think Being itself in terms of contingent beings embedded in a particular historical epoch, and the differential clearing such beings bear the trace of. It is because Being is known only through beings, because of the reciprocal causal relation binding Being to beings and vice versa, that the onto-theological project emerged. In such a project the difference is forgotten; for Being itself is other, external, transcendent, and cannot be appropriated. For this reason "The origin of the difference can no longer be thought of within the scope of metaphysics."[59] As Heidegger goes on to suggest, "The god-less thinking which must abandon the god of philosophy, god as *causa sui* is perhaps close to the divine God."[60] This would be a God thought outside of metaphysics and the project of modernity. Heidegger at several points in his work declines to embark on such thinking; presumably because of this god-less God nothing can be said – not within philosophical discourse and method anyway. For how can we think this "divine God" when, for Heidegger, metaphysics has the monopoly on representational thinking? When metaphysics is *logos* as word and reason inextricably related? With Heidegger we arrive at a place already made familiar by Nietzsche – we are bound by the nature of language itself to a metaphysical project that we need to overcome if theology is to be at all possible.

The influence of Heidegger's investigations into ontological difference has been immense, and many of the thinkers represented in Part I (and the work of the people who introduce them) and the theologians represented in Part II of this book are indebted to him. Levinas's early work was conceived in dialectical conversation with Heidegger's thinking, and several commentators have suggested that despite Levinas's own protests his project is closer to Heidegger's than Levinas claims.[61] Derrida's notion of *différance* (where differing introduces a deferral of meaning) is a rewriting of Heidegger's ontological difference with respect to Ferdinand de Saussure's understanding of semiotic difference (which we shall come to shortly). Heidegger's late work is already examining discourse as the field in which ontological difference is heard to play. Derrida's deconstruction takes this further. Gianni Vattimo has suggested that *différance* becomes an archstructure quite opposed to the Being in Heidegger, which continually empties itself (giving itself ceaselessly in the event of appropriation [*Ereignis*]) into the historical. He adds, significantly: "*Différance* as archstructure is not in history, it never comes to pass, but then again constitutes a return to the most classic qualification of metaphysical Being, eternity."[62] Derrida's work on *différance* is an ongoing dialogue between deconstruction, Heidegger's difference, and negative theology. He, like Levinas, also pushes toward a nonfoundational and heterogeneous origin. Derrida has termed this origin, after the Greek, Platonic word describing a receptacle or place which cannot be reached or touched, *Khora*. This conceiving of an unstable, mysterious, ungrounding origin is found in and employed by both Irigaray and Kristeva, who are also deeply indebted, in their own notions of difference, to Heidegger's thinking. For Irigaray, the *Khora* is a febrile, irreducible, divine spacing – like the dynamic gap between the wings of the angels which do not touch as the fold over the Ark of the Covenant – constituted by sexual difference. It is, and she uses Heidegger's word, the between or the interval. For Kristeva, the *Chora* (*sic*) is womb-like – a dark, ineffable place from which the semiotic rhythms issue which demand and yet destabilize the symbolic. For Kristeva, Heidegger's difference is located within the subject in process, torn as that subject is between the semiotic drives and the symbolic systems employed to repress and keep these drives at bay.

Among the essayists in Part II, the theologians Marion and Lacoste, the philosopher of social science Rose, and the ethicist Wyschogrod have all written comprehensively about Heidegger. Marion, in working with Heidegger, has wanted to push his work toward a theology of a God without Being. He wishes to write about the God of faith concerning whom Heidegger could only be silent. He attempts the relocation of theological discourse, founded in revelation (in Scripture) and ecclesial interpretation (in the eucharist and by the bishop), beyond the preoccupations of metaphysics. Lacoste, much more suspicious of what he believes is Heidegger's neo-paganism, nevertheless wishes to build upon Heidegger's conception of what Vattimo calls "the transitivity of Being, which dis-locates man from his metaphysical position as subject."[63] Liturgical space, for Lacoste, announces the between in the clearing in which this kenosis (and Christian discipleship) takes place. Rose, deeply suspicious also of what she believes is Heidegger's dialectic of nihilism, nevertheless in arguing against it, like Wyschogrod, demands an ethics of the other and a recognition of difference which can be found in a "holy middle."

Whatever Heidegger's influence, however, a question remains, just as it did with Nietzsche's work. Both announce an end of modernity's project, both announce a groundlessness, a nihilism, but both announce this from within metaphysics. They each seek a place beyond, a place of the other which they cannot attain while thought and language remain. In a curious act of *ressentiment*, both turn their attention toward language, toward an aesthetics of the unpresentable sublime, and each also blames language for the inability to grasp what is the nature of the case. Both thinkers view metaphysics as inevitable because grammar remains. Though pointing insistently toward a postmodern cyberspace, neither of them can enter it. Their projects remain this side of modernity. We will pursue this further, for what I wish to suggest is that only theology can complete the postmodern project. Only theology can truly occupy the postmodern condition. For the moment one more influential form of difference needs to be sketched – the semiotic difference examined by the Swiss linguist Ferdinand de Saussure.

Saussure

It was never Saussure's intention to dethrone modernity and its metaphysics. In fact, Saussure's project, although emphasizing how it is the differences between signs which construct their meaning, was thoroughly neo-Kantian. That is, a deep structure to the universe was evident and emphasized by Saussure. In setting up a system of binary oppositions – the synchronic and the diachronic, *la langue* and *la parole*, the syntagmatic relations and the associative – the system is a self-contained whole within which everything is made meaningful. Saussure's thinking, then, runs in the deep channels of modernity's interest in understanding the nature of systems and modernity's concerns with the apodictic laws governing such systems. But the linguistic system, Saussure claims, is first of all a system composed of arbitrary signs and, secondly, operates through "relations and differences." By arbitrary Saussure means not natural: "language systems are acquired and conventional."[64] He emphasized that there were degrees of arbitrariness, but fundamentally word-signs did not relate to objects out there. The signs related internally to the symbolic system itself. A principle of iteration or repetition establishes the relation between a sign (or signifier) and the idea it represents (the signified). But the principle of iteration also means that the meaning of the sign, what is signified by its use, is not stable – each repetition will alter the semantic value of the sign by placing it in a new context, a new symbolic field. The system of any language (*le langage*) Saussure calls *langue* (a tongue) and the particular use of that tongue Saussure calls *parole* (a word). And tongue develops through time and therefore it possesses a diachronic axis, but the system informing the tongue itself and which makes possible the meaningfulness of any word is the synchronic axis. Difference announces itself as a structural principle in the synchronic understanding of any tongue.

In a simple sentence like "the ship is blue," Saussure would distinguish between two sets of relations or differences. There are, first, the syntagmatic differences which enable the sentence to communicate. For example: "the" is a definite article indicating the particularity of an object (it is not "a" ship); "ship" is a noun possessing the property "blue" which is an adjective; the "is" is a verb. The syntagmatic relations are the consecutive relations in a word (*parole*): "In its place in a syntagma, any unit acquires its value simply in opposition to what precedes, or to what follows it, or to both."[65] Secondly, there are associative relations. Saussure understands these relations in terms of sound. A "ship" belongs to a group including "shipment" and "shipping," but also to another group including words like "apprenticeship" where "ship" is used as a suffix. But we might also include in associative relations connotative differences. For example, I understand the distinctiveness of "ship" because of other unspoken words like "boat," "yacht," "canoe."

The importance of Saussure's work lies in its attempt to understand the nature and operation of a symbolic system. Once other symbolic systems were identified – kinship systems (for Lévi-Strauss), the dream-work of the unconscious (for Lacan following Freud), advertisements for pasta (for Barthes) – then Saussure's analysis of the synchronic and diachronic, the syntagmatic and associative differences could be brought into play to analyze how the symbolic field arranged itself to become meaningful.

With the exception perhaps of Georges Bataille, there is not one of the thinkers represented in Part I of this volume who has not been influenced either directly by Saussure's work or the development in France of structural linguistics through thinkers like Roman Jakobson and Tzvetan Todorov. And though Saussure himself could be said to have remained a neo-Kantian idealist, a believer in the immanent wholeness of the system, his work became the watershed in the move toward a more radical critique of culture ushered in by postmodern, in this sense poststructural, thinkers. Saussure's semiotic difference fostered the development of an intratextual view of living among French thinkers. Wittgenstein's work fostered such a view elsewhere. By intratextual I refer to the symbolic field as an extension of interrelated signs. Intratextuality defines the world as known only through the operation and production of signs within this vast symbolic network. The world and its meaningfulness are known only in and through semiotic difference. The world comes to be through difference. We return to the Irigaray passage I quoted earlier: "The gods, God, first creates *space*. And time is there, more or less in the service of space. On the first day, the first days, the gods, God, make a world by separating. *Desire* occupies and designates the place of the *interval*."[66] As Irigaray goes on to show, the power of such production through differentiation can be understood as semiotic, sexual, or theological. The physical, the psychological, the linguistic, literary and theological are not independent fields of inquiry. One subject intersects with another. Jean-Luc Nancy, a more recent exponent of postmodern thinking, who is also concerned with the relations between corporeality, desire, and representation, writes: "the philosophico-theological *corpus* of bodies is still supported by the spine of *mimesis*, of representation, of the sign."[67] Saussure's work becomes important in any account of the relationship between sexuality and textuality or creation as the expression of God's Word, creation as an act of separation.

With poststructural accounts of semiotic difference a change has come about. Although Saussure is concerned in diachronic linguistics with time, movement, and history, his analysis of the synchronic axis of languages determines the importance of relations. This is his neo-Kantian perspective. But the power and attraction holding between such relations and the production and movement of that power and attraction is left unexamined. With accounts of semiotic difference in Lacan, Certeau, Barthes, Foucault, Derrida, and Kristeva, in accounts of sexual difference wedded to semiotic difference in Irigaray and Cixous, there is a concern with the dynamics, the power-lines composing, constituting and deconstructing relations between signs. The dynamism of Hegel's dialectic of desire, the dialectic also of subjectivity, is reconceived within the textual nature of the world composed of difference and relations. A philosophy of desire emerges unbounded by the holism and teleology of Hegel. Desire plays across the surface of the intratextual, transgressing the borders of distinct academic disciplines, as the libido plays upon flesh of the erogenous body and reaches out, in fantasy, toward other bodies.

The French Connection

At this point a question emerges with some insistence. It is the most obvious question, given the names of those listed above among postmodern thinkers. Why France? For all the thinkers represented as constituting the philosophy of the postmodern God in Part I are either French by birth, live in France as the country of their adoption (Levinas, Derrida, Kristeva), or write in French (Irigaray).

There can be no simple set of reasons why France becomes the ground from which much postmodern thinking which concerns itself with religious discourse takes root. It is significant that many of the thinkers have strong religious backgrounds. Levinas and Derrida (and Cixous) are Jewish; Bataille, Lacan, Foucault, Certeau, Irigaray, and Kristeva all had significant Catholic schooling; in his introduction, Valentine Cunningham draws attention to the significance of Barthes's Protestant family history. One recent scholar, writing about the reception of Heidegger into modern French philosophy, makes the more general statement about French thinking that, "More than either German or English language philosophy, French philosophy is distinguished by a strong emphasis on the relation between philosophy and religion, reason and faith."[68] There is a philosophical tradition relating the seventeenth-century philosophical and theological voices of Descartes and Pascal to the twentieth-century philosophical and theological voices of Étienne Gilson and Emmanuel Levinas.

A further characteristic of the French tradition of philosophical thinking is the way the line between literature and philosophy, imagination and reasoning, is much more fluid than in German or English language philosophy. The mixture of genres and discourses found in the work of Bataille, Girard, Derrida, and Kristeva stands in a philosophical trajectory which includes the work of Diderot, Rousseau, and Sartre. Most of the thinkers represented in Part I have written sensitively about literary texts. Such a way of proceeding to think philosophically betrays a profound love affair with the French language itself. The pleasure of the text, to employ the title of one of Barthes's famous books, is a perennial feature of French literary philosophy. Foucault will describe his own work as *récits* (stories) and Certeau will describe his own writing of history as the creation of fables. A certain interdisciplinary nature is generic to French philosophy, which partly accounts for the way a philosopher can have a voice in France outside the academic institution, even in the daily newspapers.

Even before Sartre's existentialism, there had been a consistent concern in French philosophy with human experience. Montaigne's pragmatism and anti-theorizing, Descartes's turn to the subject who meditates upon the world around him, and the skepticism of both form an influential basis. Later, the work of Henri Bergson, Maurice Blondel, and Gabriel Marcel, in their different ways, created an ethos within which the existential phenomenology of Husserl and Heidegger could find prepared soil, and where *Lebensphilosophie* as redefined by Nietzsche might flourish. Husserl's own indebtedness in his phenomenology to Descartes is evident in his *Cartesian Meditations*.[69] These lectures were first given at the Sorbonne in 1929 and were translated and published in France before being published in Germany. Indeed, Levinas assisted with their translation and publication. Although Husserl's phenomenology attacks psychologism, nevertheless it is within an intellectual context concerned with the examination of human experience that Freudian psychology too found a second home and madness became a respectable field for French intellectual enquiry.

The early reception of Husserl's phenomenology (from about 1910) prepared the ground also for the impact of Hegel's phenomenology as Kojève expounded it from 1933 to 1939. The influence of Hegel on twentieth-century French philosophy is profound. In particular a left-wing Hegelianism, with its emphases on *praxis*, dialectic, and the philosophy of history, gave intellectual strength to an emerging Communism, a Communism that flourished (coextensive with the popularity of Sartre's work) until the 1960s. It was in the sixties that the tide began to turn. The student riots of May 1968 are frequently cited as a significant event in this sea change. Jean-Luc Marion speaks of "the test of nihilism which, in France, marked the years dominated by 1968."[70] The complex history of French Marxism is not so simply charted. The in-fights between the Stalinists, the Maoists, and members of the French Communist Party, the critical role of intellectuals like Louis Althusser and *avant-garde* journals like *Tel Quel*, all contribute to a picture which is dense and multifaceted.[71] Several of the thinkers whose work has been selected for Part I were, at some point in their intellectual development, members of the Communist Party or acted at its fringes. The concern, with several of them, for analyses of violence and power owes much to their political involvements. Nevertheless, a number of the thinkers represented were writing before the '68 riots and the frontal attack upon French academic conservatism. Bataille,

Levinas, Barthes, and Lacan (not to mention the work of Maurice Blanchot) had written some of their most significant work before the late sixties.

With Bataille, Blanchot, and the early work of Deleuze a postwar nihilism is announced. Philosophically, what appears to have changed at this time had more to do with the rise of attention being paid to Heidegger's work. As one intellectual historian notes: "Increasingly, Heidegger's theory was seen as representing a viable alternative to [a Hegelian form of Marxism]."[72] Heideggerian phenomenology, rooted in ontological difference, replaced Hegelian phenomenology in which the other was assimilated into the whole. Phenomenology becomes radicalized.[73] Sartre's humanism enters a crisis. As Levinas noted in an essay entitled "Humanism and An-Archy," published in 1968: "We are witnessing the ruin of the myth of man as an end in himself, and the appearance of an order that is neither human nor inhuman."[74] Beyond all ontological categories, Levinas traces a responsibility for the other (*autre*) that ruptures all egoism (and Cartesianism): "Modern anti-humanism is no doubt right when it does not find in man understood as the individual of a genus or of an ontological region, an individual persevering in being like all substances, a privilege that would make him the goal of reality."[75] With this, Levinas announces the end of modernity as Balthasar defined it – the end of the metaphysics of being human, the metaphysics of reason and freedom; the end of the human as the measure of the whole. Jean-Luc Nancy writes of Sartre that he was driven by the desire "to restore a consistency to a traditional power of *homo metaphysicus*."[76] Heidegger and Lacan contended for Sartre's title as France's master thinker.[77]

In the light of this some rationalization is required as to why certain philosophical figures were chosen for Part I and certain other figures left out. The writers included were chosen primarily for what they have to say about "God" to students of theology and religion who take philosophy seriously. It is the omission of several important figures which takes more explaining. Of the thinkers who ought also to have been included had space allowed, the most prominent are Maurice Blanchot, Michel Serres, Gianni Vattimo, Hélène Cixous and Jean-Luc Nancy. But Blanchot's work is unsystematic and eclectic. Serres's work (other than his beautiful volume *Angels*) is not yet philosophical currency in the English-speaking world, though his work in the history of science has been partly disseminated;[78] Vattimo and Nancy are only just emerging as figures of interest to people in religious studies. Cixous is less a theorist and more a practitioner, in her writing, of a religious way of viewing the world. Cixous's work performs a spirituality.[79] She has written: "When I have finished writing, when I am a hundred and ten, all I will have ever done will have been to attempt a portrait of God. Of the God. Of what escapes us and makes us wonder ... I mean our own divinity, awkward, twisted, throbbing, our own mystery."[80] It is with genuine regret that the available space required a disciplining in which her work is not represented. I have tried to weave the very different voices of Vattimo and Jean-Luc Nancy into the text and texture of this introduction.

The Postmodern God

The work of the postmodern thinkers represented in Part I has already impacted upon the study of theology. Among the theologians who describe themselves as postmodern, Don Cupitt in Britain, Mark C. Taylor, Charles Winquist, and Carl Raschke in the United States have all been profoundly influenced by poststructural accounts of language and desire. Other "postmodern" theologians – Thomas Altizer and David Ray Griffin – are much less indebted to these thinkers. Altizer's Christian atheism owes much to Hegel and Nietzsche's accounts of the death of God, and Griffin's animistic theism is developed through an examination of quantum mechanics and process philosophy. The absence of Altizer and Griffin from the number of theologians of the postmodern God represented in Part II of this volume is, then, reasonable.[81] But the absence of the work of the other self-styled postmodern theologians does call for comment.

Their absence rests mainly upon two characteristics of their postmodern theology that make it, to my mind, not postmodern at all, but rather the theological thinking of late modernity. First, they represent the apotheosis of a liberal tradition. That is, their thinking is rooted in the liberal ethics and anthropology of modernity – its concerns remain modernity's concerns, rather than postmodern concerns. Cupitt and Taylor began as liberal theologians prior to discovering the resources of French poststructuralism. As I have observed elsewhere and in a more detailed analysis, "these theologians understand their French philosophical support to be advocating absence, nonidentity, and the unbearable lightness of being in which all is rhetoric and surface. It is also important that the relationship of postmodern philosophy to the projects of these radical theologians is epiphenomenal. Their work does not issue from postmodern philosophy, its insights and methodologies; postmodern philosophy substantiates their theses concerning contemporary culture."[82] This, again, is a liberal move – theology is demythologized and takes on the garb of present cultural concerns. Such philosophical support might be offered by the radical Nietzscheans – Gilles Deleuze, the early paganism of Jean-François Lyotard, the work on hyper-reality and seduction by Jean Baudrillard. It would not receive support from some of the postmodern thinkers they wish to enlist – Derrida, for example. Secondly, they each affirm a radical immanentalism, a nihilistic monism or ontology which is at odds with what is evidently a search for a transcendental empiricism (to use a phrase coined by Vincent Descombes[83]) in postmodern thinking. This is developed into forms of what Altizer calls "Christian atheism," Taylor "a/theology," and Cupitt "Christian humanism," "active non-realism," and "post-Christianity." The essay by Gillian Rose in Part II examines in some detail the work of Mark C. Taylor, describing it as "nomadic ecstasy" and radically antinomian. Lawlessness, the transgression of law, brings delight and freedom. Liberalism finds its cosmic framework. Existentialism is reworked, for we are still discussing the ground of our (the cosmos's now, not the subject's) being, Levinas's anonymous and indifferent *il y a*.

But it is the puncturing of the circle of immanence which the work of the postmodern philosophers of difference is attempting to sketch. This work draws attention to an aporetics – ambivalances, generated by difference – which cannot be named. This presents its own problems: difference can never be overcome. Difference offers us the trace of that which is the condition for all things, a heterogeneous origin. In the work of Bataille, Levinas, Girard, Certeau, Derrida, Irigaray, Kristeva, Cixous, and Jean-Luc Nancy discussions of this originating space, this destabilizing, differentiating source employs theological metaphors – metaphors that cannot function according to some opposition between the metaphorical and the literal, since metaphoricity is the nature of language itself. We cannot say, then, that they are simply using metaphors but they are not referring to God or the divine. The theological cannot be left out of their accounts. Their accounts call forth the theological without attempting to view the problematics of late modernity which they are alert to from an explicitly theological (that is, faith) perspective and praxis.

Yet neither can these thinkers complete the postmodern project they call for – the end of metaphysics as the ordering of what is according to human reason. They have no position from which to surmount such an overcoming. How can philosophy (even broadly conceived as interdisciplinary in the way these thinkers do conceive it) overcome itself without becoming a discourse that refuses its own legitimation? It is like the child standing in a cardboard box and attempting to lift herself off the ground by clutching the box's sides. These thinkers point toward another logic, another economy, but they can only view this logic and economy as it operates antithetically within and against their own human reasoning and their own discourse. And yet to give up all position is understood, rightly, as surrendering all possibility of an ethics – the creation of an *ethos* of love, love as not-having (Cixous says), desire without violence, an indefinitely ectopic corpus (as Nancy calls it). These different projects journey toward another city, a new corporeality, a new spacing in which the other is housed, affirmed, and necessary for any understanding of goodness. To give up all position would be to surrender to the flux and hand over what is other to a cosmic indifference. Only the aesthetics of nihilism would remain. The surrender of the subject – a certain kenosis which will bring about the final collapse of secular space itself – is both necessary and impossible for the realization of the postmodern project.

Only theology can embark upon such a project, for theology cannot conceive of a secular space at all, nor an autonomous subject. Doing theology, acting, writing, functioning theologically is not to own a voice, but to be voiced; to be spoken, not a speaker. Only as such can living theologically defeat idolatry; by surrendering, constantly, its own legitimacy. Philosophy has always sought foundations for new beginnings, new points for maximal epistemological and ontological advantage. Theology – as discourse, as praxis – proceeds groundlessly. It cannot think its own origin; it seeks and desires among the consequences of that which always remains unthought. But its seeking is not nomadic, for it seeks another city, a heteropolis. Furthermore, in its seeking it structures such a city, a cyberspatial city. The postmodern God then cannot emerge as anything other than an idol until theological discourse articulates its own spatiality and temporality, its own personhood and body, its own ethos. Theology must announce doctrines of creation and incarnation beyond the onto-theologies and humanisms of modernity. Theology must articulate this living in and journeying toward another city, a heteropolis in Greek. It must subsume postmodernism's cyberspace, writing through and beyond it, in order to establish its own orders. Not that postmodernism then becomes the anti-metaphysical philosophy theology can found itself upon. That would be akin to the liberal moves made by Tillich and Bultmann with respect to Heideggerian existentialism. That, as I have argued, is the basis for Cupitt's work and Mark C. Taylor's. They are writing a *postmodern* theology. No, I wish to argue that we have not yet attained to the postmodern until we recover for our time the world before and beyond the secular. Until then theology has constantly to engage with and critique that which calls itself postmodern. In our time, a space is being cleared and a time is being announced that only theological discourse can provide with a logic. Post-secularism makes manifest how modernity hijacked for its own purposes the theological, the premodern. Simultaneously, it traces the outline of a theological worldview yet to be recovered. We are only just beginning to see what such a postmodern *theology* might look like.

The theological essays in Part II, in rejecting modernity's cult of the new and the novel, attempt to read through the tradition and reconceive that tradition in terms of philosophy at the end of the metaphysics of modernity. Most could be termed post-liberal, if not conservative, in their theological standpoint. They are theological realists. It is this which makes them distinct from the liberal atheologians like Cupitt and Taylor. Theirs, in their different ways, is not an act of nostalgia, not a Lot's wife longing for the premodern. Theirs is a vision of another city, a kingdom of God, founded in diremption (Rose), *anthropologia crucis* (Lacoste), living under erasure (Wyschogrod) in a cultural politics issuing from difference (Chopp), Christophanic asyndeton (Pickstock), Revelation (Marion), and God as Trinity (Milbank). Living in this kingdom is liturgical – hence the place given to contemporary work on liturgy by Lacoste and Pickstock. Living in this city is political, embodied, and sexed – hence the essays on feminism, cultural politics, the law, and the city by Wyschogrod, Chopp and Rose. In being Christian, the theology of this living cannot neglect, forget, or elide the necessity of its other roots in Judaism – hence the importance of including work by the Jewish thinkers, Wyschogrod and Rose. In completing the postmodern project of overcoming metaphysics this theology does not deny or ignore the importance of philosophical analysis. Rather, current key metaphysical questions (of time, subjects, desire, phenomena, perception, language) are read critically in terms of a theological agenda – Marion reads Nietzsche, Husserl, and Heidegger; Milbank rereads Deleuze and Lyotard; Lacoste reads Hegel. There are other theologians I might have added to those represented here, space permitting. Rowan Williams would be a good example and Joseph S. O'Leary another.[84] But the major preoccupations of what I would term a proper postmodern, post-secular theology are, I hope, sketched in the essays I have chosen. The work of those who have introduced the major thinkers in Part I of this volume expands the basis of this current work.

At the end of modernity we come, I believe, to a forking of the ways. The primrose path is the aesthetics of nihilism in its various contemporary forms: a culture of seduction and flagrant, self-consuming sexuality; a culture of increasingly sophisticated drugs and drug use; a culture of virtual, video-taped realities. The thorny way is the practice of faith. The latter is a difficult path, fraught still with all the dragons, giants, and demons of *The Pilgrim's Progress*. I have mainly focused attention throughout this volume on Christian theology. This is partly because of my own standpoint and partly because the Christian tradition has a lofty library of theological investigation and reflection going back to within decades of its inception. But there are other faiths, maybe other faiths with developed theologies too. The relationship between those faiths, and the relationships between the various sectors within those faiths, make the practice of faith for this and future generations complex and problematic. We proceed by grace. We cannot take command here – forging a way through difficulties and reducing mountains to mole-hills. We have to be held in love, waiting patiently, watching constantly, tracing endlessly the invisible as the visible, the divine as the corporeal, the coming to fulfillment of the eternal Word. The task of understanding those relationships is also part of postmodernism's theological project. There is so much more of this other city, this heteropolis, yet to be built and yet to be explored.

Notes

1 *The Condition of Postmodernity: An Essay into the Origins of Cultural Change* (Oxford: Blackwell, 1990), p.112.
2 At the time Harvey was writing only Jameson's article "Postmodernism, or the cultural logic of late capitalism," *New Left Review*, 146 (Aug. 1984), pp. 53–92, was available. Later Jameson published a full-length book with the same title (London: Verso, 1991).
3 See here Lisa Jardine, *Worldly Goods* (London: Macmillan, 1996), for an account of the origins of our modern cult of ownership and consumerism in the Renaissance. She depicts the Renaissance as a "culture of consumers," a culture where developing informational technology (printing), the kudos of being a collector, and the ebb and flow of an ever-expanding market were dominant.
4 The article "Postmodernism, or the cultural logic of late capitalism."
5 *Postmodernism, or the Cultural Logic of Late Capitalism*, p. 44.
6 For a discussion of the work of Giovanni see E. H. Gombrich, *Norm and Form* (London: Phaidon, 1966), pp. 11–28. For a discussion of the work of Veronese and Tintoretto see Norbert Huse and Wolfgang Wolters, *The Art of Renaissance Venice* (Chicago: University of Chicago Press, 1990).
7 *Cosmopolis: The Hidden Agenda of Modernity* (Chicago: University of Chicago Press, 1990), p. 83.
8 See Peter French, *John Dee: The World of an Elizabethan Magus* (London: Ark Paperbacks, 1987).
9 Eamon Duffy, *The Stripping of the Altars: Traditional Religion in England 1400–1580* (New Haven: Yale University Press, 1992), p. 395.
10 Toulmin, *Cosmopolis*, p. 108).
11 *The Discovery of Time*, Stephen Toulmin and J. Goodfield (London: Hutchinson, 1965), p. 103.
12 See Éric Alliez, *Capital Times*, trans. Georges Van Den Abbeele (Minneapolis: University of Minnesota Press, 1996). He traces the meaning and changing nature of time in Plotinus, Augustine and Duns Scotus.
13 *Summa theologiæ*, 1a QQ. 91.
14 *Summa theologiæ*, 1a QQ. 66.
15 Early Church Fathers like Gregory of Nyssa understood the powerful relation between perception and lust and called for a discipline of both desire and perception accordingly. 1 John 2:6 speaks of the "lust of the eyes." It was still a dominant teaching in Dante's time – hence the leopard (symbol of the hunger of seeing) in the opening Canto of the *Inferno*.
16 *Discoveries and Opinions of Galileo*, trans. Stillman Drake (New York: Anchor, 1957), p. 182.
17 See Amos Funkenstein, *Theology and the Scientific Imagination* (Princeton: Princeton University Press, 1986) for a detailed account of the secularization of divine properties and the development of what he terms "secular theology" between the Middle Ages and the seventeenth century.
18 See Michael J. Buckley, *At the Origins of Modern Atheism* (New Haven: Yale University Press, 1987).

19 *Essay Towards a Real Character* (1668, reprinted by the Scolar Press, 1968). This essay developed the bishop's work on signs, published as *Mercury* in 1641.

20 Harvey, p. 227.

21 Toulmin, *Cosmopolis*, p. 43.

22 See Edgar Wind, *Pagan Mysteries in the Renaissance* (Oxford: Oxford University Press, 1980), p. 65.

23 See *The Glory of the Lord*, volume 5: *The Realm of Metaphysics in the Modern Age*, trans. Oliver Davies et al. (Edinburgh: T. and T. Clark, 1991), pp. 9–47. The quotation is taken from pp. 26–9.

24 See Oliver Leaman, *Averroes and His Philosophy* (Oxford: Oxford University Press, 1988), for a detailed account of Averroës' work.

25 Lauro Martines, *Power and Imagination: City-States in Renaissance Italy* (London: Penguin Books, 1983), p. 299.

26 The conception of "analogy" changes here. The conception of "analogy" in Aquinas deals with similarity in difference as a means whereby God-talk avoids the pitfalls of univocity (resulting in anthropomorphism) and equivocity (resulting in agnosticism). Aquinas concludes that only certain terms, perfection terms like "love," "pure," and "good," are analogical. But the analogy of being, as Suarez conceives it, allows all predicates to participate in a third thing (Being) which they all share. God is the top, the most beingful, in the chain of being. "Analogy" here has erased difference to exalt similarity. The ontological difference between the uncreated God and the created order, which Aquinas saw as fundamental, has disappeared.

27 "Postmodern vs. Late-Modern," in Ingeborg Hoesterey (ed.), *Zeitgeist in Babel: The Post-Modernist Controversy* (Bloomington: Indiana University Press, 1991), pp. 4–21.

28 This is how Steven Connor uses it, for example, in his *Postmodern Culture: An Introduction to the Theories of the Contemporary* (Oxford: Blackwell, 1989).

29 *The Postmodern Condition: A Report on Knowledge*, trans. Geoff Bennington and Brian Massumi (Manchester: Manchester University Press, 1984), p. xxiii.

30 Ibid., p. xxiv.

31 "Rewriting Modernity," *SubStance*, no. 54 (1987), pp. 8–9.

32 "Answering the Question: What is Postmodernism?" in Thomas Docherty (ed.), *Postmodernism: A Reader* (Hemel Hempstead: Harvester Wheatsheaf, 1993), p. 50.

33 *The Postmodern Condition*, p. 81.

34 See the work of the sociologist Zygmunt Bauman here, particularly *Legislators and Interpreters: On Modernity, Postmodernity, and the Intellectuals* (Oxford: Polity Press, 1987) and *Intimations of Postmodernity* (London: Routledge, 1992).

35 *An Ethics of Sexual Difference*, trans. Carolyn Burke and Gillian C. Gill (London: Athlone Press, 1993), p. 7.

36 *Phenomenology of Spirit*, trans. A. V. Miller (Oxford: Oxford University Press, 1977), p. 490.

37 *The Gay Science*, trans. Walter Kaufmann (New York: Vintage, 1979), p. 125.

38 See *The Essence of Christianity*, trans. George Eliot (New York: Harper Torchbook), 1957. "By his God thou knowest the man, and by the man his God; the two are identical" (p. 12).

39 *Time and the Other* (1948), trans. Richard Cohen (Pittsburgh: Duquesne University Press, 1987), p. 46.

40 "On Truth and Falsity in their Ultramoral Sense," in vol. II of *Collected Works*, ed. Oscar Levy (London and Edinburgh: T. N. Foulis, 1911), p. 180.

41 *Daybreak Thoughts on the Prejudices of Morality*, trans. R. J. Hollingdale (Cambridge: Cambridge University Press, 1982), p. 9.

42 *Ecce Homo*, trans. Walter Kaufmann (New York: Vintage, 1969), p. 272.

43 *Will to Power*, trans. Walter Kaufmann and R. J. Hollingdale (New York: Vintage, 1968), p. 481).

44 *Nietzsche*, vol. 3, trans. Joan Stambaugh et al. (New York: HarperCollins, 1991), pp. 3–9.

45 *The Philosophical Discourse of Modernity*, trans. Frederick G. Lawrence (Oxford: Polity Press, 1987), pp. 83–105.

46 *Twilight of the Idols*, trans. R. J. Hollingdale (London: Penguin, 1968), pp. 49–50.

47 *Genealogy of Morals*, trans. Walter Kaufmann and R. J. Hollingdale (New York: Vintage, 1969), p. 161.

48 *Will to Power*, p. 427.

49 Alexander Nehamas, *Nietzsche: Life as Literature* (Cambridge, MA: Harvard University Press, 1985), p. 90.

50 Henry Staten, *Nietzsche's Voice* (Ithaca, NY: Cornell University Press, 1990), p. 104. This book details the dialectical economy of logic and libido in Nietzsche's texts.

51 *The Gay Science*, trans. Walter Kaufmann (New York: Vintage, 1966), p. 343.

52 Ibid., p. 54.

53 *Identity and Difference*, trans. Joan Stambaugh (New York: Harper and Row, 1969), p. 54.

54 Ibid.

55 Ibid., p. 25.

56 Ibid., p. 51.

57 Ibid., p. 53.

58 Ibid., p. 65.

59 Ibid., p. 71.

60 Ibid., p. 72.

61 The first of such commentators was Derrida himself in his essay "Violence and Metaphysics: An Essay on the Thought of Emmanuel Levinas," in *Writing and Difference*, trans. Alan Bass (London: Routledge, 1981), pp. 79–153. I take up this analysis in my own *Barth, Derrida and the Theology of Language* (Cambridge: Cambridge University Press, 1995).

62 *The Adventure of Difference: Philosophy after Nietzsche and Heidegger*, trans. Cyprian Blamires et al. (Oxford: Polity Press, 1993), p. 144.

63 Ibid., p. 177.

64 *Course in General Linguistics*, trans. Roy Harris (London: Duckworth, 1983), p. 10.

65 Ibid. p. 121.

66 *An Ethics of Sexual Difference*, pp. 7–8.

67 *The Birth to Presence*, trans. Brian Holmes et al. (Stanford, CA: Stanford University Press, 1993), p. 192.

68 Tom Rockmore, *Heidegger and French Philosophy* (London: Routledge, 1995), p. 8.

69 *Cartesian Meditations: An Introduction to Phenomenology*, trans. Dorion Cairns (Dordrecht: Martinus Nijhoff, 1960).

70 *God Without Being*, trans. Thomas A. Carlson (Chicago: University of Chicago Press, 1991), p. xix.

71 For an introductory account of the warring see Vincent Descombes, *Modern French Philosophy*, trans. L. Scott-Fox and J. M. Harding (Cambridge: Cambridge University Press, 1980), pp. 117–35.

72 Rockmore, *Heidegger*, p. 13.

73 See here the article by Marion in Part II, for Marion's own theological work is a development in this radicalization of phenomenology.

74 *Collected Philosophical Papers*, trans. Alphonso Lingis (Dordrecht: Martinus Nijhoff, 1987), p. 130.

75 Ibid., p. 138.

76 *Experience of Freedom*, trans. Bridget McDonald (Stanford, CA: Stanford University Press, 1993), p. 98.

77 Rockmore, *Heidegger*, pp. 18–39.

78 *Angels: A Modern Myth*, trans. Francis Cowper (Paris: Flammarion, 1995). See *A History of Scientific Thought: Elements of a History of Science*, ed. Michel Serres, trans. from the French (Cambridge, MA: Blackwell Reference, 1995).

79 See my article on Hélène Cixous, "Words of Life: Hosting Postmodern Plenitude," in *The Way*, 363 (July 1996), pp. 200–14.

80 *"Coming to Writing" and Other Essays*, ed. Deborah Jenson, trans. Sarah Cornell et al. (Cambridge, MA: Harvard University Press, 1991), p. 129.

81 For a brief guide to these thinkers as self-styled postmodern theologians, see my contribution "Postmodern Theology," in David Ford (ed.), *The Modern Theologians*, second edition (Oxford: Blackwell, 1996), pp. 585–601. The list of publications by Thomas T. Altizer and David Ray Griffin is impressive, but I would refer the reader to Altizer's *The Gospel of Christian Atheism* (London: SCM, 1967); *Total Presence: The Language of Jesus and the Language of Today* (New York: Seabury Press, 1980); and *History as Apocalypse* (Albany: State University of New York Press, 1985). For Griffin see *God and Religion in the Postmodern World: Essays in Postmodern Theology* (Albany: State University of New York Press, 1989).

82 *The Modern Theologians*, p. 590. Don Cupitt has written many volumes, but perhaps representative of his thinking would be *The Long Legged Fly* (London: SCM, 1987) and, more recently, *The Last Philosophy* (London: SCM, 1995). For Mark C. Taylor's work, see *De-constructing Theology* (New York: Crossroad Publishing, 1982) and *Erring: A Postmodern A/theology* (Chicago: University of Chicago Press, 1984).

83 Descombes, *Modern French Philosophy*, pp. 152–6.

84 See the final chapter of Rowan Williams, *Arius: Heresy and Tradition* (London: Darton, Longman and Todd, 1987) and Joseph S. O'Leary, *Questioning Back: Overcoming Metaphysics in Christian Tradition* (Minneapolis: Winston Press, 1985).

PART

I

Selected Texts

I

Georges Bataille (1897–1962): Introduction

Craig James

André Breton, the leader of the French Surrealist Group in the 1920s and 1930s, described Bataille as a "case," a person whose ideas seemed distinctly "obsessive," even "pathological."[1] Sartre, similarly, thought that a psychoanalyst should be consulted. He defined Bataille disparagingly as *un nouveau mystique*.[2] Other assessments of Bataille's work were more enthusiastic. Heidegger, for example, maintained that Bataille was "one of France's best minds." And Breton himself wrote, on another occasion, that Bataille was "one of the few men in life worth taking the trouble of getting to know."[3]

What is alarming is that however we choose to discuss Bataille's life and works we are left feeling uneasy, as if, confronted with a particularly demanding riddle, we have been caught trying to cheat. "From whichever angle we approach him, he eludes us" (LE110).[4] He is a "paradoxical" philosopher, whose work is essentially unclassifiable, connecting both "metaphysics" and "the human flesh."[5] It is not satisfactory, for example, to describe Bataille as a surrealist, although he was closely associated with many members of the Surrealist Group. Nor is he a poststructuralist, despite the fact that Bataille has often come to be known as the shadowy figure (an *éminence grise*) who exerted an enormous influence on later thinkers like Foucault, Derrida, Baudrillard, Kristeva, and Lyotard: chronologically he is too early. Some think of Bataille as a fascist, but Michel Leiris, who knew him well, asserts instead that he was "profoundly anti-fascist."[6] Still others attack him on the grounds that he was a Nietzschean, a Hegelian, a Marxist, an Existentialist, or a Stalinist! And his books make him seem still more contradictory and enigmatic. Roland Barthes writes: "Is this writer a novelist, a poet, an essayist, an economist, a philosopher, a mystic? The answer is so uncertain that handbooks of literature generally prefer to leave Bataille out."[7] Bataille might playfully add: "I can also be anything you like" (AM83). Elsewhere, he writes: "I have more than one face. I don't know which is laughing at which" (ON68). Already it seems appropriate to ask: "is there a Georges Bataille?"

Certainly it is possible to weave a biographical narrative around the "life" of Bataille, and one might be tempted to suggest that, in many ways, the elusive and troublesome nature of his work is, in fact, best understood within the context of a life lived against the backcloth of turbulent historical events. Bataille was born in Billom, France, in 1897, to a blind father who was later also partially paralyzed, the result, Bataille claimed, of syphilis (although his elder brother disputed this). Despite having received no formal religious instruction, Bataille converted to Catholicism in August 1914, around the time that he and his mother fled from their home town, which was under threat of German bombardment. Bataille's sick father was left behind and died alone during the following year. In 1917 Bataille was discharged from the army and subsequently thought of becoming a priest or monk. Instead, in 1918, he entered the École des Chartes in Paris. He lost his faith in 1920 (it had made a woman he loved shed tears). He was sent in the same year to work in Madrid, where he developed a passionate interest in bull-fighting and witnessed the death of Granero, one of Spain's most popular matadors. In 1922 Bataille became a librarian at the Bibliothèque Nationale and began an extensive course of reading. In the following year he was introduced to ethnology (the comparative study of different social groups) and read Marcel Mauss's influential book *The Gift*.[8] Bataille later came into contact with the Surrealists and his first conflicts with Breton soon followed. In 1927 he underwent Freudian psychoanalysis. At last able to write, he published a black erotic text called *Story of the Eye* in 1928, under the pseudonym of Lord Auch.

Bataille became important on the Paris intellectual scene because of his involvement in a number of new literary and political groups. In 1929–30 he edited the eclectic journal *Documents* and in 1935 he set up *Contre-Attaque* with André Breton (during a brief period of reconciliation). This was a left-wing political group which aimed to counter the rise of Fascism by employing equal force, but Bataille quickly disbanded the group because it was itself accused of being fascist. Apart from the preoccupation with the rise of Fascism and the threat of war, intellectual debate in Paris was very much centered around the work of Hegel, which was being brilliantly explored in Alexandre Kojève's 1933–9 lecture series. Bataille, like most of his contemporary Parisian intellectuals, attended these lectures and was deeply influenced by them.

From 1937 to 1939 Bataille organized a secret society called *Acéphale* (which he reputedly used as a forum to call for "an irrevocable ritual gesture – the enactment of a voluntary human sacrifice" (ME202) and, jointly with Roger

Caillois, founded the famous Collège de Sociologie. Bataille's disenchantment with political activism was intensified by the death, in 1938, of his lover Colette Peignot ("Laure") and by the outbreak of war in 1939. During the war he wrote a number of deeply introspective works, especially the triad of books which constitute part of the incomplete *La Somme athéologique* (*Inner Experience*, *Guilty*, and *On Nietzsche*). In 1946 he set up *Critique*, a monthly review, and *The Accursed Share*, which Bataille considered to be his most important work, was published in 1949. Another major work, *Eroticism*, was published in 1957, five years before his death.

Writing about Bataille's life seems strange: it smacks of necrophilia. But like a faded old black and white photograph of an unknown face, it conjures up the sense of a life, no matter how misleading. That we are at least a little astray in our fantasies, however, is inevitable. Likewise as I discuss some of the disparate, shifting voices and ideas which can be detected in Bataille's work, there is a real danger of binding together a set of "meanings" in a coherent narrative, through which we can evoke an entirely bogus and erroneous "Bataille." And then we can dismiss him, having effectively emasculated the unsettling challenge which his thought presents. This tendency of language to induce lethargy is something which Bataille is very aware of. He notes that language can often substitute "the appearance of a solution for the insoluble, and a screen for violent truth" (LE94). Therefore: "any commentary which does not simply say that commentaries are useless and impossible moves us away from the truth at the very moment when it might come close to it in itself" (LE94). To this extent it is important to remember that you may not now be reading about "Bataille" (a corpse, after all): you may be reading fiction. Words should not be treated like medicine: although you may be instructed to swallow them without protest, it is healthier to struggle a little.

Much of Bataille's work could, in fact, be seen as an attempt to promote this kind of struggle. Like some crazy shaman, he dares us to slip beneath our masks, to strip naked in response to the challenge to plunge into otherness (*altérité*), while at the same time lucidly confronting the intense anguish that this movement brings. But reading him in any conventional way may prevent this dazzling laceration (*déchirement*) from occurring. Bataille subsequently writes in a style which tends generally to undermine the glib reactions that the reader might want to make about his work: he constantly raises the ante. Reading him can therefore be a deeply harrowing experience. As Sartre has observed, his ideas seem often to "melt like snow"[9] and with one slip we may find ourselves "dissolved forever in the void" (AC146). Bataille writes: "The one who writes with his blood does not want to be *read?* . . . One mustn't read me: I don't want to be covered with evasions. I propose a challenge, not a book. I offer nothing for insomnia" (IE199). Yet elsewhere Bataille asserts that to write is already to have "fallen asleep again" (AM99). So writing is itself problematical; and the paradox of the writer who denounces writing is not lost on Bataille. Rather like Epicurus, his distaste for language is often vehement: "I can't abide sentences . . . I'm only silence, and the universe is silence" (G40). And he wonders: "*How to write, except as a usually chaste woman getting undressed for an orgy?*" (AM100). His writing is an offense (true literature is always guilty), which must be compensated for by the "annihilation of what is written."[10] But at the same time Bataille has a powerful sense of the *need* to communicate. So to write is a betrayal although not to write would be a still greater act of treachery. He does not attempt to flee from this dilemma: it is one of the many "impossible" tensions which resound through his writings. Instead he warns us that "even what I say is yet another obstacle which we must remove if we want to *see*" (LE94). Now I am wielding the knife (or is it you?) so take care . . .

Before turning to look at *Theory of Religion* it is worth sketching out the most important aspects of Bataille's thinking. His work may be described as an attempt to confront the "totality of what is." So in opposition to the "scientific method," which bases knowledge on the separation of subject and object, Bataille maintains that any study which tries to extract one element from its proper place within the totality of "being" will result in misunderstanding. He is also engaging in "a voyage to the end of the possible of man" (IE7), a voyage to the end of the night (*voyage au bout de la nuit*). He writes: "To ask oneself before another: by what means does he calm within himself the desire to be everything?" (IExxxii). To this end, he grapples with the insight that human life is an experience of limits. Spurred on by desire, our existence is "an exasperated attempt to complete being" (IE89). The individual struggles, on the one hand, to find and constitute himself or herself as an autonomous entity (a necessary narcotic made up of a desire to deny death in an affirmation of a particular continuity). But the fact of limits (discontinuity) continually frustrates this desire: the isolated self is constantly contested by the existence of others (*alterity*) and by the transcendent whole. This is a transcendence that at other moments we desperately wish to embrace (a nostalgic desire for lost intimacy and for pure immanence). The only way for the self truly to achieve continuity is by losing itself in the "totality of what is"; but this involves a sudden, sacrificial negation of self and an impossible anguish (*angoisse*) which is, simply, unendurable. It ultimately heralds death. The anguish is inevitable because to be a human being is to move from a sense of the insufficiency of self to a desire to be immanent within the totality of "being" – a desire which can never be realized, of course, as a discontinuous self: it is to be condemned, blind and lost, within an endless labyrinth.

In *Eroticism*, Bataille explores these tensions in relation to human sexuality. He gives an initial definition of eroticism as the "assenting of life up to the point of death" (E11). Realizing the importance of understanding humanity in ways which incorporate its "passions," Bataille asserts a fundamental connection between sexuality, violence, and death. He notes, for example, that: "Reproduction implies the existence of *discontinuous* beings" (E12). Beings which reproduce sexually are distinct from one another: "Between one being and another, there is a gulf, a discontinuity" (E12). This discontinuity is defined in relation to the recognition of death. Death, Bataille maintains, is not essential to life.[11] But it is necessary if life is to advance because development requires a process of separation and differentiation. Development, in other words, requires my death. Matters are more complicated, however, because death does not simply constitute the violence of discontinuity. As death is necessary for human life (life rises up from death), so it also heralds an essential continuity lying beneath our existence. Bataille explains: "Sperm and ovum are to begin with discontinuous entities, but they *unite*, and consequently a continuity comes into existence between them to form a new entity from the death and disappearance of the separate beings. The new entity is itself discontinuous, but it bears within itself the transition to continuity, the fusion, fatal to both, of two separate beings" (E14). Eroticism differs from animal sexuality because of an awareness (if only vague) of this ambivalence between continuity and discontinuity, the violence of sexuality and death. Our sexuality is a question mark which, like the blade of a guillotine, hangs over us: "In human consciousness eroticism is that within man which calls his being in question" (E29). Sexuality is particularly significant because it is the forum in which birth and death coincide: our moans of delight herald the birth of a new life but later seem to have been moans of anguish, as we fearfully await our own demise. Sexuality reveals the void beneath us, on which the improbability of our being rests. It is an immense gulf, one from which we cannot escape, although we can, at least, experience the dizziness of it together (it can become the basis of communication). The gulf is death, but "death is vertiginous, death is hypnotising" (E13). Eroticism is, therefore, an impossible exuberance; it is one of the many ways in which we continually challenge the limits of our discontinuous selves, attempting vainly to go beyond ourselves toward the dark mystery of all that is other (and ultimately into continuity, intimacy, and death). The death of the individual must subsequently be seen as "but one aspect of the proliferative excess of being" (LE16).

It is helpful to understand the exuberant nature of eroticism in the context of Bataille's analysis of excess energy, or what he describes as the general, or "solar," economy (in contrast to the restricted economy of conventional economic discourse). This analysis is found in *The Accursed Share* and is an attempt to address the following question: "Should we not, given the constant development of economic forces, pose the *general* problems that are linked to the movement of energy on the globe?" (AS120). Bataille asserts that the living organism (including humanity) generally receives more energy (emanating ultimately from the "ceaseless prodigality" of the sun) than is necessary for maintaining life. This excess energy is used primarily for the growth of a life system, but "if the system can no longer grow, or if the excess cannot be completely absorbed in its growth, it must necessarily be lost without profit; it must be spent, willingly or not, gloriously or catastrophically" (ASI21). The key to Bataille's understanding of the general economy is that it is not necessity, but luxury (the "accursed share"), which is the cause of fundamental social problems: a formula which derives from his assertion that the underlying principle of the universe is one of "proliferative excess." Bataille points out that the tendency of modern, capitalist humanity, in opposition to this principle, is often to accumulate for itself, like a miser, as much of this excess energy as possible. He maintains that this is dangerous; it leads to a constipated economy which at some point must, of necessity, have relief: "eventually, like a river into the sea," the accumulated forces are "bound to escape us and be lost to us" (ASI23). If we are not able to destroy the surplus energy, this energy destroys us. So our most pressing problem is to find adequate ways to expend this surplus: solutions have included the festival, the orgy, the sacrifice, and, when no other alternative could be found: war. Bataille, on the basis of this analysis, calls for an "overturning of economic principles," and of the ethics that accompany them. By incorporating the movements of the general economy into our understanding, Bataille hopes to achieve a "Copernican transformation" in which the principal focus of economic activity would no longer be accumulation, but a frenzied expenditure (*dépense*) in which commodities would be surrendered without return. The consequence of an economy based upon the general circuit of cosmic energy would therefore be that "the possibility of pursuing growth is itself subordinated to giving" (ASI25f).[12]

Drawing on the insights of Durkheimian sociology, Bataille frequently employs the opposed concepts of "sacred" and "profane." The profane (homogeneous) world is the world of work, project, utility, tools, morality, and so on. It is a servile world: a world of "things." Humanity, as it exists within the restricted economy, occupies a place in the profane world: it defers current satisfaction in favour of accumulating excess wealth. The sacred (heterogeneous) realm, on the other hand, is made up of all that threatens to reveal the profane world for what it really is – a sham. It is the excluded element which defines and lends meaning to the profane world. But because the sacred threatens to transgress and violate the stable order of the restricted economy it must, of necessity, be deemed taboo: its violent, lacerating forces are too volatile to be domesticated within everyday life. So the sacred realm is generally ostracized to the boundaries of language and experience. All that is not easily reducible to language, all that cannot be fully grasped by reason, belongs to the sacred realm (including bodily fluids, laughter, poetry, sacrifice, festivals, religion, sexuality, violence, death, and God). True communication, in Bataille's sense, can, in fact, only occur within the sacred realm because only within the sacred realm do the limits of individual and society merge in an experience of "totality" (an experience, in other words, which cannot be reduced, by reason, to servility). Such communication always requires a radical taking of risks (like the opening up of a wound) in which the self is lost within and lacerated by desire for all that is other (*autre*): it involves a movement of glorious expenditure where excess energies are magnificently squandered. It is momentarily to touch the moral summit and to know sovereignty "suspended in the beyond of oneself, at the limit of nothingness" (ON19). It is to embrace the prospect of self-annihilation. So Bataille understands the action of giving, for example, as "sacred": it is an action which encourages "communication." But communication is also always "Evil" in that its values are opposed to the profane world (the world of declining morality and the Good): communication always shatters the world of things. Bataille therefore endorses Sartre's definition of the sacred as "subjectivity manifesting itself in and through the objective by destroying objectivity" (LE206).

Many of these notions are elaborated in *Theory of Religion*, a work which was probably written in the latter part of the 1940s but which was not published until after Bataille's death. The text begins with a discussion of "animality." The animal, Bataille claims, is "immanent" in the world because it does not know itself as a subject. Instead, "every animal is in the world like water in water" (TR19). But the human person has come to know itself as a subject through the development of the profane world. This world developed from the positing of "objects," originally in the form of tools. Bataille writes: "The developed tool is the nascent form of the non-I" (TR27). The status of the tool is subordinate to that of man because its end becomes perceived in terms of the means that it provides. A world of discontinuity based upon the object subsequently emerges and this world opposes immanence or "the flow of all that is" (TR29). Our consciousness becomes trapped in an endless chain: "The stick digs the ground in order to ensure the growth of a plant; the plant is cultivated in order to be eaten; it is eaten in order to maintain the life of the one who cultivates it" (TR28). Humanity then commits the error of placing elements which are really continuous with the world (e.g., animals, plants, other men, and finally the determining subject itself) onto this discontinuous plane of objects (tools). Humanity subsequently comes to view itself as "another": simultaneously subject and object, it is, in Hegelian terms, both "for itself" and "in itself." At the same time humanity becomes nostalgic for a lost sacred and continuous world. These tensions are further reflected in the equation of the mind with the sacred realm and the body with its profane antithesis: "Insofar as it is spirit, the human reality is holy, but it is profane insofar as it is real" (TR38). The world of things which humanity creates and rules thus succeeds in alienating us from ourselves and from our environment: "If he places the world in his power, this is to the extent that he forgets that he is himself the world: he denies the world but it is himself that he denies" (TR41). This fall from the realm of continuity to discontinuity symbolizes, for Bataille, the transition from animal to human: the intimate order is replaced by a fragmented world of things. It endorses Bataille's assertion that "man is the animal that does not just accept the facts of nature, he contradicts them" (E214).

Eventually all that belongs rightly to the realm of the sacred, including sacrifice, violence and divinity, loses its power and is reduced to the servile status of mere things (even if sacred things). The denial of violence, for example, leads to its redirection outside of a given community. A new order arises: the order of war and empire. But this new world is weighed down by utility and misplaced values: it denies the necessary consumption of a society's sacred excess in ways which do not contribute to an increase of its power (i.e., in non-utilitarian ways). Instead, the growth of empire depends wholly upon the real order: "It subordinates itself to ends that it affirms: it is the administration of reason" (TR66). And the empire itself becomes a symbol of the "universal thing" (TR67). Elevated to a similar stature as reason, morality likewise develops in order to guarantee that the values of the profane world pass unquestioned. Note that this requires a fundamental shift in the way that the divine order is perceived. If this order is to underwrite successfully the values of the empire, it must be purged of all that threatens to violate those values: all that seems irrational (or truly sacred), such as violence and useless consumption, must be expelled. This, in turn, encourages a marked tendency toward a dualism in which all that reason maintains to be "good" is deemed sacred and all that reason deems to be "bad" must, of necessity, be profane. So: "They rationalize and moralize divinity, in the very movement where morality and reason are divinized" (TR71). The intimate order is denied and humanity finds itself entirely cut off from the world: "This world is in fact immanent to him but this is insofar as he is no longer characterized by intimacy, insofar as he is defined by things, and is himself a thing, being a distinctly separate individual" (TR74). Humanity is now left only with a dim memory of lost intimacy and a fear of irrational violence which, in turn, prohibits any future access to the sacred. The principles of production, which require human duration and subsequently a constant deferral of the present moment, are all that remain. Eventually the "millenial quest for lost intimacy was abandoned by productive mankind" (TR92). Our world is almost completely reduced to the real order. This "Enlightenment" stage is that upon which modern capitalism gaily stomps, while humanity drifts ever deeper into "THE SLEEP OF REASON – WHICH PRODUCES MONSTERS" (TR112).

We have noted that the human person itself comes to be viewed as a thing: "The farmer is not a man: he is the plow of the one who eats the bread" (TR42). It is as a result of this that sacrifice is such an important notion for Bataille: sacrifice is a way of appeasing humanity's guilt at making things out of continuous beings (especially itself). Like death, it "restores a lost value through a relinquishment of that value" (TR48). It is a way of removing from the world of things that which does not rightly belong there. So note that Bataille stresses that sacrifice need not necessarily involve the victim's death. He writes: "The thing – only the thing – is what sacrifice means to destroy in the victim" (TR43). The violence of the sacrifice (like the exuberance of the festival) subsequently comes to represent a partial restoration of the intimate order; it is a revelation of continuity. Its values are the antithesis to those of the profane world; it is a "gift and relinquishment" which is concerned only with "the world of abrupt consumption" (TR49).

It is important to be clear that, by drawing on the notion of sacrifice, Bataille is *not* recommending that we reject all of the values that are associated with humanity's modern self-understanding. He is not promoting a return to some idyllic, immanent animality: romanticism and *Lebensphilosophie* are not to his taste.[13] He is fully aware of the danger that "if man surrendered unreservedly to immanence, he would fall short of humanity; he would achieve it only to lose it and eventually life would return to the unconscious intimacy of animals" (TR53). Nor should he be dismissed as an anarchist or a nihilist; his understanding of a heterogeneous society is not one which revolves entirely around chaos and self-satisfaction (such a description is better fitted to a homogeneous society). Instead it is a call for humanity to address the question of the price which it must pay for self-consciousness. He maintains that a heterogeneous society is a healthy society; it is a society which does not try to suppress or ignore the sacred aspects of our being. Rather it concedes that the sacred elements that cause us such anguish by challenging the solidity of our separate, isolated existences, lie precisely at the heart of social being. So Bataille wants a lucid (total) self-understanding, while knowing that such comprehension is impossible. He is grappling with the "constant problem posed by the impossibility of being human without being a thing and of escaping the limits of things without returning to animal slumber (TR53).

The frustration, for Bataille, is that all attempts to restore humanity to the world of intimacy (i.e., religion) are intrinsically flawed: success is always limited because the sacred realm is not "real" – it cannot be captured. This is important: once the "sacred" is objectified in language and consciousness, it becomes a thing, and is therefore no longer sacred. In other words, when we feel sure that we have captured the Grail, what we really grasp is a thing, "and what is left in our hands is only a cooking pot" (ASI130). Attempts to grasp the sacred also quickly reduce themselves to the language of project (utility, the real) and so become profane. Sacrifice, like the hope of a future salvation, ultimately exemplifies the world of project (sacrifices do, after all, tend to be prepared with great discipline). In the manner of inner experience, they are doomed attempts "to emerge through project from the realm of project" (IE46).

Likewise our notions of "God" (a thing) all too often become screens which prevent us from experiencing the sacred: they must themselves be sacrificed (crucified). So what is sacred is nothing (but if we see "nothing" as an object, a thing, not even this is true). Sacrifice and festivals may be able to bring about a "slippage" (*glissement*) which gives us a sensation of vertigo, or of looking down into nothingness (*néant*), but "the letting loose of the festival is finally, if not fettered, then at least confined to the limits of a reality of which it is the negation" (TR54). Bataille writes: "The festival is not a true return to immanence but rather an amicable reconciliation, full of anguish, between the incompatible necessities" (TR55). Like Kafka's castle, the sacred ultimately remains inaccessible to consciousness. So sacrifice is, at best, an attempt to give violence its due and thereby to limit its mortal contagion. It represents an important way of acknowledging the absolute (totality, otherness) and of ritualizing or dramatizing our painful sense of incompletion (the drama of a victim's death reminds me of my own fragmentation in the same way that a negation of another leads to the negation of self). And our inevitable misunderstanding of the nature of sacrifice and the sacred (inevitable because "understanding" already presupposes positing a "thing") remains the "basic problem of religion" (TR56).

"Man," Bataille declares, "is the being that has lost, and even rejected, that which he obscurely is, a vague intimacy" (TR56). The human tragedy is subsequently one of "clear consciousness" engaging in a futile search for "complete self-consciousness." This is an "impossible" search because "knowledge finally opens a void": at the "summit of knowledge, knowledge stops" (G89). Bataille is aware that the attempt to look directly at the blazing sun (*en plein soleil*) results in the laceration of the eye and the blindness of night: like Icarus, our attempt to soar to the heights is followed inevitably by a catastrophic fall. And the moment of sacrifice (including the sacrifice of language in poetry and the sacrifice of selfhood in eroticism) is essentially that point at which knowledge slips into non-knowledge (*non-savoir*): "I yield, and everything's vertigo" (G89). Bataille writes: "If one were to ascribe me a place within the history of thought, it would be, I believe, for having discerned the effects, within our lives, of the moments at which discursive reality disappears, and for having drawn from the description of these effects a disappearing light: this light may be blinding, but it also announces the opacity of the night; it announces only night."[14]

Are we now nearer to discerning the source of the enigma which is Georges Bataille? Perhaps Bataille has realized that, underneath "the mask of one man among others," the holding up of a mirror before one's being always reveals a fundamental continuity: "*the unknown*" (IE151). This violent revelation of sacred continuity, this *unknown*, involves a total negation of consciousness: language and clarity slip away in the plenitude of the impossible. It is to enter into a realm in which all apparent opposites are reconciled: "Life will dissolve itself in death, rivers in the sea, and the known in the unknown. Knowledge is access to the unknown. Nonsense is the outcome of every possible sense" (IE101). Bataille writes: "at the boundary of that which escapes cohesion, he who reflects within cohesion realizes that there is no longer any room for him" (TR10). For a moment Bataille mistakes himself for God: "At times it was entertaining to think I was God" (ON65). Although it is vital to remember that, like Eckhart, what we label "God" is an "absence of any object" (E23): "God is nothing if he is not a transcendence of God in every direction; in that of vulgar being, in that of horror and impurity; even in that of nothing at all in the last analysis" (E269). As with the acephalic man (the gnostic image used by Bataille to symbolize the sovereign, headless figure), the search for the center of our being results in the unraveling of our being. It leads to the realization that the truth of humanity is to be a continual questioning, a "supplication without response" (IE13). Bataille describes himself as "a cloth in tatters" (IE66), a person whose life is "an ongoing evocation of possibilities" (ON149), a tearing open before the infinite. As such, his words must be read as a song of jubilation and praise in the face of the "impossible depth of things."

Abbreviations

AC	*L'Abbé C*
AM	*The Absence of Myth*
ASI	*The Accursed Share, Vol. I*
E	*Eroticism*
G	*Guilty*
IE	*Inner Experience*
LE	*Literature and Evil*
ME	*My Mother, Madame Edwarda, The Dead Man*
ON	*On Nietzsche*
TR	*Theory of Religion*

Notes

1 "Second Manifesto of Surrealism," trans. Richard Seaver and Helen R. Lane in André Breton, *Manifestoes of Surrealism* (Ann Arbor: University of Michigan Press, 1972), p. 184.

2 "Un nouveau mystique" was the title given by Sartre to his critique, in the journal *Cahiers*

du Sud, of Bataille's *Inner Experience*.

3 Quoted by Michael Richardson in his introduction to Bataille, *The Absence of Myth*, p. 6.

4 This is a comment which Bataille makes on Sade, but it is equally applicable to himself.

5 Yukio Mishima, "Georges Bataille and Divinus Deus," in Bataille, *My Mother, Madame Edwarda, The Dead Man*, trans. Austryn Wainhouse (London: Marion Boyars, 1989), p. 11.

6 See Bernard-Henri Lévy, *Adventures on the Freedom Road: The French Intellectuals in the Twentieth Century*, trans. Richard Veasey (London: Harvill Press, 1995), p. 198.

7 "From Work to Text," in *The Rustle of Language*, trans. Richard Howard (New York: Hill and Wang, 1986), p. 58.

8 See Marcel Mauss, *The Gift: The Form and Reason for Exchange in Archaic Societies*, trans. W. D. Halls (London: Routledge, 1990).

9 Quoted in Michèle H. Richman, *Beyond the Gift: Reading Georges Bataille* (Baltimore, MD: Johns Hopkins University Press, 1982), p. 114.

10 Quoted in Nick Land, *The Thirst for Annihilation*, p. 186.

11 He notes that some basic life forms reproduce by scissiparity, or a process of cell division, in a way which does not seem to involve death in our sense.

12 Bataille's use of the notion of "The Gift" clearly originates with Mauss's influential essay, but note that Bataille's formulation of it is significantly different from that of Mauss, whose analysis centered upon an understanding of gift-giving as a largely reciprocal and reasoned activity.

13 Cf. Jürgen Habermas, *The Philosophical Discourse of Modernity*, trans. Frederick Lawrence (Cambridge, MA: MIT Press, 1987), p. 235.

14 Quoted in Michèle H. Richman: *Beyond the Gift: Reading Georges Bataille*, p. 97.

Selected Bibliography

Bataille, Georges, *Visions of Excess* (Selected Writings 1927–39), trans. Allan Stoekl (Minneapolis: University of Minnesota Press, 1985).

——*Story of the Eye by Lord Auch* (1928), trans. Joachim Neugroschal (Harmondsworth: Penguin, 1982).

——*Inner Experience* (1943), trans. Leslie Anne Boldt (Albany: State University of New York Press, 1988).

——*Guilty* (1944), trans. Bruce Boone (Venice, CA: Lapis Press, 1988).

——*On Nietzsche* (1945), trans. Bruce Boone (London: Athlone Press, 1992).

——*The Impossible: A Story of Rats followed by Dianus and by the Oresteia* (1947–62), trans. Robert Hurley (San Francisco: City Lights Books, 1991).

——*The Accursed Share* (1949), trans. Robert Hurley (New York: Zone Books, 1988).

——*L'Abbé C* (1950), trans. Philip A. Facey (London: Marion Boyars, 1988).

——*Blue of Noon* (1957), trans. Harry Mathews (London: Marion Boyars, 1986).

——*Eroticism* (1957), trans. Mary Dalwood (London: Marion Boyars, 1987).

——*Literature and Evil* (1957), trans. Alastair Hamilton (London: Marion Boyars, 1986).

—— *The Tears of Eros* (1961), trans. Peter Connor (San Francisco: City Lights Books, 1989).

—— *My Mother, Madame Edwarda, The Dead Man* (1966/7), trans. Austryn Wainhouse (London: Marion Boyars, 1988).

—— *Theory of Religion* (1973), trans. Robert Hurley (New York: Zone Books, 1989).

—— *The Absence of Myth: Writings on Surrealism*, trans. Michael Richardson (London: Verso, 1994).

Gill, Carolyn Bailey (ed.), *Georges Bataille: Writing and the Sacred* (London: Routledge, 1994).

Hollier, Denis, *Against Architecture: The Writings of Georges Bataille*, trans. Betsy Wing (Cambridge, MA: MIT Press, 1989).

Land, Nick, *The Thirst For Annihilation: Georges Bataille and Virulent Nihilism (An Essay in Atheistic Religion)*. (London: Routledge, 1992).

Richardson, Michael, *Georges Bataille* (London: Routledge, 1994).

Richman, Michèle H., *Reading Georges Bataille: Beyond the Gift* (Baltimore: Johns Hopkins University Press, 1982).

Stoekl, Allan (ed.), "On Bataille," *Yale French Studies*, 78 (1990).

From *Theory of Religion*

The Need that is Met by Sacrifice and Its Principle

The first fruits of the harvest or a head of livestock are sacrificed in order to remove the plant and the animal, together with the farmer and the stock raiser, from the world of things.

The principle of sacrifice is destruction, but though it sometimes goes so far as to destroy completely (as in a holocaust), the destruction that sacrifice is intended to bring about is not annihilation. The thing – only the thing – is what sacrifice means to destroy in the victim. Sacrifice destroys an object's real ties of subordination; it draws the victim out of the world of utility and restores it to that of unintelligible caprice. When the offered animal enters the circle in which the priest will immolate it, it passes from the world of things which are closed to man and are *nothing* to him, which he knows from the outside – to the world that is immanent to it, *intimate*, known as the wife is known in sexual consumption (*consommation charnelle*).

This assumes that it has ceased to be separated from its own intimacy, as it is in the subordination of labor. The sacrificer's prior separation from the world of things is necessary for the return to *intimacy*, of immanence between man and the world, between the subject and the object. The sacrificer needs the sacrifice in order to separate himself from the world of things and the victim could not be separated from it in turn if the sacrificer was not already separated in advance. The sacrificer declares:

> *Intimately*, I belong to the sovereign world of the gods and myths, to the world of violent and uncalculated generosity, just as my wife belongs to my desires. I withdraw you, victim, from the world in which you were and could only be reduced to the condition of a thing, having a meaning that was foreign to your intimate nature. I call you back to the *intimacy* of the divine world, of the profound immanence of all that is.

The Unreality of the Divine World

Of course this is a monologue and the victim can neither understand nor reply. Sacrifice essentially turns its back on real relations. If it took them into account, it would go against its own nature, which is precisely the opposite of that world of things on which distinct *reality* is founded. It could not destroy the animal as a thing without denying the animal's objective *reality*. This is what gives the world of sacrifice an appearance of puerile gratuitousness. But one cannot at the same time destroy the values that found reality and accept their limits. The return to immanent intimacy implies a beclouded consciousness: consciousness is tied to the positing of objects as such, grasped directly, apart from a vague perception, beyond the always unreal images of a thinking based on participation.

The Ordinary Association of Death and Sacrifice

The puerile unconsciousness of sacrifice even goes so far that killing appears as a way of redressing the wrong done to the animal, miserably reduced to the condition of a thing. As a matter of fact, killing in the literal sense is not necessary. But the greatest negation of the real order is the one most favorable to the appearance of the mythical order. Moreover, sacrificial killing resolves the painful antinomy of life and death by means of a reversal. In fact death is nothing in immanence, but because it is nothing, a being is never truly separated from it. Because death has no meaning, because there is no difference between it and life, and there is no fear of it or defense against it, it invades everything without giving rise to any resistance. Duration ceases to have any value, or it is there only in order to produce the morbid delectation of anguish. On the contrary, the objective and in a sense transcendent (relative to the subject) positing of the world of things has duration as its foundation: no *thing* in fact has a separate existence, has a meaning, unless a subsequent time is posited, in view of which it is constituted as an object. The object is defined as an operative power only if its duration is implicitly understood. If it is destroyed as food or fuel is, the eater or the manufactured object preserves its value in duration; it has a lasting purpose like coal or bread. Future time constitutes this real world to such a degree that death no longer has a place in it. But it is for this very reason that death means everything to it. The weakness (the contradiction) of the world of things is that it imparts an unreal character to death even though man's membership in this world is tied to the positing of the body as a thing insofar as it is mortal.

As a matter of fact, that is a superficial view. What has no place in the world of things, what is unreal in the real world is not exactly death. Death actually discloses the imposture of reality, not only in that the absence of duration gives the lie to it, but above all because death is the great affirmer, the wonder-struck cry of life. The real order does not so much reject the negation of life that is death as it rejects the affirmation of intimate life, whose measureless violence is a danger to the stability of things, an affirmation that is fully revealed only in death. The real order must annul – neutralize – that intimate life and replace it with the thing that the individual is in the society of labor. But it cannot prevent life's disappearance in death from revealing the *invisible* brilliance of life that is not a *thing*. The power of death signifies that this real world can only have a neutral image of life, that life's intimacy does not reveal its dazzling consumption until the moment it gives out. No one knew *it* was there when it was; it was overlooked in favor of real things: death was one real thing among others. But death suddenly shows that the real society was lying. Then it is not the loss of the thing, of the useful member, that is taken into consideration. What the real society has lost is not a member but rather its truth. That intimate life, which had lost the ability to fully reach me, which I regarded primarily as a thing, is fully restored to my sensibility through its absence. Death reveals life in its plenitude and dissolves the real order. Henceforth it matters very little that this real order is the need for the duration of that which no longer exists. When an element escapes its demands, what remains is not an entity that suffers bereavement; all at once that entity, the real order, has completely dissipated. There is no more question of it and what death brings in tears is the useless consumption of the intimate order.

It is a naive opinion that links death closely to sorrow. The tears of the living, which respond to its coming, are themselves far from having a meaning opposite to joy. Far from being sorrowful, the tears are the expression of a keen awareness of shared life grasped in its intimacy. It is true that this awareness is never keener than at the moment when absence suddenly replaces presence, as in death or mere separation. And in this case, the consolation (in the strong sense the word has in the "consolations" of the mystics) is in a sense bitterly tied to the fact that it cannot last, but it is precisely the disappearance of duration, and of the neutral behaviors associated with it, that uncovers a ground of things that is dazzlingly bright (in other words, it is clear that the need for duration conceals life from us, and that, only in theory, the impossibility of duration frees us). In other cases the tears respond instead to unexpected triumph, to good fortune that makes us exult, but always madly, far beyond the concern for a future time.

The Consummation of Sacrifice

The power that death generally has illuminates the meaning of sacrifice, which functions like death in that it restores a lost value through a relinquishment of that value. But death is not necessarily linked to it, and the most solemn sacrifice may not be bloody. To sacrifice is not to kill but to relinquish and to give. Killing is only the exhibition of a deep meaning. What is important is to pass from a lasting order, in which all consumption of resources is subordinated to the need for duration, to the violence of an unconditional consumption; what is important is to leave a world of real things, whose reality derives from a long-term operation and never resides in the moment – a world that creates and preserves (that creates for the benefit of a lasting reality). Sacrifice is the antithesis of production, which is accomplished with a view to the future; it is consumption that is concerned only with the moment. This is the sense in which it is gift and relinquishment, but what is given cannot be an object of preservation for the receiver: the gift of an offering makes it pass precisely into the world of abrupt consumption.

This is the meaning of "sacrificing to the deity," whose sacred essence is comparable to a fire. To sacrifice is to give as one gives coal to the furnace. But the furnace ordinarily has an undeniable utility, to which the coal is subordinated, whereas in sacrifice the offering is rescued from all utility.

This is so clearly the precise meaning of sacrifice, that one sacrifices *what is useful*; one does not sacrifice luxurious objects. There could be no sacrifice if the offering were destroyed beforehand. Now, depriving the labor of manufacture of its usefulness at the outset, luxury has already *destroyed* that labor; it has dissipated it in vainglory; in the very moment, it has lost it for good. To sacrifice a luxury object would be to sacrifice the same object twice.

But neither could one sacrifice that which was not first withdrawn from immanence, that which, never having belonged to immanence, would not have been secondarily subjugated, domesticated, and reduced to being a thing. Sacrifice is made of objects that could have been spirits, such as animals or plant substances, but that have become things and that need to be restored to the immanence whence they come, to the vague sphere of lost intimacy.

The Individual, Anguish, and Sacrifice

Intimacy cannot be expressed discursively.

The swelling to the bursting point, the malice that breaks out with clenched teeth and weeps; the sinking feeling that doesn't know where it comes from or what it's about; the fear that sings its head off in the dark; the white-eyed pallor, the sweet sadness, the rage and the vomiting . . . are so many evasions.

What is intimate, in the strong sense, is what has the passion of an absence of individuality, the imperceptible sonority of a river, the empty limpidity of the sky: this is still a negative definition, from which the essential is missing.

These statements have the vague quality of inaccessible distances, but on the other hand articulated definitions substitute the tree for the forest, the distinct articulation for that which is articulated.

I will resort to articulation nevertheless.

Paradoxically, intimacy is violence, and it is destruction, because it is not compatible with the positing of the separate individual. If one describes the individual in the operation of sacrifice, he is defined by anguish. But if sacrifice is distressing, the reason is that the individual takes part in it. The individual identifies with the victim in the sudden movement that restores it to immanence (to intimacy), but the assimilation that is linked to the return to immanence is nonetheless based on the fact that the victim is the thing, just as the sacrificer is the individual. The separate individual is of the same nature as the thing, or rather the anxiousness to remain personally alive that establishes the person's individuality is linked to the integration of existence into the world of things. To put it differently, work and the fear of dying are interdependent; the former implies the thing and vice versa. In fact it is not even necessary to work in order to be the *thing* of fear: man is an individual to the extent that his apprehension ties him to the results of labor. But man is not, as one might think, a thing because he is afraid. He would have no anguish if he were not the individual (the thing), and it is essentially the fact of being an individual that fuels his anguish. It is in order to satisfy the demands of the thing, it is insofar as the world of things has posited his duration as the basic condition of his worth, that he learns anguish. He is afraid of death as soon as he enters the system of projects that is the order of things. Death disturbs the order of things and the order of things holds us. Man is afraid of the intimate order that is not reconcilable with the order of things. Otherwise there would be no sacrifice, and there would be no mankind either. The intimate order would not reveal itself in the destruction and the sacred anguish of the individual. Because man is not squarely within that order, but only partakes of it through a thing that is threatened in its nature (in the projects that constitute it), intimacy, in the trembling of the individual, is holy, sacred, and suffused with anguish.

The Festival

The sacred is that prodigious effervescence of life that, for the sake of duration, the order of things holds in check, and that this holding changes into a breaking loose, that is, into violence. It constantly threatens to break the dikes, to confront productive activity with the precipitate and contagious movement of a purely glorious consumption. The sacred is exactly comparable to the flame that destroys the wood by consuming it. It is that opposite of a thing which an unlimited fire is; it spreads, it radiates heat and light, it suddenly inflames and blinds in turn. Sacrifice burns like the sun that slowly dies of the prodigious radiation whose brilliance our eyes cannot bear, but it is never isolated and, in a world of individuals, it calls for the general negation of individuals as such.

The divine world is contagious and its contagion is dangerous. In theory, what is started in the operation of sacrifice is like the action of lightning: in theory there is no limit to the conflagration. It favors human life and not animality; the resistance to immanence is what regulates its resurgence, so poignant in tears and so strong in the unavowable pleasure of anguish. But if man surrendered unreservedly to immanence, he would fall short of humanity; he would achieve it only to lose it and eventually life would return to the unconscious intimacy of animals. The constant problem posed by the impossibility of being human without being a thing and of escaping the limits of things without returning to animal slumber receives the limited solution of the festival.

The initial movement of the festival is given in elementary humanity, but it reaches the plenitude of an effusion only if the anguished concentration of sacrifice sets it loose. The festival assembles men whom the consumption of the contagious offering (communion) opens up to a conflagration, but one that is limited by a countervailing prudence: there is an aspiration for destruction that breaks out in the festival, but there is a conservative prudence that regulates and limits it. On the one hand, all the possibilities of consumption are brought together: dance and poetry, music and the different arts contribute to making the festival the place and the time of a spectacular letting loose. But consciousness, awake in anguish, is disposed, in a reversal commanded by an inability to go along with the letting loose, to subordinate it to the need that the order of things has – being fettered by nature and self-paralyzed – to receive an impetus from the outside. Thus the letting loose of the festival is finally, if not fettered, then at least confined to the limits of a reality of which it is the negation. The festival is tolerated to the extent that it reserves the necessities of the profane world.

Limitation, the Utilitarian Interpretation of the Festival, and the Positing of the Group

The festival is the fusion of human life. For the thing and the individual, it is the crucible where distinctions melt in the intense heat of intimate life. But its intimacy is dissolved in the real and individualized positing of the ensemble that is at stake in the rituals. For the sake of a *real* community, of a social fact that is given as a thing – of a common operation in view of a future time – the festival is limited: it is itself integrated as a link in the concatenation of useful works. As drunkenness, chaos, sexual orgy, that which it tends to be, it drowns everything in immanence in a sense; it then even exceeds the limits of the hybrid world of spirits, but its ritual movements slip into the world of immanence only through the mediation of spirits. To the spirits borne by the festival, to whom the sacrifice is offered, and to whose intimacy the victims are restored, an operative power is attributed in the same way it is attributed to things. In the end the festival itself is viewed as an operation and its effectiveness is not questioned. The possibility of producing, of fecundating the fields and the herds, is given to rites whose least servile operative forms are aimed, through a concession, at cuting the losses from the dreadful violence of the divine world. In any case, positively in fecundation, negatively in propitiation, the community first appears in the festival as a thing, a definite individualization and a shared project with a view to duration. The festival is not a true return to immanence but rather an amicable reconciliation, full of anguish, between the incompatible necessities.

Of course the community in the festival is not posited simply as an object, but more generally as a spirit (as a subject-object), but its positing has the value of a limit to the immanence of the festival and, for this reason, the thing aspect is accentuated. If the festival is not yet, or no longer, under way, the community link to the festival is given in operative forms, whose chief ends are the products of labor, the crops, and the herds. There is no clear *consciousness* of what the festival *actually* is (of what it is at the moment of its letting loose) and the festival is not situated distinctly in consciousness except as it is integrated into the duration of the community. This is what the festival (incendiary sacrifice and the outbreak of fire) is consciously (subordinated to that duration of the common thing, which prevents it from enduring), but this shows the festival's peculiar impossibility and man's limit, tied as he is to clear consciousness. So it is not humanity – insofar as clear consciousness rightly opposes it to animality – restored to immanence. The virtue of the festival is not integrated into its nature and conversely the letting loose of the festival has been possible only because of this powerlessness of consciousness to take it for what it is. The basic problem of religion is given in this fatal misunderstanding of sacrifice. Man is the being that has lost, and even rejected, that which he obscurely is, a vague intimacy. Consciousness could not have become clear in the course of time if it had not turned away from its awkward contents, but clear consciousness is itself looking for what it has itself lost, and what it must lose again as it draws near to it. Of course what it has lost is not outside it; consciousness turns away from the obscure intimacy of consciousness itself. Religion, whose essence is the search for lost intimacy, comes down to the effort of clear consciousness which wants to be a complete self-consciousness: but this effort is futile, since consciousness of intimacy is possible only at a level where consciousness is no longer an operation whose outcome implies duration, that is, at the level where clarity, which is the effect of the operation, is no longer given.

War: The Illusions of the Unleashing of Violence to the Outside

A society's individuality, which the fusion of the festival dissolves, is defined first of all in terms of real works – of agrarian production – that integrate sacrifice into the world of things. But the unity of a group thus has the ability to direct destructive violence to the outside.

As a matter of fact, external violence is antithetical to sacrifice or the festival, whose violence works havoc within. Only religion ensures a consumption that destroys the very substance of those whom it moves. Armed action destroys others or the wealth of others. It can be exerted individually, within a group, but the constituted group can bring it to bear on the outside and it is then that it begins to develop its consequences.

In deadly battles, in massacres and pillages, it has a meaning akin to that of festivals, in that the enemy is not treated as a thing. But war is not limited to these explosive forces and, within these very limits, it is not a slow action as sacrifice is, conducted with a view to a return to lost intimacy. It is a disorderly eruption whose external direction robs the warrior of the intimacy he attains. And if it is true that warfare tends in its own way to dissolve the individual through a negative wagering of the value of his own life, it cannot help but enhance his value in the course of time by making the surviving individual the beneficiary of the wager.

War determines the development of the individual beyond the individual-as-thing in the glorious individuality of the warrior. The glorious individual introduces, through a first negation of individuality, the divine order into the category of the individual (which expresses the order of things in a basic way). He has the contradictory will to make the negation of duration durable. Thus his strength is in part a strength to lie. War represents a bold advance, but it is the crudest kind of advance: one needs as much naïveté – or stupidity – as strength to be indifferent to that which one overvalues and to take pride in having deemed oneself of no value.

From the Unfettered Violence of Wars to the Fettering of Man-as-Commodity

This false and superficial character has serious consequences. War is not limited to forms of uncalculated havoc. Although he remains dimly aware of a calling that rules out the self-seeking behavior of work, the warrior reduces his fellow men to servitude. He thus subordinates violence to the most complete reduction of mankind to the order of things. Doubtless the warrior is not the initiator of the reduction. The operation that makes the slave a thing presupposed the prior institution of work. But the free worker was a thing voluntarily and for a given time. Only the slave, whom the military order has made a commodity, draws out the complete consequences of the reduction. (Indeed, it is necessary to specify that without slavery the world of things would not have achieved its plenitude.) Thus the crude unconsciousness of the warrior mainly works in favor of a predominance of the real order. The sacred prestige he arrogates to himself is the false pretense of a world brought down to the weight of utility. The warrior's nobility is like a prostitute's smile, the truth of which is self-interest.

Human Sacrifice

The sacrifices of slaves illustrate the principle according to which *what is useful* is destined for sacrifice. Sacrifice surrenders the slave, whose servitude accentuates the degradation of the human order, to the baleful intimacy of unfettered violence.

In general, human sacrifice is the acute stage of a dispute setting the movement of a measureless violence against the real order and duration. It is the most radical contestation of the primacy of utility. It is at the same time the highest degree of an unleashing of internal violence. The society in which this sacrifice rages mainly affirms the rejection of a disequilibrium of the two violences. He who unleashes his forces of destruction on the outside cannot be sparing of his resources. If he reduces the enemy to slavery, he must, in a spectacular fashion, make a glorious use of this new source of wealth. He must partly destroy these things that serve him, for there is nothing useful around him that can fail to satisfy, first of all, the mythical order's demand for consumption. Thus a continual surpassing toward destruction denies, at the same time that it affirms, the individual status of the group.

But this demand for consumption is brought to bear on the slave insofar as the latter is *his* property and *his* thing. It should not be confused with the movements of violence that have the outside, the enemy, as their object. In this respect the sacrifice of a slave is far from being pure. In a sense it is an extension of military combat, and internal violence, the essence of sacrifice, is not satisfied by it. Intense consumption requires victims at the top who are not only the useful wealth of a people, but this people itself; or at least, elements that signify it and that will be destined for sacrifice, this time not owing to an alienation from the sacred world – a fall – but, quite the contrary, owing to an exceptional proximity, such as the sovereign or the children (whose killing finally realizes the performance of a sacrifice twice over).

One could not go further in the desire to consume the life substance. Indeed, one could not go more recklessly than this. Such an intense movement of consumption responds to a movement of malaise by creating a greater malaise. It is not the apogee of a religious system, but rather the moment when it condemns itself: when the old forms have lost part of their virtue, it can maintain itself only through excesses, through innovations that are too onerous. Numerous signs indicate that these cruel demands were not easily tolerated. Trickery replaced the king with a slave on whom a temporary royalty was conferred. The primacy of consumption could not resist that of military force.

Translated by Robert Hurley

Jacques Lacan (1901–1981): Introduction

Cleo McNelly Kearns

Jacques Marie Émile Lacan (1901–81) was born into an upper middle-class French Catholic family, his father a businessman; his mother something of a mystic. (A brother became a Benedictine monk and a theologian.) Lacan, who dropped the Marie from his name when he became an atheist in his youth, pursued a vocation in medicine with a specialty in psychiatry. After his training, he joined the staff of St Anne's hospital (a prestigious research hospital specializing in psychiatric medicine), worked at the police infirmary in Paris, returned to St Anne's, and set up in private practice as a psychoanalyst. A flamboyant reputation won him both a high professional profile and much public attention, but caused tensions within the psychoanalytic movement, leading to a series of splits and bifurcations in the major organization for Freudians in France and the eventual establishment in 1953 of a new organization crystallizing around Lacan himself, the Société Française de Psychanalyse. After some years, this organization foundered over controversies with its parent body, the International Psychoanalytical Association – controversies also related to Lacan – and in the late sixties he started his own school, the École Freudienne de Paris. This too dissolved in the conflicts surrounding his old age some fifteen years later. In spite of these vicissitudes, Lacan's prestige was such that he was always able to obtain a forum and a following, and he died surrounded by dedicated students and colleagues prepared and willing to carry on his work.

Early in his career, while still preparing his thesis, Lacan encountered a patient who had committed an assault; she had knifed and injured an actress, someone with whom she had no previous direct acquaintance except as an object of persecutory fantasies. As Élisabeth Roudinesco, Lacan's biographer, recounts, the perpetrator of this attack suffered from what was then called erotomania, a paranoiac delusion in which someone imagines herself the lover or potential lover of a public figure. In dealing with this patient, whom he dubbed Aimée, Lacan began to lay down the directions he would follow throughout his career: a principled refusal to reduce pathology either to a medical condition or to a spiritual malaise; an acute awareness of the language of madness and of its nuances; and a profound respect for its peculiar modes of truth. In shaping Aimée's treatment, Lacan studied her writings, read the books she had read, and attempted to absorb the exact tone and temper of her modes of expression. Indeed, he wrote part of his thesis as a quasi-novelistic, quasi-Flaubertian study of her case – a tour de force on its own, but also an innovative struggle to hear and analyze another person's unique idiom. Upon publication, this thesis (which also announced its debt to the avant-garde and to surrealism) demonstrated to a wide circle Lacan's extraordinary literary and philosophical range. In dealing with Aimée, Lacan also took seriously the problem of counter transference, the problem of the function within therapeutic discourse of the analyst's own desire. In doing so, he learned to respect not only the content of a pathology but its intersubjective power, and to see analysis as a kind of dance in which both parties traced out the meaning or pattern. As Roudinesco points out, Aimée taught Lacan in many respects how to analyze himself.

Early in his practice, then, Lacan was advocating a highly self-aware and self-reflexive language-based approach to insanity, even in the treatment of serious and apparently intractable conditions. It was in this sense that he spoke of his "return to Freud," an ambiguous slogan, but one that always meant deep investment in what Freud had called the talking cure. As he developed this approach, Lacan increasingly insisted that it was designed less to cure or sublimate mental illness by strengthening the ego than to recognize and release its energies into a playful and engaged experience of language. This experience, he insisted, had its own special but not unfathomable logic. His insistence that the language of the unconscious had a logic of its own, and was thus subject to rational, even scientific scrutiny, brought Lacan's line of thought into conjunction with modern breakthroughs in structural linguistics (Jakobson) and anthropology (Lévi-Strauss), and even with formal thought experiments in mathematics (Goedel). Just as Lévi-Strauss was beginning to chart out the hidden rationality of myths and Jakobson that of morphemes, so Lacan assumed that the language of the unconscious could be decoded. Such decoding would not be dependent on idiosyncratic powers of charm and persuasion, but could be tested, taught, and transferred to others. Indeed, the development of a well-founded scientific profile for psychoanalysis (as opposed to a merely spiritualistic or charismatic one) was for Lacan a matter of some importance. When forced to choose between the dangers of a scientistic and a quasi-mystical misprision of his work, he seems to have preferred the former. Nevertheless, he fully recognized that psychoanalysis had a curious affinity for, as well as a common history with, Western religious discourse, and that this affinity could never entirely be analyzed away.

Lacan's views and methods, though fascinating to many, were nonetheless troubling when it came to such practical concerns as cure and social control, for Lacan himself made no promises of cure or normalization; indeed, he tended to heap scorn on those who did. Rather, he insisted that psychoanalysis was nothing but the science of provoking and understanding the language of the unconscious – no more and no less. Above all, it was not about an attempt to shore up the ego so that the analysand could carry on whatever society defined as business as usual. A good analyst was to elicit the speech of desire, to disconcert, for a while, the chatter of the daily self, allowing to speak instead the heterodox and surprising voice of a more complex subject, with a stranger tale to tell. In the service of this endeavor, Lacan increasingly violated various unwritten rules of psychoanalytic protocol, seeing patients at odd hours, charging apparently capricious amounts, not always respecting the boundaries among the roles of analyst, analysand, student, disciple, and/or erotic partner. Lacan remained intransigent if not always straightforward in defending these practices, which he thought he could not abandon without vitiating the point of his own work.

Lacan's controversial theory and practice put him in the center of a number of debates over the years, not only within his own profession, but in the wider context of the postmodern revaluation of the humanities and the sciences in general. Coming at a time when psychoanalysis was arousing both interest and resistance in the minds of many concerned with the care of the soul, Lacan's insistence on the strong scientific case for psychoanalysis, and yet on its fundamental entanglement with issues of power, charisma, control, and responsibility, gave his work implications which were widely felt. Lacan knew that matters of inspiration and devotion, self-assertion and obedience, mastery and discipleship were as inescapable in the analyst's office as in the pew or pulpit, and that nothing was to be gained by evading them. He was also aware (as was Freud) of the charismatic and messianic discourse into which his vocation had plunged him and of the repetition in his own life of Freud's function as father-figure and victim, a double role both men saw as ironically forecast by the fate of the prophets of Israel.

Lacan's influence is best felt and his work perhaps best understood through those who have interpreted, criticized, or revised his thought. Among these are a line of postmoderns whose voices resound with defiance of the patriarchal and repressive structures Lacan so brilliantly analyzed, and who yet accept the necessity for attending to those structures before attempting to move beyond them. In France, for instance, Jacques Derrida has articulated a closely argued philosophical critique of Lacan's position, clarifying why he seems so much more a modern than a postmodern figure, invested in the possibility, at least, of an adequate and truthful language of the soul. Nevertheless, Derrida fully understands Lacan's power and point. Julia Kristeva has extended Lacan's rigorous commitment to psychoanalysis into a form of cultural criticism which mobilizes the forces of literature and art, as well as those of analysis, to support resistance to reification, abstraction, and violence in personal and public life. Luce Irigaray has developed perhaps the most rigorous and far-reaching critique of Freudianism, and she has also made some of the most radical constructive or reconstructive theological moves of any postmodern, perhaps as a result. She has not done so, however, without a full appreciation of both Freud and Lacan, and the influence of her early training as a Lacanian analyst is everywhere in evidence.

In the Anglophone world, Lacan has suffered as much from his friends as from his enemies, with a rash of derivative and excessively baroque writings, though there are also a number of excellent expositions of his thought, including those of Elizabeth Grosz and Ellie Ragland-Sullivan. In terms of more extensive appropriations, Theresa Brennan is perhaps Lacan's most interesting philosophical and feminist heir, elaborating his model of the psyche into a general account of the development of the Western sense of self, which approaches something like a unified field theory of the individual in society. In philosophy and religion, the work of Edith Wyschogrod, David Crownfield, and Amy Hollywood indicates the important contribution Lacan's thought can make to the ongoing critique of Jewish and Christian traditions, and suggests a dimension of relevance to those traditions obvious, indeed explicit, in Lacan's thought, but rarely pursued fully enough. To reread Lacan in light of their studies is to recover an ear for the liberating possibilities of the unconscious in language without the reduction of questions of faith and religion to mere neurotic projection that often plagued Freud's own work

The text below is a translation of the more or less faithful record of part of Lacan's seminars for the academic year 1959–60. These seminars were open to the public and became fashionable to attend, even though the audience was presumed to be made up largely of analysts in training. They are cast in Lacan's difficult, allusive, and witty style and in them he is addressing at least two different constituencies: those familiar with the technical aspects of his thought and those primarily interested in its wider implications. As his opening remarks suggest, for this particular seminar Lacan had recommended as prior reading a text by Sperber on the derivation of certain words from sexual terms or functions. Once the seminar began, however, this assignment turned out to be something of a straw dog, for what Lacan really wanted to discuss was less Sperber's rather dated bit of etymologizing than his own more sophisticated observations on the connections between human sexuality, language, and the foundations of society. What interested him was not the roots of words but their functions in a signifying structure; not the supposed origin of specific terms but the general relationship of language as a system to human sexuality as a general problem. After all, he points out, as have so many others aware of the linguistic turn, the elements of vocal use "still cannot give us even the most primitive structuring element of language. There is a gap there." In other words, language is more than an extraordinary extension of onomatopoeia; it is a highly abstract system which requires, among other things, opposing terms distinguished from each other to work.

Nevertheless, Lacan suggests, although Sperber's work may appear naive, there is something going on in the interconnections between language, sex, and society that cannot easily be dismissed. Lacan explores these interconnections in the second part of the seminar, adding into the mix the question of religion, and specifically the issue of monotheism, with its thematic emphasis on God the Father. This elaboration requires him to revisit two crucial Freudian essays, *Totem and Taboo* and *Moses and Monotheism.* (Of the latter, Lacan says that every psychoanalyst ought to know it by heart.) We remember that in these works Freud speculated on the origin of ordered society in the Western sense by imagining, for heuristic purposes, a kind of phantasmagoric scenario according to which the father is murdered by his jealous sons, who are then horrified by their action into erecting monuments and cults to his memory and laws to avert further violence. The father is both erased and celebrated in this scenario, both elevated to a universal principle and rendered somewhat unreal in terms of daily life, in part so that the sexual pleasure permitted by his absence may be enjoyed along lawful or temperate lines without a paralyzing sense of guilt.

The medium through which this double inscription of erasure and celebration is accomplished is primarily the medium of the word, the language of religious worship and of moral law. Is the prominence of language in this scenario, Lacan wants to ask, an accident? Or is language itself – or at least language as conceived and deployed in Western traditions – so deeply connected to monotheism, and both to the Oedipal drama, as to make it the perfect, as if predestined instrument, both for glorifying and for distancing the Father and for deflecting sexual energy along legitimate or quasi-legitimate lines? His answer is affirmative: yes, what might be called – in a theological reference to Pauline terms to which Lacan draws explicit attention – law and sin are intertwined uniquely in language in such a way that the intensification of prohibition is also and simultaneously the intensification of transgression. As Romans 7:7 puts it, "Nay, I had not known sin, but by the law." The impossible bind into which the psyche is led by this dynamic is resolved for Paul by grace; for Lacan by a kind of bonding of desire and law, such that one supplies traction for the other, enabling pleasure, at least, if not the full transcendence of the biblical promise.

But Lacan was not simply analyzing theoretical or speculative issues here. He was also carrying on an indirect meditation on his own position as the displaced master, the absent and silenced father of Freudian analysis in France. This position was fraught with ironies, not the least of which was its pervasive description, following Freud's own example, in terms taken from religious discourse. Lacan, like Freud, felt he was experiencing the ecclesiastical and institutional victimization of the one who tells the truth about God, thus becoming a prophet without honor in his own country. A few years later, on the occasion of the condemnation of his teachings by the International Psychoanalytical Association, Lacan was to remark scathingly, "I am not telling you – but it would not be impossible – that the psychoanalytic community is a Church. And yet, uncontestably, the question arises of what within it offers a kind of echo of religious practice."[1] He went on to speak of his "excommunication," for which he found a precedent not just in Freud but in Spinoza, in whose formal interdiction from the Jewish community of Amsterdam he found a parallel to his own case. Lacan was not aligning himself here simply with Spinoza's philosophical skepticism, but with his Jewish identity, representing as he did a great tradition of dissent within Judaism against all false, idealizing, and legalistic forms of religion and self-understanding.

But what is the "truth about God," for his witness to which Lacan liked to see himself as both lauded and victimized? It is not the oft-proclaimed and by now no longer shocking news that God is dead, but rather the disturbing intimation that He (or His shadow) is alive and well – well enough, at least, to be capable of generating extremely strong psychic, social, and even political effects. Lacan knows that as a culture we have all internalized to one degree or another the modernist, the perhaps perennial notion that God the Father is a sentimentalizing fiction. This fiction, we insist, enables us to explain certain things, enjoy certain feelings, or proceed in certain ways, but it must also be distanced or deconstructed to avoid the repressions and oppressions that follow in its wake. What is remarkable for Lacan is that we continue unconsciously to invest in and to love as well as to question and to hate this absent, supposedly fictive God, and that we mobilize this love–hate to articulate, advocate, and embrace a love of self and neighbor we regard as vital to all of our social and personal lives. The result is an ironic paradox: you must, it seems, posit a single, monotheistic, male Father God and then rationalize Him as dead in order to allow the resonance of His being to modulate gender difference and sexual desire into fraternal love.

Lacan explores this paradox in the next seminar, "Love of one's neighbor."[2] In doing so, he wishes to remind us that Freud might well be counted among the great theologians of our century because he does not just generalize about some innate religious function, but rather tries to examine its exact manifestations and deformations, especially where it takes the form of the commandment to love the Lord thy God with all thy heart, mind, and soul, and to love thy neighbor as thyself. What Freud has to say on this topic, Lacan notes, should "make our ears ring and set our teeth on edge," carrying as it does the sense of vertigo we experience when we look into the dizzying regress of projections and introjections our psychic and religious life seems to entail. The same might be said of Lacan's work, which bears eloquent and dangerous witness not simply to the death of God but to what we can only call His persistent life, and His constitutive role in structuring the language of the unconscious – gender, authority, madness, and all. Lacan's is surely not the last word on the doctrine of God, as the extensive and rigorous critique of his position, especially in Irigaray, makes clear. But it is a *strong* word, and it has the potential for enabling a far more mature understanding of the soul and her desires than much of the idealizing, unsexing and vaporizing of this doctrine that passes for theology today.

Notes

1 Seminar XI, p. 8; cited by E. Roudinesco in *Jacques Lacan & Co.* (1990), p. 362.
2 See Porter's, XIV, pp. 179ff.

Selected Bibliography

Brennan, Theresa, *History after Lacan* (London and New York: Routledge, 1993).
—— *The Interpretation of the Flesh* (London and New York: Routledge, 1992).
Brennan, Theresa, and Ragland-Sullivan Ellie, *Jacques Lacan and the Philosophy of Psychoanalysis* (Champaign-Urbana; University of Illinois Press, 1986).
—— *Jacques Lacan and the Subject of Language* (New York: Routledge, 1991).
Clément, Cathérine, *The Lives and Legends of Jacques Lacan* (New York: Columbia University Press, 1983).
Derrida, Jacques, *The Post Card: Socrates to Freud and Beyond*, trans. Alan Bass (Chicago: University of Chicago Press, 1987).
Grosz, Elizabeth, *Jacques Lacan: A Feminist Introduction* (New York: Routledge, 1990).
Irigaray, Luce, *Speculum of the Other Woman*, trans. Gillian C. Gill (Ithaca, NY: Cornell University Press, 1985).
—— *This Sex which Is Not One*, trans. Catherine Porter with Carolyn Burke (Ithaca, NY: Cornell University Press, 1985).
Kristeva, Julia, *Tales of Love*, trans. Leon C. Roudiez (New York: Columbia University Press, 1987).

Lacan, Jacques, *The Ethics of Psychoanalysis, 1959–1960*, Book VII, ed. Jacques-Alain Miller, trans. with notes by Dennis Porter (London: Routledge, and New York: Norton, 1992).
—— *The Four Fundamental Concepts of Psychoanalysis*, ed. Jacques-Alain Miller, trans. Alan Sheriden (New York: Norton, 1978).
—— *The Language of the Self: The Function of Language in Psychoanalysis*, trans. with notes and commentary by Anthony Wilden (Baltimore, MD: Johns Hopkins University Press, 1968).
Lee, Jonathan *Jacques Lacan* (Boston, MA: Twayne, 1990).
Macey, David, *Lacan in Contexts* (London: Verso, 1988).
Rose, Jacqueline, *Feminine Sexuality: Jacques Lacan and the École Freudienne* (New York: Pantheon, 1982).
Roudinesco, Élisabeth, *Jacques Lacan & Co.: A History of Psychoanalysis in France, 1925–1985*, trans. Jeffrey Mehlman (Chicago: University of Chicago Press, 1990).
Turkle, Sherry, *Psychoanalytic Politics: Jacques Lacan and Freud's French Revolution* (London: Free Association Books, and New York: Guilford Press, 1992).
Wyschogrod, Edith, Crownfield, David, and Raschke, Carl A. (eds), *Lacan and Theological Discourse* (Albany: State University of New York Press, 1989).

The Death of God

If I wanted you to be acquainted with Sperber's article, it is because it is coupled to our sublimation train.

1

I will not engage in a serious critique of the text, for I hope that after several years of following my teaching here, most of you have found something irritating in the way in which Sperber proceeds. Though his goal is undoubtedly interesting, his mode of demonstration has its weaknesses. To refer to the fact that words with an original sexual meaning started to take on a series of meanings increasingly remote from their primitive meaning, as a way of proving the common sexual origin in a sublimated form of fundamental human activities, is to adopt an approach whose demonstrable value seems to me to be eminently refutable from the point of view of common sense.

That words whose meaning was originally sexual spread out so as to overlay meanings that are very remote doesn't mean as a consequence that the whole field of meaning is overlaid in that way. That doesn't mean that all the language we use is in the end reducible to the key words it contains, words whose valorization is considerably facilitated by the fact that one accepts as proven what is, in fact, most questionable, namely, the notion of a root or radical, and what in human language would be its constitutive link to sense.

This emphasis placed on roots and radicals in languages making use of inflections raises particular problems that are far from being applicable to human language universally. What would be the case with Chinese, for example, where all the signifying units are monosyllabic? The notion of a root is highly tenuous. In fact, what is involved is an illusion that is linked to the development of language, of the use of the language system, which can only seem very suspect to us.

That doesn't mean that Sperber's remarks concerning the use of words with what might be called sexual roots in Indo-European languages are of no interest. But they can hardly satisfy us from the perspective in which I believe you have been trained and formed by me, a perspective which involves distinguishing properly the function of the signifier or the creation of signification through the metonymic and metaphoric use of signifiers.

That's where the trouble begins. Why are those zones in which sexual signification spreads outward, why are those rivers through which it ordinarily flows – and, as you have seen, in a direction that isn't just random – specially chosen, so that in order to reach them one uses words that already have a given usage in the sexual sphere? Why is it precisely in connection with a half-failed act of pruning, with an act of cutting that is blocked, thwarted, messed up, that one should evoke the presumed origin of the word and find it in the hole-drilling activities of work in its most primitive of forms, with the meaning of sexual operation, of phallic penetration? Why does one resurrect the metaphor "fuck" in connection with something that is "fucked up?" Why is it the image of the vulva that surfaces to express a number of different acts, including those of escaping, of fleeing, of cutting and running (*se tailler*), as the German term in the text has often been translated?

I have, in fact, tried to find confirmation of the historical moment when that nice little expression, *se tailler* (to cut and run), in the sense of "to flee" or "to escape," first appeared. I haven't had time to find out, and I didn't discover it in the dictionaries and other sources that I have at my disposal. It is true that I don't have in Paris the dictionaries that give the popular meanings of words. I would like someone to do some research on the topic.

Thus, why in our everyday life do we find that in our metaphors a certain type of meaning is involved, certain signifiers that are marked by their primitive use in connection with the sexual relation? Why, for example, do we use some slang expression that had originally a sexual significance in order to evoke metaphorically situations that have nothing to do with sex? The metaphorical usage involved is employed to obtain a certain modification.

But if it were only a question of showing how in the normal diachronic development of linguistic usage sexual references are used in a certain metaphorical sense – that is, if I were only concerned with providing another example of certain aberrations of psychoanalytic speculation – I wouldn't have presented you with the Sperber text. If it is still interesting, it is because of what is to be found on its horizon, something that isn't demonstrated there, but which in its intention it strives for, and that is the radical relationship that exists between the first instrumental relations, the earliest techniques, the principal actions of agriculture, such as that of opening the belly of the earth, or again the principal actions in the making of a vase that I have previously emphasized, and something very precise, namely, not so much the sexual act as the female sexual organ.

It is insofar as the female sexual organ or, more precisely, the form of an opening and an emptiness, is at the center of all the metaphors concerned, that the article is of interest and is valuable in focusing our thought, for it is obvious that there is a gap in the text, a leap beyond the supposed reference.

One takes note of the fact that the use of a term that originally meant "coitus" is capable of being extended virtually infinitely, that the use of a term that originally meant "vulva" is capable of generating all kinds of metaphorical uses. And it is in this way that it began to be supposed that the vocalization presumed to accompany the sexual act gave men the idea of using the signifier to designate either the organ, and especially the female organ, in a noun form, or the act of coitus in a verbal form. The priority of the vocal use of the signifier among men is thus supposed to find its origin in the chanted calls that are assumed to be those of primitive sexual relations among humans, in the same way that they are among animals and especially birds.

The idea is very interesting. But you can sense right away the difference that exists between the more or less standardized cry that accompanies an activity and the use of a signifier that detaches a given articulatory element, that is to say, either the act or the organ. We don't find the signifying structure as such here; nothing implies that the oppositional element which forms the structure of the use of signifiers – and is already fully developed in the *Fort-Da* from which we took our original example – is given in the natural sexual call. If the sexual call can be derived from a temporal modulation of the act whose repetition may involve the fixation of certain elements of vocal activity, it still cannot give us even the most primitive structuring element of language. There is a gap there.

Nevertheless, the interest of the article is in making us see the way in which what is essential in the development of our experience and in Freud's doctrine may be conceived, that is to say, that sexual symbolism in the ordinary sense of the word may polarize at its point of origin the metaphorical play of the signifier.

That's all I have to say on the subject today, with the understanding that I may return to it later.

2

I wondered how I should take up the thread of our discussions, how I should start out again today.

As the result of conversations I have had with some of you, I said to myself that there would be some value in my giving you an idea of the lectures, comments, and conversations in which I engaged in Brussels. The fact is, when I have something to communicate to you, it is always related to the line of thought I am pursuing, and even when I take it out into the world, I do little more than take it up more or less at the point I have reached.

But to suppose that you already know implicitly what I said up there, which isn't the case, would be to take too great a leap forward. It is, in fact, important that the issues raised not be ignored.

That may seem to you to be an unconventional way of proceeding, but given the distance we still have to go, I don't have time to indulge in professorial scruples. Mine is not a professor's role. I don't even like to put myself in the teaching situation, since a psychoanalyst who speaks to an initiated audience is in the position of a propagandist. If I agreed to talk at the Catholic University of Brussels, I did so in a spirit of mutual assistance; it was in order to support the presence and the activities of those who are our friends and colleagues in Belgium. This concern is not for me the primary one, of course, but it is a secondary one.

I thus found myself in front of an audience that was very large and of which I had a very good impression, summoned there by the Catholic University. And that alone is enough to explain my motivation for speaking to them of what Freud has to say about the function of the Father.

As you might expect from me, I didn't mince my words or censor my language. I didn't attempt to attenuate Freud's position on religion. Moreover, you know what my position is concerning the so-called religious truths.

It is perhaps worthwhile to be more precise on the subject for once, although I believe I have made it clear enough. Whether from personal conviction or in the name of a methodological point of view, the so-called scientific point of view – a point of view that is by the way reached by people who otherwise consider themselves to be believers, but who in a certain sphere assume they are required to put aside their religious point of view – there is a paradox involved in practically excluding from the debate and from analysis things, terms, and doctrines that have been articulated in the field of faith, on the pretext that they belong to a domain that is reserved for believers.

You once heard me make a series of remarks on a passage from St Paul's Epistle to the Romans in connection with the theme that it is the Law which causes sin. And you saw that, thanks to an artifice I could have done without, namely, the substitution of the term the Thing for what the text calls sin, I was able to achieve a very precise formulation of what I had to say at the time on the subject of the knot of the Law and desire. Well, that particular example was not chosen by chance – it belonged to a certain order of effectiveness in relation to a special case, and by means of a kind of sleight of hand it was unusually helpful in leading to something I needed at the time to bring to your attention.

We analysts, who claim to go beyond certain conceptions of pre-psychology relative to the phenomena of our own field or who approach human realities without prejudice, do not have to believe in these religious truths in any way, given that such belief may extend as far as what is called faith, in order to be interested in what is articulated in its own terms in religious experience – in the terms of the conflict between freedom and grace, for example.

A notion as precise and articulate as grace is irreplaceable where the psychology of the act is concerned, and we don't find anything equivalent in classic academic psychology. Not only doctrines, but also the history of choices, that is, of heresies that have been attested to in this sphere, and the succession of emotional outbursts that have motivated a certain number of directions taken in the concrete ethics of generations, all belong to our sphere of inquiry; they, so to speak, demand all of our attention in their own register and mode of expression.

It is not enough that certain themes be raised only by those who believe they believe – after all, how can we know? – for the whole field to be reserved for them alone. If we accept that they truly believe, then they are not beliefs for them but truths. What they believe in, whether they believe they believe in it or they don't – nothing is more ambiguous than belief – one thing is certain, they believe they know. The knowledge in question is like any other, and for this reason it falls into the field of inquiry that we should conduct on all forms of knowledge; and such is the case, because as analysts we believe that there is no knowledge which doesn't emerge against a background of ignorance.

That is the reason why we accept as such the idea of other forms of knowledge than the kind that is founded scientifically.

It was not useless, then, for me to confront an audience that represents an important sector of the public. Whether or not I may have caused an ear or two to prick up is problematic; the future alone will reveal that. Moreover, it won't have the same impact on a very different audience, like you.

Freud himself took an unequivocal position on the subject of religious experience. He said that everything of that kind that implied a sentimental approach meant nothing to him; it was literally a dead letter for him. Yet if we in this assembly have the position on the letter that we do, that doesn't solve a thing; however dead it might be, that letter was nevertheless definitely articulated. Well now, faced with people who are supposed not to be able to dissociate themselves from a certain message concerning the function of the Father – given that it is at the heart of the experience defined as religious – I had no discomfort in affirming that as far as that matter was concerned, "Freud had what it took," as I put it in a subtitle that was found a little startling.

You only have to open the little book entitled *Moses and Monotheism* that Freud cogitated over for some ten years, for after *Totem and Taboo* he thought of nothing but that, of Moses and the religion of his fathers. And if it weren't for the article on the *Spaltung* of the ego, one might say that the pen fell from his hands at the end of *Moses and Monotheism*. Contrary to what has been suggested to me over the last few weeks in connection with Freud's intellectual production toward the end of his life, I don't at all think that there was a decline. Nothing seems to me to be more firmly articulated in any case and more in conformity with all Freud's previous thought than this work.

It bears on the monotheistic message as such; and for him there is no doubt that it contains an uncontestable weight of superior value over any other. The fact that Freud was an atheist doesn't make any difference. For the atheist that Freud was, if not necessarily for all atheists, the goal of the radical core of this message was of decisive value. On the left of this message, there are some things that are henceforth outdated, obsolete; they no longer hold beyond the manifestation of the message. On the right, things are quite different.

The situation is quite clear from the spirit of Freud's argument. That doesn't mean that there is nothing at all outside of monotheism, far from it. He doesn't give us a theory of the gods, but enough is said concerning the ambiance that is usually connoted by "pagan," a late connotation linked to its retreat to the milieu of the peasantry. In that pagan ambiance at the time when it was flourishing, the *numen* rises up at every step, at the corner of every road, in grottoes, at crossroads; it weaves human experience together, and we can still see traces of it in a great many fields. That is something that contrasts greatly with the monotheistic profession of faith.

The numinous rises up at every step and, conversely, every step of the numinous leaves a trace, engenders a memorial. It didn't take much for a new temple to be erected, for a new religion to be established. The numinous proliferates and intervenes on all sides in human experience; it is, moreover, so abundant that something in the end must be manifested through man; its power cannot be overcome.

It is to this immense envelopment and at the same time to a degradation that the genre of the fable bears witness. Ancient fables are full of meanings that remain richly rewarding, but we have trouble realizing that they could have been compatible with something like a faith in the gods, because, whether they are heroic or vulgar, they are shot through with a kind of riotousness, drunkenness, and anarchy born of divine passions. The laughter of the Olympians in the *Iliad* sufficiently illustrates this on the heroic plane. There's a lot to be said about this laughter. From the pen of the philosophers, on the other hand, we have the other side of this laughter, of the derisory character of the adventures of the gods. It is difficult for us to conceive this.

In opposition to this we have the monotheistic message. How is it possible? How did it rise to this level? The way in which Freud articulates it is crucial if we are to appreciate the level at which its progress is to be situated.

For him everything is founded on the notion of Moses the Egyptian and of Moses the Midianite. I believe that an audience of people like you, 80 percent of whom are psychoanalysts, should know this book by heart.

Moses the Egyptian is the Great Man, the legislator, the politician, the rationalist, the one whose path Freud claims to discover with the historical appearance in the fourteenth century BC of the religion of Akhenaton – something that has been attested by recent discoveries. This religion promotes a unitarianism of energy, symbolized by the sun from which it radiates and spreads out across the earth. This first attempt at a rationalist vision of the world, which is presupposed in the unitarianism of the real, in the substantive unification of the world centered on the sun, failed. Hardly had Akhenaton disappeared, when religious ideas of all kinds begin to multiply again, especially in Egypt; the pandemonium of the gods returns to take charge once more and utterly wipes out the reform. One man keeps the flame of this rationalist cause alight, Moses the Egyptian; it is he who chooses a small group of men and leads them through the test that will make them worthy to found a community based on his principles. In other words, someone wanted to create socialism in a single country, except, of course, there was in addition no country but just a bunch of men to carry the project through.

That's Freud's conception of the true Moses, the Great Man; and what we need to know is how his message has come down to us.

You will perhaps respond that this Moses was after all a bit of a magician. How otherwise did he produce the swarms of locusts and frogs? But that was his business. It's not an essential question from the point of view that concerns us here, that of his place in religion. Let's leave the question of magic aside, although it doesn't seem to have hurt him with anyone.

On the other hand, there is Moses the Midianite, the son-in-law of Jethro, whom Freud also calls the one from Sinai, from Horeb, and Freud teaches us that this one was confused with the other. It is this one who claims to have heard the decisive word emerge from the burning bush, the word that cannot be eluded, as Freud eludes it: "I am," not as the whole Christian gnosis has attempted to interpret it, "he who is" – thereby exposing us to difficulties relative to the concept of being that are far from being over, and which have perhaps contributed to compromising exegesis – but "I am what I am." Or, in other words, a God who introduces himself as an essentially hidden God.

This hidden god is a jealous God. He seems to be very difficult to dissociate from the one who, according to the Bible, proclaims in that same ambiance of fire which makes him inaccessible the famous ten commandments to the assembled people, who are required to remain at a certain distance. Given that these commandments turn out to be proof against anything – and by that I mean that whether or not we obey them, we still cannot help hearing them – in their indestructible character they prove to be the very laws of speech, as I tried to show you.

Moses the Midianite seems to pose a problem of his own – I would like to know whom or what he faced on Sinai and on Horeb. But after all, since he couldn't bear the brilliance of the face of him who said "I am what I am," we will simply say at this point that the burning bush was Moses's Thing, and leave it there. In any case, we still have to calculate the consequences of that revelation.

By what means is the problem resolved for Freud? He considers that Moses the Egyptian was assassinated by his little people, who were less docile than ours relative to socialism in a single country. And then these people went on to devote themselves to all kinds of paralyzing observances at the same time that they caused trouble for countless neighbors – for we shouldn't overlook what is, in effect, the history of the Jews. One only has to read a little into these ancient works to realize that they knew all about colonial ambition in Canaan. They even managed to induce neighboring populations to have themselves circumcised on the quiet, and then they profited from the paralysis that that operation between your legs causes for a time, in order to wipe them out. But I don't mention that simply to record grievances about a stage of the religion that is now far behind us.

Having said that, however, it's clear that Freud doesn't for a moment doubt that the major interest of Jewish history is that of being the bearer of the message of one God.

And that's where things stand. We have the dissociation between the rationalist Moses and the inspired, obscurantist Moses, who is scarcely ever discussed. But basing his argument on the examination of historical evidence, Freud finds no other path adapted to the transmission of the rationalist Moses's message than that of darkness; in other words, this message is linked through repression to the murder of the Great Man. And it is precisely in this way, Freud tells us, that it could be transmitted and maintained in a state of efficacy that can be historically measured. It's so close to the Christian tradition that it's really remarkable; it is because the primordial murder of the Great Man re-emerges in a second murder that in a sense translates and brings it to light, the murder of Christ, that the monotheistic message is completed. It is because the secret malediction of the murder of the Great Man – which itself only draws its power from the fact that it echoes the inaugural murder of humanity, that of the primitive father – it is because this event emerges into the light of day, that what, in the light of Freud's text, we are obliged to call Christian redemption may be accomplished.

That tradition alone pursues to the end the task of revealing what is involved in the primitive crime of the primordial law.

How after that can one avoid taking note of the originality of Freud's position relative to all that is to be found in the field of the history of religions? The history of religions consists essentially of establishing the common denominator of religiosity. We stake out the religious region in man within which we are required to include religions as different as one from Borneo, Confucianism, Taoism, and the Christian religion. It's not without its difficulties, although, when one sets out to produce typologies, there's no reason why one shouldn't end up with something. And this time, one ends up with a classification of the imaginary, which is in opposition to that which characterizes the origin of monotheism, and which is integrated into the primordial commandments insofar as they are the laws of speech: "Thou shalt not make a carved image of me," and so as to avoid that risk altogether, "Thou shalt not make any image at all."

And since I have happened to talk to you about the primitive sublimation of architecture, let me say that the problem of the temple that was destroyed without trace remains. To which symbolic order, to which set of precautions, to which exceptional circumstances did it appeal for everything to be destroyed, everything down to the remotest corner that might have made possible the reappearance, on the sides of a vase – and it wouldn't have been difficult – of images of animals, plants, and all those forms that were outlined on the walls of the cave? This temple was, in effect, only supposed to be the cover of what was at its center, of the Ark of union, that is, the pure symbol of the pact, of the tie that bound him who said "I am what I am," and gave the commandments, to the people who received them, so that among all peoples it might be distinguished as the one that had wise and intelligent laws. How was this temple to be constructed so as to avoid all the traps of art?

It's a question that cannot be answered by any document, by any material image. I simply leave it open.

3

What is involved here is discussed by Freud in *Moses and Monotheism* in connection with the business of the moral law. He thoroughly integrates it there into the adventure which, as he writes in his text, only found its further development and its fulfillment in the Judeo-Christian story.

As far as other religions are concerned – he vaguely defines these as Oriental, thereby alluding apparently to a whole range that includes Buddhism, Lao-Tsu, and others – he affirms, with a boldness that one can only wonder at, that they are all nothing more than the religion of the Great Man. Thus things there remained stuck halfway, more or less aborted, without reaching the point of the primitive murder of this Great Man.

I am far from agreeing with all that. Yet in the history of the avatars of Buddhism, one can find a great many things which, legitimately or not, can be made to illustrate Freud's theory; in other words, it is because they did not push the development of the drama through to the end that they stayed where they are. But it is, needless to say, odd to find this strange Christocentrism in Freud's writings. There must have been a reason for him to have slipped into it almost without realizing it.

In any case, we find ourselves brought back to following the path to the end.

So that something like the order of the law may be transmitted, it has to pass along the path traced by the primordial drama articulated in *Totem and Taboo*, that is to say, the murder of the father and its consequences, the murder at the origin of culture of the figure about whom one can say nothing, a fearful and feared as well as dubious figure, an all-powerful, half-animal creature of the primal horde, who was killed by his sons. As a result of which – and the articulation here is important – an inaugural pact is established that is essential for a time to the institution of that law, which Freud does his best to tie to the murder of the father and to identify with the ambivalence that is thus at the basis of the relations between son and father or, in other words, involves the return of love once the act is accomplished.

All the mystery is in that act. It is designed to hide something, namely, that not only does the murder of the father not open the path to *jouissance* that the presence of the father was supposed to prohibit, but it, in fact, strengthens the prohibition. The whole problem is there; that's where, in fact as well as in theory, the fault lies. Although the obstacle is removed as a result of the murder, *jouissance* is still prohibited; not only that, but the prohibition is reinforced.

This fault that denies is thus sustained, articulated, made visible by the myth, but at the same time it is also camouflaged by it. That is why the important feature of *Totem and Taboo* is that it is a myth, and, as has been said, perhaps the only myth that the modern age was capable of. And Freud created it.

It is important to grasp what is embodied in this fault. Everything that passes across it is turned into a debt in the Great Book of debts. Every act of *jouissance* gives rise to something that is inscribed in the Book of debts of the Law. Furthermore, something in this regulatory mechanism must either be a paradox or the site of some irregularity, for to pass across the fault in the other direction is not equivalent.

Freud writes in *Civilization and Its Discontents* that everything that is transferred from *jouissance* to prohibition gives rise to the increasing strengthening of prohibition. Whoever attempts to submit to the moral law sees the demands of his superego grow increasingly meticulous and increasingly cruel.

Why isn't it the same in the other direction? It is a fact that it isn't the case at all. Whoever enters the path of uninhibited *jouissance*, in the name of the rejection of the moral law in some form or other, encounters obstacles whose power is revealed to us every day in our experience in innumerable forms, forms that nevertheless perhaps may be traced back to a single root.

We are, in fact, led to the point where we accept the formula that without a transgression there is no access to *jouissance*, and, to return to St Paul, that that is precisely the function of the Law. Transgression in the direction of *jouissance* only takes place if it is supported by the oppositional principle, by the forms of the Law. If the paths to *jouissance* have something in them that dies out, that tends to make them impassable, prohibition, if I may say so, becomes its all-terrain vehicle, its half-track truck, that gets it out of the circuitous routes that lead man back in a roundabout way toward the rut of a short and well-trodden satisfaction.

That is the point that our experience leads us to, on condition that we are guided by Freud's articulation of the problem. Sin needed the Law, St Paul said, so that he could become a great sinner – nothing, of course, affirms that he did, but so that he could conceive of the possibility.

Meanwhile, what we see here is the tight bond between desire and the Law. And it is in the light of this that Freud's ideal is an ideal tempered with civility that might be called patriarchal civility, in the full idyllic sense. The father is as sentimental a figure as you can imagine, the kind of figure suggested by the humanitarian ideal that resonates in Diderot's bourgeois dramas, or indeed in the figures that are the favorites of eighteenth-century engravings. That patriarchal civility is supposed to set us on the most reasonable path to temperate or normal desires.

Yet what Freud is proposing through his myth is, in spite of its novelty, not something that wasn't from a certain point of view a response to a demand. The demand to which it was, in fact, a response is not difficult to see.

The myth of the origin of the Law is incarnated in the murder of the father; it is out of that that the prototypes emerged, which we call successively the animal totem, then a more or less powerful and jealous god, and, finally, the single God, God the Father. The myth of the murder of the father is the myth of a time for which God is dead.

But if for us God is dead, it is because he always has been dead, and that's what Freud says. He has never been the father except in the mythology of the son, or, in other words, in that of the commandment which commands that he, the father, be loved, and in the drama of the passion which reveals that there is a resurrection after death. That is to say, the man who made incarnate the death of God still exists. He still exists with the commandment which orders him to love God. That's the place where Freud stops, and he stops at the same time – the theme is developed in *Civilization and Its Discontents* – at the place that concerns the love of one's neighbor, which is something that appears to be insurmountable for us, indeed incomprehensible.

I will attempt to explain why next time. I just wanted to emphasize the fact today that there is a certain atheistic message in Christianity itself, and I am not the first to have mentioned it. Hegel said that the destruction of the gods would be brought about by Christianity.

Man survives the death of God, which he assumes, but in doing so, he presents himself before us. The pagan legend tells us that at the moment when the veil of the temple was rent on the Aegean Sea, the message resounded that "The great Pan is dead." Even if Freud moralizes in *Civilization and Its Discontents*, he stops short at the commandment to love thy neighbor. It is to the heart of this problem that his theory of the meaning of the instinct brings us back. The relationship of the great Pan to death was, then, a stumbling block for the psychologism of his current disciples.

That's why my second lecture in Brussels turned on the question of love of one's neighbor. It was another theme I had in common with my audience. What I did, in fact, come up with, I will allow you to judge next time.

March 16, 1960
Translated by D. Porter

Emmanuel Levinas (1906–1995): Introduction

Robert Gibbs

Emmanuel Levinas's work effects a critical challenge to the prominent philosophical tradition of his time: phenomenology. That challenge arises through the crises of this century, crises of unimagined violence and cruelty, crises which interrupted and devastated his own life. Levinas frames the challenge to philosophy in philosophical terms and through the philosophical tradition, but he draws richly on another tradition, the Jewish tradition arising from the Bible through rabbinic sources, in order to disrupt the complacency and self-sufficiency of philosophy. His texts are not Jewish dogmatic theology, nor are they fashioned as reflections on his personal experiences of suffering. They remain, curiously and almost intractably, philosophy – abstract, theoretical, complex, and addressed to readers trained to read philosophy. To turn to Levinas for instruction about God, therefore, is not to look for an almost romantic personal testimony to God's presence; nor is it to look for a rationalist account of God's predicates, but also it is not to find a nice Jewish sermon, or even a not so nice threatening Jewish prophet. It is to read an essay called "God and Philosophy" – an interrogation of philosophy and philosophy's ways of thinking about and writing about God – conducted in an intensely philosophical idiom.

Levinas was born in 1906 in Lithuania. His family were liberal Jews in a thoroughly Jewish milieu. He studied the Hebrew Scriptures, but was not given a traditional Talmudic education. He moved to Strasbourg to matriculate at the university (1923). He soon became engaged with philosophy, and studied with Husserl and Heidegger, publishing the first French translation of Husserl in 1931. Throughout the 1930s he lived in Paris, published essays on phenomenology, and taught at a Jewish teacher-training school. He survived the Second World War and the Shoah as a prisoner of war in a hard labor camp, while his parents and relatives in Lithuania were murdered and his wife and daughter were hidden, thanks in part to Maurice Blanchot, in a convent in the south of France.

After liberation, Levinas began to develop his own voice, a voice that was still phenomenological but strikingly critical of Heidegger. The early work, *From Existence to the Existant,* was rich with analyses of the labor camps and raised issues of ethics. At the same time, Levinas began to study Jewish sources with much greater intensity. His major philosophical work, *Totality and Infinity* (1961), explored the ethical relation as a face-to-face encounter, in which my responsibilities for the other person break apart my own world. Following its publication, Levinas received a university appointment, and eventually taught in Paris. His second major work, *Otherwise than Being, or Beyond Essence* (1974), redeveloped many earlier themes, but focused both on the extreme passivity of being assigned responsibility for another person and on the way that philosophical discourse itself could perform ethical responsibilities. These philosophical texts insist on the primacy of ethics and responsibility for the other person and give a metaphysics that breaks with the ontological tradition of thought.

During these later years, Levinas also published several works in Jewish thought. The genre he developed most was readings of Talmudic passages, published in four collections. In the third collection, *Beyond the Verse* (1982), Levinas explores the way that texts bear abundant meanings for generations of readers. His Jewish writings also discover within traditional Jewish sources many of the themes found in his philosophical works. Indeed, the relation of his Jewish and his philosophical works is much more complex and interrelated than one might suspect. Levinas died in December 1995.

The Overlay of Ontology and Semiotics

"God and Philosophy" developed from a series of presentations at the same time that Levinas was concluding *Otherwise than Being.* It is his most extensive treatment of theological themes, and it also represents many of his later phenomenological analyses (insomnia, trauma, the trace, saying, and testimony). Like most of Levinas's essays, it devotes extensive concern to a position he labels philosophy and rejects. That position is occupied by a totalizing ontology and a semiotics where language merely replicates reality: signs are mirrors of what is. When Levinas disrupts this concept of philosophy, he will insert a God who is infinite, a God who "comes to mind" – which is the title of the volume in which this essay was collected. Philosophy will be changed, but not discarded; ontology challenged; semiotics transformed.

At the outset, Levinas presents philosophy as a mode of reflection that reduces everything to immanence. Levinas draws on the phenomenological school, where a transcendental reflection governs thought. Following from Kant and developed again in Husserl, the claim is that all experience arises in consciousness and that there is a correlation between my thoughts and what I think about. For anything to be it must become present to a consciousness. Consciousness is an act that synthesizes the field of experience, representing it for the "I" that now holds the field and its contents. Levinas focuses on the act of transcendental apperception, the way that a consciousness itself sets the stage onto which all experience must come. For Levinas, this act forces all that transcends me to become immanent for me. While in an earlier stage of philosophy, the identity of being and thinking held that being was the norm for thinking, in the phenomenological school, both arise in consciousness.

Representations manage to hold the past and the future as present in consciousness. Levinas interprets the apperception of consciousness as a unified temporal horizon, in which everything that is real is (still) present. The authority to represent the past strips the past of its shadow, the aspect that is immemorial. Even the present is exposed to full presence, unable to shelter any ambiguity or enigmatic excess. The temporality of representation is one of synchrony, in which what is present is bound in immanence.

Levinas challenges not only this presence of representation, but also what Heidegger would have called the presencing of the present being. Indeed, Levinas interprets this act of being as binding being too tightly with the immanence of consciousness. The act by which things take their being is connected to the authority of consciousness, itself justified in its relation to what does appear. Philosophy, then, becomes the reflection that not only knows what is immanent; philosophy is the reflection that binds reality to immanence.

Some would object that this only goes for what is objective and scientific. Surely, they would say, religious experience or experience of the numinous transcends the immanence of this equation of being and thinking. Levinas regards the *experience* in religious experience as located clearly within consciousness and within the bounds set by transcendental reflection. Indeed, he is suspicious of arguments, such as Otto's, that claim one can go from some sort of experience to a correlate numinous being. The being to which the experience corresponds is limited as such by the field of consciousness. Like all other experiences of reality, the religious ones have purchased their presence at the expense of what could transcend the subject who has the experience.

More important than the ontological critique of philosophy is the correlate interpretation of meaning and of language. Levinas explores a semiotic in which ideas and words signify in a close approximation to the reduction to immanence we have just seen in ontology; that is, the correlation of being and thinking is determined as the correlation of reality and its meaning. The adequacy of a thought to what it thinks about is assumed to be the meaning of the thought. Signs, then, are interpreted as primarily semantically determined, referring to the *realia*, whether percept or concept. But this leads Levinas into an altogether traditional philosophic problematic: how to talk (and think) about God? For if God transcends us radically, then no correlation can be formed between our thoughts and God's being. In the context of language, we are in the contested terrain of ineffability. The choice that seems closest to Levinas's work is the *via eminentia*: the path of refining or reducing an excellence until, for instance, the goodness of the goodness of a good becomes God. The highest height within the realm of philosophical ontology turns out to be the being whose being is being in the highest sense. Hence, Levinas wonders whether the terms used to describe God will only reinstate the immanence of our thought. Indeed, he hints early in the essay that the task will have to be to cancel or exclude the sense of being as an entity, and even of an act of Being, from the language about God.

Moreover, just as religious experience encloses God within the horizon of the subject's reality, so even ejecting God from rational discourse will not sufficiently check our impulse to render God immanent. Levinas criticizes Pascal and others, even those who reject God as dwelling beneath reason, for presuming to leave reason and its field of thought intact. To consign God to outside consciousness, or to a consciousness outside reason, ˙ to allow philosophy to persist as immanence. Levinas contests the restricted options: God as a being or God as an object of faith outside reason. Levinas's title is "God and Philosophy," and the issue is first to see how philosophy has been unable to bear God, but secondly to rethink what reason and philosophy are, precisely because God does come to mind, and does not merely abandon it.

The God Who Comes to Mind

Levinas draws directly and extensively on Descartes, in what is at once a curious reading and a challenging one. It challenges us by allowing the most modern of modern thinkers, the father of modernity, the villain of Heidegger's narrative as well as of others', to be a resource for what we may call postmodern philosophy. Worse still, Levinas plunges directly into the *Meditations*, and there finds a rupture of immanence, a rupture at the very heart of immanence, at the very center of consciousness, in the idea of God. For it is a resurrected Cartesian idea of God that provides the breakup of immanent ontology in Levinas. The idea, quite simply, is the infinite, an idea that thinks more than it can think. The basic structure of correlation is shattered not by something that stays beyond consciousness, but by something that invades it. In the idea of the infinite, I think more than I am able to, and so discover my passivity, my lack of control, in my own thinking. My ability to think does not control my thoughts; rather, there are thoughts which exceed my capacities and in so doing unseat my authority and autonomy. What transcends me is not something so big that I cannot think it, something that lurks outside my horizon, but rather something that turns my world inside out by coming into my world. Levinas plays with the way that the *in-* of infinity does not only mean negation (the not-finite), but also means within, that the infinite comes into the finite. As transcendent, however, the infinite cannot be thought, cannot be represented in my consciousness under the rules of transcendental apperception. What passes as my thought of the infinite is not the infinite, but a reduction of it (again). Hence, the infinite is not present – "is" not-present, but turns inside out the structure of the present that is represented by a subject. The subject comes back, stuffing everything it can back into its tube, contesting the infinite, calling for evidence, for presence. The infinite cannot appear on the subject's stage, but calls for the drama. The subject's game of rigging the stage now is itself part of a larger dramaturgy, where it is called to set the stage by something it cannot conceive: the infinite.

Levinas is clear, in one footnote, that this essay is about transcendence, not primarily an essay on ethics. But not surprisingly for readers of Levinas, it just happens to turn out that the way that the infinite interrupts consciousness is in my ethical responsibilities for another person. Levinas argues from an infinite that challenges consciousness to a desire that has no satisfaction – a desire for the non-desirable. But this quickly leads to the set of his most well-known themes. The neighbor, the one who draws near me, is the one whom I am responsible for. Levinas explores the way that I am bound in a responsibility without limits, a responsibility that increases the more I do – an infinitization of responsibility. The instigation of this responsibility, moreover, precedes my consciousness and indeed calls consciousness in. The metaphysical structure of the infinite, beyond being, is performed in relation to another person, a person with material needs. Elsewhere, Levinas cites a traditional Jewish saying that "my neighbor's material needs are my spiritual needs."[1] The question of God and Philosophy becomes, in line with a long tradition in Jewish thought, a matter for interhuman relations, for ethics.

Consequent to the discussion of the infinite, the issue is not merely how other is the other person, but rather, how that otherness enters into my world, turning my world inside out. Levinas makes use of excessive themes in order to examine these responsibilities. The key theme is substitution. I am a substitute for the other person, responsible in her place. Levinas writes of being a hostage for the other. Such responsibility, to the point of suffering or dying for the other person, is asymmetric. I am a substitute for the other person, but no one is reciprocally a substitute for me. Indeed, characteristic of this ethics is the moral revulsion from any claim that others are responsible for me in the same way that I am responsible for them. Independent of the complex relations to many other people, prior to any considerations of justice, I am responsible for this neighbor, this near one, regardless of the other's behavior, attitudes, even responsibilities toward me. Such a being-for-the-other instigates my entry into society, where there are other others and justice is at issue. But we join society, says Levinas, because before joining, we are already responsible excessively for one other person, the neighbor.

In this social context, semiotics is radically transformed. Levinas insists on a distinction between the saying and the said. The saying is not what is said but is the giving of myself in giving words to another. We might examine that by distinguishing between the semantic content, the power of signs to refer to their objects, and the pragmatic function, the way that signs relate to those who use them (the speaker and listener, reader and writer). The key dimension of semiotics becomes pragmatics, the way that a person can be for another person and can signify that ethical relation. Levinas calls the saying the signifying, in giving a sign. It is a performative dimension of language, and it justifies the semantic dimension. Elsewhere, Levinas will justify the semantic element,[2] but in this essay he focuses on the way that using words can allow for meanings that exceed the correlation of thinking and being. Language is not a mere doubling of reality, but is the way to make myself available for the other, for whom I am already responsible. In addition, saying leads to a vital activity in the life of responsibility: witnessing. Not only am I responsible for the other, but I speak in order to signify that responsibility. And what I testify to is the infinite, to the miracle that exceeds my own capacity in my responsibilities for the others. Through my action of testifying, and not as a referent of my discourse, the infinite comes to signify.

The final issue, which returns with still greater force, is the role of philosophy. For while philosophy appeared at first as the reduction of transcendence to immanence, philosophy now can also appear as a discourse that attends to what cannot be thought – in thinking itself. It can witness and speak of not what is simply inexpressible, but of the saying in which what exceeds what can be said has happened. Levinas calls this mode of discourse prophecy but refuses to locate it in the confines of religious experience. Instead, prophecy is a way to testify not by presenting a theme called responsibility but by speaking in my responsibility to others. The need to theorize becomes not a mode of cognition but a requirement of responsibility in relation to others. And philosophical thinking itself must recall its own gesture of reducing the saying to a said by then unsaying its said. Philosophy testifies to the call to thought in the face of the other, an ethical call, by saying a theme (ethics, transcendence, saying itself) and then unsaying what it has said. It refuses neither the said – a presence for others in words – nor the unsaying – a re-opening of the philosopher for others. Without the said, philosophy would consign transcendence to an outside, leaving the inside of the system intact; without the unsaying, philosophy would again reduce the God who comes to mind to merely what the mind can think. Philosophy itself becomes philosophy and God. God and Philosophy.

Notes

1 Cited in Salomon Malka, *Lire Levinas* (Paris: Les Éditions du CERF, 1984), p. 52.
2 *Otherwise than Being, or Beyond Essence*, trans. Alphonso Lingis (Dordrecht: Martinus Nijhoff, 1981), pp. 153–62.

Selected Bibliography

Bernasconi, Robert, and Critchley, Simon, *Re-reading Levinas* (Bloomington: Indiana University Press, 1991).
Cohen, Richard, *Elevations: The Height and the Good in Rosenzweig and Levinas* (Chicago: University of Chicago Press, 1994).
Cohen, Richard A. (ed.), *Face to Face with Levinas* (Albany: State University of New York Press, 1986).
Handelman, Susan A., *Fragments of Redemption: Jewish Thought and Literary Theory in Benjamin, Scholem, and Levinas* (Bloomington: Indiana University Press, 1991).
Levinas, Emmanuel, *Totality and Infinity*, trans. Alphonso Lingis (Pittsburgh: Duquesne University Press, 1969).
——*Difficult Freedom: Essays on Judaism*, trans. Sean Hand (Baltimore, MD: Johns Hopkins University Press, 1990).
——*Beyond the Verse: Talmudic Readings and Lectures*, trans. Gary D. Mole (London: Athlone Press, 1994).

God and Philosophy

The Priority of Philosophical Discourse, and Ontology

"Not to philosophize is still to philosophize." The philosophical discourse of the West claims the amplitude of an all-encompassing structure or of an ultimate comprehension. It compels every other discourse to justify itself before philosophy.

Rational theology accepts this vassalage. If, for the benefit of religion, it reserves a domain from the authority of philosophy, one will know that this domain will have been recognized to be philosophically unverifiable.

The dignity of being the ultimate and royal discourse belongs to Western philosophy because of the strict coinciding of thought, in which philosophy resides, and the idea of reality in which this thought thinks. For thought, this coinciding means not having to think beyond what belongs to "being's move" (*geste d'être*), or at least not beyond what modifies a previous belongingness to "being's move," such as formal or ideal notions. For the being of reality, this coinciding means: to illuminate thought and the conceived by showing itself. To show oneself, to be illuminated, is just what having meaning is, what having intelligibility par excellence is, the intelligibility underlying every modification of meaning. Then we should have to understand the rationality of "being's move" not as some characteristic which would be attributed to it when a reason comes to know of it. That a thought comes to know of it is intelligibility. Rationality has to be understood as the incessant emergence of thought from the energy of "being's move" or its manifestation, and reason has to be understood out of this rationality. Meaningful thought, and thought about being, would be pleonasms and equivalent pleonasms, which, however, are justified by the vicissitudes and privations to which this identification of the thought of the meaningful and of being is de jure exposed.

Philosophical discourse therefore should be able to include God, of whom the Bible speaks – if this God does have a meaning. But as soon as he is conceived, this God is situated within "being's move." He is situated there as the *entity* par excellence. If the intellectual understanding of the biblical God, theology, does not reach to the level of philosophical thought, this is not because it thinks of God as *a being* without first explicating the "being of this being," but because in thematizing God it brings God into the course of being. But, in the most unlikely way – that is, not analogous with an idea subject to *criteria*, or subject to the demand that it show itself to be true or false – the God of the Bible signifies the beyond being, transcendence. It is not by chance that the history of Western philosophy has been a destruction of transcendence. Rational theology, fundamentally ontological, strives to take account of transcendence in the domain of being by expressing it with adverbs of height applied to the verb being; God is said to exist eminently or par excellence. But does the height, or the height above all height, that is thus expressed belong to ontology? And does not the modality which this adverb, borrowed from the dimension of the sky over our heads, expresses modify the verbal meaning of the verb to be to the point of excluding it from the thinkable as something inapprehendable, excluding it from the *esse* showing itself, that is, showing itself meaningfully in a theme?

One can also, to be sure, claim that the God of the Bible does not have meaning, that is, is not properly speaking thinkable. This would be the other term of the alternative. "The concept of God is not a problematical concept; it is not a concept at all," writes Mme Delhomme in a recent book, continuing a major tradition of philosophical rationalism which refuses to accept the transcendence of the God of Abraham, Isaac, and Jacob among the concepts without which there would be no thought. What the Bible puts above all comprehension would have not yet reached the threshold of intelligibility!

The problem which is thus posed, and which will be ours, is whether the meaning that is equivalent to the *esse* of being, that is, the meaning which is meaning in philosophy, is not already a restriction of meaning. Is it not already a derivative or a drifting of meaning? Is not the meaning equivalent to essence – to being's move, to being *qua* being – first broached in presence, which is the time of the same? This supposition can be justified only through the possibility of going back from this allegedly conditioned meaning to a meaning which could no longer be put in terms of being or in terms of beings. We must ask if beyond the intelligibility and rationalism of identity, consciousness, the present, and being – beyond the intelligibility of immanence – the signifyingness, rationality, and rationalism of transcendence are not understood. Over and beyond being does not a meaning whose priority, translated into ontological language, would have to be called *antecedent* to being, show itself? It is not certain that in going beyond the terms and beings one necessarily relapses into speaking of opinion or faith. In fact, in staying or wanting to be outside of reason, faith and opinion speak the language of being. Nothing is less opposed to ontology than opinion and faith. To ask, as we are trying to do here, if God can be expressed in a rational discourse which would be neither ontology nor faith is implicitly to doubt the formal opposition, established by Yehouda Halévy and taken up by Pascal, between the God of Abraham, Isaac, and Jacob, invoked in faith without philosophy, and the god of philosophers. It is to doubt that this opposition constitutes an alternative.

The Priority of Ontology and Immanence

We said that for Western philosophy meaning or intelligibility coincide with the manifestation of being, as if the very doings of being led to clarity, in the form of intelligibility, and then became an intentional thematization in an experience. Pressing toward or waiting for it, all the potentialities of experience are derived from or susceptible to such thematization. Thematic exposition concludes the business of being or truth. But if being *is* manifestation, if the exertion of being amounts to this exhibition, the manifestation of being is only the manifestation of this "exertion," that is, the manifestation of manifestation, the truth of truth. Philosophy thus finds in manifestation its matter and its form. In its attachment to being, to beings or the being of beings, it would thus remain a movement of knowledge and truth, an adventure of experience between the clear and the obscure. It is certain that this is the sense in which philosophy is the bearer of the spirituality of the West, where spirit is taken to be coextensive with knowing. But knowing – or thought, or experience – is not to be understood as a kind of reflection of exteriority in an inner forum. The notion of reflection, an optical metaphor taken from thematized beings and events, is not the proper trope for knowing. Knowing is only understood in its proper essence when one begins with consciousness, whose specificity is lost when it is defined with the concept of knowing, a concept which presupposes consciousness.

It is as a modality or modification of *insomnia* that consciousness is consciousness of . . ., a gathering into being or into presence, which, at a certain depth of vigilance where vigilance has to clothe itself with justice, is essential to insomnia.[1] Insomnia, wakefulness, or vigilance, far from being definable as the simple negation of the natural phenomenon of sleep, belongs to the categorial, antecedent to all anthropological attention and stupor. Ever on the verge of awakening, sleep communicates with vigilance; while trying to escape, sleep stays tuned in, an *obedience to the wakefulness* which threatens it and calls to it, which *demands*. The categorial proper to insomnia is not reducible to the tautological affirmation of the same, dialectical negation, or the ecstasy of thematizing intentionality. Here being awake is not equivalent to *watching over* . . ., where already the identical, rest, sleep, is sought after. It is in consciousness alone that the *watching*, already petrified, bends over toward a content which is identified and gathered into a presence, into a "move of being," and is absorbed in it. Insomnia as a category – or as a meta-category (but the *meta* – becomes meaningful through it) – does not get inscribed in a table of categories from a determining activity exercised on the other as *given* by the unity of the same (and all activity is but the identification and crystallization of the same against the other, upon being affected by that other), in order to ensure to the other, consolidated into a being, the gravity of being. Insomnia – the wakefulness in awakening – is disturbed in the core of its formal or categorical *sameness* by the *other*, which tears away at whatever forms a nucleus, a substance of the same, identity, a rest, a presence, a sleep. Insomnia is disturbed by the other who breaks this rest, breaks it from this side of the state in which equality tends to establish itself. The irreducible categorical character of insomnia lies precisely in that. The other is in the same, and does not alienate the same but awakens it. Awakening is like a demand that no obedience is equal to, no obedience puts to sleep; it is a "more" in the "less." Or, to use an obsolete language, it is the spirituality of the soul, ceaselessly aroused from its state of soul, in which wakefulness itself already closes over upon itself or falls to sleep, resting within the boundaries it has as a state. We find here the passivity of inspiration, or the subjectivity of the subjectivity of the subject aroused, sobered up, out of its being. There is a formalism in insomnia, a formalism more formal than that of any defining, delimiting, confining form, more formally formal than that of a form that closes into a presence and an *esse*, filling with content. Insomnia is wakefulness, but a wakefulness without intentionality, disinterested. Its indeterminatedness does not call for a form, is not a materiality. It is a form that does not *terminate* the drawing out of a form in it, and does not condense its own emptiness into a content. It is uncontained – infinity.

Consciousness has already broken with this disinterestedness. It is the identity of the same, the presence of being, the presence of presence. We must think of consciousness beginning with the emphasis of presence.[2] Presence is only possible as a return of consciousness to itself, outside of sleep – and consciousness thus goes back to insomnia. That is so even though this return to itself, in the form of self-consciousness, is only a forgetting of the other which awakens the same from within, and even if the freedom of the same is still only a waking dream. Presence is only possible as an incessant taking up of presence again, an incessant re-presentation. The incessance of presence is a repetition, its being taken up again an apperception of representation. Representation is not to be described as a taking up again. Representation is the very possibility of a return, the possibility of the *always*, or of the presence of the present. The unity of apperception, the "I think," which is discovered and acquired its role in re-presentation, is not a way to make presence purely subjective. The synthesis effected by the unity of the *I think* behind experience constitutes the act of presence, presence as an act, or presence in act. This encompassing movement is accomplished by the unity formed into a nucleus in the "I think," a synopsis which is a structure necessary for the actuality of the present. The "activity of the mind," the operative concept of transcendental idealism, is not based on an empirical experience of the deployment of intellectual energy. It is rather the extreme purity – to the point of tension – of the presence of presence, which is Aristotle's being in act, a presence of presence, an extreme tension breaking up *presence* into an "experience of a subject," where precisely presence returns upon itself and is filled up and fulfilled. The psychic nature of consciousness is this emphasis of being, this presence of presence, a presence outdoing itself, without loopholes, without hedging, without any possible forgetting in the folds of what would be only implicit and could not be unfolded. The "incessance" is an explication without any possible shading off; it refers to an awakening that would be lucidity, but also to a watching over being, an attention to . . . and not an exposedness to the other (and already a modification of the formalism without intentionality of insomnia). It is always true that because of consciousness nothing can be dissimulated in being. Consciousness is a light which illuminates the world from one end to the other; everything which goes off into the past is recalled or recovered by history. Reminiscence is the extreme consciousness which is also the universal presence and the universal ontology; whatever is able to fill the field of consciousness was, in its time, received or perceived, had an origin. Through consciousness the past is only a modification of the present. Nothing can happen and nothing could have happened without presenting itself, nothing could be smuggled by without being declared, without being shown, without being inspected as to its truth. Transcendental subjectivity is the figure of this presence; no signification precedes that which I give to myself.

Thus the process of the present unfolds through consciousness like a "held note" held in its *always*, in its identity of being the same, in the simultaneity of its moments. The process of the subjective does not come from the outside; the presence of the present involves consciousness. And philosophy, then, in search of the transcendental operations of the apperception of the *I think*, is not some unhealthy and accidental curiosity; it is representation, the reactualization of representation, that is, the emphasis of presence, being's remaining-the-same in the simultaneity of its presence, in its always, in its immanence. Philosophy is not merely the knowledge of immanence; it is immanence itself.[3]

Immanence and consciousness, as gathering up the manifestation of manifestation, are not disturbed by the phenomenological interpretation of affective states or of the voluntary psyche, which puts in the very heart of consciousness the emotion or the anxiety which upset its imperturbability – nor by that interpretation that starts from fear or trembling before the sacred, and understands them as primary lived states. It is not accidental that the axiological and practical strata in Husserl cover over a representational ground.

The axiological and the practical strata remain experiences – experiences of values, or experiences of the willed *qua* willed. The representational ground, which Husserl brings out in them, consists, moreover, less in some serenity of the theoretical intention than in the identification of the identical in the form of ideality, in the assembling, in the representation in the form of a presence, a lucidity which allows nothing to escape. In short, it consists in immanence.

But let us take note of this: the interpretation of affectivity as a modification of representation, or as founded on a representation, succeeds in the measure that affectivity is taken at the level of a tendency, or concupiscence, as Pascal would say – at the level of an aspiration which can be satisfied in pleasure or, when unsatisfied, remains a pure lack which causes suffering. Beneath such an affectivity is found the ontological activity of consciousness – wholly investment and comprehension, that is, presence and representation (of which the specifically theoretical thematization is but a modality). This does not exclude the possibility that, in another direction besides that of a tendency going to its term, there may break out an affectivity which breaks with the form and purpose of consciousness, and leaves immanence, is a transcendence. We are going to try to speak of this "elsewhere."

A religious thought which appeals to religious experiences allegedly independent of philosophy already, inasmuch as it is founded on experience, refers to the "I think," and is wholly connected on to philosophy. The "narration" of religious experience does not shake philosophy and cannot break with presence and immanence, of which philosophy is the emphatic completion. It is possible that the word God has come to philosophy out of religious discourse. But even if philosophy refuses this discourse, it understands it as a language made of propositions bearing on a theme, that is, as having a meaning which refers to a disclosure, a manifestation of presence. The bearers of religious experience do not conceive of any other signification of meaning. Religious "revelation" is therewith already assimilated to philosophical disclosure; even dialectical theology maintains this assimilation. That a discourse can speak otherwise than to say what has been seen or heard on the outside, or previously experienced, remains unsuspected. From the start then a religious being interprets what he lived through as an experience. In spite of himself he already interprets God, of whom he claims to have an experience, in terms of being, presence, and immanence.

Then the first question has to be: Can discourse signify otherwise than by signifying a theme? Does God signify as the theme of the religious discourse which names God – or as the discourse which, at least to begin with, does not name Him, but says Him with another form of address than denomination or evocation?

The Idea of the Infinite

The thematization of God in religious experience has already avoided or missed the inordinate plot that breaks up the unity of the "I think."[4]

In his meditation on the idea of God, Descartes, with an unequalled rigor, has sketched out the extraordinary course of a thought that proceeds on to the breakup of the *I think*. Although he conceives of God as a being, he conceives of him as an eminent being or being that *is* eminently. Before this rapprochement between the idea of God and the idea of being, we do indeed have to ask whether the adjective *eminent* and the adverb *eminently* do not refer to the elevation of the sky above our heads, and whether they do not go beyond ontology. Be that as it may, interpreting the immeasurability of God as a superlative case of existing, Descartes maintains a substantialist language. But for us this is not what is unsurpassable in his meditation. It is not the proofs of God's existence that matter to us here, but the breakup of consciousness, which is not a repression into the unconscious, but a sobering up or an awakening, jolting the "dogmatic slumber" which sleeps at the bottom of every consciousness resting on its object. The idea of God, the *cogitatum* of a *cogitatio* which *to begin with* contains that *cogitatio*, *signifies the non-contained par excellence*. Is not that the very absolution of the absolute? It overflows every capacity; the "objective reality" of the *cogitatum* breaks up the "formal reality" of the *cogitatio*. This perhaps overturns, in advance, the universal validity and primordial character of intentionality. We will say that the idea of God breaks up the thought which is an investment, a synopsis, and a synthesis, and can only enclose in a presence, re-present, reduce to presence, or let be.

Malebranche knew how to gauge the import of this event; there is no idea of God, or God is his own idea. We are outside the order in which one passes from an idea to a being. The idea of God is God in me, but God already breaking up the consciousness which aims at ideas, and unlike any content. This difference is certainly not an emergence, which would be to imply that an inclusion of God in consciousness had been possible, nor some sort of escaping the realm of consciousness, which is to imply that there could have been *comprehension*. And yet there is an idea of God, or God is in us, as though the being-not-includable were also an ex-ceptional relationship with me, as though the difference between the Infinite and what ought to include and comprehend it were a non-indifference of the Infinite to this impossible inclusion, a non-indifference of the Infinite to thought. There is a putting of the Infinite into thought, but this is wholly different from what is structured as a comprehension of a *cogitatum* by a *cogitatio*. This putting is an unequalled passivity, because it is unassumable. (It is perhaps in this passivity – beyond all passivity – that we should recognize awakening.) Or, conversely, it is as though the negation of the finite included in In-finity did not signify any sort of negation resulting from the formal structure of negative judgment, but rather signified the *idea of the Infinite*, that is, the Infinite in me. Or, more exactly, it is as though the psyche in subjectivity were equivalent to the negation of the finite by the Infinite, as though – without wanting to play on words – the *in* of the Infinite were to signify both the *non* and the *within*.[5]

The actuality of the *cogito* is thus interrupted by the unincludable, not thought but undergone in the form of the idea of the Infinite, bearing in a second moment of consciousness what in a first moment claimed to bear it. After the certainty of the *cogito*, present to itself in the second Meditation, after the "halt" which the last lines of this Meditation mark, the third Meditation announces that "in some way I have in me the notion of the infinite earlier than the finite – to wit, the notion of God before that of myself." The idea of the Infinite, *Infinity in me*, can only be a passivity of consciousness. Is it still consciousness? There is here a passivity which cannot be likened to receptivity. Receptivity is a collecting that takes place in a welcome, an assuming that takes place under the force of the blow received. The breakup of the actuality of thought in the "idea of God" is a passivity more passive still than any passivity, like the passivity of a trauma through which the idea of God would have been put into us. An "idea put into us" – does this stylistic turn suit the subjectivity of the cogito? Does it suit consciousness and its way of holding a content, which is always to leave some traces of its grasp on it? Does not consciousness, in its present, get its origin and its contents from itself? Can an idea be put into a thought and abjure its letters patent of Socratic nobility, its immanent birth in reminiscence, that is, its origin in the very presence of the thought that thinks it, or in the recuperation of this thought by memory? But in the idea of the Infinite there is described a passivity more passive still than any passivity befitting consciousness: there is the surprise or susception of the unassumable, more open still than any openness – wakefulness – but suggesting the passivity of someone created.[6] The putting into us of an unincludable idea overturns that presence to self which consciousness is, forcing its way through the barrier and checkpoint, eluding the obligation to accept or adopt all that enters from the outside. It is then an idea signifying with a signifyingness prior to presence, to all presence, prior to every origin in consciousness and thus an-archical, accessible in its trace. It signifies with a signifyingness from the first older than its exhibition, not exhausting itself in exhibiting itself, not drawing its meaning from its manifestation, and thus breaking with the coinciding of being with appearance in which, for Western philosophy, meaning or rationality lie, breaking with synopsis. It is more ancient than the rememberable thought which representation retains in its presence. What can this signification more ancient than exhibition mean? Or, more exactly, what can the antiquity of a signification mean? In exhibition, can it enter into another time than that of the historical present, which already annuls the past and its dia-chrony by representing it? What can this antiquity mean if not the trauma of awakening – as though the idea of the Infinite, the Infinite in us, awakened a consciousness which is not awakened enough? As though the idea of the Infinite in us were a demand, and a signification in the sense that an order is signified in a demand.

Divine Comedy

We have already said that it is not in the negation of the finite by the Infinite, understood in its abstraction and logical formalism, that the idea of the Infinite, or the Infinite in thought, is to be interpreted. On the contrary, the idea of the Infinite, or the Infinite in thought, is the proper and irreducible figure for the negation of the finite. The *in* of infinity is not a *not* like any other; its negation is the subjectivity of the subject, which is behind intentionality. The difference between the Infinite and the finite is behind intentionality. The difference between the Infinite and the finite is a non-indifference of the Infinite to the finite, and is the secret of subjectivity. The figure of the Infinite put in me, and, according to Descartes, contemporaneous with my creation,[7] would mean that the not being able to comprehend the Infinite by thought is somehow a positive relationship with this thought – but with this thought as passive, as a *cogitatio* as though dumbfounded and no longer, or not yet, commanding the *cogitatum*, not yet hastening toward adequation between the term of the spontaneous teleology of consciousness and this term given in being. Such an adequation is the destiny of the essential teleology of consciousness, which proceeds to its intentional term, and conjures up the presence of re-presentation. Better yet, the not-being-able-to-comprehend-the-Infinite-by-thought would signify the condition – or the unconditionality – of thought, as though to speak of the non-comprehension of the Infinite by the finite did not amount to simply saying that the Infinite is not finite, and as though the affirmation of the difference between the Infinite and the finite had to remain a verbal abstraction, without consideration of the fact that through the non-comprehension of the Infinite by thought, thought is posited as thought,[8] as a posited subjectivity, that is, is posited as self-positing. The Infinite has nothing to add on to itself so as to affect subjectivity; its very in-finity, its difference from the finite, is already its non-indifference to the finite. This amounts to a *cogitatio not comprehending the cogitatum* which affects it utterly. The Infinite affects thought by devastating it and at the same time calls upon it; in a "putting it back in its place" it puts thought in place. It awakens it. The awakening of thought is not a welcoming of the Infinite, is not a recollecting, not an assuming, which are necessary and sufficient for *experience*. The idea of the Infinite puts these in question. The idea of the Infinite is not even taken up as love, which is awakened when the arrow strikes, but then the subject stunned by the trauma finds himself forthwith in the immanence of a state of soul. The Infinite signifies precisely prior to its manifestation; here the meaning is not reducible to manifestation, the representation of presence, or teleology. Here meaning is not measured by the possibility or impossibility of the truth of being, even if this antecedent signification should, in one way or another – and if only through its trace – show itself in the enigmas involved in saying.

What then is the plot of meaning, other than that of re-presentation and of empirical experience, which is hatched in the idea of the Infinite – in the monstrosity of the Infinite *put* in me – an idea which in its passivity over and beyond all receptivity is no longer an idea? What is the meaning of the trauma of awakening, in which the Infinite can neither be posited as a correlate of the subject, nor enter into a structure with it, nor become its contemporary in a co-presence – but in which it transcends him? How is transcendence as a relationship thinkable if it must exclude the ultimate and the most formal co-presence which a relationship guarantees to its terms?

The *in* of the Infinite designates the depth of the affecting by which subjectivity is affected through this "putting" of the Infinite into it, without prehension or comprehension. It designates the depth of an undergoing that no capacity comprehends, that no foundation any longer supports, where every process of investing fails and where the screws that fix the stern of inwardness burst. This putting in without a corresponding recollecting devastates its site like a devouring fire, catastrophying its site, in the etymological sense of the word.[9] It is a dazzling, where the eye takes more than it can hold, an igniting of the skin which touches and does not touch what is beyond the graspable, and burns. It is a passivity or a passion in which desire can be recognized, in which the "*more* in the *less*" awakens by its most ardent, noblest, and most ancient flame a thought given over to thinking more than it thinks.[10] But this desire is of another order than the desires involved in hedonist or eudaemonist affectivity and activity, where the desirable is invested, reached, and identified as an object of need, and where the immanence of representation and of the exterior world is restored. The negativity of the *in* of the Infinite – otherwise than being, divine comedy – hollows out a desire which cannot be filled, nourishes itself with its very augmentation, and is exalted as a desire, withdraws from its satisfaction in the measure that it approaches the desirable. It is a desire that is beyond satisfaction, and, unlike a need, does not identify a term or an end. This endless desire for what is beyond being is dis-inter*estedness*, transcendence – desire for the Good.

But if the Infinite in me means a desire for the Infinite, is one certain of the transcendence which *passes* there? Does not desire restore the contemporaneousness of desiring and the desirable? Or, in other words, does not the desiring being derive from the desirable a complacency in desiring, as though it had already grasped it by its intention? Is not the disinter*estedness* of the desire for the Infinite an inter*estedness*? We have spoken of a desire for the Good beyond being, a transcendence, without giving our attention to the way interestedness is excluded from the desire for the Infinite, and without showing how the transcendent Infinite deserves the name Good, when its very transcendence can, it seems, only mean indifference.

Love is possible only through the idea of the Infinite – through the Infinite put in me, through the "more" which devastates and awakens the "less," turning away from teleology, destroying the moment and the happiness of the end. Plato forces out of Aristophanes an admission which, coming from the lips of the master of comedy, is striking indeed: "These are the people who pass their whole lives together; yet they could not explain what they desire of one another."[11] Hephaestus will say that they want to become "one instead of two,"[12] and he thus assigns an end to love and reduces it to a nostalgia for what was in the past. But why can the lovers themselves not say what they ask from one another beyond pleasure? Diotima will put love's intention beyond this unity, but will find love to be indigent, needy, and subject to vulgarity. The celestial and the vulgar Venus are sisters. Love is complacent in waiting for the lovable, that is, it enjoys the lovable through the representation which fills up the waiting. Perhaps pornography is that, arising in all eroticism, as eroticism arises in all love. Losing in this enjoyment the inordinateness of desire, love is concupiscence in Pascal's sense of the term, an assuming and an investing by the *I*. The *I think* reconstitutes presence and being, inter*estedness* and immanence, in love.

Is a transcendence of the desirable beyond the inter*estedness* and eroticism in which the beloved abides possible? Affected by the Infinite, desire cannot proceed to an end which it would be equal to; in desire the approach distances, and enjoyment is but the increase of hunger. Transcendence or the disinter*estedness* of desire "passes" in this reversal of terms. How? And in the transcendence of the Infinite what dictates to us the word Good? For dis-inter*estedness* to be possible in the desire for the Infinite, for the desire beyond being, or transcendence, not to be an absorption in immanence, which would thus make its return, it is necessary that the desirable or Good remain separated in the desire; as desirable it is near but different: holy. This can only be if the desirable orders me to what is the non-desirable, the undesirable par excellence – the other. The reference to the other is an awakening, an awakening to proximity, and this is responsibility for the neighbor, to the point of substituting for him. Elsewhere[13] we have shown that substitution for another lies in the heart of responsibility, an undoing of the nucleus of the transcendental subject, the transcendence of goodness, the nobility of a pure *supporting*, an ipseity of pure election. Such is love without Eros. Transcendence is ethics, and subjectivity which is not, in the last analysis, the "I think" (which it is at first) or the unity of "transcendental apperception" is, as a responsibility for another, a subjection to the other. The I is a passivity more passive still than any passivity because it is from the first in the accusative – oneself (*soi*) – and never was in the nominative; it is under the accusation of the other, even though it be faultless. It is a hostage for the other, obeying a command before having heard it, faithful to a commitment that it never made, to a past that has never been present. This wakefulness or openness to oneself is completely exposed, and sobered up from the ecstasy of intentionality. We have designated this way for the Infinite, or for God, to refer, from the heart of its very desirability, to the non-desirable proximity of others, by the term "illeity"; it is the extraordinary reversal of the desirability of the desirable, the supreme desirability, calling to itself the rectilinear straightforwardness of desire. Through this reversal the desirable escapes desire. The goodness of the Good – the Good which never sleeps or nods – inclines the movement it calls forth, to turn it from the Good and orient it toward the other, and only thus toward the Good. Here is an obliqueness that goes higher than straightforwardness. The desirable is intangible and separates itself from the relationship with desire which it calls for; through this separation or holiness it remains a third person, the *he* in the depth of the you. He is good in just this eminent sense; He does not fill me up with goods, but compels me to goodness, which is better than goods received.[14]

To be good is a deficit, waste, and foolishness in a being; to be good is excellence and elevation beyond being. Ethics is not a moment of being; it is otherwise and better than being, the very possibility of the beyond.[15] In this ethical reversal, in this reference of the desirable to the non-desirable, in this strange mission that orders the approach to the other, God is drawn out of objectivity, presence, and being. He is neither an object nor an interlocutor. His absolute remoteness, his transcendence, turns into my responsibility – non-erotic par excellence – for the other. And this analysis implies that God is not simply the "first other," the "other par excellence," or the "absolutely other," but other than the other (*autre qu'autrui*), other otherwise, other with an alterity prior to the alterity of the other, prior to the ethical bond with another and different from every neighbor, transcendent to the point of absence, to the point of a possible confusion with the stirring of the *there is*.[16] In this confusion the substitution for the neighbor gains in dis-inter*estedness*, that is, in nobility, and the transcendence of the Infinite arises in glory. Such transcendence is true with a dia-chronic truth and without any synthesis, higher than the truths that are without enigma.[17] For this formula "transcendence to the point of absence" not to mean the simple explicitation of an ex-ceptional word, this word itself has to be put back into the significance of the whole plot of the ethical or back into the divine comedy without which it could not have arisen. That comedy is enacted equivocally between temple and theatre, but in it the laughter sticks in one's throat when the neighbor approaches – that is, when his face, or his forsakeness, draws near.

Phenomenology and Transcendence

The exposition of the ethical signification of transcendence and of the Infinite beyond being can be worked out, beginning with the proximity of the neighbor and my responsibility for the other.

Until then a passive subjectivity might seem something constructed and abstract. The receptivity of finite knowledge is an assembling of a dispersed given in the simultaneity of presence, in immanence. The passivity "more passive still than any passivity" consisted in undergoing – or more exactly in having already undergone, in a non-representable past which was never present – a trauma that could not be assumed; it consisted in being struck by the "*in*" of infinity which devastates presence and awakens subjectivity to the proximity of the other. The non-contained, which breaks the container or the forms of consciousness, thus *transcends* the essence or the "move" of knowable being which carries on its being in presence; it transcends the inter*estedness* and simultaneity of a representable or historically reconstitutable temporality; it transcends immanence.

This trauma which cannot be assumed, inflicted by the Infinite on presence, or this affecting of presence by the Infinite – this affectivity – takes shape as a subjection to the neighbor. It is thought thinking more than it thinks, desire, the reference to the neighbor, the responsibility for another.

This abstraction is nevertheless familiar to us in the empirical event of obligation to another, as the impossibility of indifference – impossible without fail – before the misfortunes and faults of a neighbor, the unexceptionable responsibility for him. It is impossible to fix limits or measure the extreme urgency of this responsibility. Upon reflection it is something completely astonishing, a responsibility that even extends to the obligation to answer for another's freedom, to be responsible for his responsibility, whereas the freedom which would demand an eventual commitment or even the assuming of an imposed necessity cannot find a present that includes the possibilities which belong to the other. The other's freedom can neither constitute a structure along with my freedom, nor enter into a synthesis with it. Responsibility for the neighbor is precisely what goes beyond the legal and obliges beyond contracts; it comes to me from what is prior to my freedom, from a non-present, an immemorial. A difference gapes open between me and the other that no unity of transcendental apperception can undo. My responsibility for the other is precisely the non-indifference of this difference – the proximity of the other. An absolutely extra-ordinary relation, it does not re-establish the order of representation in which every past returns. The proximity of a neighbor remains a dia-chronic break, a resistance of time to the synthesis of simultaneity.

The biological human brotherhood – conceived with the sober coldness of Cain – is not a sufficient reason for me to be responsible for a separated being. The sober coldness of Cain consists in conceiving responsibility as proceeding from freedom or in terms of a contract. But responsibility for another comes from what is prior to my freedom. It does not come from the time made up of presences, nor presences that have sunk into the past and are representable, the time of beginnings or assumings. It does not allow me to constitute myself into an *I think*, substantial like a stone, or, like a heart of stone, existing in and for oneself. It ends up in substitution for another, in the condition – or the unconditionality – of being a hostage. Such responsibility does not give one time, a present for recollection or coming back to oneself; it makes one always late. Before the neighbor I am summoned and do not just appear; from the first I am answering to an assignation. Already the stony core of my substance is dislodged. But the responsibility to which I am exposed in such a passivity does not apprehend me as an interchangeable thing, for here no one can be substituted for me; in calling upon me as someone accused who cannot reject the accusation, it obliges me as someone unreplaceable and unique, someone chosen. Inasmuch as it calls upon my responsibility it forbids me any replacement. Unreplaceable in responsibility, I cannot, without defaulting, incurring fault, or being caught up in some complex, escape the face of a neighbor; here I am pledged to the other without being able to take back my pledge.[18] I cannot evade the face of the other, naked and without resources. The nakedness of someone forsaken shows in the cracks in the mask of the personage, or in his wrinkled skin; his being "without resources" has to be heard like cries not voiced or thematized, already addressed to God. There the resonance of silence – *Geläut der Stille* – certainly sounds. We here have come upon an imbroglio that has to be taken seriously: a relationship to . . . that is not represented, without intentionality, not repressed; it is the latent birth of religion in the other, prior to emotions or voices, prior to "religious experience" which speaks of revelation in terms of the disclosure of being, when it is a question of an unwonted access, in the heart of my responsibility, to an unwonted disturbance of being. Even if one says right away, "It was nothing." "It was nothing" – it was not being, but otherwise than being. My responsibility in spite of myself – which is the way the other's charge falls upon me, or the way the other disturbs me, that is, is close to me – is the hearing or understanding of this cry. It is awakening. The proximity of a neighbor is my responsibility for him; to approach is to be one's brother's keeper; to be one's brother's keeper is to be his hostage. Immediacy is this. Responsibility does not come from fraternity, but fraternity denotes responsibility for another, antecedent to my freedom.

To posit subjectivity in this responsibility is to catch sight of a passivity in it that is never passive enough, that of being consumed for the other. The very light of subjectivity shines and illuminates out of this ardour, although the ashes of this consummation are not able to fashion the kernel of a being existing in and for itself, and the I does not oppose to the other any form that protects itself or provides it with a measure. Such is the consuming of a holocaust. "I am dust and ashes," says Abraham in interceding for Sodom.[19] "What are we?" says Moses more humbly still.[20]

What is the meaning of this assignation in which the nucleus of the subject is uprooted, undone, and does not receive any form capable of assuming this? What do these atomic metaphors mean, if not an I torn from the concept of the ego and from the content of obligations for which the concept rigorously supplies measure and rule, and thus left to an unmeasured responsibility, because it increases in the measure – or in the immeasurableness – that a response is made, increasing gloriously. This is the I that is not designated, but which says "here I am." "Each of us is guilty before everyone, for everyone and for each one, and I more than others," writes Dostoyevsky in *The Brothers Karamazov*. The I which says I is not that which singularizes or individuates a concept or a genus. It is I, unique in its genus, who speaks to you in the first person. That is, unless one could maintain that it is in the individuation of the genus or the concept of the ego that I myself awaken and expose myself to others, that is, begin to speak. This exposedness is not like self-consciousness, the recurrence of the subject to himself, confirming the ego by itself. The recurrence in awakening is something one can describe as a shudder of incarnation through which *giving* takes on meaning, as the primordial dative of the *for another*, in which a subject becomes a heart, a sensibility, and hands which give. But it is thus a position already deposed of its kingdom of identity and substance, already in debt, "for the other" to the point of substitution for the other, altering the immanence of the subject in the depths of its identity. This subject unreplaceable for the responsibility assigned to him finds in that very fact a new identity. But in extracting me from the concept of the ego, the fission of the subject is a growth of obligation in proportion as obedience grows, the augmentation of guilt that comes with the augmentation of holiness, the increase of distance proportionate to the approach. Here there is no rest for the self sheltered in its form, in its ego–concept! There are no conditions, not even those of servitude. There is an incessant solicitude for solicitude, the extreme of passivity in responsibility for the responsibility of the other. Thus proximity is never close enough; as responsible, I am never finished with emptying myself of myself. There is infinite increase in this exhausting of oneself, in which the subject is not simply an awareness of this expenditure, but is its locus and event and, so to speak, its goodness. The *glory of a long desire*! The subject as a hostage has been neither the experience nor the proof of the Infinite, but a witness borne of the Infinite, a modality of this glory, a testimony that no disclosure has preceded.

This growing surplus of the Infinite that we have ventured to call *glory* is not an abstract quintessence. It has a signification in the response to the summons which comes to me from the face of a neighbor, and which could not be evaded; it is the hyperbolic demand which at once exceeds that response. This comes as a surprise for the respondent himself by which, ousted from his inwardness as an ego and a "being with two sides," he is awakened, that is, exposed to the other without restraint or reserve. The passivity of such an exposure to the other is not exhausted in some sort of being open to the other's look or objectifying judgment. The openness of the ego exposed to the other is the breakup or turning inside out of inwardness. Sincerity is the name of this extra-version.[21] But what else can this inversion or extra-version mean but a responsibility for others such that I keep nothing for myself? A responsibility such that everything in me is debt and donation and such that my being-there is the ultimate being-there where the creditors find the debtor? It is a responsibility such that my position as a subject in its *as for me* is already my substitution or expiation for others. Responsibility for the other – for his distress and his freedom – does not derive from any commitment, project, or antecedent disclosure, in which the subject would be posited for itself before being-in-debt. Here passivity is extreme in the measure (or inordinateness) that the devotion for the other is not shut up in itself like a state of soul, but is itself from the start given over to the other.

This excess is *saying*. Sincerity is not an attribute which eventually receives the saying; it is by saying that sincerity – exposedness without reserve – is first possible. Saying makes signs to the other, but in this sign signifies the very giving of signs. Saying opens me to the other before saying what is said, before the said uttered in this sincerity forms a screen between me and the other. This saying without a said is thus like silence. It is without words, but not with hands empty. If silence speaks, it is not through some inward mystery or some sort of ecstasy of intentionality, but through the hyperbolic passivity of giving, which is prior to all willing and thematization. Saying bears witness to the other of the Infinite which rends me, which in the saying awakens me.

Language understood in this way loses its superfluous and strange function of doubling up thought and being. Saying as testimony precedes all the said. Saying, before setting forth a said, is already the testimony of this responsibility – and even the saying of a said, as an approach to the other, is a responsibility for him. Saying is therefore a way of signifying prior to all experience. A pure testimony, it is a martyr's truth which does not depend on any disclosure or any "religious" experience; it is an obedience that precedes the hearing of any order. A pure testimony, it does not testify to a prior experience, but to the Infinite which is not accessible to the unity of apperception, non-appearing and disproportionate to the present. Saying could neither include nor comprehend the Infinite; the Infinite concerns and closes in on me while speaking through my mouth. And the only pure testimony is that of the Infinite. This is not a psychological wonder, but the modality in which the Infinite *comes to pass*, signifying through him to whom it signifies, understood inasmuch as, before any commitment, I answer for the other.

Like someone put under leaden skies that suppress every shadowy corner in me, every residue of mystery, every mental reservation, every "as for me . . ." and every hardening or relaxing of the plot of things by which escape would be possible, I am a testimony, or a trace, or the glory of the Infinite, breaking the bad silence which harbors Gyges's secrecy. There is extraverting of a subject's inwardness; the subject becomes visible before becoming a seer! The Infinite is not "in front of" me; I express it, but precisely by giving a sign of the giving of signs, of the "for-the-other" in which I am dis-interested; here I am (*me voici*)! The accusative (*me* voici!) here is remarkable: here I am, under your eyes, at your service, your obedient servant. In the name of God. But this is without thematization; the sentence in which God gets mixed in with words is not "I believe in God." The religious discourse that precedes all religious discourse is not dialogue. It is the "here I am" said to a neighbor to whom I am given over, by which I announce peace, that is, my responsibility for the other. "Creating . . . the fruit of the lips. Peace, peace to the far and to the near, says the Lord."[22]

In the description which has been elaborated up to now there has been no question of the transcendental condition for some sort of ethical experience. Ethics as substitution for the other, giving without reserve, breaks up the unity of transcendental apperception, that condition for all being and all experience. Disinter*estedness* in the radical sense of the term, ethics designates the improbable field where the Infinite is in relationship with the finite without contradicting itself by this relationship, where on the contrary it alone *comes to pass* as Infinity and as awakening. The Infinite transcends itself in the finite, it *passes* the finite, in that it directs the neighbor to me without exposing itself to me. This order steals into me like a thief, despite the outstretched nets of consciousness, a trauma which surprises me absolutely, always already *passed* in a past which was never present and remains un-representable.

One can call this plot of infinity, where I make myself the author of what I understand by inspiration. It constitutes, prior to the unity of apperception, the very psyche in the soul. In this inspiration, or prophesying, I am the go-between for what I set forth. God has spoken "that you shall not prophesy," says Amos,[23] comparing the prophetic reaction to the passivity of the fear which takes hold of him who hears the roaring of wild beasts. Prophesying is pure testimony, pure because prior to all disclosure; it is subjection to an order before understanding the order. In the recoverable time of reminiscence, this anachronism is no less paradoxical than a prediction of the future. It is in prophesying that the Infinite passes – and awakens. As a transcendence, refusing objectification and dialogue, it signifies in an ethical way. It *signifies* in the sense in which one says *to mean an order*; it *orders*.

In sketching out, behind philosophy where transcendence is always reduced, the outlines of prophetic testimony, we have not entered into the shifting sands of religious experience. To say that subjectivity is the temple or the theatre of transcendence, and that the understanding of transcendence takes on an ethical meaning, does indeed not contradict the idea of the Good beyond being. This idea guarantees the philosophical dignity of an undertaking in which the signifyingness of meaning is separated from the manifestation or the presence of being. But one can only wonder if Western philosophy has been faithful to this Platonism. It discovered intelligibility in terms in conjunction, posited by relation with one another, signifying one another; for Western philosophy being, thematized in its presence, is illuminated in this way. The clarity of the visible signifies. The appropriate trope for the signifyingness of signification is: the one-for-the-other. But signifyingness becomes visibility, immanence, and ontology, inasmuch as the terms unite into a whole, and even their history is systematized, so as to be clarified.

On the pages of this study transcendence as the ethical structure, the one-for-the-other has been formulated in terms of signifyingness and intelligibility.[24] The trope of intelligibility takes form in the ethical one-for-the-other, a signifyingness prior to that which terms in conjunction in a system acquire. But does this signifyingness more ancient than all patterns really *take form?* We have shown elsewhere the latent birth of systems and philosophy out of this august intelligibility; we shall not return to that here.[25]

The intelligibility of transcendence is not something ontological. The transcendence of God cannot be stated or conceived in terms of being, the element of philosophy, behind which philosophy sees only night. But the break between philosophical intelligibility and the beyond being, or the contradiction there would be in comprehending infinity, does not exclude God from signifyingness, which, if it is not ontological, does not simply amount to thoughts bearing on being in decline, to views lacking necessity and word-plays.

In our times – is this its very modernity? – a presumption of being an ideology weighs on philosophy. This presumption cannot claim to be a part of philosophy, where the critical spirit cannot content itself with suspicions, but owes it to itself that it bring forth proofs. This presumption, which is irrecusable, draws its force from elsewhere. It begins in a cry of ethical revolt, bearing witness to responsibility; it begins in prophecy. Philosophy does not become suspect at just any moment in the spiritual history of the West. To recognize with philosophy – or to recognize philosophically – that the real is rational and that the rational is alone real, and not to be able to smother or cover over the cry of those who, the morrow after this recognition, mean to transform the world, is already to move in a domain of meaning which the inclusion cannot comprehend and among reasons that "reason" does not know, and which have not begun in philosophy. A meaning thus seems to bear witness to a beyond which would not be the no man's land of non-sense where opinions accumulate. *Not to philosophize would not be "to philosophize still,"* nor to succumb to opinions. There is meaning testified to in interjections and outcries, before being disclosed in propositions, a meaning that signifies as a command, like an order that one signifies. Its manifestation in a theme already devolves from its signifying as ordering; ethical signification signifies not *for* a consciousness which thematizes, but *to* a subjectivity, wholly an obedience, obeying with an obedience that precedes understanding. Here is a passivity still more passive than that of receptivity in knowing, the receptivity that assumes what affects it. In this signification the ethical moment is not founded on any preliminary structure of theoretical thought, on language or on any particular language. Language then has over signification only the hold a form has, clothing matter. This recalls the distinction between form and signification, which shows itself in that distinction and through its references to a linguistic system. The distinction holds even if this *said* has to be *unsaid* – and it will have to so as to lose its linguistic alternation. The signification will indeed have to be reduced and lose the "stains" to which it owed its exposition to the light or its sojourn in shadow. An alternating rhythm of the said and the unsaid, and the unsaid being unsaid in its turn, will have to be substituted for the unity of discourse. There is here a breakup of the omnipotence of the logos, that of system and simultaneity. The logos breaks up into a signifier and a signified which is not *only* a signifier. This negates the attempt to amalgamate signifier and signified and to drive transcendence from its first or last refuge, in con-signing all thought to language as a system of signs. Such an attempt was elaborated in the shadow of a philosophy for which meaning is equivalent to the manifestation of being, and manifestation equivalent to being's *esse*.

Transcendence as signification, and signification as the signification of an order given to subjectivity before any statement, is the pure one-for-the-other. Poor ethical subjectivity deprived of freedom! Unless this would be the trauma of a fission of the self that occurs in an adventure undergone with God or through God. But in fact this ambiguity also is necessary to transcendence. Transcendence owes it to itself to interrupt its own demonstration and monstration, its phenomenality. It requires the blinking and dia-chrony of enigma, which is not simply a precarious certainty, but breaks up the unity of transcendental apperception, in which immanence always triumphs over transcendence.

Notes

1 Cf. *Otherwise than Being, or Beyond Essence*, trans. A. Lingis (Dordrecht: Martinus Nijhoff, 1981), pp. 153–62.
2 Which is required by justice, itself required by vigilance, and thus by the Infinite in me, by the idea of infinity.

3 The notion of experience is inseparable from the unity of presence, or simultaneity. It thus refers to the unity of apperception which does not come from the outside and "become conscious" of simultaneity. It belongs to the very "way" of presence, for presence, being, is only possible as a thematization or gathering of the transitory, and thus as a phenomenon, which is thematic exhibition itself. But all signification does not derive from experience, does not resolve into a manifestation. The formal structure of signifyingness, the one-for-the-other, does not from the first amount to a "showing oneself." Suffering for another, for example, has a meaning in which knowing is adventitious. The adventure of knowledge which is characteristic of being, ontological from the first, is not the only mode, nor the preliminary mode, of intelligibility or meaning. Experience as the souce of meaning has to be put into question. It is possible to show that meaning *qua* knowing has its motivation in a meaning that at the start is not a knowing at all. This is not to deny that philosophy is itself knowledge. But the possibility for knowing to take in all meaning does not reduce all meaning to the structures that its exhibition imposes. This then suggests the idea of a dia-chrony of truth in which the said has to be unsaid, and the unsaid unsaid in its turn. In this sense the sceptical essence of philosophy can be taken seriously: scepticism is not an arbitrary contestation; it is a doctrine of inspection and testing, although not reducible to testing of the scientific sort.

4 This possibility of conjuring away or missing the division of truth into two times – that of the *immediate* and that of the *reflected* – deserves consideration and prudence. It does not necessarily lead to the subordination of one to the other. Truth as *dia-chrony*, as refusal of synchronization and synthesis, is perhaps proper to transcendence.

5 The latent birth of negation occurs not in subjectivity, but in the idea of the Infinite. Or, if one prefers, it is in subjectivity *qua* idea of the Infinite. It is in this sense that the idea of the infinite, as Descartes affirms, is a "genuine idea" and not merely what I conceive "by the negation of what *is* finite."

6 Translator's note. Inquiring after the "manner in which I have acquired this idea," the sense of this receptivity, Descartes says in the third Meditation: "For I have not received it through the senses, and it is never presented to me unexpectedly, as is usual with the ideas of sensible things when these things present themselves, or seem to present themselves, to the external organs of my senses . . ." In the ideas of sensible things, the surprise of the experience is taken up by the understanding, which extracts from the sense the clear and distinct intelligible, and this allows one to say that the sensible things "seem to present themselves to the external organs of my senses." This is the very process of receptivity! "Nor is it [the idea of infinity]," Descartes continues, "likewise a fiction of my mind, for it is not in my power to take from or add anything to it; and consequently the only alternative is that it is innate in me, just as the idea of myself is innate in me" (*The Philosophical Works of Descartes*, vol. 1, trans. E. S. Haldane and G. R. T. Ross (Cambridge: Cambridge University Press, 1969), p. 170).

7 Cf. preceding note.

8 Or, as Descartes says, "which is *created*."

9 "For behold, the Lord is coming forth out of his place, and will come down and tread upon the high places of the earth. And the mountains will melt under him, and the valleys will be cleft, like wax before the fire, like waters poured down a steep place"

(Micah 1: 3–4). "What sustains yields to what is sustained," is overwhelmed or gives way. This "structure" (which is, so to speak, destructure itself) is what is announced and expressed in this text, which we cite independently of considerations of its authority and "rhetoric" as Holy Writ.

10 Cf. *Totality and Infinity*, pp. 33–104 and *passim*.

11 *Symposium*, 192c.

12 Ibid., 192e.

13 Cf. *Otherwise than Being, or Beyond Essence*, ch. 4.

14 Franz Rosenzweig interprets the *response* given by man to the love with which God loves him as the movement unto the neighbor (*The Star of Redemption*, trans. William W. Hallo (Boston: Beacon, 1964), Part III). This takes up the structure which commands a homiletic theme in Jewish thought. The "fringes" on the corners of their garments, whose sight should remind the faithful of "all the commandments of the Lord" (Numbers 15: 38–40), are in Hebrew called *tzitzit*. The ancient rabbinical commentary *Siphri* connects this word with the verb *tsouts* of which one form, in the Song of Songs 2: 9, means "to observe" or "to look" as in "My beloved . . . looking through the lattice." The faithful looking at the "fringes" which remind him of his obligations, thus returns the gaze of the beloved who observes him. This would be the *vis-à-vis* or the face-to-face with God!

15 It is the meaning of the beyond, of transcendence, and not ethics, that our study is pursuing. It finds this meaning in ethics. There is *signification*, for ethics is structured as the-one-for-the-other; there is signification, of the beyond being, for one finds oneself outside of all finality in a responsibility which ever increases, in a dis-interestedness where a being undoes itself of its being.

16 Trace of a past which was never present, but this absence still disturbs.

17 Dia-chronic truth; that is, the dia-chrony of truth that is without any possible synthesis. Contrary to what Bergson teaches us, there would be "a disorder" which is not another order, there where the elements cannot be made contemporary, in the way, for example (but is this an example or the ex-ception?), in which God contrasts with the presence of re-presentation.

18 A devotedness as strong as death, and in a sense stronger than death. In *finitude* death outlines a destiny which it interrupts, but there can be no dispensation from the response which I am *passively* held to. The tomb is not a refuge; it is not a pardon. The debt remains.

19 Genesis 18: 27.

20 Exodus 16: 7.

21 The-one-for-the-other, the formal structure of signification, the signifyingness of rationality of signification, here does not begin by being exposed in a theme. It is my openness to the other, my sincerity or *veracity*.

22 Isaiah 57: 18-19.

23 Amos 2: 12.

24 It is quite remarkable that the word signifyingness (*signifiance*) has empirically the meaning of a mark of attention given to someone.

25 Cf. *Otherwise than Being, or Beyond Essence*, pp. 46 and 153.

Translated by Richard A. Cohen and Alphonso Lingis

Roland Barthes (1915–1980): Introduction

Valentine Cunningham

Roland Barthes's interpretative struggle in 1971 with the story of the patriarch Jacob's struggle with the angel established this small portion of biblical narrative right at the enticing center of the burgeoning world of new post-Saussurean criticism. After Barthes's demonstration of how certain highly formalist strategies for textual engagement could open up the inner dynamics even of a biblical text so manifestly geared to the political-historical, to the tribal, ritual, and theological needs of an ancient people as the Jacob story is, critics rushed to recruit Genesis 32 to their particular researches and programs of a more or less structuralist and poststructuralist kind. Because of Barthes, Wrestling Jacob has become a main icon of poststructuralist critique, the text of his story one of the most versatile and necessary of critical sites. So Harold Bloom read Jacob as the ancestor and type of Freud and the Freudian struggles for meaning, the oldest manifestation of, and manifesto for, Bloomian notions of how poetic influence works, the belief that "the aesthetic and the agonistic are one." Jacques Derrida seized on Jacob as an ancient exemplum of the Joycean war (all at once modernist and deconstructionist) with Jahwe and Christian textuality. For Geoffrey Hartman, Jacob's struggle became the key to all our struggles with text, but especially in the light of the midrashic perspectives and practices Hartman and others have wanted to revive as keys to postmodernist critical labour.[1] The offspring Barthes's essay has engendered are numerous. In showing there was great signifying life left in this old canonical story, Barthes was initiating a trend. The effect of his piece has been, not least, greatly to stimulate the return to the biblical text as canonical for literary study in our postmodernist reading times.

Barthes's piece began life, like so many of his texts, as an invited contribution, this time to two evenings of dialogue between structuralists and biblical exegetes in the Protestant Faculty of Theology at Geneva in February 1971. The other invited structuralist was Jean Starobinski, who offered an analysis of Mark 5: 1–20. Presenting a more conventional exegesis of the Jacob story, as an exemplary counter to Barthes's reading, was the professional exegete Robert Martin-Achard. (Starobinski's interlocutor was Franz I. Leenhardt.) The proceedings were published as *Structuralisme et exégèse biblique* in 1971, and as *Analyse structurale et exégèse biblique* in 1972. An American translation of this second volume appeared in 1974 as *Structural Analysis and Biblical Exegesis*. Further translations of Barthes's contribution, by Stephen Heath and by Richard Howard, appeared in 1977 and 1988.[2] Richard Howard's is the one used in this present volume.

Barthes's strategies for reading the Jacob story hark back to principles he set down at some length in his 1966 essay "Introduction to the Structural Analysis of Narratives." He opens his Jacob reading with a refusal to repeat the introductory "account of the principles, perspectives, and the problems of the structural analysis of narrative" with which he had opened an earlier biblical reading – Acts 10–11, the story of St Peter and the Roman centurion Cornelius – given at the annual congress of the French Catholic Bible Studies Association at Chantilly, 6 September 1969.[3] Analysis of narrative is not "a science, nor even a discipline (it is not taught)," Barthes insists, in nearly the very same words he had used at Chantilly. But science and discipline or not, Barthes clearly considers the structuralist ground rules to have been clearly laid down – and, of course, by himself. Structuralism is already a wisdom and a praxis, and all according to Roland Barthes. The curious student must look him up. The time for merely theoretical prologomena has gone by. Barthes is now ready, and on the face of it eager, to show how to practice a structuralist analysis. He wants to get across the river Jabbok with Jacob, to open his account with the Genesis account of that crossing, or rather, to grapple with the arrestingly cross-eyed beginning of the Jacob story.

The story's opening, or apparent opening, is doubled, repetitive, self-contradictory. Jacob crosses, but then seems not to have done. Barthes goes on to suggest that this hesitancy is characteristic of all the text – perhaps, by implication, of all texts, not least the biblical ones. "Where to begin?" As Jacques Derrida and others would repeatedly do, Barthes wants us to pause, and feel the extent to which we're being given pause, as the text pauses, hovering, stammering, at its putative threshold. We're waylaid, a brake is put on our interpretative progress, friction is applied to the acquisition of meaning. On such a reckoning, soon after this to become utterly typical interpretative reasoning, the textual border, the entry place that appears to solicit one's passage through and in, is proving a considerable hazard, a place of stumbling.

And if beginnings are to prove such trouble to locate, define, and negotiate, what price then middles and endings? Readers and reading on this plan are, by definition, in for an uneasy time.

Mixed signals are, of course, what Barthes will find the text giving off throughout. As he was still willing – up to a point – to practice it in 1971, his structuralism is a mixed bag of approaches – a collage, in fact, of hermeneutic devices culled in particular from Lévi-Strauss, from Barthes's friend Algirdas Julien Greimas, and from the Russian formalist Vladimir Propp. Barthes is right to insist on the unscientific nature of his proceeding, if by science is meant procedural rigor. Even as he seeks to include what he calls a "canonical structural analysis," he admits his current practice as a reader has taken him outside a pure structuralism. His reading of the Jacob story keeps being invaded by echoes from that ongoing methodological progress. Barthes certainly had moved on by 1971. One of his books of the year before, *S/Z*, a bit by bit trawl through a story by Balzac, had been, as he declares in a note in the Jacob piece, more textual than structuralist. His other 1970 book, *Empire of Signs*, is a stunning mish-mash about Japan, a kind of neo-anthropological notebook with semiotic tendencies, an attempt to define the discourse, the signifying practices of a real place – what, in fact, Barthes had always understood by mythology and semiology. His new book of 1971, *Sade/Fourier/Loyola*, would attempt something similar with three great historical systems-builders (the Loyola material pokes through into the Jacob essay's illustration of Jacob's marking, his laming, with reference to the Ignatian *ascesis*). The way was clearly being prepared in the early seventies for the important personal books to come, the ones uniting confession with analytical reflections on how personal histories get textualized, *Roland Barthes by Roland Barthes* (1975), *A Lover's Discourse* (1977), and *Camera Lucida* (1980).[4]

No wonder the Jacob piece shows pure structuralist principles loosening their hold on Barthes's critical imagination. But, in any case, he had already allowed in his earlier enunciation of structuralist principle in the Acts piece for the analyst to express his own personality and to respond sensitively to the particular demands of the text, whatever they might be. *Pertinence*, he had said there, should be the analyst's guide.[5] Barthes says of Jacob's story that he could mount an *indicial* analysis. This method had featured prominently in the "Introduction to the Structural Analysis of Narratives." It has to do with the composing of character and atmosphere, and is important in the reading of realist novels. But Barthes has concluded that the Jacob story is rather folkloric, and a *functional* analysis is apter to that.[6] So it's clearly a mistake to suppose structuralism had done away with the critic's conventional need to weigh the implicit textual relevance of approaches. It's evidently an error, too, to suppose structuralism had replaced the personality of the reader by some purely mechanical, impersonal moves. What structuralism involves, Barthes says in the

Acts piece, is "an enterprise of *finesse* . . . there is no machine for reading meaning":

> there must still be an individual operation of reading . . . one investigator cannot speak in another's name. Further, this individual research is, on the level of each researcher, *in process*: each investigator has his own history.[7]

And the personal stake in Barthes's reading of Jacob, the personalized nature of his particular structuralist operation – the tendency that will lead to his later highly personal writings, and which is enough to demonstrate both the difficulty of a "pure" structuralism and also the way the would-be scientific methods of structuralism are always collapsing into a messier poststructuralism – are all instructively manifest.

Both the occasion and the text in question clearly appealed to a main aspect of Barthes's selfhood, his inherited Protestantism. Brought up by a Protestant mother, Barthes tended to take up Protestant invitations to write and to speak – for "sentimental reasons," as he said.[8] And this Protestant Barthes had long been fascinated by wrestling. His early essay on French wrestling had helped make his name as a semiologist.[9] Wrestling clearly had Protestant implications. Jacob, the lone wrestler, struggling with God, is a kind of archetypal Protestant. Analyzing Jacob's struggle was a Barthesian reading encounter waiting to happen. Jacob's limp, the mark of his agon, a kind of analogue for the burdened Protestant conscience, is the sort of mixed blessing Barthes's reflections on his Protestant heritage are inevitably drawn to. Barthes's long critical war upon "the illusion of the natural" in texts and text-making began, he suggested in *Barthes by Barthes*:

> in the minority situation of R.B. himself; he has always belonged to some minority, to some margin – of society, of language, of desire, of profession, and even of religion (it was not a matter of indifference to be a Protestant in a class of Catholic children); in no way a severe situation, but one which somewhat marks the whole of social existence: who does not feel how *natural* it is, in France, to be Catholic, married, and properly accredited with the right degrees?[10]

This particular outsider's special mark included, of course, his homosexuality – which was part of his lifelong attraction to André Gide, another French Protestant homosexual ("Gide . . . my original language, my *Ursuppe*, my literary soup").[11] What's more, the wrestler as type of the Protestant self doomed to a life of unremitting and probably unrewarded struggle, is evidently a central figure for the belief amounting to a private mythology of Barthes's, that language itself is all an intimidating matter of combat. "Language is the field of *Mache: pugna verborum*."[12] The binaries that Saussure defined as language's essence are, crucially, at odds across their binary line, signifier against signified, *langue* against *parole*, synchrony against diachrony. *Difference* is a matter of conflict: "Wrestling is like a diacritic writing."[13] Acts of naming are inevitably wrapped up in narratives of struggle, as Jacob's is. (Barthes's long obsession with *onomastics*, the business of naming and of the proper noun, that "sovereign signifier" as he called it,[14] began in his very first published article, which was (naturally enough) on Gide, and continued in his meditations on the nicknames of wrestlers and competitive cyclists.)[15] And the critical act is always in Barthes's rhetoric a doing of necessary violence – it's a matter of *ungluing* the text,[16] of tearing off its protective shells (*décortiquer* in French, hulling, de-husking, the word used in Barthes's invited meditation on violence in – yes – the French Protestant journal *Réforme*).[17] The Tour de France, Barthes wrote,

> resolutely rejects anything which might seem to affect in advance the naked brutal risks of combat. *The die is not cast*, the Tour is a confrontation of characters, it requires a morality of the individual, of solitary combat for life.[18]

The race of cyclists to the finish, so Protestant, so Jacob-like in its individualism, is an ethical struggle which could go either way right to the end – and Barthes evidently relishes that uncertain protractedness. The wrestler's determination likewise defines his moral strength. Hence Barthes's awed reading of the low blow by which Jacob's antagonist brings the fight to a crisis. He compares this would-be winning blow to the dirty tricks of the villain in French wrestling which rather preoccupy his "World of Wrestling" essay – the stagey nastiness of the "bastard," the *salaud* or even *salope*, whose bad behavior nonetheless contributes greatly to what Barthes claims is the strongly ethical world of the French wrestling hall.

The bastard generally loses. The one in the Jacob story wins, at least eventually. The divine low blow is intended to be decisive, but isn't utterly so. This *coup de Jarnac*, as Barthes calls it, using the proverbial French expression (spelled out in Richard Howard's translation), celebrates the hamstringing thrust to the knee by which the Comte de Jarnac won a famous duel in 1547. The victory was legal but still morally dubious. Jarnac was also the name of the place, etched on French Protestant memory, where twenty-two years after the notorious duel, the Huguenot general Louis, Prince de Conde, was defeated and killed in battle against his Catholic enemies – the Protestant good guy losing to the Catholic bastard. Clearly, when it comes to *coups* by and at Jarnac, morality and victory do not fit readily together. So too in the biblical story, as read by Barthes. Jacob, the habitual trickster, appears to win, but still loses and is marked for life. His apparently good opponent uses a low move, is checked, but still wins.

In reading these struggles, at the Jabbok, at Jarnac, with Jarnac, in the wrestling ring, Barthes appears to be mindful (for these fights are all being taken as allegories of reading and interpretation) of what he considered to be the ethical imperative of criticism to heterology and heterodoxy. For him the critic should always be a kind of trickster, like Jacob, and a deployer of the *coup de Jarnac* like Jacob's antagonist – a bit of a bastard in the critical wrestle, in fact. *Doxa*, of every kind, was Barthes's steady target. Criticism must be *heteroclite*, he said; critical discourse should be *acratic*, i.e., anti-doxal.[19] The task of reading is to uncover precisely the aberrant item, to expose scandals orthodox writing and reading would rather stayed concealed in the text:

> The good analyst of narrative must have a sort of imagination of the counter-text, an imagination of the aberration of the text, of what is narratively scandalous; he must be sensitive to the notion of logical, narrative "scandal."[20]

And so Barthes is with the Jacob story. God comes out of Barthes's reading looking like a cheat. He was even at the point of defeat. On the Greimasian actantial plan which Barthes deploys, God the Sender is also God the Opponent, and the only narrative structure which Barthes knows of where that is usual is in tales of blackmail. God as blackmailer. It's a strikingly unorthodox narrative structure to have uncovered, "audacious" indeed as Barthes calls it, and one "which corresponds to the 'scandal' represented by God's defeat." And it's Jacob, the scandalous if momentary winner, type of the unorthodox bastard wrestler, who bears the mark of a sort of victory. But still he is only grudgingly allowed his victory, so he's still, in effect, one of wrestling's bad ones, among the *salopes*. And *salope*, *bitch*, a term of "ultimate degradation" as Barthes's wrestling essay points out, abusively denotes effeminacy in the wrestling ring.

> Orsano (an effeminate teddy-boy first seen in a blue-and-pink dressing-gown) . . . a vindictive *salope*, or bitch (for I do not think that the public of the Elysée-Montmartre, like Littré, believes the word *salope* to be a masculine).[21]

The clear implication is that Barthes, the wrestling outsider, the one with what he feels to be the winning unorthodox analysis, is unlikely to get wholehearted orthodox acceptance – as he did not from his Protestant interlocutor on the first evening with Jacob in 1971; even if he was eventually luckier with the Collège de France, which narrowly elected the critical outsider to a chair of literary semiology in 1976.

The form, then, of Barthes's wrestle with the Jacob story, and with the Bible and orthodox readings of the biblical text, keeps on being shaped by his current concerns, anxieties, and neuroses. Like most readings of any value, this one shows the reader's particular selfhood put *en jeu*, at stake, at risk. There's always a critical wager. Barthes thought of it as being like Pascal's wager on the existence of God.[22] And perhaps even more obviously at risk here are the structuralist assumptions and practice Barthes had been invited to put into play.

For he never quite succeeds in making convincing the mere formalism, the utter linguisticism, the desired textual *ascesis* of the pure sort of structural analysis that wanted to stick, for example, as he put it, to the synchronic effects of the text and to eschew diachrony ("Our object is not the philological or historical document," "The problem . . . is in effect not to reduce the text to a signified, whatever it may be (historical, economic, folkloric, or kerygmatic)"; and so on).

And, to be sure, as Barthes himself admits, he will keep on transgressing the desired structuralist waivers and restrictions, will keep on indicating other lines of seemingly appropriate, even desirable, enquiry. But still, nonetheless, the purely structuralist parts of Barthes's analysis require of him some difficult and obviously artificial constraints and contrivances which he seems temporarily eager to go along with. He pretends, for instance, that he's dealing, as structuralism requires, with a properly bounded portion of text – despite his proper worries over where the narrative begins, and his occasional forays into other parts of Genesis and the Bible. And he enthusiastically keeps up the structuralist practice of reducing text to diagram, demonstrating structure by static maps and charts, a miniaturizing affair of coordinates and grids, a geometry that begs the question of boundedness and of coherences within a given boundedness, which, of course, the narrative is refusing to abide by. And how, in fixing the textual material for analysis, can the problem of translation be ignored? Barthes was happy to take the Jerusalem Bible's French version as read. In his Acts piece he even dismissed "the problems of translation" as "not systematically pertinent." But the kinds of Hebrew punning, for example, that Robert Martin-Achard dwelt on in his reply to Barthes, especially in the names Jacob and Israel, are not to be simply waived, certainly not without argument.

Just so, Barthes never once questions the basic assumptions of linguistic homology that structuralism is built on – the idea that narratives have a grammar because they're made out of grammatical stuff, or that sentences or phonemic distribution or morphological structure can serve as models for narrative because narratives are made out of such linguistic bits. Barthes takes over without demur Greimas's sentence, or communication, model and Propp's morphological model for Russian folk tale. So Barthes's reading acts on the structuralist assumption that narrative may be thought of as being purely and only in language, and that reading is thus an entering deeper and deeper into mere linguisticity. Hence the intense splashing about of linguistic metaphors, the *mark* and *difference* of the low blow to the hip, the *binary* or linguistic coupling of the fighters, God as *logothete*, Jacob as the *morpheme* of a new language.

It's a linguistic concentration, this insistence on stopping analysis at what Barthes calls the *dissemination*, the merely *signifying* level of the structure, that radically thins meaning, because it derives from a theoretical reducing of language to only a handful of its normal functions – synchrony, *langue*, the signifier – at the expense of diachrony, philology, speech acts of real persons, reference, semantics, and so on. It's not only Robert Martin-Achard who knew better, with his insistence on textual issues, and questions of genre and context. Barthes knew better too, as did Saussure, at least the Saussure who also announced the prospect of semiology, the study of signs in their social aspects. Barthes can't – of course he can't; how could he not? – can't help slipping occasionally out of the tight structuralist frame, to indicate where the Jacob story points to textual problems (that reference to the now traditional exegetical suggestion that the narrative's opening blurs together two originally separate textual versions), or to the implied history, economics, politics, psychology, and theology of the text, to the way the narrative, in other words, supposes various contexts. And it's not only a fuller linguistics than the Saussurean, a linguistics Barthes is plainly alert to, the paying of attention to, say, philology as a further model for text that Lévi-Strauss urged on the structuralist world,[23] which is inciting such deviations from purist structuralist linguistifying. It's also, clearly, the old and continuing semiologist in him, his old Foucauldian desire to decode discourse as a social and historical as well as a merely linguistic matter that was prevailing in his work on Japan, and on Sade and Loyola and Fourier, and which would continue in a steady series of implicit and explicit disavowals of structuralist purism.

In a most impressive passage in his inaugural lecture to the Collège de France in 1977 Barthes dwelt on the improper purity of Saussurean linguistics and of the structuralism it inspired. Armed with those Saussurean assumptions, Barthes had at first felt he 'could reduce discourse, miniaturize it into a grammatical example, and thereby hope to hold all human communication under my net':

> But the example is not "the thing itself," and the matter of language cannot be held or contained in the limits of the sentence. It is not only the phonemes, the words, and the syntactical articulations which are subject to a system of controlled freedom, since we cannot combine them arbitrarily; it is the whole stratum of discourse which is fixed by a network of rules, constraints, oppressions, repressions, massive and blurred at the rhetorical level, subtle and acute at the grammatical level. Language flows out into discourse; discourse flows back into language ... And linguistics now seems to me to be working on an enormous imposture, on an object it makes improperly clean and pure by wiping its fingers on the skein of discourse, like Trimalchio on his slaves' hair. Semiology would consequently be that labour which collects the impurity of language, the waste of linguistics, the immediate corruption of the message: nothing less than the desires, the fears, the appearances, the intimidations, the advances, the blandishments, the protests, the excuses, the aggressions, the various kinds of music out of which active language is made.[24]

And, of course, in the Acts piece, meditating on whether language and texts, as well as being held in language, can also refer beyond themselves to the world, to things and beings outside of text, not least to the divine "final signified," Barthes had already come close to his inaugural lecture's fuller sense of how language and signification work. The Bible, he suggested, is a sharp case of the text that is available to an internalizing structuralist analysis but that also clearly lays claim to the extra-linguistic relations a pure structuralism eschews:

> the realm which brings us together here, to wit Scripture, is a privileged domain for the problem, because, on the one hand, theologically, it is certain that a final signified is postulated: the metaphysical definition or the semantic definition of theology is to postulate the Last Signified; and because, on the other hand, the very notion of Scripture, the fact that the Bible is called Scripture, Writing, would orient us toward a more ambiguous comprehension of the problems, as if effectively, and theologically too, the base, the *princeps*, were still a Writing, and always a Writing.[25]

The reader of the Jacob essay is left to work out that Barthes might actually hold this "ambiguous comprehension" of writing, and of text and the Bible. But at least Barthes refers his "Jacob" readership back to the Acts piece where he explains the ambivalence. He was still Protestant enough, we might say, for that.

Notes

1 Harold Bloom, "Wrestling Sigmund: Three Paradigms for Poetic Originality," *The Breaking of the Vessels* (Chicago and London: Chicago University Press, 1982), pp. 47ff; idem, *The Western Canon: The Books and School of the Ages* (London: Macmillan, 1995), p. 6. Jacques Derrida, "Two Words for Joyce," *Post-structuralist Joyce: Essays from the French*, ed. Derek Attridge and Daniel Ferrer (Cambridge: Cambridge University Press, 1984), pp. 145–59; idem, "Des Tours de Babel," in *Difference in Translation*, ed. and trans. Joseph F. Graham (Ithaca, NY, and London: Cornell University Press, 1985), p. 170; idem, *La Carte postale de Socrate à Freud et au-delà* (Paris: Flammarion, 1980), pp. 257–8. Geoffrey Hartman, "The Struggle for the Text," in *Midrash and Literature*, ed. Hartman and Sanford Budick (New Haven and London: Yale University Press, 1986), pp. 3–18.

2 Alfred M. Johnson, ed. and trans., *Structural Analysis and Biblical Exegesis: Interpretational Essays*, Pittsburgh Theological Monograph Series no. 3 (Pittsburgh: Pickwick Press, 1974). "The Struggle with the Angel," in Stephen Heath, ed. and trans., *Image-Music-Text* (Glasgow: Fontana/Collins, 1977). "Wrestling with the Angel," in Roland Barthes, *The Semiotic Challenge*, trans. Richard Howard (Oxford: Blackwell, 1988): trans. of *L'Aventure sémiologique* (Paris: Seuil, 1985).

3 "The Structural Analysis of Narrative: Apropos of Acts 10–11" (originally in *Exégèse et*

Herméneutique (Paris: Seuil, 1971)), in *The Semiotic Challenge*, pp. 217–45. See also idem, pp. 95–135, for the "Introduction to the Structural Analysis of Narratives."

4 *S/Z* (Paris: Seuil, 1970), trans. Richard Miller (New York: Hill and Wang, 1974). *L'Empire des signes* (Geneva: Skira, 1970), trans. Richard Howard, *Empire of Signs* (New York: Farrar, Straus and Giroux, 1982; London: Cape, 1983). *Sade, Fourier, Loyola* (Paris: Seuil, 1971), trans. Richard Miller, *Sade/Fourier/Loyola* (New York: Hill and Wang, 1976). *Roland Barthes par Roland Barthes* (Paris: Seuil, 1975), trans. Richard Howard, *Roland Barthes by Roland Barthes* (New York: Hill and Wang, 1977). *Fragments d'un discours amoureux* (Paris: Seuil, 1977), trans. Richard Howard, *A Lover's Discourse: Fragments* (New York: Farrar, Straus and Giroux, 1978; London: Cape, 1979). *La Chambre claire: Note sur la photographie* (Paris: Cahiers du Cinéma/Gallimard/Seuil, 1980), trans. Richard Howard, *Camera Lucida: Reflections on Photography* (New York: Hill and Wang, 1981; London: Cape, 1982).

5 *The Semiotic Challenge*, p. 225.

6 Ibid., pp. 107–8.

7 Ibid., p. 222.

8 Roland Barthes, *Le Grain de la voix: entretiens 1962–1980* (Paris: Seuil, 1981), p. 284.

9 "The World of Wrestling," in *Mythologies* (London: Cape, 1972), pp. 15ff – selected and trans. Annette Lavers from *Mythologies* (Paris: Seuil, 1975).

10 *Roland Barthes by Roland Barthes*, pp. 130–1.

11 Ibid., p. 99.

12 "The Image," in Roland Barthes, *The Rustle of Language* (Blackwell, 1986), pp. 350–2: trans. Richard Howard from *Le Bruissement de la langue* (Paris: Seuil, 1984).

13 *Mythologies*, p. 18.

14 *Sade/Fourier/Loyola*, p. 168.

15 "Onomastics of Gide's characters," in Barthes, "On Gide and His Journal," in *Barthes: Selected Writings*, ed. and introd. Susan Sontag (London: Fontana/Collins, 1983), pp. 14f: trans. Richard Howard from "Notes sur Gide et son Journal," *Existence*, July 1942. "There is an onomastics of the tour de France": Barthes, "The Tour de France as Epic," in *The Eiffel Tower and Other Mythologies*, trans. Richard Howard (New York: Hill and Wang, 1979), pp. 79ff. *Mythologies*, p. 18.

16 *Sade/Fourier/Loyola*, p. 9.

17 "Propos sur la violence," *Réforme*, 2 Sept. 1978, in *Le Grain de la voix*, pp. 284–90.

18 "The Tour de France as Epic," p. 85.

19 *Heteroclite: Barthes by Barthes*, p. 93; *acratic*, in "The War of Languages" (1973), in *The Rustle of Language*, pp. 107–8.

20 "The Structural Analysis of Narrative: Apropos of Acts 10–11," p. 227.

21 "The World of Wrestling," pp. 17–18, 24.

22 "Neither-Nor Criticism," in *Mythologies*, p. 82 (and footnote).

23 Claude Lévi-Strauss, "Structure and Form: Reflections on a Work by Vladimir Propp," in *Structural Anthropology*, vol. 2, trans. Monique Layton (Harmondsworth: Peregrine, 1978), pp. 115–45.

24 "Inaugural Lecture, Collège de France," in Susan Sontag (ed.) *Barthes: Selected Writings*, pp. 470–1: trans. Richard Howard of *Leçon* (Paris: Seuil, 1978).

25 "Apropos of Acts 10–11," p. 242.

Wrestling with the Angel:
Textual Analysis of Genesis 32: 23–32

[23]That same night he rose, and taking his two wives and his two slave-girls and his eleven children he crossed the ford of the Jabbok. [24]He took them and sent them across the stream and sent all his possessions over too. [25]And Jacob was left alone.

And there was one that wrestled with him until daybreak [26]who, seeing that he could not master him, struck him in the socket of his hip, and Jacob's hip was dislocated as he wrestled with him. [27]He said, "Let me go, for day is breaking." But Jacob answered, "I will not let you go unless you bless me." [28]He then asked, "What is your name?" "Jacob," he replied. [29]He said, "Your name shall no longer be Jacob, but Israel, because you have been strong against God, you shall prevail against men." [30]Jacob then made this request, "I beg you, tell me your name," but he replied, "Why do you ask my name?" And he blessed him there.

[31]Jacob named the place Peniel, "Because I have seen God face to face," he said, "and I have survived." The sun rose as he left Peniel, limping because of his hip. [32]That is the reason why to this day the Israelites do not eat the sciatic nerve which is in the socket of the hip; because he had struck Jacob in the socket of the hip on the sciatic nerve.[1]

The particulars – or the precautions – which will serve as an introduction to our analysis will in fact be largely negative. First of all, I must acknowledge that I shall not be providing any preliminary account of the principles, the perspectives, and the problems of the structural analysis of narrative: that analysis is certainly not a science, nor even a discipline (it is not taught), but in the context of the nascent semiology, it is an area of research which is beginning to be well known, to the point where one would risk an impression of redundance by offering its prolegomena on the occasion of each new analysis. Furthermore, the structural analysis presented here will be anything but a pure one; of course I shall refer in essentials to the principles common to all the semiologists concerned with narrative, and even, in conclusion, shall show how our text sustains a very classical, even canonical structural analysis; this orthodox inquiry (from the point of view of the structural analysis of narrative) will be all the more justified in that we are dealing here with a mythic narrative which may have entered writing (Scripture) by an oral tradition; but I shall occasionally permit myself (and perhaps continuously, in an underhanded way) to orient my investigation toward an analysis with which I am more comfortable, Textual Analysis ("textual" is used here in reference to the present theory of the *text*, which is to be understood as a signifying production and not at all as a philological object, custodian of the Letter); this textual analysis seeks to "see" the text in its difference – which does not mean in its ineffable individuality, for such difference is "woven" in the known codes; for this analysis, the text is caught in an *open* network, which is the very infinity of language, itself structured without closure; textual analysis seeks to say, no longer where the text *comes from* (historical criticism), nor even *how* it is made (structural analysis), but how it is unmade, how it explodes, disseminates: according to what coded avenues it *goes*. Finally, a last precaution, in order to forestall any disappointment: there will be no question in the text which follows of a methodological confrontation between structural or textual analysis and biblical exegesis: I should have no competence there whatever.[2] I shall confine myself to analyzing the text of Genesis 32 (traditionally known as "Jacob Wrestles with the Angel"), as if I were in the first stage of an investigation (which is indeed the case): it is not a "result" I offer here, nor even a "method" (which would be too ambitious and would imply a "scientific" view of the text I do not have), but simply a "way of proceeding."

1. Sequential analysis

Structural analysis includes by and large three types – or three objects – of analysis, or, to put it differently, involves three tasks: 1. to proceed to the inventory and classification of the "psychological," biographical, characterial, social attributes of the characters involved in the narrative (age, sex, external qualities, social situation or rank, etc.); structurally, this is the instance of *indices* (notations, of infinitely varied expression, which serve to transmit a signified – for example "nervousness," "grace," "power" – which the analyst names in his metalanguage, it being understood that the metalinguistic term may very well not figure directly in the text, which will never use "nervousness" or "grace," etc.: this is the case here); if we establish a homology between the narrative and the (linguistic) sentence, the *index* corresponds to the adjective, to the *epithet* (which, let us not forget, was once a figure of rhetoric): this is what we might call *indicial analysis*; 2. to proceed to the inventory and classification of the *functions* of the characters: what they do according to their narrative status, their quality as subject of a constant action: the Sender, the Seeker, the Emissary, etc.; at the level of the sentence, this would correspond to the *present participle*: it is the *actantial analysis* of which A. J. Greimas was the first to offer a theory; 3. to proceed to the inventory and classification of *actions*: this is the level of *verbs*; these narrative actions are organized, as we know, in sequences, in series apparently organized according to a pseudo-logical schema (such logic is purely empirical, cultural, and results from an experience which may be ancestral, but not from reasoning): this is *sequential analysis*.

Our text lends itself, if briefly, to indicial analysis. The combat which is staged can be read as an index of Jacob's strength (attested in other episodes of the chronicle of this hero); the index leads toward an anagogical meaning, which is the (invincible) strength of God's Chosen. Actantial analysis is also possible; but since our text is essentially composed of actions which are apparently contingent, it would be better to proceed directly to a sequential (or actional) analysis of the episode, merely adding in conclusion a few remarks on the actantial. We shall divide the text (and I believe this is not forcing matters) into three sequences: 1. the Crossing; 2. the Wrestling; 3. the Namings.

1. *The Crossing* (vv. 23–25). Let us immediately give the sequential schema of this episode; this is a double schema, or at the very least, one may say, "strabismic" (what is at stake will be immediately apparent):

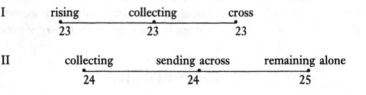

Let us note at once that structurally, *rising* is a simple *operator of beginning*; we might say, as a short cut, that by *rising* we are to understand not only that Jacob gets under way, but also that *the discourse gets under way*; the beginning of a narrative, of a discourse, of a text, is a very sensitive place: *where to begin?* The *said* must be wrenched away from the *not-said*: whence a whole rhetoric of beginning *markers*. Yet the most important thing is that the two sequences (or subsequences) seem in a state of redundance (this may be habitual in the discourse of that time: a piece of information is given and repeated; but our rule is reading, not the historical, philological determination of the text: we are not reading the text in its "truth," but in its "production" – which is not its "determination"); paradoxically, moreover (for usually redundance serves to homogenize, to clarify, and to strengthen a message), when we read it after two thousand years of Aristotelian rationalism (since Aristotle is the principal theoretician of classical narrative), the redundance of the two subsequences creates an abrasion, a grating of readability. The sequential schema can in fact be read in two ways: *a*. Jacob himself crosses the ford – if need be after having made several such trips – and therefore the wrestling occurs on the left bank of the stream (he is coming from the north), after having *definitively crossed over*; in this case, *sending across* is to be read: *crossing, oneself*; *b*. Jacob sends across but does not cross, himself; he wrestles on the right bank of the Jabbok *before crossing*, in a rearguard position. Let us not look for a *true* interpretation (our very hesitation will perhaps seem ridiculous in the eyes of the exegetes); let us acknowledge rather two different pressures of readability: *a*. if Jacob remains alone *before* having crossed the Jabbok, we are led to a "folkloristic" reading of the episode; indeed the mythic reference is overwhelming here, one that desires a trial by combat (for example, with a dragon or the genius of the river) be imposed upon the hero before he overcomes the obstacle, i.e., *so that*, being victorious, he can overcome it; *b*. if, on the contrary, Jacob (and his tribe) having crossed, he remains alone on the right side of the stream (that of the country where he wants to go), the crossing is without structural finality; on the other hand, it acquires a religious finality: if Jacob is alone, it is not in order to regulate and obtain the crossing, it is to *mark himself* by solitude (this is the familiar *setting apart* of the chosen of God). A historical circumstance here augments the undecidability of the two interpretations: the question for Jacob is to return home, to enter the land of Canaan: crossing the Jordan would then be more understandable than crossing the Jabbok; we find ourselves, in short, confronting the crossing of a neutral site; this crossing is "strong" if Jacob must make it against the genius of the place; it is indifferent if what matters is Jacob's solitude, his mark; but perhaps we have here the mingled vestige of two stories, or at least of two narrative instances: one, the more "archaic" (in the simple stylistic sense of the term), makes the crossing itself a test; the other, more "realistic," gives a "geographical" expression to Jacob's journey by mentioning the places he passes through (without attaching a mythic value to them).

If we project back onto this double sequence what occurs subsequently, to wit the Wrestling and the Naming, the double reading continues, coherent to the end, in each of its two versions; let us consider the diagram again:

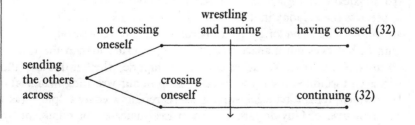

If the Combat separates the "not crossing" and the "having crossed" (folkloristic, mythic reading), the mutation of Names corresponds to the very project of every etymological saga; if, on the contrary, the Combat is merely a halt between a position of immobility (of meditation, of election) and a continuing movement, the mutation of the Name has the value of a spiritual renaissance (of "baptism"). We can summarize all this by saying that, in this first episode, there is sequential readability but cultural ambiguity. The theologian would no doubt be distressed by this indecision; the exegete would acknowledge it, hoping that some element, factual or argumentative, would allow him to bring it to an end; the textual analyst, it must be said, if I may judge by my own impression, will savor this sort of *friction* between two intelligibilities.

2. *The Combat* (vv. 25–30). Here again, for this second episode, we must start from an indetermination (I am not saying: a doubt) of readability – we know that textual analysis is based on *reading* rather than on the objective structure of the text, which is more the concern of structural analysis. This indetermination has to do with the interchangeable character of the pronouns which refer to the two partners of the wrestling match: a style which a purist would call *confused*, but whose vagueness no doubt raised no difficulty for Hebrew syntax. Who is "one"? Remaining on the level of v. 26, is this "one" who does not manage to overcome Jacob, or Jacob who cannot manage to overcome this "one"? Is the "he" of "he could not master him" (26) the same as the "he" of "he said" (27)? Doubtless it is all eventually clarified, but this requires a kind of retroactive reasoning, of the syllogistic type: You have defeated God. Now, he who speaks to you is the one whom you have defeated. Hence he who speaks to you is God. The identification of the partners is oblique, the readability is *deviated* (whence occasional commentaries which verge on misapprehension; this one for instance: "He wrestles with the Angel of the Lord and, defeated, obtains thereby the certainty that God is with him").

Structurally, this amphibology, even if it is subsequently illuminated, is not without significance; it is not, in our opinion (which, I repeat, is that of a contemporary reader), a simple awkwardness of expression due to a crude, archaizing style; it is linked to a paradoxical structure of the combat (paradoxical with regard to the stereotype of mythical combats). In order to appreciate the paradox in its structural *finesse*, let us imagine for a moment an endoxical (and no longer paradoxical) reading of the episode: A wrestles with B, but does not manage to defeat him; in order to gain the victory at all costs, A then resorts to an exceptional technique, whether this is an illegal and even forbidden hold (the forearm chop in our wrestling matches) or a hold which, remaining legal, supposes a secret knowledge, a "ploy" (as was the maneuver of Guy de Jarnac, who in 1547 defeated his opponent by an unlooked-for hold); such a hold, generally said to be "decisive" *in the very logic of narrative*, accords victory to the wrestler who uses it: the mark of which this hold is structurally the object cannot be reconciled with its ineffectiveness: it *must*, by the god of narrative, succeed. Now, it is the contrary which occurs here: the decisive hold fails; A, who has employed it, is not the victor: this is the structural paradox. The sequence then takes an unexpected course:

Wrestling (durative)	A's impotence	Decisive hold	(Ineffectiveness)	Negotiation
25	26	26		27

A's request	Bargaining	Acceptance
27	27	30

It will be noted that A (it is of little consequence, from the structural point of view, whether this is *one*, *a man*, *God*, or *the Angel*) is not, strictly speaking, defeated, but *checked*; for this check to be regarded as a defeat, there must be the addition of a *time limit*: this is daybreak ("for day is breaking," 27); this notation takes up from v. 25 ("until daybreak"), but this time in the explicit context of a mythic structure: the theme of the combat by night is structurally justified by the fact that at a certain moment, foreseen ahead of time (as is the sunrise, and as is the length of a boxing match), the rules of the combat will no longer be valid: the structural play will cease, the supernatural play as well (the "demons" withdraw at dawn). We thereby see that it is in a "regular" combat that the sequence establishes an unexpected readability, a logical surprise: the one who possesses the knowledge, the secret, the special hold, is nonetheless defeated. In other words, the sequence itself, entirely actional, entirely anecdotal as it is, has its function to *unbalance* the opponents in the combat, not only by the unexpected victory of one over the other, but above all (let us note the *formal* delicacy of this surprise) by the illogical, *inverted* character of this victory; in other words (and we recognize here an eminently structural term, familiar to linguists) the struggle, as it is inverted in its unexpected outcome, *marks* one of the combatants: the weaker defeats the stronger, *in exchange for which* he is marked (on the hip).

It is plausible (but here we depart somewhat from pure structural analysis and approach textual analysis, which is a vision *without barriers* of meanings) to fill this schema of the mark (of the imbalance) by contents of an ethnological type. The structural meaning of the episode, let us once more recall, is as follows: a situation of balance (the struggle at its outset) – such a situation is necessary for any marking: the Ignatian ascesis, for example, has for its function to establish the *indifference* of the will, which permits the divine mark, choice, election – is disturbed by the undue victory of one of the combatants: there is an inversion of the mark, there is a counter-mark. Then let us turn to the family configuration: traditionally, the line of brothers is in principle balanced (they are all located on the same level in relation to the parents); equigeniture is normally unbalanced by the right of primogeniture: the oldest is marked; now, in the story of Jacob, there is an inversion of mark, there is a counter-mark: it is the youngest who supplants the oldest (Genesis 27: 36), taking his older brother by the heel to turn time backward: it is the youngest, Jacob, who marks himself. Jacob having just been marked in his struggle with God, we can say in a sense that A (God) is the substitute of the oldest Brother, who is once again defeated by the youngest: the conflict with Esau is *displaced* (every symbol is a *displacement*; if the "struggle with the Angel" is symbolic, it is because it has displaced something). The commentary – for which I am inadequately equipped – would no doubt have to enlarge, here, the interpretation of this *inversion of the mark*: by placing it either in a historico-economic field – Esau is the eponym of the Edomites; there were economic links between the Edomites and the Israelites; perhaps what has been figured here is an overthrow of the alliance, the inception of a new league of interests? – or in the symbolic field (in the psychoanalytic sense of *symbolic*) – the Old Testament seems to be the world less of the Fathers than of the Enemy Brothers: the elder are ousted in favor of the younger; Freud has pointed out in the myth of the Enemy Brothers the narcissistic theme of *the smallest difference*: the blow on the hip, on that thin tendon – is that not just such a *smallest difference*? Whatever the case, in this universe, God marks the youngest, he acts as a counter-nature: his (structural) function is to constitute a *counter-marker*.

To be done with this extremely rich episode of the Struggle, of the Mark, I should like to make a semiologist's observation. We have just seen that in the binary opposition of combatants, which is perhaps the binary of the Enemy Brothers, the younger is marked both by the inversion of the expected relation of forces and by a bodily sign, lameness (which cannot fail to remind us of Oedipus, the Swollen Foot, the Lame One). Now, the mark is a creator of meaning; in the phonological representation of language, the "equality" of the paradigm is unbalanced to the benefit of a marked element, by the presence of a feature which remains absent from its correlative and oppositional term: by marking Jacob (Israel), God (or Narrative) permits an anagogic development of meaning: he creates the formal conditions for the functioning of a new "language," of which Israel's election is the "message," God is a logothete, Jacob is here a "morpheme" of the new language.

3. *The Namings or Mutations* (vv. 28–33). The object of the last sequence is the exchange of names, i.e., the promotion of a new status, of new powers; Naming is obviously linked to Blessing: to bless (to receive the homage of a kneeling suppliant) and to name are a suzerain's actions. There are two namings:

I   Request for name,   Jacob's   Result:
     from God to Jacob   answer   mutation
         28   28   29

II Request for name,   Indirect   (Result:
     from Jacob to God   answer   decision)
        30   30   ( )

                                            Mutation:
                                          Peniel
                                          (31)

The mutation concerns Names; but as a matter of fact, it is the entire episode which functions as *the creation of a multiple trace*: in Jacob's body, in the status of the Brothers, in Jacob's name, in the name of the place, in eating (the creation of an alimentary taboo: the whole story can also be interpreted *a minimo* as the mythic foundation of a taboo). The three sequences we have analyzed are homological: in all three there is a question of a *crossing*: of the place, of the parental line, of the name, of the alimentary rite: all this remaining very close to a language activity, to a transgression of the rules of meaning.

Such is the sequential (or actional) analysis of our episode. We have attempted, as is evident, to remain on the level of structure, i.e., of the systematic correlation of the terms denoting an action; if we have happened to mention certain possible meanings, this has not been in order to discuss the probability of these meanings, but rather to show how structure "disseminates" contents – which each reading can deal with on its own. Our object is not the philological or historical document, custodian of a truth to be found, but the text's *signifying* volume.

2. Structural Analysis

The structural analysis of narrative having already been partially con-stituted (by Propp, Lévi-Strauss, Greimas, Bremond), I should like, in closing – and perhaps more modestly – to confront our text with two practices of structural analysis, in order to show the interest of these practices

– though my own work is oriented in a somewhat different direction[3] – Greimas's actantial analysis and Propp's functional analysis.

1. *Actantial analysis.* The actantial grid conceived by Greimas[4] – to be employed, as its creator himself has said, with discretion and flexibility – distributes the characters, the actors of a narrative, into six formal classes of actants, defined by what they do according to their status and not by what they are psychologically (the actant can unite several characters, but also a single character can unite several actants; a character can also be represented by an inanimate entity). The Struggle with the Angel constitutes a familiar episode of mythic narratives: the overcoming of an obstacle, the Ordeal. At the level of this episode (since, for the whole chronicle of Jacob, this might be different), the actants are "filled" as follows: Jacob is the *Subject* (subject of the demand, of the search, of the action); the *Object* of this same demand, search, action) is the crossing of the guarded, forbidden place, the stream, the Jabbok; the *Sender*, who puts into circulation the stake of the search (to wit, the crossing of the stream), is obviously God; the *Receiver* is again Jacob (two actants are here present in one and the same figure); the *Opponent* (the one or ones who hamper the Subject in his search) is God himself (it is he who, in mythic terms, guards the crossing); the *Helper* (the one or ones who assist the Subject) is Jacob, who helps himself by his own strength, which is legendary (an indicial feature, as we have seen).

The paradox, or at least the anomic character, of the formula is immediately apparent: that the subject be identified with the receiver is banal enough: that the subject be his own helper is rarer; this usually happens in "voluntarist" narratives and novels; but that the sender be the opponent is extremely rare; there is only one type of narrative which can stage this paradoxical formula: narratives which relate a blackmail; of course, if the opponent were merely the (temporary) custodian of the stake, there would be nothing extraordinary about it: it is the opponent's role to defend the ownership of the object which the hero seeks to conquer: as in the case of the dragon which guards a crossing; but here, as in any blackmail, God, at the same time that he guards the stream, dispenses the mark, the privilege. As we see, the actantial formula of our text is far from being conciliatory: it is structurally very audacious – which corresponds to the "scandal" represented by God's defeat.

2. *Functional analysis.* As we know, Propp was the first[5] to have established the structure of the folk tale by dividing it up into *functions*,[6] or narrative actions; according to Propp, the functions are stable elements, their number is limited (to about thirty), their concatenation is always the same, even if certain functions are occasionally missing from one narrative or another.

Now, it so happens – as we shall see below – that our text honors quite perfectly a portion of the functional schema revealed by Propp: this author could not have conceived of a more convincing application of his discovery.

In a preparatory section of the folk tale as analyzed by Propp, there must be an instance of the Hero's absence; and this is just what occurs in the chronicle of Jacob: Isaac sends Jacob far from his country, to Laban (Genesis 28: 2, 5). Our episode actually begins with no. 15 of Propp's narrative functions; we shall therefore encode it in the following manner, showing at each stage the impressive parallelism between Propp's schema and the Genesis narrative:

Propp & the folk tale	*Genesis*
15. Transfer from one place to another (by birds, horses, boats, etc.).	Setting out from the North, from the Aramaeans, from Laban's house, Jacob journeys home to his father (29: 1, Jacob sets out).
16. Combat of the Hero against the Enemy.	This is our sequence of the Combat (32: 25–28).
17. Marking of the Hero (usually a mark on his body, but in other cases, merely the gift of a jewel, of a ring).	Jacob is marked on the hip (32: 27).
18. Victory of the Hero, defeat of the Enemy.	Jacob's victory (32: 26).
19. Liquidation of disaster or of some lack: the disaster or the lack had been posited in the Hero's initial absence: this absence is done away with.	After having succeeded in crossing Peniel (32: 32), Jacob reaches Shechem in Canaan (33: 18).

There are other points of parallelism. In Propp's function 14, the Hero receives a magical object; for Jacob, this talisman is doubtless the blessing he tricks his blind father into giving him (Genesis 27). Further, Propp's function 29 stages the Hero's transfiguration (for example, the Beast is transformed into a handsome nobleman); this transfiguration seems to be present in the change of Name (Genesis 32: 29) and the rebirth it implies. No doubt the narrative model assigns God the role of the Enemy (his *structural* role: no question of a psychological role): in our episode of Genesis can be read a veritable stereotype of the folk tale: the difficult crossing of a ford guarded by a hostile genius of the place. Another analogy with the tale is that in both cases the motivations of the characters (their reasons for acting) are not indicated: the ellipsis of notations is not a phenomenon of style, it is a structural, pertinent characteristic of the narration. Structural analysis, in the strict sense of the term, would therefore conclude that Wrestling with the Angel is a true fairy tale – since, according to Propp, all fairy tales belong to the same structure, the one he has described.

As we see, what might be called the structural exploitation of our episode is quite possible: it is even indispensable. Yet I shall say, in conclusion, that what most interests me in this famous passage is not the "folklore" model, but the frictions, the breaks, the discontinuities of readability, the juxta-position of narrative entities which manage to escape an explicit logical articulation: we are dealing here (at least, for me, this is the relish of the reading) with a sort of *metonymic montage*: the themes (Crossing, Struggle, Naming, Alimentary Rite) are *combined* and not "developed." This abrupt-ness, this asyndetic character of the narrative is well expressed by Hosea (12: 3): "In the very womb he supplanted his brother, in maturity he wrestled against God. He wrestled with the Angel and beat him." Metonymic logic, as we know, is that of the unconscious. It is therefore perhaps in this direction that we should continue our research, i.e., I repeat, the *reading* of the text, its dissemination, not its truth. Of course, we then risk weakening the economico-historical range of the episode (it certainly exists, on the level of the exchanges of tribes and of the problems of power); but it also reinforces the symbolic explosion of the text (which is not necessarily of a religious order). The problem, at least the one I raise for myself, is in effect not to reduce the Text to a signified, whatever it may be (historical, economic, folkloric, or kerygmatic), but to keep its signifying power open.

Translated by Richard Howard

Notes

1 *The Jerusalem Bible* (New York: Doubleday, 1966).
2 I want to express my gratitude to Jean Alexandre, whose exegetic, linguistic, socio-historical competence, and whose openness of mind have helped me understand the text here analyzed; many of his ideas will appear in this analysis; only the fear of having distorted them keeps me from acknowledging them on each occasion.
3 My work on Balzac's *Sarrasine* (*S/Z*, Paris: Seuil, 1970; English trans., New York: Hill and Wang, 1975) belongs more to textual than to structural analysis.
4 See especially A. J. Greimas, *Sémantique structurale* (Paris: Larousse, 1966), and *Du sens* (Paris: Seuil, 1970).

5 Vladimir Propp, *Morphologie du conte* (Paris: Seuil, 1970).
6 The word "function" is unfortunately ambiguous in all cases; we used it initially to define the actantial analysis which assesses a character by his role in the action (which is precisely his "function"); in Propp's terminology, there is a displacement from the character to the action itself, apprehended as it is *linked* to the actions surrounding it.

René Girard (b. 1923):
Introduction

Gerard Loughlin

One might ask: What is René Girard (b. 1923) doing in a book on postmodern divinity? For Girard would appear to be an anthropologist in the grand, armchair manner of those eminent gentleman-scholars who, seated in their studies, perused the texts of others and espied the hidden workings of human society (for example: William Robertson Smith, James George Frazer, Émile Durkheim, and Sigmund Freud). Girard, one might think, is a latter-day Edward Casaubon, the character in George Eliot's *Middlemarch* (1871–2) who hunts for the "key to all mythologies," for the "elements which made the seed of all tradition";[1] except that Girard, unlike Casaubon, claims to have found the key, to have actually discovered the elements that make for tradition, culture, and religion.

Girard has described himself as a man of few ideas, perhaps only of a single one, but an idea so powerful that Girard finds in it the foundation of all others; except that it is not really an idea – a concept – at all. It is rather what Girard calls a "mechanism," a non-conscious working of the social body, operative everywhere, but until now – until Girard – largely *unthought*. Such a claim must seem the very epitome of rationalist science with its desire to find the one thing that will make sense of all – whether it is the Darwinists with their "principle of natural selection," the Freudians with their "Oedipus complex," or the physicists with their search for the "theory of everything." Surely it is this kind of totalizing fantasy that postmodernism seeks to subvert and leave behind? I will return to this question, having first articulated Girard's *idée fixe*, the mechanism that is said to found society, culture, and religion: the murder of the innocent.

The Helmet of Mambrino

Girard is an armchair anthropologist insofar as he is first and last a reader of texts, a literary critic. His first book, *Deceit, Desire, and the Novel*, was a study of "triangular" or "mediated" desire in the novels of Cervantes, Stendhal, Flaubert, Proust, and Dostoyevsky. Desire is the dominant concern in all Girard's work, whether writing on European novels, the texts of Sophocles and Freud, or on the Gospels and the plays of Shakespeare. All the texts that Girard considers are ranked according to how close they come to revealing the mediated structure of desire and – most important – its power to create society.

For Girard, Cervantes (1547–1616) is paradigmatic, since *Don Quixote* (1604–14), and in particular its story of "foolish curiosity" (Part I, chapters 33–6), already displays the insights of the later novelists. Quixote desires to do the things that chivalrous knights do, to fight battles and win glory; but his desire is not spontaneous, it has been mediated by a model of errantry, an exemplar of chivalrous ambition. Quixote desires after Amadis of Gaul; for Amadis – Quixote tells his squire Sancho Panza – is "the pole-star, the morning star, the sun of all valiant knights and lovers, and all of us who ride beneath the banner of love and chivalry should imitate him."[2]

Girard claims that the triangular structure of subject (Quixote), object (chivalry), and model/mediator (Amadis) is the structure of all desire and, ultimately, the engine of all social life. No one simply desires an object spontaneously, but first learns the desire from another. We are each desirous of other people's desired objects; indeed, desirous of their desiring. Freud was to say that the boy first desires his mother, a dual desire of subject for object; but Freud was nearer the mark – Girard contends – when he wrote that a "little boy will exhibit a special interest in his father; he would like to grow like and be like him, and *take his place everywhere*."[3] All children learn how and what to desire from miming the desires of others; for the structure of desire is always triangular, always *mimetic*. When Quixote sees the barber approaching with the shaving basin on his head and mistakes it for the helmet of Mambrino, he wants it because a fine helmet is what all knights errant want.[4] There is a question of how a child – or anyone – adopts his or her mimetic models, as also a question of origin: How does the chain of mimesis begin? It would seem that at some point one must appeal either to a basic animality, an instinct, or to an object's intrinsic desirability; but Girard insists that Oedipal desire is first and last mimetically produced and socially inscribed, and thus historically contingent.

There is an important difference between Quixote's miming of Amadis and the boy whose desire follows that of his father, for the latter is a real person, while Quixote's ideal is only a fictional character. Quixote can never meet his mediator of desire, and so can never come into conflict with him as with a rival who desires the same as he does. But the father, who is a real person, becomes – or can become – a rival in pursuit of the child's objects of affection (e.g., the mother). Both wish to be in the same place and have the same things. Thus the model can become an obstacle to desire, a rival desirer. Subject (child) and model (father) become doubles, caught in desire's double bind ("desire as I do"/ "don't desire as I do").

Desire – the energy of our wanting – is secondary to our instinctual mimesis of others, and it is our miming of their desires that leads to conflict. When mimetic rivalry becomes extreme, the subject attends more to the model/ obstacle of desire than to the desired object. It is then the mediating rival who dominates the triangle of desire (*Violence and the Sacred*, pp. 145–6). In Cervantes's tale of "foolish curiosity," Anselmo desires only the same as his friend, Lothario, and keeps him as rival and obstacle even when he attains his desired object – Camilla – for it is Lothario who constitutes and confirms Camilla's desirability. At one point in the story, Camilla's maid insists that there "is no reason why a thing should lose its value because it is easily given, if in fact the gift is a good one and valuable in itself."[5] But the story teaches that nothing is valuable in itself but only as it is desired by another, and that the fulfillment of desire is not the attaining of its object but the denial of the rival.

Things Hidden since the Foundation of the World

After Darwin, Freud postulated that the founding event of society was the collective murder of the father by the brothers in the primal horde.[6] Guilt-stricken by what they had done, the brothers divinized their father and denied themselves the very thing for which they committed patricide: the sexual use of the horde's females, previously reserved to the father alone. By this postulation Freud accounted for religion (the totemic representation of the father), exogamy, and the centrality of Oedipal desire.[7] While most commentators have sought to save this story as a representation of psychic truth, Freud insisted on its historicity, and in so doing – Girard argues – knew better than his followers. For what we should discount is not the claim for an original collective murder, but its construal as patricide.

In thinking the idea of an original – originating – collective murder, Freud came close to knowing what Sophocles knew much better, and Girard knows best of all, that society results from the collective murder of an arbitrary victim (*Violence and the Sacred*, pp. 204–5). This is the fundamental truth – hidden since the foundation of the world – that Girard announced in his second major book, *Violence and the Sacred*, first published in 1972. He made his discovery through reading Sophocles in the light of his theory of triangular desire. As we have already seen, triangular desire becomes rivalry when the model of desire becomes an obstacle to its fulfillment, which can in turn lead to contagious and potentially endless violence, obeying the simple law of mimetic reciprocation (vengeance). But at some point in the past – Girard hypothesizes – groups riven by violent reciprocation discovered that peace was re-established through finding and killing a single and common enemy to whom all attributed their misfortune. It is this simple event – the killing of one by all – which Girard contends founds society, religion, and all other major social institutions, and which he names the victimage or scapegoat mechanism, using "scapegoat" in the popular sense of a victim unjustly blamed for the deeds of others.

Yet because the death of the victim brings peace, he or she undergoes an apotheosis in death, becoming the savior of the group. Thus the death of the victim becomes the site of the "sacred," the latter being no more than the salvific violence that produces peace. It is this sense of the sacred – which is the experience of peace through collective murder – that gives rise to religion, when the victim is deified and the peace brought by his or her death is maintained through the ritual re-enactment of the saving murder – which becomes the institution of "sacrifice." Girard insists that this process is both historical and mechanical, in the sense that it happened (and happens) and operates at a non-conscious social level, unrecognized at the level of religious interpretation.

However, there are certain texts which disclose the victimage mechanism, and Girard classifies these as more or less *mythological* depending on how far they conceal the mechanics of scapegoating. As already indicated, these texts range from the tragedies of Sophocles to the psychoanalytic papers of Freud, but the most important are the "Judeo-Christian" Scriptures, which, as Girard reads them, progressively reveal the lineaments of social violence and the ruse of victimage.

The Old Way Trodden by the Victim

Things Hidden since the Foundation of the World contains Girard's principal discussion of biblical texts. However, Girard has also written on biblical texts in *The Scapegoat* and *Job the Victim of His People*, which is perhaps the most succinct statement of Girard's reading of the biblical corpus, presenting a developmental contrast between the Hebraic and Christian "revelations" in the figures of Job and Jesus.

Girard's audacious reading of the Book of Job displays the ability of his mimetic theory to transform and enliven texts of which one might have thought no more could be said. The twist that Girard gives to the story is very simple and is displayed in the English title of *Job the Victim of His People*. By discounting the prologue to the Book of Job, Girard is able to attend to the dialogues between Job and his "comforters," and ask anew whence comes Job's misfortune. The answer – according to Girard – is explicit and unequivocal: Job has been "ostracized and persecuted by the people around him." He has become the "scapegoat of his community" (p. 4).

The true story of Job is that he was once the idol of his people, a man who was successful, wealthy, and powerful, a man who was admired, emulated, and desired. For to desire Job's success was to desire the successful Job. But this in turn provoked envy and rivalry, first among the "friends" and then among the people at large. As a result, the unanimity of adulation around Job became a unanimity of hatred against him, and he was made the victim of his people, the scapegoat blamed for their misfortunes (p. 60).

As ever, this process is mystified, and Job's "friends" believe that he is the cause of his own misfortune, and seek his assent to their judgment. "He is expected to acknowledge the justice of his own martyrdom" (p. 114). This mystification is profound and widespread, and it accounts for why Girard has to take certain liberties with the text, since it is already partly mythology, denying the real cause of Job's misfortune. Not only does the text as we have it trace the final cause to God, as do Job's "friends," but Job himself often thinks he is being persecuted by God. "Fear comes over me, at the thought of all I suffer, for such I know is not your treatment of the innocent" (Job 9: 28). And this interpretation has been maintained by commentators ever since, who refuse to take seriously the proclamation of Job's innocence.

Job maintains his innocence. He refuses to admit that he is the cause of his own and his people's misfortune, and thus refuses to acquiesce in the process of victimage, and thereby reveals it for what it is: the killing of an innocent for the good of society. The Book of Job is thus a powerful, if partial, revelation of what has been hidden since the foundation of the world. It is partial because the received text obscures the guilt of the people, suggesting that perhaps Job, perhaps God, is the cause of his misfortune. For the complete revelation of humanity's guilt and God's response to its violence, we must turn to the texts of the New Testament, and in particular the Gospels.

Like Job, Jesus is made a scapegoat; an innocent who is first the admired hero of his people and then the abjected victim of their censure, the "sacrifice" who resolves social tensions and quells the threat of mass violence. Jesus is portrayed by his persecutors as the cause of the people's misery, as the one who endangers their security; his impieties tempting divine wrath. Like Job before him, Jesus is made to follow "the ancient trial trodden by the wicked" (Job 22: 15): first raised up and adulated, then cast down and destroyed. And like Job, Jesus too refuses the accusations of his persecutors; but unlike the Book of Job, the Gospels support his revelation of the scapegoat mechanism, refusing to place the responsibility for violence anywhere except on those who are its perpetrators.

Girard resists the charge of anti-semitism often brought against the Gospels

– that they are persecutory texts scapegoating the Jews – by arguing that the Jews repeat a violence that has encompassed all human societies from the foundation of the world. Christians who scapegoat the Jews (or any other group or person) are no different, though perhaps more culpable, because inheritors of the Scriptures that reveal their evil. Girard defends the passivity of Jesus – and of those disciples who follow his example – against the Nietzschean charge of masochistic *ressentiment*, insisting that Jesus simply enacts the logic of the God who refuses violence. God is with the victims – with the Christ who "shares their lot until the end" – and so cannot act as do the persecutors, reciprocating their violence (p. 157). God's response is completely contrary, utterly pacific: the return of forgiveness for violence (Luke 23: 34).

The Barber's Basin

At the beginning of this essay I questioned Girard's postmodern credentials, likening his project to that of his anthropological forebears and George Eliot's Casaubon. The epigraph to the chapter in *Middlemarch* that introduces Casaubon is taken from *Don Quixote*, and describes Quixote's first sighting of the barber's basin, which he mistakes for the helmet of Mambrino. The reader is to understand that Casaubon is to Dorothea Brooke – the heroine of Eliot's novel – what the barber's basin is to Quixote. Reading Girard's detractors and admirers it is clear that he has become what the basin-cum-helmet figures in Eliot: model and obstacle, mediator and rival. The simplicity and fecundity of his theses attract both avid attention and disgruntled suspicion.

Girard is postmodern in that he rejects the modern "subject" – the autonomous Cartesian consciousness – and accepts the radical mediation of all human knowledge. Against Freud's familial drama, he insists upon a social triangularity which is at all times in the public domain, albeit non-conscious and unrecognized, a mechanism like that of language itself, an ever-present syntax of desire. That which has been hidden since the foundation of the world has not been secreted in the depths but is staring us in the face. We have not seen it because it is so close to us; right up alongside of us, like the air we breathe and the words we inhabit.

Can we also think Girard a postmodern *theologian*? He writes, of course, as a literary anthropologist. Furthermore, his reading of the Gospels offers a severe criticism of much Christian theology concerning the death of Christ, for Girard insists that any sacrificial interpretation of Christ's death ignores the Gospels' absolute refusal of such an interpretation. The mob may sacrifice Jesus; but there can be no question of Jesus paying a ransom to Satan or propitiating a vengeful God. Jesus dies by the hands of men, not by divine ordinance.

Given the prominence of sacrificial theology in Christianity, one might think Girard's reading of the New Testament somewhat high-handed. Is there no sense in which Christ's death is sacrificial? Is it not a sacrifice in that Jesus gives up his life rather than compromise his rendering of God's love? Girard allows as much, in that "Christ agrees to die so that mankind will live." But Girard resists calling this sacrificial, "even if we then have no words or categories to convey its meaning." Girard is so concerned to avoid any suggestion that Jesus acts out of masochistic or thanatic desire that he refuses the most obvious name for Jesus' death (*Things Hidden*, pp. 241–3).

Equally Girard overlooks the ancient idea of the sacrificial meal – the sharing of food with the gods[8] – which is present in the New Testament accounts of the Last Supper and central in the life of the Church, formed by and around the celebration of the eucharistic meal, when – so the Church believes – Christ is again present with his disciples. This meal may be thought sacrificial, not as a rite of identification with the sacrificial victim become totem, as parodied by Frazer, Robertson Smith, and Freud,[9] but as the enactment of that self-giving which is also a receiving: the self-giving of Christ to his disciples so that they, in imitation of him, might give themselves to the Father, in order to receive again their very life, thus enacting the ceaseless creative expenditure of the divine love, which is received only as it is given away.

Girard's "theology" has been described as gnostic, as offering only knowledge of our plight, of the scapegoat mechanism by which societies secure a violent peace (including the "vengeance" of judicial process), and offering little in its place. It is true that Girard has chiefly attended to the horror of the social body – the violence of our inescapable mimeticism – leaving it to his disciples to articulate the prospect of a good mimesis which does away with rivalry, conflict and destruction.[10] But Girard's disciples develop his own venture of the *imitatio Christi*, for he takes with full seriousness Jesus' injunction to love the enemy and not resist the one who is evil (Luke 6: 33–35; Matthew 5: 38–40). Girard insists that this teaching is rigorously objective and "completely realistic," being the only way to rid humanity of violence, which is the project of God's Kingdom (*Things Hidden*, pp. 197–8).

To be rid of violence we must refuse the illusion that there can be a legitimate, safe violence, the violence of just retribution. We tell ourselves that our violence is only reactive, protective, educative, undertaken in self-defense or just retaliation. But this is an illusion, for all violence is mimetic. To truly renounce violence we must renounce all forms of vengeance. Of course people will say this is unrealistic, a doctrine for a perfect world. In the real world matters are different. Girard would agree, but the "real world" is the Kingdom of Violence, while the Gospels announce the possibility of a different Kingdom, which we can choose if we want it. But while the latter Kingdom will fully arrive only when everyone chooses it, that choice has to be made by each individual alone

(p. 199). The choice is made possible through the mediation of Jesus, who can become the model of our desire (and here Girard needs supplementing with an account of Jesus' "attractiveness"). Jesus has come for no other purpose than that we might do as he does. The Word of the Father, which is identical with the Father, consists in telling mankind what the Father is, so that people may be able to imitate him: "Love your enemies, pray for your persecutors; so shall you be sons of your Father" (p. 269).

Rene Girard reworks St Paul's theology of the two Adams, founding society upon an "original sin" – the collective murder of an innocent victim – and witnessing to an original grace – the victim's pacific "refusal" of the violence done to him. Just as for Paul the second Adam recapitulates and undoes the work of the first, so Girard's Christ displays the founding murder from the other side, from the victim's point of view, displaying its inability to procure true peace, and refusing its invitation to reciprocate in kind. The persecutors, who, like all of us, kill in order to secure peace, are forgiven, and in return offered a model for the practice of true peaceableness. We cannot avoid mimesis, but we can choose our models. The choice before us is simple enough; making it is another matter.

Notes

1 *Middlemarch* (Harmondsworth: Penguin, 1965), pp. 87, 520.
2 *Don Quixote* (Penguin, 1950), p. 202.
3 Freud, *Group Psychology* (Penguin, 1985), p. 134.
4 *Don Quixote*, pp. 160–71.
5 Ibid., p. 304.
6 Freud, *Totem and Taboo* (Penguin, 1990), pp. 185–6.
7 Ibid., pp. 203–8.
8 See Detienne and Vernant, *The Cuisine of Sacrifice among the Greeks*, trans. P. Wissing (Chicago University Press, 1989).
9 Freud, *Totem and Taboo*, p. 217.
10 See James Alison's books listed below.

Selected Bibliography

Alison, James, *Knowing Jesus* (London: SPCK, 1993). *Raising Abel: The Recovery of the Eschatological Imagination* (New York: Crossroad Herder, 1996).
Bailie, Gil, *Violence Unveiled: Humanity at the Crossroads* (New York: Crossroad, 1995).
Cervantes Saavedra, Miguel de, *The Adventures of Don Quixote*, trans. J. M. Cohen (Harmondsworth: Penguin, 1950).

Detienne, Marcel, and Vernant, Jean-Pierre, *The Cuisine of Sacrifice Among the Greeks*, trans. Paula Wissing (Chicago and London: University of Chicago Press, 1989). [First published in 1979.]

Diacritics (special issue on the work of René Girard), 8 (1985).

Dumouchel, Paul (ed.), *Violence and Truth: On the Work of René Girard* (London: Athlone Press, 1987). [First published in 1985.]

Eliot, George, *Middlemarch*, ed. W. J. Harvey (Harmondsworth: Penguin, 1965).

Freud, Sigmund, *Group Psychology and the Ego* (1921). In *The Penguin Freud Library*. Vol. 12: *Civilization, Society and Religion*, ed. A. Dickson (Harmondsworth: Penguin, 1985).

—— *Totem and Taboo: Some Points of Agreement Between the Mental Lives of Savages and Neurotics* (1913). In *The Penguin Freud Library*. Vol. 13: *The Origins of Religion*, ed A. Dickson (Harmondsworth: Penguin, 1990).

Girard, René, *Deceit, Desire and the Novel: Self and Other in Literary Structure*, trans. Yvonne Freccero (Baltimore and London: Johns Hopkins University Press, 1996). [First published in 1961.]

—— *Violence and the Sacred*, trans. Patrick Gregory (Baltimore, MD: Johns Hopkins University Press, 1977). [First published in 1972.]

—— *"To Double Business Bound": Essays on Literature, Mimesis and Anthropology* (Baltimore, MD: Johns Hopkins University Press, 1978).

—— *Things Hidden since the Foundation of the World*, trans. Stephen Bann and Michael Metteer (London: Athlone Press, 1987). [First published in 1978.]

—— *Job the Victim of His People*, trans. Yvonne Freccero (Stanford, CA: Stanford University Press, 1987). [First published in 1985.]

—— *The Scapegoat*, trans. Yvonne Freccero (London: Athlone Press, 1986). [First published in 1982.]

—— *A Theater of Envy: William Shakespeare* (New York and Oxford: Oxford University Press, 1991).

—— *To Honor René Girard: Presented on the Occasion of His Sixtieth Birthday by Colleagues, Students, Friends*. Stanford French and Italian Studies 34 (Saratoga, CA: Anima Libri, 1986).

Hamerton-Kelly, Robert G., *Sacred Violence: Paul's Hermeneutic of the Cross* (Minneapolis: Fortress Press, 1992).

Hamerton-Kelly, Robert G. (ed.), *Violent Origins: Ritual Killing and Cultural Formation* (Stanford, CA: Stanford University Press, 1987).

Kerr, Fergus, "Rescuing Girard's Argument?" *Modern Theology*, 8 (1992), pp. 385–99.

McKenna, Andrew J., *Violence and Difference: Girard, Derrida and Deconstruction* (Urbana and Chicago: University of Illinois Press, 1992).

Milbank, John, *Theology and Social Theory: Beyond Secular Reason* (Oxford: Blackwell, 1990), pp. 392–8.

—— "Stories of Sacrifice," *Modern Theology*, 12 (1996), pp. 27–56.

Semeia (special issue on René Girard and biblical studies, ed. Andrew J. McKenna), 33 (1985).

Williams, James G., *The Bible, Violence and the Sacred: Liberation from the Myth of Sanctioned Violence* (San Francisco: HarperCollins, 1991).

The God of Victims

The God of the Gospels is clearly a candidate for the role of the God of victims. The Father sends his Son into the world to defend the victims, the poor, and the disinherited. In the Gospel according to John, Jesus calls both himself and the Holy Ghost a Paraclete. The word signifies advocate for the defence in a law court. It should be compared with the word that the Jerusalem Bible translates as "avenger" in the last text of Job I quoted, the Hebrew word *goel*, a legal term with a similar significance.

Jesus is systematically presented as the Avenger of victims. He proclaims that we cannot come to the aid of the least among them without coming to his aid, too. We cannot refuse to give aid without also refusing it to him.

Is the God of the Gospels the God of victims? The title is not necessarily warranted simply because it is claimed. It is appropriate to consider whether the logic of this God that has so far escaped us is truly developed in the Gospels.

As we have seen, a God of victims cannot impose his will on men without ceasing to exist. He would have to resort to a violence more violent than that of the wicked. He would again become the God of persecutors, supposing he had ever ceased to be. Every persecutor believes he knows the true God of victims: for them he is their persecuting divinity.

If there is a God of victims, we cannot count on him to bring about a world that everyone would agree to call just. Otherwise, the agreement of men is based on poor reasons. Even their most pacific agreement is mixed with mimesis. However just, their injustice is mixed with vengeance, which again is another word for mimesis.

When Job proves that justice does not hold sway in the world, when he says that the sort of retribution Eliphaz implies does not exist for most men, he thinks he is attacking the very concept of God. But in the Gospels, Jesus very explicitly claims as his own all Job's criticisms of retribution. And clearly the conclusion is not atheism:

> It was just about this time that some people arrived and told him about the Galileans whose blood Pilate had mingled that of their sacrifices. At this he said to them, "Do you suppose these Galileans who suffered like that were

greater sinners than any other Galileans? They were not, I tell you. No; but unless you repent you will all perish as they did. Or those eighteen on whom the tower at Siloam fell and killed them? Do you suppose that they were more guilty than all the other people living in Jerusalem? They were not, I tell you. No; but unless you repent you will all perish as they did." (Luke 13: 1–5)

According to the Jerusalem Bible, "the meaning of both is clear; sin is not the immediate cause of this or that calamity" (note 13a to Luke 13: 1–5). The atheists who take up Job's arguments against retribution are closer to the Gospels than Christians who are tempted to use the arguments of Eliphaz in favour of that same retribution. There is no necessary connection between the evils that strike men and any specific judgment of God.

Persecutions are real persecutions and accidents are real accidents. As for hereditary weaknesses, that is all they are – hereditary weaknesses. Because they attract the attention of persecutors, they are always seen as the sign of divine condemnation. Jesus rejects such a religion. To the disciples who ask him whether the blind man was born blind because either his parents or he had sinned, Jesus answers: "Neither he nor his parents sinned . . . he was born blind so that the works of God might be displayed in him" (John 9: 2–3).

All the parables have much the same meaning. God always plays the role of the absent master, the owner who has gone on a long journey. He leaves the field free for his servants, who prove themselves either faithful or unfaithful, efficient or timid. He does not allow the wheat to be separated from the tares, even to encourage the growth of good grain, whereas Aeschylus does the reverse. God makes his sun shine and his rain fall on the just as well as on the unjust. He does not arbitrate the quarrels of brothers. He knows what human justice is.

Does this mean that the God of victims is some kind of lazy god who refuses to intervene in the world, the *deus otiosus*, traces of whom are believed by certain ethnologists to be found in the pantheons of many primitive religions, the god to whom no sacrifice is made because he can do nothing for men?

Absolutely not. This God spares nothing in order to rescue victims. But if he cannot force men, what can he do? First he tries to persuade them. He shows them that they are dedicating themselves to *scandal* by their desires that are crisscrossed and thwarted by imitation.

Jesus enjoins men to imitate him and seek the glory that comes from God, instead of that which comes from men. He shows them that mimetic rivalries can lead only to murders and death. He reveals the role of the scapegoat mechanism in their own cultural system. He does not even conceal from them that they are dependent on all the collective murders committed "since the beginning of the world," the generative murders of that same world. He demands that they recognize the sons of Satan, devoted to the same lie as their father, the accuser, "murderer since the beginning."

Jesus scarcely convinces anyone. His revelation receives just enough acceptance to invite suppression by those who hear it. By revealing the truth, Jesus threatens the domination of Satan, the accuser, who in turn exerts on him the greater force of the unanimous mimesis of the accusation, the scapegoat mechanism. He becomes, inevitably, the victim of that same satanic force that, as accuser and persecutor, controls the world and has already killed all the prophets from Abel to the last victim mentioned in the Bible.

And that is what happens. All hate *with one soul*. Like Job, Jesus is condemned without being guilty and, this time, it is he who becomes the *"bloodshed for bloodshed . . . given our state to prey upon."* Thus yet again there is reproduced, in the Passion, "the ancient trail" that we have been discussing from the beginning.

If the God of victims intervenes on their behalf in the human world, then he cannot "succeed." All that can happen to him is what happens to Jesus and has already happened to Job and all the prophets. Jesus must find himself in Job's place, and not by chance. He is as innocent as Job and even more so, but by revealing how the world functions, he threatens its foundations more seriously than Job. That he finds himself in the position of a single victim results from a rigorous logic.

For an understanding of that logic, we must consider the implications of violent unanimity when it occurs. In that fundamental moment for human culture, there are only persecutors and a victim confronting them. There is no third position, no way out. Where would the God of victims be, if he were to find himself among men at that point in time? Obviously he would not be on the side of the persecutors, so he would have to be the victim. Rather than inflict violence, the Paraclete would prefer to suffer.

Christ is the God of victims primarily because he shares their lot until the end. It takes little thought to realize that nothing else is possible. If the logic of this God shares nothing in common with that of the God of persecution and its mystifying mimesis, the only possible means of intervention in the world is that illustrated by the Gospels.

According to the logic of the world, which is also that of the God of persecution and his cohorts, the failure is total. It would be better not to intervene at all than to choose this method of intervention. This God is worse than *otiosus*. He is the most miserable, ridiculous, least powerful of all the gods. It is not surprising that his "impact" on the world decreases the less he is confused with the God of Eliphaz.

This God cannot act with a strong hand in a way that men would consider divine. When men worship him they are almost always, unwittingly, honoring the God of persecutors. This God does not reign over the world. Neither he nor his real name is sanctified. His will is not obeyed.

Do I exaggerate this God's impotence? I am only repeating, verbatim, the words of Jesus to his Father:

> Hallowed be thy name.
> Thy kingdom come,
> Thy will be done on earth as it is in heaven.

This prayer would make no sense if the divine will – while remaining divine in the sense of the God of victims, while remaining itself – could break the obstacle created by men's will.

These words are prayers. God does not reign, but he will reign. He reigns already for those who have accepted him. Through the intermediary of those who imitate him and imitate the Father, the Kingdom is already among us. It is a seed that comes from Jesus and that the world cannot expel, even if it does all it can.

Another proof that God does not claim to rule over the world is that he reveals its king to us, and it is not himself but his adversary who is always eagerly in pursuit – Satan, the accuser and the persecutor. A little thought reveals that the defender of victims, the Paraclete, must have as adversary the prince of this world, but does not oppose him with violence.

The teaching of Jesus and the Passion in the Gospels constitute the strict development of a paradoxical logic. Jesus wants nothing to do with all that makes someone divine in the eyes of men: the power to seduce or constrain, the ability to make oneself indispensable.

He would seem to want the very opposite. In reality, it is not that he desires failure but that he will not avoid it if that is the only way he may remain true to the Logos of the God of victims. He is not secretly motivated by a taste for failure, but rather by the logic of the God of victims that unerringly leads him to death.

This logic permeates the Gospels through and through. The way it works is presented as a manifestation of the divine that is still hidden and radically different from the sacred of the persecutors. We are, then, confronted with yet another paradoxical aspect of the Logos of victims.

In a world of violence, divinity purified of every act of violence must be revealed by means of the event that already provides the sacrificial religion with its generative mechanism. The epiphany of the God of victims follows the same "ancient trail" and goes through the exact same phases as all the epiphanies of the sacred of persecutors. As a result, from the perspective of violence, there is absolutely no distinction between the God of victims and the God of persecutors. Our pseudoscience of religions is based entirely on the conviction that there is no essential difference between the different religions.

This confusion has affected historical Christianity and, to a certain degree, determined it. Those who are opposed to Christianity today endeavor to perpetuate it by clinging desperately to the most sacrificial theology in order not to lose that which nourishes it and to be able always to say: Christianity is only one among many religions of violence, and possibly the worst of them.

The Logos of the God of victims is almost invisible in the eyes of the world. When men reflect on the way in which Jesus conducts his enterprise, they see little other than his failure, and this they see ever more clearly so that, inevitably, it is perceived as definitive and final.

Instead of denying that failure, Christian theology affirms it in order to convert it into a startling victory. Death becomes resurrection. The Logos that has been expelled "makes it possible to become children of God" for all those who did not expel it, all who "receive" him or – what amounts to the same – any victim rejected by men. The expulsion of the Logos is the beginning of the end of the "reign of Satan." Defeat in the world is really victory over the world.

The wisdom of the world sees in this reversal a deception that is easily demystified. Thus one says this is a compensatory figment of the imagination, an imaginary revenge on an uncompromising reality. Many modern Christians are more or less openly in agreement with this interpretation.

If Jesus' defeat were turned into a victory only in the afterworld, the question would be totally one of religious belief or disbelief. From our perspective, there would be nothing to add.

But according to the Gospels, the very world is threatened and the kingdom of Satan is about to disintegrate. If these words are in agreement with the Logos of the God of victims, then they must hold some significance within the context of our analyses.

It can be shown – or rather, we have just shown – that in fact these words have a meaning in the domain we are currently studying, the comparative analysis of religious texts. They are quite different from the imaginary revenge postulated by those who remain blind to the Logos of victims. The demystification they think they achieve is merely another scapegoat mystification.

Here and now, on the plane of ethnological and religious texts, the victorious reversal of the Passion provides us with something tangible that can be understood rationally. To understand this, one need only return to the exegetical advance in progress and extract from it the essential result.

We have discovered, at the heart of every religion, the same single central event that generates its mythical significance and its ritual acts: the action of a crowd as it turns on someone it adored yesterday, and may adore again tomorrow, and transforms him into a scapegoat in order to secure by his death a period of peace for the community.

This central event is decisive and yet so little known that there are no words to describe it. The human and social sciences have never discovered it. In order to describe it, we have borrowed the periphrases of the texts we were reading: "the ancient trail trodden by the wicked . . . the bloodshed for bloodshed given our state to prey on . . ."

This event is also present in the Gospels, but on this occasion it does not just appear in transit: it is not only clearly described, but named. It is called the Passion. Jesus is the perfect victim, because he has always spoken and behaved in accordance with the Logos of the God of victims. He provides the only perfect image of the event which is at the root of all our myths and religions.

The passages of the Dialogues I have quoted form an amazing sequence that is very similar to what is called the "public life" of Jesus, the "public life" to which the Crucifixion, of course, belonged.

Job and Jesus differ on many points, but they are alike in that both tell the truth about what is happening to them. The resemblance lies not so much in the individuals as in the relationship of these individuals to the people around them. For reasons that are different but similar in result, it is the same for Job face to face with his people as it is for Jesus face to face with the crowds in Jerusalem and the various authorities who finally crucify him.

Like Job, Jesus enjoys a period of great popularity. The crowd wants to make him a kind of king, until the day when, through the mimesis of persecution, it turns against its idol with the same unanimity as Job's community did against him. The hour of violent unanimity has struck, the hour of absolute solitude for the victim. Friends, relatives, neighbors, all those whom Jesus has most helped, those he has cured, those he has saved, the disciples most dear to him – all of them leave him alone and, at least passively, join in society's outburst.

In the first texts I quoted, Job's neighbors, his servants, his slaves, and even his wife criticize him, abandon him and ill-treat him. This is much the same as the agony of Jesus. It is the same effort on the part of the authorities, represented in the Dialogues by the friends, to make Job confess his guilt; and the same effort to consolidate the hostile opposition to the suspect.

In order to perceive the structural resemblances of the two relationships, we must see what they have in common and ignore the anecdotal and local differences. (My reference is to events, not to people.)

If the Christian text is allowed to intervene in the interpretation of the

Dialogues, we immediately achieve decisive results. The futility of the boils and the lost cattle is apparent. The incredible originality of the Dialogues becomes more visible. The enigma of this text comes to light. And the Gospels provide what is needed to resolve that enigma, the knowledge of the Passion that is responsible for the essential articulation of the text, and reveals the true nature of the drama of Job's life.

Everything that Job's readers, with the help of the prologue and the epilogue, have managed not to see for two thousand years or more we will be forced to see through the accounts of the Passion, unless we yet again barricade ourselves against its message.

But this time, the meaning will penetrate. It is easy to fail to understand the experience encountered in reading only the Book of Job. But once we recognize the similarities between the experience of Jesus and those of the scapegoat Job, they cannot be forgotten.

The accounts of the Passion gather into one tight bundle all the threads of a structure scattered throughout Job. In the Gospels there are no cattle to distract us, no ostrich or hippopotamus to play hide-and-seek with the real problem.

If I have managed to recognize in Job a crowd that turns on its former idol and gathers in unanimity against a scapegoat – a sinister trial intended to stifle Job's protests – and if I attach importance to these aspects, if I emphasize them by drawing out their social and religious drama, it is because I have been guided from the beginning by the accounts of the Passion.

By this I do not mean that during these analyses, the Passion was explicitly present in my mind. That is not necessary. Whether we like it or not, the Passion is a part of our cultural horizon: it provides, as scholars would say, the "structural model" through which the Dialogues can become ever more legible.

When we examine the Book of Job in the light of the Passion, we are immediately able to isolate the essential text, the Dialogues. The excrescences are no longer apparent that cling like warts to the face of Job and prevent us from perceiving the beauty, from discarding what is parasitical in the message about the scapegoat – all that conceals the guilt of all men, including our own, in seeking out scapegoats: the satanic principle on which not only this community, but all human communities are based.

There is an anthropological dimension to the text of the Gospels. I have never claimed that it constitutes the entirety of Christian revelation, but without it Christianity could scarcely be truly itself, and would be incoherent in areas where it need not be. Without this dimension, an essential aspect of the very humanity of Christ, his incarnation, would be missing; we would not perceive fully in Christ the victim of the men we all represent, and there would be the risk of relapsing into the religion of persecution.

For the Dialogues to be interpreted as they should be, as I have already mentioned, we must choose the side of the victim against the persecutors, identify with him, and accept what he says as truth . . . As it has come down to us, the Book of Job does not insist enough on our hearing the complaint of Job: many things divert us from the crucial texts, deforming and neutralizing them with our secret complicity.

We need, therefore, another text, something else, or rather someone else to come to our aid: the text of the Passion, Christ, is the one to help us understand Job, because Christ completes what Job only half achieves, and that is paradoxically what in the context of the world is his own disaster, the Passion that will soon be inscribed in the text of the Gospels.

For the true significance of the Dialogues to become apparent we must follow the recommendation of the Gospels: pay attention to the victim, come to his aid, take note of what he says. Following the example of the Gospel text, Job's complaints must become the anchor for every interpretation and, very quickly, we will understand why Job speaks as he does, we will recognize his role as scapegoat, the double phenomenon of the crowd, the myth of the celestial armies, and the true nature of the social and religious mechanism that prepares to devour another victim. We can see how everything is linked and organized with extraordinary precision.

The only true reading is that in which Job's outcry becomes the indestructible rock of interpretation; but only through the Gospels can it be developed, only the Spirit of Christ permits the defence of the victim: he is therefore truly the Paraclete.

Most interpreters have always suspected that to do justice to the Book of Job, one must take the part of the unfortunate. Everyone therefore tries to defend Job, identify with him and praise him.

It would not be an exaggeration to identify this as the aim of the additions to the text, but they all fall short of that aim because of their lack of understanding of the community's role in Job's misfortune. Subsequent interpreters fall equally short, and will continue to do so as long as they do not turn to the one on whom even Job calls in the supreme moment of the Dialogues: the defender who is found at God's side, whom Christianity says is God himself, the Paraclete, the all-powerful advocate of all wrongfully condemned victims.

In saying this, it becomes clear that we are not dreaming, we are not falling into "compensatory illusions." The symbols we are using are actually in the text since they resolve the problems, rehabilitate the victims, free the prisoners and, above all, reveal that the God of this world is truly the accuser, Satan, the very first murderer. By coming to the help of Job and reinforcing the revelation of this unusual victim who is Christ, we are striking a death blow to a world system that can be traced in a straight line back to the most primitive forms of violence against scapegoats, the persecution of Job and the murder of "Abel, the righteous."

For centuries, now, the Passion has turned itself about as a triumph at the level of cultural understanding. It provides the interpretative grid by means of which we prevent texts of persecution from crystallizing into sacrificial mythology. In our own time all modernist culture, that bastion of anti-Christianity, begins to disintegrate on contact with the Gospel text. We owe all the real progress we have made in interpreting cultural phenomena to that one Revelation whose effect continues to deepen among us.

Far from being too ridiculous to be worthy of attention, the Christian idea that out of Christ's defeat comes victory has already been realized among us in the collapse of the culture of Marx, Freud, and Nietzsche and in the heightened crisis of all the values that the post-Christian era believed were successful in their opposition to Christianity. "The stone rejected by the builders has become the cornerstone."

The relevance of the Christian text to the interpretation of Job has always been recognized, vaguely, by the doctrine that makes of the work a "prophetic" book in the Christian sense, a book that heralds and prefigures Christ. The depth of this doctrine is apparent only in its earliest applications, the Gospels and the epistles of Paul. As we move forward in time and as these applications are multiplied in the Middle Ages, they become increasingly superficial.

The "allegorical" readings are wrong in that they are satisfied with similarities between simple words, common names, and even proper names, characters isolated from their context and thought to be prophetic of Christ because they are morally exemplary.

The more intellectually and materially comfortable Christianity became, the less it retained the memory of mimetic relationships between men and the processes that result. Hence the tendency of the early Christian exegetes to fabricate an imaginary Job who passes for a prefiguration of Christ for his moral goodness and his virtues, especially for his patience, even though Job in reality was the personification of impatience.

It is easy to ridicule the Christian concept of the prophetic. Yet, like all authentically Christian ideas, the *figure Christi* reveals a great truth, one that has been gradually discredited so that in our day it is completely rejected by Christians themselves, who alone are responsible for its relative sterility. They did not know how to take hold of the idea concretely and make it truly useful. On this point, as on so many others, the inability to maintain the Logos of the God of victims in all its purity paralyzes the revelation. It contaminates with violence the nonviolence of the Logos and makes the latter a dead letter.

The truth of prophecy in the Christian sense appears from the moment mimetic processes are emphasized rather than characters treated as Christ figures.

Job foretells Christ in his participation in the struggle against the God of persecutors. He foretells Christ when he reveals the scapegoat phenomenon that envelops him, when he attacks the system of retribution, and above all when he briefly eludes the logic of violence and the sacred in the two last texts quoted.

Job goes a long way along the path that leads from one logic to the other, from one divinity to the other. But he cannot really swing from one system into the other. Thus the solution that perceives in him a "prefiguration" of Christ seems to me the most profound – providing, of course, the concept is supported by analyses that emphasize human relationships, as instructed by the Gospels.

The "prophetic" becomes significant at the heart of an approach that is in no way retrogressive to "traditional values," in the face of what would be the audacity of the modern subversive and *critique du soupçon*. For a new approach to the Christian text, that criticism must be radicalized: which is precisely the effect of the mimetic-scapegoat thesis. It cannot be said to make use of established values. There is nothing about it that is "pious" in the traditional sense of the word.

Nothing is both more disturbing and more exciting than the irresistible resurgence of the Christian text, at a time and place when it is least anticipated.

In the New Testament, particularly Luke, knowledge of Christ is frequently achieved in two phases. There is a first contact that results from a movement of curiosity and a purely superficial sympathy.

This is followed by disenchantment and disaffection. The disciple who is not completely converted feels he has been mistaken and distances himself. This movement of retreat will not be stopped, it is truly without return; yet it will put the person who despairs in contact with the truth, but a truth so profound that it is transfigured.

The eunuch of Queen Candace came to Jerusalem to have the Gospels explained to him. He returns discouraged, for he does not yet know who could be the Servant of Yahweh in the Book of Isaiah, that unjustly condemned scapegoat who saves the community. But Philip happens to come along and explains to him that Christ is the person in question. After being baptized, the eunuch "went on his way rejoicing" (Acts 8: 26–40).

There is the same movement in the story of Emmaus. Two disciples are leaving Jerusalem after the Passion and are talking on the way about the collapse of their hope. Here again is the same attitude of sceptical and suspicious discouragement with regard to a revelation that has clearly failed.

The discouragement even brings about its own reversal: at the destructive moment of suspicious criticism, suddenly Christ is walking with the disciples and explaining to them the Scriptures. But "their eyes were prevented from recognizing him."

We may one day understand that the entire history of Western thought conforms to the model of these two stories and to a third similar one, also found in Luke: that of the Prodigal Son.

Of these three texts, by far the most precious for those of us who spend so much time writing commentaries on them, interpreting them, and comparing them, is the one about the road to Emmaus. It seems orientated toward the "work of the text"; it does not even forget to include the rewards of this work, which the interpreter receives when the light finally dawns, coldly and even, in one sense, implacably rational and at the same time just the contrary, unacceptable in the world's eyes, mad, truly demented, since it speaks of Christ, since Christ speaks through it, since it emphatically validates the most apparently absurd hopes, hopes that are considered culpable in our day. Does it not suggest that all our real desires are gratified simultaneously?

> Then they said to each other, "Did not our hearts burn within us as he talked to us on the road and explained the scriptures to us?" (Luke 24: 32)

Translated by Yvonne Freccero

Michel Foucault (1926–1984): Introduction

Mary McClintock Fulkerson and
Susan J. Dunlap

Born in Poitiers, France, in 1926, Paul-Michel Foucault was the son of a respected surgeon and a woman of independent means. Raised as a Roman Catholic and educated by Jesuits, he received advanced training in psychology and philosophy and taught both subjects. In 1970 Foucault was elected to the Collège de France, occupying a chair in the history of systems of thought. In addition to his scholarly pursuits, Foucault was involved in various activist causes, including the Groupe d'Information sur les Prisons. He died of AIDS in Paris on June 25, 1984. From 1970 until his death Foucault was an international figure, and his work continues to fascinate thinkers across many disciplines.

Few would deny Foucault's brilliance as a thinker. From madness to the "sciences of man" to prisons and sexuality, his writings are rich in the variety of topics they take up and provocative in their challenges to conventions about truth, power, and the subject. It is difficult, however, to categorize his work. It contains historical, philosophical, and political analyses, but cannot be confined within traditional disciplinary bounds. Foucault's thought is quintessentially postmodern, blurring boundaries between disciplines, theory, and practice, and disrupting fundamental Western truths.

Foucault himself warned against unifying his work with an overarching idea or system, by challenging a basic assumption of intellectual work, i.e., that writing is an entity unified/caused by a subject. In this he was similar to other French intellectuals of the late 1950s (L. Althusser, R. Barthes, C. Lévi-

Strauss, J. Lacan), who rejected humanism and the autonomous subject, preferring to explore the processes and structures that produce it. Unlike these thinkers, however, Foucault created an analytic of the specific and the marginal and refused the labels of structuralism and poststructuralism, as well as the methodologies of phenomenology and hermeneutics.

Foucault did describe his work as a "history of the present," meaning that his investigations of historic practices of knowledges were motivated by a judgment about an intolerable situation in the contemporary world (*Discipline and Punish*, pp. 30–1). Since he was not a conventional historian, we might see Foucault as an intellectual artisan, who produced discrete and valuable artifacts rather than a system or method. His analyses of insanity, sexuality, health, and confinement, for example, are the result not of prefabricated general methods but of craftsman-like skills honed by attending to the complexities of a specific historical configuration, and only retrospectively identified in methodological terms as a structuralist-like procedure called "archaeology" and a genealogy reminiscent of Nietzsche.

Foucault's corpus includes over 300 books, edited volumes, essays, interviews, and reviews. In it he challenges the way modern thinking relates us to the world. Modernity's turn away from God to "man" and its grounding of causality and freedom in the unfettered rational human consciousness appear as new forms of hegemony to Foucault. For a postmodern alternative, he coins new terms. With expressions like "discursive formations" and "epistemes," he calls attention to the way objects, subjects, and truth are not the result of objective reflection but are produced by the interrelation of language, social institutions, and power. Foucault's analyses of particular discursive formations often focus on the discourse of "experts." He explores what counts as madness or unreason in relation to reason in Western history in *Madness and Civilization*, and discursive practices that distinguish health and disease in *The Birth of the Clinic*. His (very difficult) archaeologies take more abstract positions and theorize about the analytical character of the early books and what makes the objective study of human beings possible.

In the 1970s, Foucault became more explicit about the way all discursive formations are permeated with power relations through genealogical inquiry. Thus, rather than asking what objective truth the sciences of penology offer us, Foucault asks what connecting logics and social arrangements came together at a particular time to create the notion that the modern prison is more humane than ancient forms of torture. What domesticating effects of power, he asks, are hidden by these arrangements (*Discipline and Punish*, 1975)? In *The History of Sexuality*, he asks what kinds of bodies are outlawed and disciplined by modern scientific discourses on sexuality. A Foucaultian postmodern inquiry, then, concerns the relation of practices and languages and institutions that produce "truth" about reality while "subjugating" other possibilities.

The History of Sexuality

The excerpt is from the first of what was originally planned as a six-volume project, *The History of Sexuality*. Published in 1976, volume 1 introduced the project Foucault intended to develop. It treats the emergence of technologies that produce sexualized identities for subjects. In it Foucault suggested that later volumes would treat topics of early Christian attitudes to sex, and eighteenth- and nineteenth-century issues such as children's sexuality, the sexualization of women, and perverts. When volumes 2 and 3 came out in 1984, they were on the somewhat surprising topics of classical Greek practices of the self (*The Use of Pleasure*), and first- and second-century Greek and Latin texts (*Care of the Self*). With their focus on an ethics of the self, these works are difficult to square with Foucault's previous rejection of the autonomous subject. Volumes 2 and 3 represent possibilities for future interpretations of Foucault.

Volume 1 is thematically related to *Discipline and Punish*. Both books are concrete genealogies of modes of domination that arose with modernity. The themes of these texts identify what Foucault calls the techniques of modern "bio-power," a pervasive set of strategies, practices, and forms of organization that emerged at the end of the eighteenth century with the "humanizing" modern prison and later techniques that medicalized the confessing self. More subtle than either physical violence or absolute monarchy, "bio-power" is ubiquitous, hidden, and qualitatively more comprehensive and effective than its predecessors. Unlike previous conceptions of power, it is productive rather than negative. Although the techniques of the *scientia sexualis* described here are not identical with the disciplinary techniques of the modern prison, both are aimed at the body and the normalization of persons. Foucault thought that normalizing techniques carry out the "objectifying" work of the sciences of "man," which first made it possible to categorize, delimit, and divide human beings into populations. Rendering subjects docile, they extend beyond the settings of the prison and the psychiatrist's office.

Foucault's analyses of sexuality and prisons resonate with another theme that continually concerned him: the "othering" effects of Western discourse. His work can be read as an investigation of processes that create the other – the mad, the sick, objectifiable populations in the works of the fifties and sixties. The prisoner and the homosexual, the "pervert," the masturbating child, and the sexualized woman are the "others" of the seventies. If we look for accounts of resistance or liberation in his work, however, Foucault is elusive. By writing a history of the present he invites readers to see the contingency of the definitions and technologies that divide the normal from the "other," or the marginal and resistance in the knowledges uncovered by his genealogical and archaeological investigations. As discussed below, the sexuality excerpt refutes the conventional wisdom that liberation is freedom of expression, the revelation of the "true self." However, the ubiquity of power makes it difficult to imagine an alternative. On this count Foucault's work may be more artistic than systematic, offering us pieces to admire and use in new ways rather than a comprehensive proposal complete with answers.

The Text

This excerpt from volume 1 is part of Foucault's effort to discredit the "Repressive Hypothesis," a conventional interpretation of the past 400 years of Western history. According to this view, the early seventeenth century was a time of relative openness about sex, bodies, and sensuality. As the West moved into the Victorian era, so the hypothesis goes, sex became hidden, banished from everyday life either to the realm of the secret and hushed, or to the realm of the whore, the idiot, the madwoman, and other segregated domains.

The banishment or repression of sex served an economic purpose, according to the hypothesis. It coincided with the rise of capitalism and promoted the interests of the bourgeoisie by harnessing the productive capacities of the working class, preventing the waste of their energies on sex. Repression, then, is the effect of a relationship of domination between power and sex. Liberation from this domination comes from exploring sex and pleasure without restraint, from casting off the chains of repression and reveling in free discovery and talk of things sexual. Open sexual speech and behavior are coupled with liberation, silence and segregation with domination. The fact that sex is coming out of hiding is a positive indication that the banishment of sex to the guarded and controlled is giving way to greater human freedom in the twentieth century.

Foucault offers an alternative account of history in this reading. Rather than seeing sex as repressed, hidden, or rendered mute, he sees a multiplication of sex and talk of sex. He sees a society permeated with explorations, explications, and excitations of sex. Furthermore, sex became linked to confession and thus to the compulsion to speak of the deepest corners of desire to authority, be it priest, physician, or psychiatrist. "Not only will you confess to acts contravening the law, but you will seek to transform your desire, your every desire, into discourse." Through confession, this transformation of sex into speech, Foucault says, sex became discourse. As opposed to a society where sex has been cordoned off into the realm of the clandestine, it has been multiplied and extended to the far reaches of the society.

How did this come to be?

Foucault answers this question by outlining two different "procedures for producing the truth of sex." The first, in cultures remote in time and space from the modern West, is an *ars erotica* (an erotic art), in which pleasure itself is the source of truth and whose guarded secrets are passed from the master to a few deserving students. The erotic delights were not constituted by other imperatives, but were savored and transmitted for their own sake, by their own truth. By contrast, the West practices a *scientia sexualis* (science of sex), a procedure for producing the truth of sex that merges two practices of the West: confession and scientific discourse.

Contrary to the view that sex has been banished to secrecy, Foucault claims that talk of sex has multiplied as practices of confession moved from religious penance to judicial process, medical diagnosis, and psychiatric exploration of the corners of the psyche. Behind confession is the claim that it is through self-scrutiny that the truth of oneself, the deep self, is known. This revelation of the truth of the self happens in the context of a "power relationship" in which the confessor's words are authenticated and given definitive interpretation by the expert. Yet, Foucault says, confession is a "ruse." Under the guise of freeing the self, the practice of confession furthers hegemonic power. Speaking the truth of oneself is not a route to liberation; it is an effect of power and extends its domain. The privileged topic of confession was sex. Thus, rather than something to be hidden, kept secret, as the Repressive Hypothesis had it, sex was something to confess, to divulge in all its contours. Sex was transformed into discourse, and a great pool or "archive" of sex accumulated.

The pivotal event, argues Foucault, occurred when *scientia sexualis* emerged as the merging of confessional practices with scientific discourse. The two methods of producing truth, confession and science, combined to create the truth of sex. More precisely, scientific discourse colonized or reconstituted the centuries-old practice of confession. Foucault describes five ways this reconstitution occurred. First, the imperative to self-revelation became articulated in clinical terms. The compulsion to "tell" was appropriated by the scientific medical realm. Second, sex came to be understood as the cause of a vast array of problems that plague human beings, from a skin rash to insanity to bad social skills. In order to uncover the cause of these and countless other human problems, the sexual origins had to be considered. Third, because the truth of sex is recalcitrant and loath to appear, it must be extricated from the recesses of the psyche, by force if necessary. It is evasive, slippery by nature, and does not give itself up without scientific methods of extraction. Fourth, sex requires interpretation. Its truth is not immediately apparent. It is produced in two stages; first spoken by the confessor, then deciphered by an authorized officer of science. Finally, sex was medicalized and placed on a continuum of the normal to the pathological. If healing was necessary, it was the medical realm that was invoked. With these five procedures the occupation of confession by scientific discourse was accomplished. In this way "sexuality" emerged.

Having described this process, Foucault counters the Repressive Hypothesis with his own "general working hypothesis." Far from repressing sex, nineteenth-century society put into place a grand mechanism for producing the truth of sex. And sex achieved the status of that which bears the deep truth of ourselves. Through the twofold process of revealing itself with authorized interpretation and revealing the deep truth of ourselves, sex has become key to the sciences of the human subject. "[T]he project of a science of the subject has gravitated, in ever narrowing circles, around the question of sex".

The excerpt ends with an indication of the direction of Foucault's argument. He points toward an exploration of power that produces, not simply represses, of power that creates, not simply silences. He will go on to show how power is thoroughly implicated in the press to produce the truth of sex. "In short, we must define the strategies of power that are immanent in this will to knowledge."

Implications for Theological and Religious Studies

Foucault's themes are of great interest for theological and religious studies. Confession has long been central to many religious traditions. Sex is a topic of no small concern for religions as well. In this excerpt Foucault's startling claim that Western technologies of power have produced a uniquely modern subjectivity, *sexual identity*, creates important questions for religious, particularly Christian, thinkers. A first question this work raises is the validity of sexual identity. Foucault suggests that the contemporary obsession with sexual identity is itself a form of subjugation, the further extension of the normalizing effects of the social sciences. If he is correct, religious communities obsessed with the status of "homosexuals" are being normalized and disciplined by modern bio-power, not faithful and moral.

The potentially debilitating stakes of self-examination must also be taken seriously. When is the effect of confession the endless search for the deep and true self? Does it contribute to a subtle capitulation to normalization and docility? Or has Foucault simply missed some of the liberating effects of confessional practices that include self-identification, submission, repentance, and forgiveness? A more serious question still is the *subject* of the confessional: Does contemporary Christianity require a "deep self"? To do justice to these questions requires religious thinkers to attend to power and the contingency of modern subjectivity in more serious ways.

The broader implications of his work differ for religious studies and for theology. For religious studies, a Foucaultian approach requires that a religion be analyzed as a formation of discursive practices. Pertinent questions include how its rule-ordered practices operate, how they produce social effects of truth, what they subjugate. For theologians, Foucault raises the thorny question of truth. With Nietzsche, Foucault assumes the death of God. What makes his anti-foundationalist challenge most pointed, however, is the notion that truth is an effect of power. His challenge is not historical relativism – already an issue in theological studies – but the notion that truth/knowledge is internally related to power. Not only must would-be Foucaultian postmodern theology be done without epistemological foundations, it requires renunciation of deeply in-grained habits of treating religious belief and practice separately from issues of power.

Although some interpreters judge him a nihilist, Foucault has admirers in religious and nonreligious ethics. Given his continuing fascination with the marginal and his exposure of "subjugated knowledges," he is helpful for liberation-type thinking that defines truth as praxis. Others use his later writing on self-production for an ethic of aesthetic self-creation or use bio-power to reconceive theological conceptions of power and liberation/oppression. Any route taken on these issues faces formidable problems but will be of great import to postmodern religious faith.

Selected Bibliography

Castelli, Elizabeth A., *Imitating Paul: A Discourse of Power* (Louisville, KY: Westminster/ John Knox Press, 1991).

Diamond, Irene, and Quinby, Lee (eds), *Feminism and Foucault: Reflections on Resistance* (Boston: Northeastern University Press, 1988).

Dreyfus, Hubert L., and Rabinow, Paul, *Michel Foucault: Beyond Structuralism and Hermeneutics* (Chicago: University of Chicago Press, 1982).

Foucault, Michel, *Madness and Civilization: A History of Insanity in the Age of Reason*, trans. Richard Howard (New York: Pantheon, 1965). [First published in 1961.]

—— *Discipline and Punish: The Birth of the Prison*, trans. Alan Sheridan (New York: Pantheon, 1977). [First published in 1975.]

—— *The History of Sexuality*. Vol. 1: *An Introduction*, trans. Robert Hurley (New York: Random House, 1990). [First published in 1978.]

—— *Power/Knowledge: Selected Interviews and Other Writings, 1972–1977*, ed. Colin Gordon (New York: Pantheon, 1980).

—— *The Foucault Reader*, ed. Paul Rabinow (New York: Pantheon, 1984).

Fulkerson, Mary McClintock, *Changing the Subject: Women's Discourses and Feminist Theology* (Minneapolis: Fortress Press, 1994).

Grenz, Stanley J., *A Primer on Postmodernism* (Grand Rapids, MI: Eerdmans, 1996).

Gutting, Gary (ed.), *The Cambridge Companion to Foucault* (Cambridge: Cambridge University Press, 1984).

Hoy, David Couzens, *Foucault: A Critical Reader* (New York: Blackwell, 1986).

May, Melanie A., *Bonds of Unity: Women, Theology, and the Worldwide Church*. AAR

Academy Series, no. 65, ed. Susan Thistlethwaite (Atlanta: Scholars Press, 1989).

Moore, Stephen, *Poststructuralism and the New Testament: Derrida and Foucault at the Foot of the Cross* (Minneapolis: Fortress Press, 1996).

Pasework, Kyle, *A Theology of Power: Being Beyond Domination* (Minneapolis: Fortress Press, 1993).

Ray, Stephen Alan, *The Modern Soul: Michel Foucault and the Theological Discourse of Gordon Kaufman and David Tracy* (Minneapolis: Fortress Press, 1987).

Sheridan, Alan, *Michel Foucault: The Will to Truth* (London: Tavistock, 1980).

Welch, Sharon, *Communities of Resistance and Solidarity: A Feminist Theology of Liberation* (Maryknoll, NY: Orbis Books, 1985).

From *The History of Sexuality*

Historically, there have been two great procedures for producing the truth of sex.

On the one hand, the societies – and they are numerous: China, Japan, India, Rome, the Arabo-Moslem societies – which endowed themselves with an *ars erotica*. In the erotic art, truth is drawn from pleasure itself, understood as a practice and accumulated as experience; pleasure is not considered in relation to an absolute law of the permitted and the forbidden, nor by reference to a criterion of utility, but first and foremost in relation to itself; it is experienced as pleasure, evaluated in terms of its intensity, its specific quality, its duration, its reverberations in the body and the soul. Moreover, this knowledge must be deflected back into the sexual practice itself, in order to shape it as though from within and amplify its effects. In this way, there is formed a knowledge that must remain secret, not because of an element of infamy that might attach to its object, but because of the need to hold it in the greatest reserve, since, according to tradition, it would lose its effectiveness and its virtue by being divulged. Consequently, the relationship to the master who holds the secrets is of paramount importance; only he, working alone, can transmit this art in an esoteric manner and as the culmination of an initiation in which he guides the disciple's progress with unfailing skill and severity. The effects of this masterful art, which are considerably more generous than the spareness of its prescriptions would lead one to imagine, are said to transfigure the one fortunate enough to receive its privileges: an absolute mastery of the body, a singular bliss, obliviousness to time and limits, the elixir of life, the exile of death and its threats.

On the face of it at least, our civilization possesses no *ars erotica*. In return, it is undoubtedly the only civilization to practice a *scientia sexualis*; or rather, the only civilization to have developed over the centuries procedures for telling the truth of sex which are geared to a form of knowledge-power strictly opposed to the art of initiations and the masterful secret: I have in mind the confession.

Since the Middle Ages at least, Western societies have established the confession as one of the main rituals we rely on for the production of truth: the codification of the sacrament of penance by the Lateran Council in 1215, with the resulting development of confessional techniques, the declining importance of accusatory procedures in criminal justice, the abandonment of tests of guilt (sworn statements, duels, judgments of God) and the development of methods of interrogation and inquest, the increased participation of the royal administration in the prosecution of infractions, at the expense of proceedings leading to private settlements, the setting up of tribunals of Inquisition: all this helped to give the confession a central role in the order of civil and religious powers. The evolution of the word *avowal* and of the legal function it designated is itself emblematic of this development: from being a guarantee of the status, identity, and value granted to one person by another, it came to signify someone's acknowledgment of his own actions and thoughts. For a long time, the individual was vouched for by the reference of others and the demonstration of his ties to the commonweal (family, allegiance, protection); then he was authenticated by the discourse of truth he was able or obliged to pronounce concerning himself. The truthful confession was inscribed at the heart of the procedures of individualization by power.

In any case, next to the testing rituals, next to the testimony of witnesses, and the learned methods of observation and demonstration, the confession became one of the West's most highly valued techniques for producing truth. We have since become a singularly confession society. The confession has spread its effects far and wide. It plays a part in justice, medicine, education, family relationships, and love relations, in the most ordinary affairs of everyday life, and in the most solemn rites; one confesses one's crimes, one's sins, one's thoughts and desires, one's illnesses and troubles; one goes about telling, with the greatest precision, whatever is most difficult to tell. One confesses in public and in private, to one's parents, one's educators, one's doctor, to those one loves; one admits to oneself, in pleasure and in pain, things it would be impossible to tell to anyone else, the things people write books about. One confesses – or is forced to confess. When it is not spontaneous or dictated by some internal imperative, the confession is wrung from a person by violence or threat; it is driven from its hiding-place in the soul, or extracted from the body. Since the Middle Ages, torture has accompanied it like a shadow, and supported it when it could go no further: the dark twins.[1] The most defenseless tenderness and the bloodiest of powers have a similar need of confession. Western man has become a confessing animal.

Whence a metamorphosis in literature: We have passed from a pleasure to be recounted and heard, centering on the heroic or marvelous narration of "trials" of bravery or sainthood, to a literature ordered according to the infinite task of extracting from the depths of oneself, in between the words, a truth which the very form of the confession holds out like a shimmering mirage. Whence too this new way of philosophizing: seeking the fundamental relation to the true, not simply in oneself – in some forgotten knowledge, or in a certain primal trace – but in the self-examination that yields, through a multitude of fleeting impressions, the basic certainties of consciousness. The obligation to confess is now relayed through so many different points, is so deeply ingrained in us, that we no longer perceive it as the effect of a power that constrains us; on the contrary, it seems to us that truth, lodged in our most secret nature, "demands" only to surface; that if it fails to do so, this is because a constraint holds it in place, the violence of a power weighs it down, and it can finally be articulated only at the price of a kind of liberation. Confession frees, but power reduces one to silence; truth does not belong to the order of power, but shares an original affinity with freedom: traditional themes in philosophy, which a "political history of truth" would have to overturn by showing that truth is not by nature free – nor error servile – but that its production is thoroughly imbued with relations of power. The confession is an example of this.

One has to be completely taken in by this internal ruse of confession in order to attribute a fundamental role to censorship, to taboos regarding speaking and thinking; one has to have an inverted image of power in order to believe that all these voices which have spoken so long in our civilization – repeating the formidable injunction to tell what one is and what one does, what one recollects and what one has forgotten, what one is thinking and what one thinks he is not thinking – are speaking to us of freedom. An immense labor to which the West has submitted generations in order to produce – while other forms of work ensured the accumulation of capital – men's subjection: their constitution as subjects in both senses of the word. Imagine how exorbitant must have seemed the order given to all Christians at the beginning of the thirteenth century, to kneel at least once a year and confess to all their transgressions, without omitting a single one. And think of that obscure partisan, seven centuries later, who had come to rejoin the Serbian resistance deep in the mountains; his superiors asked him to write his life story; and when he brought them a few miserable pages, scribbled in the night, they did not look at them but only said to him, "Start over, and tell the truth." Should those much-discussed language taboos make us forget this millennial yoke of confession?

From the Christian penance to the present day, sex was a privileged theme of confession. A thing that was hidden, we are told. But what if, on the contrary, it was what, in a quite particular way, one confessed? Suppose the obligation to conceal it was but another aspect of the duty to admit to it (concealing it all the more and with greater care as the confession of it was more important, requiring a stricter ritual and promising more decisive effects)? What if sex in our society, on a scale of several centuries, was something that was placed within an unrelenting system of confession? The transformation of sex into discourse, which I spoke of earlier, the dissemination and reinforcement of heterogeneous sexualities, are perhaps two elements of the same deployment: They are linked together with the help of the central element of a confession that compels individuals to articulate their sexual peculiarity – no matter how extreme. In Greece, truth and sex were linked, in the form of pedagogy, by the transmission of a precious knowledge from one body to another; sex served as a medium for initiations into learning. For us, it is in the confession that truth and sex are joined, through the obligatory and exhaustive expression of an individual secret. But this time it is truth that serves as a medium for sex and its manifestations.

The confession is a ritual of discourse in which the speaking subject is also the subject of the statement; it is also a ritual that unfolds within a power relationship, for one does not confess without the presence (or virtual presence) of a partner who is not simply the interlocutor but the authority who requires the confession, prescribes and appreciates it, and intervenes in order to judge, punish, forgive, console, and reconcile; a ritual in which the truth is corroborated by the obstacles and resistances it has had to surmount in order to be formulated; and finally, a ritual in which the expression alone, independently of its external consequences, produces intrinsic modifications in the person who articulates it: It exonerates, redeems, and purifies him; it unburdens him of his wrongs, liberates him, and promises him salvation. For centuries, the truth of sex was, at least for the most part, caught up in this discursive form. Moreover, this form was not the same as that of education (sexual education confined itself to general principles and rules of prudence); nor was it that of initiation (which remained essentially a silent practice, which the act of sexual enlightenment or deflowering merely rendered laughable or violent). As we have seen, it is a form that is far removed from the one governing the "erotic art." By virtue of the power structure immanent in it, the confessional discourse cannot come from above, as in the *ars erotica*, through the sovereign will of a master, but rather from below, as an obligatory act of speech which, under some imperious compulsion, breaks the bonds of discretion or forgetfulness. What secrecy it presupposes is not owing to the high price of what it has to say and the small number of those who are worthy of its benefits, but to its obscure familiarity and its general baseness. Its veracity is not guaranteed by the lofty authority of the magistery, nor by the tradition it transmits, but by the bond, the basic intimacy in discourse, between the one who speaks and what he is speaking about. On the other hand, the agency of domination does not reside in the one who speaks (for it is he who is constrained), but in the one who listens and says nothing; not in the one who knows and answers, but in the one who questions and is not supposed to know. And this discourse of truth finally takes effect, not in the one who receives it, but in the one from whom it is wrested. With these confessed truths, we are a long way from the learned initiations into pleasure, with their technique and their mystery. On the other hand, we belong to a society which has ordered sex's difficult knowledge, not according to the transmission of secrets, but around the slow surfacing of confidential statements.

The confession was, and still remains, the general standard governing the production of the true discourse on sex. It has undergone a considerable transformation, however. For a long time, it remained firmly entrenched in the practice of penance. But with the rise of Protestantism, the Counter Reformation, eighteenth-century pedagogy, and nineteenth-century medicine, it gradually lost its ritualistic and exclusive localization; it spread; it has been employed in a whole series of relationships: children and parents, students and educators, patients and psychiatrists, delinquents and experts. The motivations and effects it is expected to produce have varied, as have the forms it has taken: interrogations, consultations, autobiographical narratives, letters; they have been recorded, transcribed, assembled into dossiers, published, and commented on. But more important, the confession lends itself, if not to other domains, at least to new ways of exploring the existing ones. It is no longer a question simply of saying what was done – the sexual act – and how it was done; but of reconstructing, in and around the act, the thoughts that recapitulated it, the obsessions that accompanied it, the images, desires, modulations, and quality of the pleasure that animated it. For the first time no doubt, a society has taken upon itself to solicit and hear the imparting of individual pleasures.

A dissemination, then, of procedures of confession, a multiple localization of their constraint, a widening of their domain: A great archive of the pleasures of sex was gradually constituted. For a long time this archive dematerialized as it was formed. It regularly disappeared without a trace (thus suiting the purposes of the Christian pastoral) until medicine, psychiatry, and pedagogy began to solidify it: Campe, Salzmann, and especially Kaan, Krafft-Ebing, Tardieu, Molle, and Havelock Ellis carefully assembled this whole pitiful, lyrical outpouring from the sexual mosaic. Western societies thus began to keep an indefinite record of these people's pleasures. They made up a herbal of them and established a system of classification. They described their everyday deficiencies as well as their oddities or exasperations. This was an important time. It is easy to make light of these nineteenth-century psychiatrists, who made a point of apologizing for the horrors they were about to let speak, evoking "immoral behavior" or "aberrations of the genetic senses," but I am more inclined to applaud their seriousness: They had a feeling for momentous events. It was a time when the most singular pleasures were called upon to pronounce a discourse of truth concerning themselves, a discourse which had to model itself after that which spoke, not of sin and salvation, but of bodies and life processes – the discourse of science. It was enough to make one's voice tremble, for an improbable thing was then taking shape: a confessional science, a science which relied on a many-sided extortion, and took for its object what was unmentionable but admitted to nonetheless. The scientific discourse was scandalized, or in any case repelled, when it had to take charge of this whole discourse from below. It was also faced with a theoretical and methodological paradox: The long discussions concerning the possibility of constituting a science of the subject, the validity of introspection, lived experience as evidence, or the presence of consciousness to itself were responses to this problem that is inherent in the functioning of truth in our society: Can one articulate the production of truth according to the old juridico-religious model of confession, and the extortion of confidential evidence according to the rules of scientific discourse? Those who believe that sex was more rigorously elided in the nineteenth century than ever before, through a formidable mechanism of blockage and a deficiency of discourse, can say what they please. There was no deficiency, but rather an excess, a redoubling, too much rather than not enough discourse, in any case an interference between two modes of production of truth: procedures of confession, and scientific discursivity.

And instead of adding up the errors, naïvetés, and moralisms that plagued the nineteenth-century discourse of truth concerning sex, we would do better to locate the procedures by which that will to knowledge regarding sex, which characterizes the modern Occident, caused the rituals of confession to function within the norms of scientific regularity: How did this immense and traditional extortion of the sexual confession come to be constituted in scientific terms?

1   *Through a clinical codification of the inducement to speak.* Combining confession with examination, the personal history with the deployment of a set of decipherable signs and symptoms; the interrogation, the exacting questionnaire, and hypnosis, with the recollection of memories and free association: All were ways of reinscribing the procedure of confession in a field of scientifically acceptable observations.

2   *Through the postulate of a general and diffuse causality.* Having to tell everything, being able to pose questions about everything, found their justification in the principle that endowed sex with an inexhaustible and polymorphous causal power. The most discrete event in one's sexual behavior – whether an accident or a deviation, a deficit or an excess – was deemed capable of entailing the most varied consequences throughout one's existence; there was scarcely a malady or physical disturbance to which the nineteenth century did not impute at least some degree of sexual etiology. From the bad habits of children to the phthises of adults, the apoplexies of old people, nervous maladies, and the degenerations of the race, the medicine of that era wove an entire network of sexual causality to explain them. This may well appear fantastic to us, but the principle of sex as a "cause of any and everything" was the theoretical underside of a confession that had to be thorough, meticulous, and constant, and at the same time operate within a scientific type of practice. The limitless dangers that sex carried with it justified the exhaustive character of the inquisition to which it was subjected.

3   *Through the principle of a latency intrinsic to sexuality.* If it was necessary to extract the truth of sex through the technique of confession, this was not simply because it was difficult to tell, or stricken by the taboos of decency, but because the ways of sex were obscure; it was elusive by nature; its energy and its mechanisms escaped observation, and its causal power was partly clandestine. By integrating it into the beginnings of a scientific discourse, the nineteenth century altered the scope of the confession; it tended no longer to be concerned solely with what the subject wished to hide, but with what was hidden from himself, being incapable of coming to light except gradually and through the labor of a confession in which the questioner and the questioned each had a part to play. The principle of a latency essential to sexuality made it possible to link the forcing of a difficult confession to a scientific practice. It had to be exacted, by force, since it involved something that tried to stay hidden.

4   *Through the method of interpretation.* If one had to confess, this was not merely because the person to whom one confessed had the power to forgive, console, and direct, but because the work of producing the truth was obliged

to pass through this relationship if it was to be scientifically validated. The truth did not reside solely in the subject who, by confessing, would reveal it wholly formed. It was constituted in two stages: Present but incomplete, blind to itself, in the one who spoke, it could only reach completion in the one who assimilated and recorded it. It was the latter's function to verify this obscure truth: The revelation of confession had to be coupled with the decipherment of what it said. The one who listened was not simply the forgiving master, the judge who condemned or acquitted; he was the master of truth. His was a hermeneutic function. With regard to the confession, his power was not only to demand it before it was made, or decide what was to follow after it, but also to constitute a discourse of truth on the basis of its decipherment. By no longer making the confession a test, but rather a sign, and by making sexuality something to be interpreted, the nineteenth century gave itself the possibility of causing the procedures of confession to operate within the regular formation of a scientific discourse.

5   *Through the medicalization of the effects of confession.* The obtaining of the confession and its effects were recodified as therapeutic operations. Which meant first of all that the sexual domain was no longer accounted for simply by the notions of error or sin, excess or transgression, but was placed under the rule of the normal and the pathological (which, for that matter, were the transposition of the former categories); a characteristic sexual morbidity was defined for the first time; sex appeared as an extremely unstable pathological field: a surface of repercussion for other ailments, but also the focus of a specific nosography, that of instincts, tendencies, images, pleasure, and conduct. This implied furthermore that sex would derive its meaning and its necessity from medical interventions: It would be required by the doctor, necessary for diagnosis, and effective by nature in the cure. Spoken in time, to the proper party, and by the person who was both the bearer of it and the one responsible for it, the truth healed.

Let us consider things in broad historical perspective: Breaking with the traditions of the *ars erotica*, our society has equipped itself with a *scientia sexualis*. To be more precise, it has pursued the task of producing true discourses concerning sex, and this by adapting – not without difficulty – the ancient procedure of confession to the rules of scientific discourse. Paradoxically, the *scientia sexualis* that emerged in the nineteenth century kept as its nucleus the singular ritual of obligatory and exhaustive confession, which in the Christian West was the first technique for producing the truth of sex. Beginning in the sixteenth century, this rite gradually detached itself from the sacrament of penance, and via the guidance of souls and the direction of conscience – the *ars artium* – emigrated toward pedagogy, relationships between adults and children, family relations, medicine, and psychiatry. In any case, nearly 150 years have gone into the making of a complex machinery for producing true discourses on sex: a deployment that spans a wide segment of history in that it connects the ancient injunction of confession to clinical listening methods. It is this deployment that enables something called "sexuality" to embody the truth of sex and its pleasures.

"Sexuality": the correlative of that slowly developed discursive practice which constitutes the *scientia sexualis*. The essential features of this sexuality are not the expression of a representation that is more or less distorted by ideology, or of a misunderstanding caused by taboos; they correspond to the functional requirements of a discourse that must produce its truth. Situated at the point of intersection of a technique of confession and a scientific discursivity, where certain major mechanisms had to be found for adapting them to one another (the listening technique, the postulate of causality, the principle of latency, the rule of interpretation, the imperative of medicalization), sexuality was defined as being "by nature": a domain susceptible to pathological processes, and hence one calling for therapeutic or normalizing interventions; a field of meanings to decipher; the site of processes concealed by specific mechanisms; a focus of indefinite causal relations; and an obscure speech (*parole*) that had to be ferreted out and listened to. The "economy" of discourses – their intrinsic technology, the necessities of their operation, the tactics they employ, the effects of power which underlie them and which they transmit – this, and not a system of representations, is what determines the essential features of what they have to say. The history of sexuality – that is, the history of what functioned in the nineteenth century as a specific field of truth – must first be written from the viewpoint of a history of discourses.

Let us put forward a general working hypothesis. The society that emerged in the nineteenth century – bourgeois, capitalist, or industrial society, call it what you will – did not confront sex with a fundamental refusal of recognition. On the contrary, it put into operation an entire machinery for producing true discourses concerning it. Not only did it speak of sex and compel everyone to do so; it also set out to formulate the uniform truth of sex. As if it suspected sex of harboring a fundamental secret. As if it needed this production of truth. As if it was essential that sex be inscribed not only in an economy of pleasure but in an ordered system of knowledge. Thus sex gradually became an object of great suspicion; the general and disquieting meaning that pervades our conduct and our existence, in spite of ourselves; the point of weakness where evil portents reach through to us; the fragment of darkness that we each carry within us: a general signification, a universal secret, an omnipresent cause, a fear that never ends. And so, in this "question" of sex (in both senses: as interrogation and problematization, and as the need for confession and integration into a field of rationality), two processes emerge, the one always conditioning the other: we demand that sex speak the truth (but, since it is the secret and is oblivious to its own nature, we reserve for ourselves the function of telling the truth of its truth, revealed and deciphered at last), and we demand that it tell us our truth, or rather, the deeply buried truth of that truth about ourselves which we think we possess in our immediate consciousness. We tell it its truth by deciphering what it tells us about that truth; it tells us our own by delivering up that part of it that escaped us. From this interplay there has evolved, over several centuries, a knowledge of the subject; a knowledge not so much of his form, but of that which divides him, determines him perhaps, but above all causes him to be ignorant of himself. As unlikely as this may seem, it should not surprise us when we think of the long history of the Christian and juridical confession, of the shifts and transformations this form of knowledge-power, so important in the West, has undergone: The project of a science of the subject has gravitated, in ever narrowing circles, around the question of sex. Causality in the subject, the unconscious of the subject, the truth of the subject in the other who knows, the knowledge he holds unbeknown to him, all this found an opportunity to deploy itself in the discourse of sex. Not, however, by reason of some natural property inherent in sex itself, but by virtue of the tactics of power immanent in this discourse.

Scientia sexualis versus *ars erotica*, no doubt. But it should be noted that the *ars erotica* did not disappear altogether from Western civilization; nor has it always been absent from the movement by which one sought to produce a science of sexuality. In the Christian confession, but especially in the direction and examination of conscience, in the search for spiritual union and the love of God, there was a whole series of methods that had much in common with an erotic art: guidance by the master along a path of initiation, the intensification of experiences extending down to their physical components, the optimization of effects by the discourse that accompanied them. The phenomena of possession and ecstasy, which were quite frequent in the Catholicism of the Counter Reformation, were undoubtedly effects that had got outside the control of the erotic technique immanent in this subtle science of the flesh. And we must ask whether, since the nineteenth century, the *scientia sexualis* – under the guise of its decent positivism – has not functioned, at least to a certain extent, as an *ars erotica*. Perhaps this production of truth, intimidated though it was by the scientific model, multiplied, intensified, and even created its own intrinsic pleasures. It is often said that we have been incapable of imagining any new pleasures. We have at least invented a different kind of pleasure: pleasure in the truth of pleasure, the pleasure of knowing that truth, of discovering and exposing it, the fascination of seeing it and telling it, of captivating and capturing others by it, of confiding it in secret, of luring it out in the open – the specific pleasure of the true discourse on pleasure.

The most important elements of an erotic art linked to our knowledge about sexuality are not to be sought in the ideal, promised to us by medicine, of a healthy sexuality, nor in the humanist dream of a complete and flourishing sexuality, and certainly not in the lyricism of orgasm and the good feelings of bio-energy (these are but aspects of its normalizing utilization), but in this multiplication and intensification of pleasures connected to the production of the truth about sex. The learned volumes, written and read; the consultations and examinations; the anguish of answering questions and the delights of having one's words interpreted; all the stories told to oneself and to others, so much curiosity, so many confidences offered in the face of scandal, sustained – but not without trembling a little – by the obligation of truth; the profusion of secret fantasies and the dearly paid right to whisper them to whoever is able to hear them; in short, the formidable "pleasure of analysis" (in the widest sense of the latter term) which the West has cleverly been fostering for several centuries: all this constitutes something like the errant fragments of an erotic art that is secretly transmitted by confession and the science of sex. Must we conclude that our *scientia sexualis* is but an extraordinarily subtle form of *ars erotica*, and that it is the Western, sublimated version of that seemingly lost tradition? Or must we suppose that all these pleasures are only the by-products of a sexual science, a bonus that compensates for its many stresses and strains?

In any case, the hypothesis of a power of repression exerted by our society on sex for economic reasons appears to me quite inadequate if we are to explain this whole series of reinforcements and intensifications that our preliminary inquiry has discovered: a proliferation of discourses, carefully tailored to the requirements of power; the solidification of the sexual mosaic and the construction of devices capable not only of isolating it but of stimulating and provoking it, of forming it into focuses of attention, discourse, and pleasure; the mandatory production of confessions and the subsequent establishment of a system of legitimate knowledge and of an economy of manifold pleasures. We are dealing not nearly so much with a negative mechanism of exclusion as with the operation of a subtle network of discourses, special knowledges, pleasures, and powers. At issue is not a movement bent on pushing rude sex back into some obscure and inaccessible region, but on the contrary, a process that spreads it over the surface of things and bodies, arouses it, draws it out and bids it speak, implants it in reality and enjoins it to tell the truth: an entire glittering sexual array, reflected in a myriad of discourses, the obstination of powers, and the interplay of knowledge and pleasure.

All this is an illusion, it will be said, a hasty impression behind which a more discerning gaze will surely discover the same great machinery of repression. Beyond these few phosphorescences, are we not sure to find once more the somber law that always says no? The answer will have to come out of a historical inquiry. An inquiry concerning the manner in which a knowledge of sex has been forming over the last three centuries; the manner in which the discourses that take it as their object have multiplied, and the reasons for which we have come to attach a nearly fabulous price to the truth they claimed to produce. Perhaps these historical analyses will end by dissipating what this cursory survey seems to suggest. But the postulate I started out with, and would like to hold to as long as possible, is that these deployments of power and knowledge, of truth and pleasures, so unlike those of repression, are not necessarily secondary and derivative; and further, that repression is not in any case fundamental and overriding. We need to take these mechanisms seriously, therefore, and reverse the direction of our analysis: Rather than assuming a generally acknowledged repression, and an ignorance measured against what we are supposed to know, we must begin with these positive mechanisms, insofar as they produce knowledge, multiply discourse, induce pleasure, and generate power; we must investigate the conditions of their emergence and operation, and try to discover how the related facts of interdiction or concealment are distributed with respect to them. In short, we must define the strategies of power that are immanent in this will to knowledge. As far as sexuality is concerned, we shall attempt to constitute the "political economy" of a will to knowledge.

Translated by Robert Hurley

Note

1 Greek law had already coupled torture and confession, at least where slaves were concerned, and Imperial Roman law had widened the practice.

Michel de Certeau (1925–1986): Introduction

Frederick Christian Bauerschmidt

In one of Kafka's parables the narrator tells of mounting a horse and hearing a distant bugle call unheard by others. When a servant asks the narrator where he is going, he replies, "I don't know, . . . only away from here, away from here. Always away from here, only by doing so can I reach my destination." The servant asks the narrator whether he knows his destination and he replies, "Yes, . . . didn't I say so? Away-From-Here, that is my destination." When asked about his lack of provisions, he replies that he needs none, for "the journey is so long that I must die of hunger if I don't get anything on the way. No provisions can save me. For it is, fortunately, a truly immense journey."[1] This parable captures something of the restlessness which moves the work of Michel de Certeau. His writings both explore and embody the "movement of perpetual departure" (*The Mystic Fable*, p. 299) which knows its destination only – and precisely – as Away-From-Here. For it is only Away-From-Here that one encounters the other.

In many ways the work of Certeau displays a sensibility which seems characteristically postmodern: an awareness of the inescapableness of linguistic representation, an overturning of traditional hierarchies of presence and absence, a recognition of the shattering of meta-narratives, and, perhaps above all, a concern with otherness. Yet unlike many postmodern thinkers, Certeau's sensibilities are profoundly marked by Christian faith and tradition, making his thought of particular interest to theologians, even though he himself seems to have come to view theology as one of those provisions which must be left behind on the journey to Away-From-Here.

The movement of Certeau's life reflects that journey. The path of his intellectual itinerary moves through the diverse fields of anthropology, history, philosophy, psychology, sociology, semiotics, and theology. Both a Roman Catholic priest and a founding member of Jacques Lacan's École Freudienne, Certeau wove a web of institutional alliances yet resisted any institutional identification. Born in 1925, he entered the Society of Jesus in 1950, hoping to become a missionary in China. While this desire was never realized, it is emblematic of Certeau's impulse to leave behind any homeland and to move toward that which is unknown and different. After his ordination to the priesthood in 1956, he immersed himself in the study of spirituality in early modern France, establishing himself as an expert in the field. This historical investigation introduced Certeau to an alterity defined not by space – the distant land of China – but by time – our own past which we are compelled to confront as irreducibly other than the present. His painstaking work bore fruit in the 1960s in critical editions of the writings of the seventeenth-century Jesuit Jean-Joseph Surin, and in 1970 in *La Possession de Loudun*, an exploration of a celebrated case of demonic possession in which an entire convent of Ursuline nuns was "diagnosed" in 1632 as being under diabolic attack. In this book, Certeau presents the voices of the possessed in all their disruptive power as an example of an alterity which ruptures the classificatory schemes not only of their exorcists but also of their modern interpreters. *La Possession de Loudun* both brings the first, classically "historical" phase of his intellectual work to a culmination and presages the work that was to follow.

During the late 1960s and the 1970s, Certeau's efforts moved into diverse areas, of which I shall mention three. The first is his critical reflection on historiography. As I have noted, historical work was for Certeau a "heterological" task in which one encountered the past as other. Yet he was also keenly aware that historians did not simply passively apprehend the past as *given*, but were actively engaged in the *writing* of history, the construction of the past of which they spoke. Thus the otherness of the past is constantly in danger of being obscured, because it is inevitably classified and organized according to the interests of the present. At the same time, the past constantly resists the historian's attempt to capture it for the present and insinuates otherness into historical discourse. As Certeau wrote: "Thus founded on the rupture between a past that is its object, and a present that is the place of its practice, history endlessly finds the present in its object and the past in its practice" (*The Writing of History*, p. 36).

The colonization of the past by the present and its simultaneous evasion of the present's grasp is emblematic of a second area of Certeau's work: the analysis of everyday practices. Explicitly in *The Practice of Everyday Life* and implicitly in all his later works, Certeau sought to display the logic of the practices by which those without power evaded and resisted the mechanisms of control within which their lives were situated.[2] He explored the myriad forms of resistance enacted by people in their everyday practices, the often unknowing cleverness with which they *use* the system which seems to control them. His writings employ a variety of distinctions to describe the logic of those practices which resist systemic totalization. Such practices are "tactical" rather than "strategic." They are maneuvers accomplished in the dark, on alien territory, which do not seek to conquer the enemy or take his land, but rather to seize opportunities to cross his borders on poaching missions. Resistant practices must "vigilantly make use of the cracks that particular conjunctions open in the surveillance of the proprietary powers." Operating in the "spaces" (*espaces*) it creates in the interstices of totalizing systems, a tactical maneuver has no "place" (*lieu*) in which to consolidate its gains: "What it wins it cannot keep" (*The Practice of Everyday Life*, p. 37).[3] In their very "weakness," their inability to operate in the same way as a strategic gaze, tactics insinuate alterity into panoptic systems. Whereas the strategic place marked out by totalizing practices ceaselessly seeks to turn everything that is "other" into the "same," the "guileful ruses" of resistant practices create spaces at whose frontiers the other is encountered. As in Kafka's parable, the "immense journey" to the other is one for which we cannot stockpile provisions, whether material or conceptual, but must "poach," living off the land which is not our own.

Certeau's work in the fields of historiography and of everyday practices is well known today, but the third strand of his work in the middle period of his career is less well known: his attempt to grasp the situation of Christianity in modernity and to rethink Christian theology in light of that situation. It is this aspect of his work which is represented by the essay "How is Christianity Thinkable Today?"[4] The essay first takes up themes which are drawn from Certeau's historiographical investigations: Christianity is a relationship to a past event – the event of Jesus Christ – to which it must seek to be *faithful*, while at the same time being irreducibly and unavoidably *different*. Jesus is the *archè* which cannot be objectified in knowledge, but can only be registered in his effects upon the Christian communities which issue from him. As such, he is known precisely as unknown, as the one who "*effaces himself* to give faithful witness to the Father who authorizes him, and to 'give rise' to different but faithful communities which he makes possible." As the *sine qua non* of Christianity, the condition for its possibility, Jesus appears within it only in being disseminated in a multiplicity of interpretations. The second part of the essay expands the dialectic of manifestation and effacement, arguing that the *form* of Jesus' death and resurrection is reproduced with different *content* in every Christian experience. It is what Certeau calls an "*inter*-locution: (something 'said-*between*')" which cannot be identified with any one particular practice, institution, experience or concept, but which haunts the gaps between "a multiplicity of practices and discourses which neither 'preserve' nor repeat the event," yet which "would not exist without it." This "not without"

(Heidegger's *nicht ohne*) expresses the form of Christian experience: "In the organization of the community, no one is a Christian without the others – it is impossible to be a Christian alone."

In this, Christian experience *repeats differently* the experience of Jesus, who is "not without the Father (who speaks in him), nor without the disciples (who will perform other works – and greater than his), though he is different from the Father ('greater than me') and though the disciples cannot be identified with him." The notion of repeating differently is crucial to how Certeau answers the question of how Christianity is thinkable today. Christianity is clearly *not* thinkable today in the *same* way in which it was thinkable in the past; it must always be thought *differently*, yet in such a way that it perpetually repeats the difference of its founding event. Christianity is a practice of alterity: One is faithful to the event of Jesus Christ precisely in accepting the risk of being Christian differently. It is this event which constantly returns in permitting new "spaces" in which Christianity is enacted differently, not only differently from the way in which it was enacted in the past, but in a heterogeneous plurality in the present.

In the third part of the essay, Certeau explores the way in which "[e]very figure of authority in Christian society is stamped by the absence of that which founds it." The event which "authorizes" Christianity and which it is always "not without" implies "an irreducible *plurality of authorities*," none of which can function without the others; "it leaves behind only a multiplicity of signs: an historical network of interconnected places, rather than a hierarchical pyramid." This heterogeneity of Christian authorities can be seen within the canon of Scriptures ("they are a collection of texts which do not say the same thing") as well as in the boundary drawn between the canon itself and subsequent authorities ("[t]he 'closing' of the New Testament makes differences possible and even preserves the necessity of such differences"). Every Christian authority must accept its limitation so as to open itself to the other: "the limit plays a role of differentiation which constantly restores a Christian relationship with the other as necessary but ungraspable." This acceptance of limits applies not just to authorities within Christianity, but to Christianity's authority as a whole. For Certeau, Christians must have a sense of the boundaries of their community not in order to exclude, but to register the alterity of those experiences which are not Christian. He identifies a covert triumphalism in the modern Christian tendency to identify itself with all people of good will, the "anonymous Christians" of whom Karl Rahner spoke. "This poor universalism is a mask; it is a compensation against the fact of the Christian particularity." Christianity must acknowledge its limitations; it must recognize that there are other spaces which open to encounter the other and which Christian discourse cannot position or name.

In the fourth and final section, Certeau stresses that the interlocution of

Christian experience is not primarily a *saying* but a *doing*, by which the boundaries which necessarily delimit Christianity are perpetually transgressed. "A particular place – our present place – is required if there is to be a departure." In terms of Certeau's analysis in *The Practice of Everyday Life*, his claim here seems to be that Christianity has both a strategic place, defined by the boundaries which delimit it, as well as tactical actions which displace it through the praxis of departure. "Boundaries are the place of Christian work, and their displacements are the result of this work." Christianity is both locution (speaking) marking out boundaries and interlocution (action) slipping through the cracks in the walls: "When it comes to an objective, readable, communicable, and understandable Christianity, action articulates the immense silence of Christian experiences, works, and departures with regard to those things that limit and specify such experiences."

Christian action has for Certeau a specific logic, a consistent "formality,"[5] which manifests itself in relation to various "contents." This action is not defined by a binary structure of opposition – either "the one *or* the other" which excludes, or "the one *and* the other" which includes by denying alterity – but by the logic of "neither the one nor the other." This double negation "creates, proportioned to a given term and to its juxtaposed contrary, a third hypothesis but without determining it." It is the logic of a Christianity which is neither without the event of Jesus nor the same as that event. It is the logic of "neither Jewish nor heathen; neither circumcised nor uncircumcised, but spiritually circumcised." It is the logic of the Christian risk, which must be taken precisely out of fidelity to others (Jesus, the community, the unnameable) and without which Christianity can only be "a (perhaps beautiful) museum, a (perhaps glorious) cemetery."

"How is Christianity Thinkable Today?" captures a particular phase in Certeau's thinking in which he sought to articulate a Christianity which was "thinkable" and livable in the context of modernity. This was a project which he abandoned, at least in any obvious sense. In 1971 he had written that "Jesus is the Other. He is the vanished one [le disparu] living ('verified') in his Church."[6] However, two years later he wrote that while a relation to the other remained an essential constituent of the modern self and modern society, "this other is no longer God."[7] Having described Christianity as both a doing *and* a saying, Certeau came to question the possibility of theology speaking a truth which could define an identifiably Christian praxis. He increasingly saw the formality of Christian faith breaking free from its content; practices of departure are no longer tied to a determinable vocabulary of faith, nor to an institutional Christian place.[8] In the face of this abandonment of its institutions and language, Christian faith discovers its own "weakness," as its own practice of alterity is now enacted upon different contents. This "weakness of faith" (*faiblesse de croire*) was reproduced in Certeau's own life, and can be seen in what Luce Giard describes as "a tertiary position between the 'inside' and the 'outside'" of the Christian community which he sought in the last decade of his life.[9] No longer engaged in a project which could be described as "theological" in any traditional sense, Certeau continued to pursue his passion for the other and his reflection on Christian texts in his writing of *The Mystic Fable*. One can see this same passion in the remarkably personal text "White Ecstasy," first published in 1983.[10]

In this essay one can feel quite palpably the tension between the call of Kafka's infinite journey to Away-From-Here ("the millennial march") and the desire for provisions which might save us. The gaze of God, the "universal transparency" which conquers all opacity, the absolute vision which sees *everything*, finally sees *no-thing*, sees no thing in its stubborn particularity. Such a gaze both exhilarates and terrifies, and in the face of it we cling to the "minuscule remains of night" which we futilely hope will shield us. Even the statement "God sees us" cannot protect us, for everything is obliterated, even the subject "God" and the object "us." "Only the act remains, unbound, absolute. It fuses subjects seeing and objects seen into itself." Here we find articulated the formality of otherness, honed to a purity which excises even alterity. Same and other become impossible categories in the "white eschatology" depicted here: *neither* the same, *nor* the other. "That which *is* without us" is not only beyond the name "God," but beyond even the category of "other." And yet . . . an ineradicable alterity insinuates itself again in the spoken response of the visitor from "Panoptie": "I have known this in my country." The monologue of Simeon finds its confirmation in the voice of the other. The universality of the absolute gaze which obliterates particular objects paradoxically can be registered only in the particular other of the visitor whom we encounter, who speaks to us of his own country. As Certeau puts it in another context, it is only "an oceanic rumor of 'me too'" which "changes the private hallucination into a thought of the infinite."[11]

The thought of the infinite born from the sea of voices which murmur "me too" haunts every page of Michel de Certeau's work and forms a fitting "rupture" to mark his departure. Luce Giard says that when she first read "White Ecstasy" she felt "this mystical poem announced the close arrival of the angel of death."[12] And indeed, Certeau fell seriously ill in July of 1985. Despite his illness, he struggled to finish the second volume of *The Mystic Fable*, but when he died on January 9, 1986, it remained unfinished. As such, *The Mystic Fable* is an appropriate testament to a life devoted to ambiguous texts, a provision left behind on the fortunately immense journey to Away-From-Here.

Notes

1 Franz Kafka, "My Destination," in *The Complete Stories and Parables*, ed. Nahum Glatzer (New York: Quality Paperback Book Club, 1983), p. 489.
2 It is instructive to distinguish him from Michel Foucault on this point. See Michel de Certeau, "Micro-techniques and Panoptic Discourse: A Quid pro Quo," in *Heterologies: Discourse on the Other*, pp. 185–92.
3 On the distinction between *espace* and *lieu*, see *The Practice of Everyday Life*, pp. 115–30.
4 The essay was originally a lecture given in the United States at St Louis University on May 16, 1971, and appeared in *Theology Digest*, 19 (1971), pp. 334–45. It is in large part based on the second half of his essay "La Rupture instauratrice" ("The Inaugurating Rupture"), originally published in *Esprit* (June 1971) and reprinted in *La Faiblesse de croire*.
5 Certeau speaks of the "formality of practices" by which he means operations which remain consistent, though they may be carried out with respect to varying contents. See *The Writing of History*, pp. 147–205.
6 "La Rupture instauratrice," in *La Faiblesse de croire*, p. 225.
7 "Lieux de transit," *Esprit* (February 1973), reprinted in *La Faiblesse de croire*, p. 244.
8 See "La Faiblesse de croire," *Esprit* (April–May 1977), reprinted in edited form in *La Faiblesse de croire*, pp. 307–14.
9 Luce Giard, "Cherchant Dieu," introduction to *La Faiblesse de croire*, p. iv. As Giard makes clear, to describe Certeau as a "former Jesuit" is far too simple.
10 Certeau was known for his personal reticence and Giard notes that he hesitated to publish this essay ("Cherchant Dieu," p. xix).
11 "The Gaze: Nicholas of Cusa," p. 34. This essay illumines many aspects of "White Ecstasy."
12 "Cherchant Dieu," p. xix.

Selected Bibliography

For an almost complete bibliography up to 1988, see Luce Giard, "Bibliographie complète de Michel de Certeau," *Recherches de Science Religieuse*, 76/3 (1988), pp. 405–57.

Ahearne, Jeremy, *Michel de Certeau: Interpretation and its Other* (Oxford: Polity Press, 1995).
Bauerschmidt, F. C., "The Abrahamic Voyage: Michel de Certeau and Theology," *Modern Theology*, 12/1 (1996), pp. 1–26.
—— "Walking in the Pilgrim City," *New Blackfriars*, 77 (1996), pp. 504–18.
Certeau, Michel de, "Is There a Language of Unity?" trans. Lancelot Sheppard, *Concilium*, 51 (1970), pp. 79–93.
—— *The Practice of Everyday Life*, trans. Steven Rendall (Berkeley: University of California Press, 1984).
—— *The Writing of History*, trans. Tom Conley (New York: Columbia University Press, 1988).

—— *Heterologies: Discourse on the Other*, trans. Brian Massumi (Minneapolis: University of Minnesota Press, and Manchester: Manchester University Press, 1986).

—— *The Mystic Fable*. Vol. 1: *The Sixteenth and Seventeenth Centuries*, trans. Michael B. Smith (Chicago: University of Chicago Press, 1992).

—— *La Faiblesse de croire*, ed. Luce Giard (Paris: Seuil, 1987).

—— "The Gaze: Nicholas of Cusa," trans. Catherine Porter. *Diacritics* (Fall, 1987), pp. 2–38.

Frow John, "Michel de Certeau and the Practice of Representation," *Cultural Studies*, 5/1 (1991), pp. 52–60.

Giard, Luce, "Epilogue: Michel de Certeau's Heterology and the New World," trans. Katherine Streip. *Representations*, 33 (1991), pp. 212–21.

Moingt, Joseph, "L'ailleurs de la théologie," *Recherches de Science Religieuse*, 76/3 (1988), pp. 365–80.

Ward, Graham (ed.), *Michel de Certeau, S. J.* Special issue of *New Blackfriars*, 77 no. 909 (1996).

How is Christianity Thinkable Today?

I propose to stress how the Christian experience *works*, or rather to stress its own peculiar *operation* and some structural features which characterize its process. It is a means of stating a little more precisely how Christianity is thinkable in our *epistemological situation*. If, however, this statement should fail to win the recognition of other Christians, then my work will be simply the record of an individual search. Only by recognition can a particular investigation be changed into a Christian testimony.

It is possible to distinguish within Christianity four aspects, which will be the four parts of this presentation.

1. Christianity and History: The Event as "Permission"

However it is taken, Christianity implies a *relationship to the event* which inaugurated it: Jesus Christ. It has had a series of intellectual and historical social forms which have had two apparently contradictory characteristics: the will to be *faithful* to the inaugural event: the necessity of being *different* from these beginnings.

This contradiction calls "permission" into question. The experience and reality of "permission" can today regain its epistemological and historical importance.

(a) *A simple experience.* "Permission" refers initially to simple experiences. Thus, when he comes out of the theater after seeing Jacques Tati's *Play-Time*, a comic movie on modern life, the viewer notices humor in the streets as if he now had Tati's gift of seeing. The seeing of the film has *made this possible.* The reading of a poem, a meeting with a person, or the movement of a group can produce similar changes. If the register of our perception or understanding is modified, it is because the event in question *makes possible* or in a very real sense *permits* another type of relationship to the world.

(b) *The history of science.* The history of science exemplifies this problem and possibility in certain "authors" (bringing about or "permitting" new beginnings in the sciences) or in certain "epistemological breaks," as G. Bachelard has pointed out. This is the case, for example, with Sigmund Freud or Karl Marx.

Freud made possible a new theoretical and practical method of analysis. This remains undeniable even though the effort to determine his thought exactly has given rise to a variety of interpretations, and even though it is difficult – or, rather, impossible – to fix his "truth" in one or other of these or in an objective knowledge of his work. For example, should that part of his writings which concerns culture be judged secondary or irrelevant in regard to a psychoanalysis of individual relationships? Or again, in the genesis of the ego, as Freud explains it, what should be seen as central or as most important – a differentiation of psychic energy or a dialectic of representation and identification? There are divergent views on this among psychoanalytic groups.

The fact is that Freud cannot be reduced to an object of knowledge. The Freud-event escapes all "objective" definition. It is disseminated in a multiplicity of interpretations. It cannot be grasped as an object, but this is precisely because it "permits" all these interpretations. With reference to them, Freud is not only that which is *known* by specialists, but that which *makes possible* different ways of knowing after him. He is an "author," then, for he *authorizes* a series of investigations which, however, are not identifiable with his own. The "return to Freud" is the index of a development which creates differences, while specifying the possibilities opened by this epistemological break. Such a break opens new and different possibilities.

(c) *Jesus: The event as permission.* This conception of permission (compare the German word *lassen*) clarifies the relationship that links the successive and different forms of Christianity to an inaugural event. Here there is no longer a matter of aesthetic perceptions or scientific practices, but a question which radically concerns the reference of our existence to its irreducible "other". All the elaborations which are made by Christians in response to this question *presuppose* the Jesus Christ event. Those elaborations are historically specified in being *permitted* by this beginning; but none is identical with it. Whatever types of transmission or of reading of the "origins" exist, they never repeat the Gospel, but they would be impossible without the Gospel.

A universal and objective representation, therefore, cannot be given of this beginning in the past. Insofar as it is inaugural, an event cannot be grasped in objective knowledge. It is historical indeed. But for us, in our knowledge, it is not an objective fact.

Evidently, the life, words, death, and resurrection of Jesus left traces in the organization of the early Christian communities or writings. But the map of these traces is not a "proof" nor the "truth," but only an effect. It is, in present historiography and in accord with our contemporary conception of historical research, one more trace of the relationship which from the beginning believers have fashioned when what they heard and learned *became* for them an *event* by "opening their hearts" to new possibilities. And the writings of those believers express not the event itself, but that which the event made possible in the first believers.

(d) *Relationship to the absence of the past.* The early documents of the Christ event give us in writing only the reverse side of what is essential. They all speak of an event which they efface by substituting *different* consequences for it. But they *manifest* the nature of this event by virtue of the fact that they refer to it as that which "permits" new possibilities.

The event is "historical" not because of its preservation outside time owing to a knowledge of it that supposedly has remained intact, but because of its introduction into time with various discoveries about it for which it "makes room."

The successive creations of faith relate to new situations. They also specify, in proportion to the distance traveled from the origins, on the one hand the *meaning* of the initial "break" (a meaning expressed in other languages than the first ones), and on the other hand the *rules* of a fidelity that is defined in terms of compatibility and incompatibility. (This fidelity is not a repetition or an objective survival of a past.) Each explication postulates the reference to a past event which makes other expressions possible.

Christian belief is never in any way to be identified with the sum total, with a theoretical corollary, or with a practical conclusion, of the work done during the time that has elapsed since the start of such belief. Of course, it leaves each time the *objective trace* of a "fidelity." But this fidelity itself is not of an objective kind. It is linked with *the absence of the object* or of the particular past which inaugurated it. The past is not our security.

Besides, the first statement of this fidelity (possible only after the disappearance of Jesus) is the Scripture, supposing as its own condition, the death of the "Son of man." The Christian language begins with the disappearance of its "author." That is to say that Jesus *effaces himself* to give faithful witness to the Father who authorizes him, and to "give rise" to different but faithful communities, which he makes possible. There is a close bond between the absence of Jesus (dead and not present) and the birth of the Christian language (objective and faithful testimony of his survival).

2. The Spiritual Experience: Opening of a New Dimension

(a) *Disappearance and manifestation.* The "truth" of the beginning of an event is revealed only through new possibilities which it opens. That truth is both *shown* by the differences in relation to the initial event and *hidden* by new elaborations (differing from the first evangelical testimony). In this respect, this "truth" appears as alienated in what it permits, because in himself God remains always other than what he permits. The Jesus event is irreducible to a particular knowledge or experience. It is the *condition* and not the object of the operations which flow from it. Thus the event is lost precisely in what it authorizes. It somehow dies to its own historical specificity, but this happens in the very discoveries which it provokes.

The process of the death (the absence) and the survival (the presence) of Jesus continues in each Christian experience: What the event makes possible is different each time, as a new remoteness from the event and a new way of erasing it.

There is a relation of kenosis to glory, of disappearance to manifestation. It is not simply according to an order of succession, for there is a necessary articulation of one with the other: "It was necessary that he die."

The empty tomb is the condition of possibility for a spiritual knowledge, i.e., for a "verification" which expresses itself and extends into the era of the word and the Spirit. Each Christian language refers to the same event, but does not give us what disappeared to make it possible.

Thus, the initial event becomes an *inter-locution*: something *said-between*, implied by all the Christian languages but given by no one of them. Not that it is untouchable and taboo. But the founder disappears; he is impossible to grasp and "hold," to the extent that he is incorporated and takes on meaning in a plurality of "Christian" experiences, operations, discoveries, and inventions. Just as the fire before Moses was a manifestation destroying all the particular religious representations, so the Christian manifestation suppresses the possibility of identifying Jesus with an object, a knowledge, an experience. This manifestation is no more than a multiplicity of practices and discourses which neither "preserve" nor repeat the event.

The Christian event is thus an *inter*-locution (something "said-*between*") insofar as it is neither said nor given anywhere in particular, except in the form of those interrelations constituted by the network of expressions which would not exist without it.

(b) *"Not without him."* With this last expression – "not without" – we have the most modest, and also the most rigorous, formulation of the relation between the plurality of Christian languages and "the inter-locution" which they designate. It is, if you will, the negative side of a truth objectively announced in the manner of an absence. We may ascertain: "You are no longer (or not yet) *there*." But to this enunciation of a fact corresponds the enunciation proper to the faith: "Not without you" – or, according to the liturgical formula: "Let me never be separated from you."

Analogously, the lover cannot reduce the other to an object of knowledge or possession. However, he cannot tolerate being separated from the other. He says: "I miss you."

The category of "not without" was suggested by Heidegger. It enters in a hundred ways into the functioning of the Christian experience:

- In the organization of the community no one is Christian without the others – it is impossible to be a Christian alone. And no community could call itself Christian without being thus "authorized" by a necessary relation to the differences of past, present, or future and to other groups as other (coexisting societies, different cultures, and so forth).
- Likewise, in the Gospels, Jesus is not without the Father (who speaks in him), nor without the disciples (who will perform other works – and greater than his), though he is different from the Father ("greater than me") and though the disciples cannot be identified with him.

Thus, through community practice and Trinitarian theology, the death of Jesus becomes the condition for the new Church to arise and for new languages of the Gospel to develop. The true relation of Jesus to the Father (who gives him his authority) and to the Church (which he "permits") is verified (i.e., manifested) by his death. The Jesus event is extended (verified) in the manner of a disappearance in the *differences* which that event renders possible. Our relation to the origin is in the function of its increasing absence.

The beginning is more and more hidden by the multiple creations which reveal its significance.

(c) *Manifestation and multiplicity*. Through all its history, the relation of the beginning of the Jesus event to its verification has no other form but a plural one. The structure of the manifestation is pluralist, in its Scriptural form just as in the form of the community.

Indeed, there is the disappearance of an "idol" which would freeze our view and give us the truth in a singularity. There is a fading away of any "primitive" object capable of being delimited by a knowledge and possessed as in an ownership. There is a *loss* of anything "essential" immediately given in the image or in the voice. On the contrary, *the "kenosis" of presence gives rise to a plural, communitarian language*. A series of places, works, or historical formations which the absence of Jesus has made possible are the only traces of the incarnate God, and may leave free, within the present, a different place for the inventions which we risk.

"Verification" is not given by an objective proof or by the reference to a singular guarantee, today any more than yesterday. It is that which Christianity (through different ways of discovering it) makes possible within us and between us. It is a new dimension or "spaces" open to our enunciation and practice: an unveiling which relates to our situation; a discovering which opens a future; an experience made possible by an event, but never identical with a past, with a doctrine, or with a law.

You might even speak of a syntax of these "spaces," since they are joined together among themselves. But this interconnection cannot be identified in terms of a common culture, or an ideological or practical element which would define these "spaces." Nor is it a question of relating it to a homogeneous and linear development, as if a new step was a consequence of a former one. This interconnection is due to the relation – which organizes them all – between a singularity which gradually disappears insofar as it "permits" these spaces open to our enunciation and practice, and their very multiplicity which reveals its meaning in the act of becoming differentiated.

Christianity is still capable of opening a new space; it can make possible a change in the practice of speaking and in the relation of a speaker to others and to his social language; it "permits" today a faith as the discovering of a living necessity (linked to the disappearance of an objective security because this truth has the form of a creative, risked freedom); "it works" creating always other figures of the same movement. All these aspects are ultimately its real "verification," whatever may be the manner or the place.

3. The Community Structure: Authority in the Plural

Every figure of authority in Christian society is stamped by the absence of that which founds it. Whether it is a question of Scripture, or tradition, or councils, the pope, or anything else among the Christian "authorities," that which "permits" them is missing. Each authority reveals what it is not, because it refers to God as he is historically manifested in Jesus.

Thus it is impossible for any one to be the whole, the "central," or the unique authority. Only an irreducible *plurality of authorities* can indicate the relation which exists among them and what each one postulates as "Christian." Considered precisely as authority, neither the pope, nor Scripture, nor any particular tradition is sufficient to itself. The others are not part of it; as different, they are necessary to it. A necessary relation of each one to others establishes and signifies its relation to the other (God) who authorizes it. The plural is the manifestation of the Christian meaning.

(a) *Communitarian structure.* Christian language has (and must have) a communitarian structure. This connection of witnesses, of signs or different roles announces a "truth" which cannot be reduced to unity by one member, or by a particular function.

Because this "truth" belongs to no one individual or group (even theological), it is proclaimed by several. Because this truth is the ungraspable condition of that which it makes possible, it leaves behind only a multiplicity of signs: a historical network of interconnected places, rather than a hierarchical pyramid.

The first writings after the death and disappearance of Jesus already present the peculiarity of being what Kasemann called a "connection of opposites," *complexio oppositorum.* They are a collection of texts which do not say the same thing. The Gospel of Mark cannot be reduced to that of John any more than to the Epistles of Jude or Paul. Non-identity is characteristic of the language of the New Testament. No one of these differences can be excluded in the name of a privilege granted to any one among them. Paul would not be more "Christian" without Jude or Peter, who are so different from him and in certain respects his opposite.

This network of texts, which is interconnected but not unified, thus obeys another kind of coherence than that found in philosophical discourse. It does not reduce the many to the one. On the contrary, the plural is maintained. Differences permit the other. They are the condition of a future and of a historical manifestation. The plural indicates the "Christian" relation with regard to which each apostolic text offers a distinct treatment by speaking in its own way of the faith in the dead and risen Jesus.

(b) *The limit, a permissive function.* By his death, Jesus "made room" for the Christian communities and for the Church as different. That is the law of the Christian development.

If the corpus of the testament is closed (i.e., limited), it is because it has to allow, *outside* of itself and *after* itself, *other* compilations: patristic, liturgical, theological, and so forth, which will become multiple and often more and more different. The "closing" of the New Testament makes differences possible and even preserves the necessity of such differences. The corpus of Scripture would not be Christian without this reference back to others. To recognize its limits is to recognize the necessity of other testimonies.

The limit has a permissive function. In every synchronic space (between contemporary communities, languages, theologies, and so forth) and in diachronic development (between successive generations, periods, and ages of Christianity), the limit plays a role of differentiation which constantly restores a Christian relationship with the other as necessary but ungraspable. By recognizing its limits and its proper task, each collective or individual testimony or authority manifests that it is *not* possible to be Christian *without* the other – in the form of faith (relationship with God) or charity (relationship with men). Like Jesus, it must "make room" for others.

(c) *The temptation of uniformity.* Thus it is not permitted to reduce everything to one element. Those who have tried have simply brought about a reduction to something else. Some tried to reduce Christianity to the *sola Scriptura*: others, in opposition, identified it with the pronouncements of an individual (the pope) or limited it to an institutional body (as did the Catholic traditionalists) or to a body of doctrine (as does fundamentalism). These are all variations of the same structure: *identification*. None of them is compatible with the structure of *limit*. In this structure, each one of the above-mentioned authorities is necessary but Christianity cannot be identified with any one of them alone. Every confession of faith is regulated socially, theoretically, and practically by the limit. The limit is the ultimate law of *death* (the irreducible existence of the other is manifested in the experience of one's own limit and death), of *solidarity* (each one is needed by the others), and of *meaning* (which cannot be identified with an individual presence or with knowledge or an objective property because it is given by the very relationships of faith and charity as an inter-locution).

The death of Jesus, the development of the Church, the Spirit of the risen

Jesus within the relationships of charity designate these three aspects of the same law.

Authorities as well as communities must be organized by this interconnection. This law defines the community by differentiating the members who are necessary to one another but never reducible to one another. It establishes each community in a necessary relation with the others.

(d) *A Christianity recognizing its limits*. Even more, a clear separation of groups or properly "Christian" ways of speaking is the means of avowing what they do not have, what they miss, and by this very fact, of confessing the necessity of the others and the meaning of the Christian faith.

Of course, it is understandable that communities tend to take refuge in the indifferentiation of "dialogue" or syncretism. The revelation of their differences would bind them to their limits. Every group wants to constitute itself as the whole because it refuses, with its limits, any articulation with others. It would want to be all. Today a Christian group protects itself often by hiding its particularity, by speaking as the testimony of all good wills, by identifying itself with positions held in common, by announcing only the insignificant truths of every man. This poor universalism is a mask; it is a compensation against the fact of the Christian particularity.

Whenever it is a question of faith or of God, every Christian, every community, and Christianity as a whole is called on to be the *sign of that which is lacking*. This "lack" is not some wide region to conquer or to be filled in. It is a *limit* by means of which every witness publicly confesses his relation with the "author" of the faith and with the others (believers or non-believers). This is so because, since Jesus, an internal law links his death to the necessity of making room for others. It expresses an essential covenant of Christianity with the unforeseeable or unknown spaces which God opens elsewhere and in other ways.

The important thing is not to speak about the death of God, but to accept the limits of Christianity and the death of universalism as a way of recognizing our bond with the others and, through them, with God. "God is greater than we." The problem is less the death of God than the death of our ideological reassurance of our missionary totalism.

(e) *To make room for others*. Recognizing our limits articulates Christian language – social, liturgical, theoretical, etc. It posits the meaning of Christianity as a *necessary relation to the necessarily different*. It is referred to the act which made the Gospels possible and which they recount, the death of Jesus. For Jesus to die, is to "make room" for the Father and at the same time "make room" for the polyglot and creative community of Pentecost, for the plurality of the Scriptures, for the multiplicity of the future Christian generations.

The gesture of making room for the multiplicity of Christian languages in relation to the invisibility of the Spirit inaugurates a structure of communication where a plurality of members (or of authorities) is the only revelation of spiritual meaning.

With this gesture begins a history in which, each time, to *"permit" means to "disappear"* and, at last, to die. Whether it be in a personal itinerary, pedagogical transmission, educational task or social organization, the mark of spiritual truth is henceforward the effective relation between the fading away of a singularity and that which it makes possible. It is to say that a spiritual authority may be recognized according to the nature of its relationships with other such authorities in a plurality of authorities.

4. To Step Forward: The Risk of Doing

(a) *The risk of being different.* The Christian movement is always the recognizing of a particular situation and the necessity of a new step forward. There is always a necessary risk in being different. It requires simultaneously a place and a "further," a "now" and an "afterwards," a "here" and an "elsewhere." Thus in the Gospel, it is to this category that belongs the relationship, established by his death, between Jesus living and Jesus resurrected. He had to be "here" in order that it might be possible for him to be "not here" but "elsewhere"; he had to be present so that his disappearance might become the sign of a different future (Matthew 28: 1–8).

Within the Christian experience, the boundary or limit is a place for the action which ensures the step from a particular situation to a progress (opening a future and creating a new past), from a being "there" to a being "elsewhere," from one stage to another. Our situation is that of working on the present social and intellectual frontiers. A particular place – our present place – is required if there is to be a departure. Both elements, the place and the departure, are interrelated, because it is the withdrawal from a place that allows one to recognize the enclosure implicit in the initial position, and as a result it is this limited field which makes possible a further investigation. Boundaries are the place of the Christian work, and their displacements are the result of this work.

In order to pass from one place to another, something must be *done* (not only *said*) that affects the boundary: namely, *praxis*. It is this action which transcends, whereas speeches and institutions circumscribe each place successively occupied. Praxis is linked to the particular circumstances of an act, but insofar as the critical step makes them out-of-date, those circumstances are things of the past.

(b) *Praxis and speech.* In relation to speech, therefore, praxis is *silence*: It belongs to a different order from the institutionalized or theological statements from which it starts, and which it may condition. It is impossible to contain praxis within such statements as their content or object. Praxis is not a "thing" that can be "expressed" in a "formula."

It would be a mistake to think that the necessary relationship between speech and practice must involve a verbal formulation which will be a description or an analysis, of the experience. Any account of analysis of a particular praxis must be "unfaithful" to that action simply because it speaks of it. Moreover, often the more a thing can be said, the less it can be done. At least, the relation of saying to doing is not the relation of container to contained, or of formulation to experience. It is the breaking–down into different elements. The out-going implied by *doing* is related to the defining or limiting of positions required by *saying*, just as departure is related to place though neither can be reduced to the other.

(c) *Primary function of action.* Within the Gospels, there is a close connection between decision and truth: "He who *does* the truth will come to the light." His actions are the way of knowing (John 3: 21). A "conversion" is a condition of possibility for the faith.

Doing is not the "application" of a doctrine and its putting into practice, or its justification. Even less is it an object determined and already depicted by a particular language. It is not a consequence of a knowledge, but a beginning and a risk.

Moreover the history of religions has gradually shown, as it has become more and more sensitive to the contribution of sociology, that the practice of Christians has always been, and remains today, something other than official laws and theological teaching. Is this anything to cause scandal? Let us leave this scandal to a certain elite or to certain clergymen who are inclined to identify truth with what they say, or who believe that ideas alone guide history. As a matter of fact, praxis always brings about, in relation to what is present and pointed out, gradual or abrupt displacements which will make possible other laws or other theologies. In itself, action is a permanent divergence, but a divergence with a relation to an institution which is the reference point of new movements and which will then be changed by such movements.

On the other hand, language is not just the simple "reflection" of what is done. It follows rules of organization which, for example, one can set forth in a series of dogmatic or exegetical treatises. Language keeps the necessary role of specifying, criticizing, and elucidating the Christian initiative. But without practice, language would not be what it is. It would be the indefinite repetition of the same thing. The new level from which language directs the implications of practice results in a critical divergence from former levels.

Hence there results a connection between the differing functions of praxis and language. This connection is a coordination between necessary grounding points (languages, theories, institutions) and critical divergences (inventions, "prophetic" actions, or displacements hidden within each Christian experience). But both of these functions are equally necessary.

Here we have a new form of the *complexio oppositorum*. It does not deal any more only with the connection between different languages of faith, but with the relation of saying and doing.

When it comes to an objective, readable, communicable, and understandable Christianity, action articulates the immense silence of Christian experiences, works, and departures with regard to those things that limit and specify such experiences. The practice of Christianity has often not stopped to put such experiences (prophets, new missions, social movements, political protests) into proportion with the limiting factors of institutions or theologies. The multiform operation of practical steps which are taken is brought to light when we see how such steps sometimes diverge from orders and instructions already received and in force. Seeing this divergence then "makes room" for yet further elaborations of praxis and teaching. Irreducible directly to language, yet finding its meaning in language and providing yet new levels of meaning to language, this praxis, formed by separation from and transcending language, is fundamentally a necessary and permanent conversion.

(d) *The conversion of the Old Testament into the New Testament: a "model."* That this conversion takes place today in the data of the sacred, or in political life, or in the arena of a profession, or in the field of a science, is of little importance. It cannot be isolated into any one of these sectors, and it ought to be suited to the actual and current grounding points, the languages, theories, and institutions, of the particular culture. The determination of these important and relevant grounding points will depend on vitality and lucidity; Christians take as much a risk here as do others. But whatever might be its form, Christian praxis holds on equally to the effectiveness of a realistic determination of just where we are and the necessity of stepping forward from that position.

By that double movement alone it conforms to the way in which the entire Christian faith is articulate in the conversion of the Old Testament into the New Testament. The praxis of Jesus (which has its fulfillment in the silence of his death) is the point of articulation between these two languages of Old and New Testament. It is, between the two halves of the Bible, the opening up of an *action*. What is that? Jesus does not cease to hold to the uniqueness of the Jewish institution, while he creates the beginning of another meaning for it. His act is a "distance" with respect to the old law; it brings about a displacement which gives birth to a new law. A new practice of the "letter" of the old law opens up that letter to a spirit from which another scripture (another "letter") is now set forth.

Globally, this New Testament Scripture does not mean a replacing of the former truth by a new one. Jesus does not replace one religion by another. It is always the same religion. But a new practice changes the nature of the relationships of that religion with its institutions, laws, or texts. This type of conversion inaugurated by the act of Jesus is to be continued indefinitely, to be reproduced, with respect to the same (Jewish) institutions or to others. The essential here is not a new content, new institutions, or new Scriptures, but the conversion of relationships with respect to each institution.

(e) *A logic of action.* The Gospels, the first apostolic texts, point up this movement of transcendence even by the very organization of their story. In this way they indicate the process of a Christian action or conversion.

The confrontation or the dialogues which constitute their framework are not governed by a binary structure. They do not set up in exact opposition to each other one position (which is good) against another (which is bad or annulled). Using present-day categories, we might describe their logic thus:

— It is not the logic of "the one *or* the other." (This kind of structure situates the "truth" as one of two contrary terms: for example, either circumcised or uncircumcised; either Jew or Greek; either Jewish or heathen; either clean or unclean; and so forth.)
— It is not the logic of "the one *and* the other." (This "logic" pretends to overcome the differences, to give a synthesizing statement, to reconcile all the former positions within a new and particular truth.)
— It is the logic of "neither the one nor the other." (For example: neither Jewish nor heathen; neither circumcised nor uncircumcised, but spiritually circumcised; neither clean nor unclean, but pure in heart; neither the tradition of the Pharisees nor the power of Pilate, but the reference to another kind of "truth"; and so forth.) This dialogue is a movement. It creates, proportioned to a given term and to its juxtaposed contrary, a third hypothesis but without determining it. It opens a future but without fixing that future. It "permits" a spiritual action, but without identifying it with an objective statement, institution, or law. It makes necessary a risk, a conversion, a doing which cannot be a priori specified or said within a text. It makes room for a decision which will be the unforeseeable decision of the Christian reader of these Scriptures.

This kind of spiritual displacement by an action will always be necessary.

It is the condition of possibility of a Christian language, i.e., of an actual, contemporary production proportioned to the living experiences, the risks undertaken, and the real communications among believers. Otherwise, the Christian language would be only the consequence of a past – a (perhaps beautiful) museum, a (perhaps glorious) cemetery. "Leave the dead to bury their own dead; you must go . . ." (Luke 9: 60).

No life without risk

The Christian faith has no security other than the *living* God discovered by communities which are alive and which undergo the experience of *losing* objective securities. In the last analysis, Christianity is thinkable only if it is alive. And there is no life without new risks in our actual situation. The death of Jesus and his resurrection within a multiplicity of Christian languages made and continues to make a faithful freedom *possible*. But only new departures manifest and will continue to manifest Christianity as still *alive*. That is the first question: no longer to know whether God exists, but to *exist* as Christian communities. It is impossible to be Christian without a common risk, without the creation of a new divergence in relation to our past and to our present, without being alive.

White Ecstasy

How can I explain? says Simeon the monk to his visitor, who had come from Panoptie (Simeon could not have said where this distant land was; he knew only his mountains). How to describe the exorbitant goal of the millennial march – many times millennial – of travelers who have set out to see God? I am old and I still do not know. Yet our authors talk a lot about it. They tell of marvels that will perhaps seem to you more disturbing than illuminating. According to what they write – I am relating what they themselves have received, so they say, from an ancient tradition that goes back to who knows who – the vision coincides with the disappearance of things seen. They separate what appears to us to be one and the same: the act of seeing and the things that one sees. They claim that the more vision there is, the less there are of things seen; that the one grows to the degree that the other is effaced. *We* suppose that sight improves as objects are conquered. For them, it is perfected in their loss. To see God is, in the end, to see *nothing*; it is to see nothing in particular; it is to participate in a universal visibility that no longer is comprised of the cutting out of the individual, multiple, fragmentary, and mobile scenes which make up our perceptions.

Perhaps you think that the paradox that opposes "seeing" and objects seen has an air of trickery about it, and that better vision must in fact necessarily diminish the number of things one does not see. For these authors this makes no difference, because objects are only perceived in distinction from what is invisible. Suppress what you do not see and you suppress what you see as well. Then a great dazzling blindness is created: the extinction of things seen.

Seeing is devouring. The things we see are less the emblems of its victories than the limits of its expansion. They protect us, like a skiff whose fragile sides prevent – but for how long? – its oceanic inundation. Painters know the danger. They play with this fire. You must know artists where you come from who draw a luminous line around certain opaque objects, in the same way that the whiteness of a wave limits the solar omnipotence of the sea at the shore. There are those who combat clarity by throwing down shadows. Yet among painters there are also captives of the passion of seeing; they hand things over to light and lose them there, shipwrecked in visibility. Ultimately, we are all painters, even if we do not construct theaters where this struggle between seeing and things unfolds. Some resist this voracious fascination; others yield to it only for a moment, seized by a vision that no longer knows what it perceives; many hasten – unconsciously? – toward the ecstasy that will be the end of their world.

You seem surprised. It is true, it is terrible to see. Scripture says that one cannot see God without dying. No doubt it means by this that seeing presupposes the annihilation of all things seen. Should I confess to you that I am myself stricken with fear? With age, with the pettiness that old age learns, I become more and more attached to secrets, to stubborn details, to spots of shadow that protect things, and ourselves, from universal transparency. I cling to these minuscule remains of night. The very miseries that old age multiplies become precious because they slow the course of light. I do not speak of pain, because it belongs to no one. It clarifies too much. Suffering dazzles. It is already seeing, just as there are no visionaries but those stripped of self and of things by fascination with the misfortunes that occur. No, I speak of odd intimacies: there in the belly, here in the head, trembling, twitching, deformity, the brute brusqueness of a body unknown to others. Who would dare to surrender them? Who would take them from us? They preserve us from strange retreats. They are our scraps of history, of secret rites, of ruses, and of habits with shadows lurking in the hidden places of the body. But you are too young to know the ways of these clandestine times.

Let us return to our authors. They do not mince words. They say they know what it is about: It is a leveling of history, a white eschatology that suppresses and "confuses" all secrets. To the initial "tohu-bohu" that preceded all distinction, according to the first chapter of Genesis, they seem to contrast an ultimate obliteration of all things in the "universal and confused" light of vision. To refer to this they mostly use the verb "to see," which names an agent that is always operative. For example, they say: God is Seeing. Hence their way of expressing themselves, which is a little strange to us. As they explain it, the subject and the object of this verb are unstable; they pivot around the verb. We can say, "we see God" or "God sees us." It comes to the same thing. The subject and the object can replace each other, interchangeable and unstable, inhaled by a domineering verb. Who sees? Who is seen? We no longer know. The act alone remains, unbounded, absolute. It fuses subjects seeing and objects seen into itself. How could it be otherwise? The difference between seeing and seen no longer holds if no secret distances seeing from what it sees, if no obscurity serves seeing as a refuge from which to constitute a scene before it, if there is no longer a night from which a representation is detached.

Here is what the final bedazzlement would be: an absorption of objects and subjects in the act of seeing. No violence, only the unfolding of presence. Neither fold nor hole. Nothing hidden and thus nothing visible. A light without limits, without difference; neuter, in a sense, and continuous. It is only possible to speak of it in relation to our cherished activities, which are utterly annihilated there. There is no more reading where signs no longer are removed from and deprived of what they indicate. There is no more interpretation if no secret sustains and summons it. There are no more words if no absence founds the waiting that they articulate. Our works are gently engulfed in this silent ecstasy. Without disaster and without noise, simply having become futile, our world – the immense apparatus born of our obscurities – ends.

It is understandable that fear is mingled with fascination for the walkers gone in quest of vision. What foreboding hastens them toward clarity? I am of two minds and cannot really say. Sometimes I have terrible thoughts. I imagine that these pilgrims are searching for something they are certain not to find. And then, *voilà*: one fine day, one blinding day, it happens. If they escape, from that moment on they bear this dazzling death, speechless from having seen without knowing it. Other times I let myself be caught in the desire to see – like everyone, I suppose. I forget the warnings of our authors, for when all is said and done, in writing of this sublime and terrible thing, they protect themselves and they put us on our guard. Thus the inveigling of that which *is* without us creeps in, the whiteness that is beyond all division, the ecstasy that kills consciousness and extinguishes all spectacles, an illuminated death – a "fortunate shipwreck," as the Ancients said.

I have known this in my country, said the visitor at last. The experience you speak of is commonplace there. Everything there is already overcome by clarity. I traveled hoping to find a place, a temple, a hermitage, to house vision. Then my country would immediately be transformed into a land of secrets, simply by being distanced from manifestation. But your misgivings send me back to my shadowless plain. There is no other end of the world.

Translated by Frederick Christian Bauerschmidt and Catriona Hanley

Jacques Derrida (b. 1930): Introduction

Kevin Hart

Jacques Derrida was born in 1930, in El-Biar, just outside Algiers. His philosophical studies began in *lycées* in Algiers and Paris, and were continued at the École Normale Supérieure where he later served as Maître-assistant until 1984. Since then he has been Directeur d'Études at the École des Hautes Études en Sciences Sociales. Although he spends most of the year in Paris, Derrida is a regular visitor to other European cities and far beyond. In particular, since the 1970s, he has frequently taught at universities in the United States, where his work has been rapidly translated and intensely discussed. In the English-speaking world, the king wave of his influence was in literary studies, while later waves of influence have passed through architecture and law, as well as the humanities.

As a *lycée* student, Derrida was introduced to the writings of Maurice Merleau-Ponty and Jean-Paul Sartre. Yet it was the more severe phenomenology of their master, Edmund Husserl, that attracted the young philosopher. He found there both a "discipline of incomparable rigour" and an "un-thought-out axiomatics."[1] And it was by a painstaking identification of gaps in Husserl's reasonings and an inventive filling of them that Derrida began to form styles of reading and writing that would distance him from philosophy as traditionally understood. These styles were complicated, from the very beginning, by critical relations with other practices and theories. In his first maturity, during the early to mid-1960s, Derrida followed the structuralists in focusing on the linguistic sign. A study of Husserl's theory of signs helped him to clarify what had remained unthought in phenomenology. At no time was Derrida a structuralist, however. On the contrary, he showed that theories of the sign, including

Husserl's, covertly rely on a "metaphysics of presence" and that this metaphysics can be shown to founder when the concept "sign" is carefully exfoliated. It was Martin Heidegger who first drew attention to this metaphysics, and although Derrida has learned from other thinkers – the genetic critiques of Freud and Nietzsche, on the one hand, and the writings of Blanchot, Celan, Joyce, and Ponge, on the other – his richest, most enduring, and most tense dialogue has been with Heidegger. "Deconstruction," which has come to name Derrida's styles, translates *Destruktion*, one of the words Heidegger used to indicate the task of loosening up the Western philosophical tradition in order to expose how being has been variously determined as presence.

Derrida agrees with Heidegger that at root there is only *one* metaphysics and that it shapes all Western thought. So, while there are many philosophies, they all share a deep assumption that, more often than not, must be uncovered by a close reading of specific texts. It is this: Something *is* if and only if it is present or presentable. In the last analysis, objects are construed as present beings, while consciousness is regarded as self-presence. The assumption also guides a common understanding of time in which the past is no longer present while the future is not yet present. On Heidegger's account, philosophers from Plato to Nietzsche offer competing versions of this "metaphysics of presence." And yet there are people who stand outside or slightly aside from this tradition. The Pre-Socratics experienced being before it became hardened into an essence; some mystics have encountered a God beyond the categories of presence; and poets like Hölderlin and Trakl have broken the concordat between truth and presence. On Derrida's account, though, this tradition exceeds these limits in both directions so as to encompass the Pre-Socratics and Heidegger himself. For while Heidegger sought to overcome metaphysics he was drawn at times, despite himself, to recover the proper name of being, as in his broodings on *Ereignis*. That said, it would be misleading to speak of a writer simply being "included" in the metaphysical tradition. For while Derrida maintains there is just the one metaphysics, he stresses that it is not a homogeneous unity. No sooner is a limit to metaphysics determined than it can be shown to be divisible, and this situation troubles any idea of there being an "inside" and an "outside" to metaphysics.

Since he does not preach an end to metaphysics, Derrida is not proposing an apocalyptic discourse.[2] And since he does not proclaim an outside to metaphysics, he is not speaking as a prophet.[3] His claim is both more modest and more radical: that we can discern a closure to metaphysics, and that this has been made possible by attending to "the movement of language" hidden by the sign and especially by the prevailing conception of writing as "*the signifier of the signifier*."[4] It is by a meditation on the scope and status of writing, then, that we can review Western history and question the determination of being as presence. "Writing," as used here, stands for any kind of inscription. It includes painting and athletics, cinema and audio- or video-tape, as well as phonetic script. And lest it seem that "writing" is value-free, it includes systems of social differentiation: Hence Derrida's insistence on the originary violence of writing. Leaving aside the ethical and political questions that begin to form here (and that Derrida takes up in his later work), let us look at how he puts the notion of writing to work. Very roughly, his argument is that all objects – even ideal ones, like geometrical figures – presume in their very constitution the possibility of being inscribed. Were this not so, there could be no guarantee of their intelligibility for other people at other times. To inscribe an object, though, is to allow that the mark be repeatable in any context whatsoever, where it can be ironized or parodied, divided or supplemented. Whether or not it is inscribed in fact, it will always be *possible* for the being of an object to diverge from its meaning. Or, to say the same thing in another way, equivocity can never in principle be reduced.

This conclusion upsets the metaphysics of presence, which posits an identity of being and meaning as a ground or as an end, and which regards equivocity as a regrettable deviation that in fact could always be avoided. From Derrida's standpoint, however, there is no question of avoidance or regret. There is no fall from presence, no failure to reach it, and deconstruction is to be valued as affirmative criticism. Interpretation may be freed from the simple call or recall of presence, yet no one is thereby licensed to engage in a hermeneutic free for all. One can remove univocity from its metaphysical home as a ground or an end, but it immediately springs into place as a horizon. We can better appreciate the status and scope of "affirmative" when we realize that what is affirmed in deconstruction is the non-coincidence of being and meaning. Derrida dubs this non-coincidence *différance*, and maintains that it precedes all grounds while resisting becoming another ground precisely because it forbids self-identity of any sort. *Différance* provides Derrida with a (non)-site from which to question metaphysics because, on his reading, it produces both the discourse of metaphysics and the means of ungrounding it. *Différance* may help us to glimpse "the yet unnameable glimmer beyond the closure" but it cannot disentangle itself wholly from metaphysics.[5] Deconstruction shows how meaning overflows limits; it does not erase limits.

Let us shift focus for a moment and see how deconstruction stands with respect to theology. At first the picture seems clear enough. Since God is "the name and the element of that which makes possible an absolutely pure and absolutely self-present self-knowledge" any God talk, any theology, would be thoroughly shaken by *différance*.[6] Not only is the sign complicit with metaphysics but also it is "essentially theological."[7] All talk of a center is "theological," and *différance* "blocks every relationship to theology."[8] For all that, deconstruction is neither proposing a "return to finitude" nor calling for "God's death."[9] And a closer inspection of Derrida's texts reveals that he is concerned solely with the metaphysics in theology, and would be sympathetic to those theologies, if any, that do not "appropriate the resources of Greek conceptuality."[10] There is at least one, it seems, a contemporary deconstructive theology. The point of this movement, Derrida tells us,

> would seem to be to liberate theology from what has been grafted on to it, to free it from its metaphysico-philosophical super ego, so as to uncover an authenticity of the "gospel", of the evangelical message. And thus, from the perspective of faith, deconstruction can at least be a very useful technique when Aristotelianism or Thomism are to be criticized or, even from an institutional perspective, when what needs to be criticized is a whole theological institution which supposedly has covered over, dissimulated an authentic Christian message. And [the point would also seem to be] a real possibility for faith both at the margins and very close to Scripture, a faith lived in a venturous, dangerous, free way.[11]

Is this the only theology that unsettles metaphysics? Not at all. In Christianity alone many names could be offered, from Paul to Tertullian, from Eckhart to Luther, from Barth to Marion. There are mystics who call philosophy into question, and complex traditions of negative theology that propose a God beyond being. Does Derrida have anything to say about these?

Yes: in several texts, all listed in the bibliography, Derrida examines questions relating to apocalypse, mysticism, negative theology, "religion today," and the sacred. At the same time, Derrida is careful to avoid speaking in an improper way about these things; and that is a motif of the paper introduced here, "How to Avoid Speaking." Let me begin by pointing out what Derrida means by "avoid speaking" in this lecture. First, although he has long been fascinated by negative theology, he has thus far not examined it in detail; and now, invited to a conference to be held in Jerusalem in 1986, he has an opportunity to treat the topic in a thorough manner. Second, while at this conference, he will not speak about "negative theology," because the expression is misleading: There are negative theolog*ies*, and they are entwined with positive theologies, whose predications of God they deny, limit, question, or suspend. Third, he will remain silent about Islamic and Jewish theology, preferring to limit himself to three paradigms: Greek, Christian, and Heideggerian. (This silence can be read "autobiographically," he concedes: a Jew born among Arabs, Derrida has never been able to speak directly about his "origins.") Fourth, he will not be able to speak simply of a promise – to reflect on the difficulties of affirming a God beyond being – since he is already committed, as everyone is, also to speak in a promise that precedes any present contract. This is the promise of *différance*: Any speech or writing will have divided. And fifth, he will avoid speaking, as he always has done, in the register of negative theology; for deconstruction is not a negative theology.

This last consideration determines the polemic stratum of "How to Avoid

Speaking." From early on deconstruction has been mistaken as a negative theology, despite warnings to the contrary. For example, in "Différance," a paper read to the Société Française de Philosophie in January 1968, Derrida maintains that *différance* is "not theological, not even in the order of the most negative of negative theologies."[12] And the reason is clear: Not only is *différance* not a divine being but also it is the condition for thinking God (and the death of God). Even so, Brice Parain observed in the discussion, "I begin to wonder what this differance might be since, in short, it is the source of everything. It is the source of everything and one cannot know it: it is the God of negative theology . . ." To which Derrida responded, "It is and it is not . . . It is above all not."[13] A few minutes later he returned to the issue and added, with respect to the paper he had just read, "nothing in such a discourse strikes me as more alien to negative theology. And yet, as often happens, this infinite distance is also an infinitesimal distance. That is why negative theology fascinates me . . . negative theology is also an *excessive* practice of language (*langue*)."[14] Thus prompted, let us distinguish negative theology from deconstruction.

All negative theologies promise to pass from talk about God to His immediate presence, from language to silence. Yet in doing so each has to traverse an entire positive theology: every predication of God offered in revelation (beauty, good, light, love . . .) must be crossed out in order to glimpse the unknowable divinity beyond being. But can we ever exhaust the predications appropriate to God? His sheer transcendence makes the task of negative theology interminable. By contrast, *différance* is transcendental, not transcendent; it concerns conditions of possibility and impossibility, not eminent or hyper-eminent modes of being. In a sense, both God and *différance* precede Creation; but whereas God was always present to Himself, *différance* "was" neither a being nor self-present. As soon as there is writing, though, there has always been *différance*, and it has immemorially promised that we are inscribed in language, even when we remain silent. "This promise is older than I am," Derrida observes, alluding to an ongoing argument with speech act theorists.[15] Why is this promise "older" than he is? Because it is the condition of possibility for any speech or writing whatsoever. And what is promised? First, that any piece of writing, in Derrida's extended sense of the word, can always be repeated in foreseen and unforeseen contexts. Second, that its meaning will change if repeated, sometimes subtly (if you quote a prayer in an essay after praying it before beginning to write), and sometimes dramatically (if you parody the prayer). And third, that the writing will retain a performative power; it is always possible that it will be found by an unintended reader who will choose to find himself or herself addressed there, and may even change his or her life on the basis of the unexpected encounter.[16]

Negative theology is driven to an "*excessive* practice of language," as Derrida puts it, in order to approach the God revealed in positive theology. A syntax of "neither–nor" is called for because the divinity transcends the world and the language appropriate to it. Deconstruction, by contrast, shows that language is excessive in that equivocity cannot be eliminated in fact or in principle. There is always a possibility of textual contamination, grafting, or supplementation. In or behind language there is *différance*, which cannot be positively described. It too calls for a syntax of "neither – nor," but only because it is transcendental: a condition of possibility (for talk of identity and presence, as much as difference and equivocity) that is also a condition of impossibility (for talk of self-identity, undivided presence, absolute difference, unbounded equivocity). So deconstruction is not a negative theology. The more interesting question, which preoccupies Derrida in the latter part of "How to Avoid Speaking," is what happens to negative theologies when they are exposed to a deconstructive reading. I will restrict myself to the central part of Derrida's discussion, the opening passage of *The Mystical Theology* by Dionysius the Areopagite.

Dionysius begins *The Mystical Theology* with a prayer. He cannot properly do otherwise. For unless the "hyperessential and more than divine Trinity" guides him, Dionysius runs the risk of "manipulating . . . negations like empty and purely mechanical phrases." Yet, as Derrida points out, there is no pure prayer, no "address to the other as other," for it is supplemented by an encomium. The God beyond being is determined in advance to be the Christian God. Could a Christian do otherwise? No; the supplement is essential. Reading closely, we also find that Dionysius does not just pray, he quotes his prayer; and he does so while addressing Timothy, who wishes to be initiated into mystical contemplation. Far from being a pure address, then, Dionysius's prayer falls short of immediate presence by dint of repetition and by having multiple addressees. Were it uttered in complete silence, the prayer still could not erase the possibility of its inscription and all that follows from this. And so, Derrida concludes, one cannot approach God, as negative theology promises, by passing from language to silence. Even silence is marked by the effects of *différance*.

What consequences does this argument have for theology? Derrida points out that *différance* does not annul positive and negative theologies but rather renders them possible *as discourses*. At first this might seem like small consolation for a theologian. After all, what is the point of a theology without God? Yet to show that God does not abide in the immediacy and simplicity of a present moment is not to deny God. It is to demonstrate that God is conceived metaphysically within theology, even within negative theologies. To be sure, a negative theology may partially deconstruct the metaphysics that shapes the God of a positive theology. But to the extent it conceives approaching the God beyond being without recourse to language, this negative theology will itself call for deconstruction. To turn to another point. The theologian should remember that Derrida nowhere rejects the notion of presence. He argues that presence cannot present itself; the possibility of inscription is a necessary one, and one that ensures the possibility of division. There may be a God, and this God may be pure self-presence; but He cannot be intuited or revealed in the present. Derrida himself inclines to atheism – "I quite rightly pass for an atheist," he says[17] – and this is consistent with his argument. It would be equally consistent, though, for someone who believes in God not to convert to atheism on finding Derrida's case valid.

I will conclude by quickly sketching this believer. He or she would trust in God's presence while not expecting to experience it in the present. The life of faith would center on the interpretation of traces. It would be a negative way, not necessarily by virtue of accepting a "negative theology" but by dint of experiencing an aporia, an inexorable demand to choose between legitimate alternatives. One would look to the God rendered possible by exegesis and philosophy, while at the same time answering to the God who upsets the realm of the possible, who arrives in a singular manner outside the known and the expected. "Why this language, which does not fortuitously resemble that of negative theology? How to justify the choice of a *negative form (aporia)* to designate a duty that, through the impossible or the impracticable, nonetheless announces itself in an affirmative fashion? Because one must avoid good conscience at all costs."[18] Thus Derrida on law and justice. In the same spirit one could say that unless an impossible God belongs to a life of faith it would not be a life of faith at all but only the performance of a program. Perhaps Derrida's most important legacy for theology is not his reading of negative theology, fascinating though it is, but the thought that theology must be maintained or recast in a "negative form."

Notes

1 Jacques Derrida, "The Time of a Thesis: Punctuations," in *Philosophy in France Today*, ed. Alan Montefiore (Cambridge: Cambridge University Press, 1983), pp. 38, 39.

2 See Derrida's essay, "On a Newly Arisen Apocalyptic Tone in Philosophy," trans. John Leavey, Jr., in *Raising the Tone of Philosophy: Late Essays by Immanuel Kant, Transformative Critique by Jacques Derrida*, ed. Peter Fenves (Baltimore, MD: Johns Hopkins University Press, 1993), pp. 117–71.

3 See Derrida's remarks on prophecy in "Deconstruction and the Other," in *Dialogues with Contemporary Continental Thinkers: The Phenomenological Heritage*, by Richard Kearney (Manchester: Manchester University Press, 1984), pp. 117–19.

4 Derrida, *Of Grammatology*, trans. Gayatri Chakravorty Spivak (Baltimore, MD: Johns Hopkins University Press, 1976), p. 7.

5 Ibid., p. 14.

6 Ibid., p. 98.

7 Ibid., p. 14.

8 Derrida, *Positions*, trans. Alan Bass (University of Chicago Press, 1981), pp. 14, 40.

9 Derrida, *Of Grammatology*, p. 68; cf. *Positions*, p. 6.
10 Derrida, *Of Grammatology*, p. 13.
11 James Creech, Peggy Kamuf, and Jane Todd, "Deconstruction in America: an interview with Jacques Derrida," *Critical Exchange* 17 (1985), p. 12.
12 Derrida, *Margins of Philosophy*, trans. Alan Bass (University of Chicago Press, 1982), p. 6.
13 Derrida et al., "Original discussion (1968) of La 'Différance' [sic]", in *Derrida and Différance*, ed. David Wood and Robert Bernasconi (Warwick: Parousia Press, 1985), p. 130.
14 Derrida et al., "Original discussion," p. 132. First ellipsis mine.
15 Derrida, "How to Avoid Speaking," in *Languages of the Unsayable: The Play of Negativity in Literature and Literary Theory*, ed. Sanford Budick and Wolfgang Iser (New York: Columbia University Press, 1989), p. 14. For Derrida's arguments with J. L. Austin and John Searle, especially over the assumption that all promises must be made in the present, see Derrida's *Limited Inc*, trans. Samuel Weber (Evanston, IL: Northwestern University Press, 1988).
16 Derrida makes this point in "Telepathy," trans. Nicholas Royle, *Oxford Literary Review*, 10 (1988), pp. 5–6.
17 Derrida, "Circumfession," in *Jacques Derrida*, by Geoffrey Bennington and Jacques Derrida, trans. Geoffrey Bennington (University of Chicago Press, 1993), p. 155.
18 Derrida, *Aporias*, trans. Thomas Dutoit (Stanford, CA: Stanford University Press, 1993), p. 19. I offer an account of the figure of the aporia in "Impossible Marx," *Arena Journal*, 5 (1995), pp. 185–208.

Selected Bibliography

Bennington, Geoffrey, and Derrida, Jacques, *Jacques Derrida*, trans. Geoffrey Bennington (Chicago: University of Chicago Press, 1993).
Caputo, John D., "Mysticism and Transgression: Derrida and Meister Eckhart," in *Derrida and Deconstruction*, ed. Hugh J. Silverman (New York; Routledge, 1989), pp. 24–39.
—— *The Prayers and Tears of Jacques Derrida: Religion without Religion* (Bloomington: Indiana University Press, 1997).
Derrida, Jacques, "Violence and Metaphysics: An Essay on the Thought of Emmanuel Levinas," in *Writing and Difference*, trans. and introd. Alan Bass (London: Routledge and Kegan Paul, 1978), pp. 79–153.
—— "A Number of Yes," trans. Brian Holmes, in *Qui Parle*, 2/2 (1988), pp. 120–32.
—— "On a Newly Arisen Apocalyptic Tone in Philosophy," trans. John Leavey, Jr., in *Raising the Tone of Philosophy: Late Essays by Immanuel Kant, Transformative Critique by Jacques Derrida*, ed. Peter Fenves (Baltimore, MD: Johns Hopkins University Press, 1993), pp. 117–71.
—— *The Gift of Death*, trans. David Wills (Chicago: University of Chicago Press, 1995).
—— *On the Name*, ed. Thomas Dutoit, trans. David Wood, John P. Leavey, Jr., and Ian McLeod (Stanford, CA: Stanford University Press, 1995).
—— "Foi et savoir: Les deux sources de la 'religion' aux limites de la simple raison," in *La Religion: Séminaire de Capri sous la direction de Jacques Derrida et Gianni Vattimo* (Paris: Seuil, 1996), pp. 9–86.

Dufrenne, Mikel, "Pour une philosophie non théologique," in *Le Poétique* (Paris: Presses Universitaires de France, 1973), pp. 7–57.

Foshay, Toby, "Introduction: Denegation and Resentment," in *Derrida and Negative Theology*, ed. Harold Coward and Toby Foshay (Albany: State University of New York Press, 1992), pp. 1–24.

Gasché, Rodolphe, "God, for example," in *Inventions of Difference: On Jacques Derrida* (Cambridge, MA: Harvard University Press, 1994), pp. 150–70.

Handelman, Susan A., "Reb Derrida's Scripture," in *The Slayers of Moses: The Emergence of Rabbinic Interpretation in Modern Literary Theory* (Albany: State University of New York Press, 1982), pp. 163–78.

Hart, Kevin, *The Trespass of the Sign: Deconstruction, Theology and Philosophy*, 2nd edn (Cambridge: Cambridge University Press, 1991).

—— "The God Effect," in *Beyond Secular Philosophy*, ed. Phillip Blond (Routledge, London, forthcoming).

Marion, Jean-Luc, *L'Idole et la distance* (Paris: Grasset, 1977).

O'Leary, Joseph S., *Questioning Back: The Overcoming of Metaphysics in Christian Tradition* (Minneapolis: Winston Press, 1985).

Scharlemann, Robert P. (ed.), *Negation and Theology* (Charlottesville: University Press of Virginia, 1992).

Taylor, Mark C., "Rewriting," in *Altarity* (Chicago: University of Chicago Press, 1987), pp. 255–303.

Vattimo, Gianni, *Les Aventures de la différance* (Paris: Minuit, 1985).

Ward, Graham, *Barth, Derrida, and the Language of Theology* (Cambridge: Cambridge University Press, 1995).

TEXT

From *How to Avoid Speaking*

The passage through the negativity of discourse on the subject of the *khora* is neither the last word nor a mediation in service of a dialectic, an elevation toward a positive or proper meaning, a Good or a God. This has nothing to do with negative theology; there is reference neither to an event nor to a giving, neither to an order nor to a promise, even if, as I have just underscored, the absence of promise or of order – the barren, radically nonhuman, and atheological character of this "place" – obliges us to speak and to refer to it in a certain and unique manner, as to the wholly other who is neither transcendent, absolutely distanced, nor immanent and close. Not that we are obliged to speak of it; but if, stirred by an obligation that does not come from it, we think and speak of it, then it is necessary to respect the singularity of this reference. Although it is nothing, this referent appears irreducible and irreducibly other: one cannot invent it. But since it remains alien to the order of presence and absence, it seems that one could only invent it in its very otherness, at the moment of the address.

But this unique address is not a prayer, a celebration, or an encomium. It does not speak to You.

Above all, this "third species" that the *khora* also is does not belong to a *group of three*. "Third species" is here only a *philosophical* way of naming an X that is not included in a group, a family, a triad or a trinity. Even when Plato seems to compare it to a "mother" or to a "nurse," this always virginal *khora* in truth does not couple with the "father" to whom Plato "compares" the paradigms; the *khora* does not *engender* the sensible forms that are inscribed in it and that Plato "compares" to a child (*Timaeus*, 50d).

To ask what *happens* between this type of experience (or the experience of the typos) and the Christian apophases is neither necessarily nor exclusively to think of history, of events, of influences. Indeed, the question that arises here concerns the historicity or eventuality (*événementialité*), that is, of significations foreign to the *khora*. Even if one wishes to describe "what happens" in terms of structures and relations, it is no doubt necessary to recognize that what happens between them is, perhaps, precisely the event of the event, the story, the thinking of an essential "having-taken-place," of a revelation, of an order and of a promise, of an anthropo–theologicalization which – despite the extreme rigor of the negative hyperbole – seems to dominate anew, even closer to the *agathon* than to the *khora*. And in Dionysius' works, for example, the trinitarian schema appears absolutely indispensable to ensure the passage through or crossing between discourses on the divine names, between the symbolic and mystical theology. The affirmative theologemes celebrate God as the Good, the intelligible Light, even the Good "beyond all light" (it is a "principle of all light and hence it is too little to call it light"; *DN*, ch. 4:701ab). Even if this Good is called formless (like the *khora*), this time it itself gives form: "But if the Good transcends all being, as is in effect the case, then it is necessary to say that it is the formless that gives form, and that the One who remains in Himself without essence is the height of the essence, and the reality without supreme life" (*DN*, ch. 4:697a). This Good inspires an entire erotics, but Dionysius warns us: it is necessary to avoid using the word *erôs* without first clarifying the meaning, the intention. It is always necessary to start from the intentional meaning and not from the mere words (*DN*, ch. 4: 708bc): "one should not imagine that we oppose Scripture in venerating this word of amorous desire [erôs]. . . . It even seemed to some of our sacred authors that 'amorous love' [*erôs*] is a term more worthy of God than 'charitable love' [*agapè*]. For the divine Ignatius wrote: 'It is the object of my amorous love that they crucified'" (*DN*, ch. 4.708c–709b). The holy theologians attribute the same import, the same power of unification and gathering to *erôs* and to *agapè*, which the many poorly understand, which assigns desire to the body, to the division, to the carving up (ibid.). In God, desire is at once ecstatic, jealous, and condescending (*DN*, ch. 4:712a et seq.). This erotics leads forward and hence leads back to the Good, circularly, that is, toward what "is situated far beyond both being considered in itself and non-being" (*DN*, ch. 4:716d). As for Evil, "it belongs neither to Being nor to non-Being. Rather, it is more absent and estranged from the Good than non-Being; it is more greatly without being than non-Being" (ibid.). What is the more of this less in regard to what is already without essence? Evil is even more without essence than the Good. If possible, one should draw the full consequences of this singular axiomatics. For the moment, this is not my concern.

Between the theological movement that speaks and is inspired by the Good beyond Being or by light and the apophatic path that exceeds the Good, there is necessarily a passage, a transfer, a translation. An experience must yet guide the apophasis toward excellence, not allow it to say just anything, and prevent it from manipulating its negations like empty and purely mechanical phrases. This experience is that of prayer. Here prayer is not a preamble, an accessory mode of access. It constitutes an essential moment, it adjusts discursive asceticism, the passage through the desert of discourse, the apparent referential vacuity which will only avoid empty deliria and prattling, by addressing itself from the start to the other, to you. But to you as "hyperessential and more than divine Trinity."

I will distinguish at least two traits in the experiences and in the so manifold determinations of what one calls prayer. I isolate them here even if at the neglect of everything else, in order to clarify my talk. 1. In every prayer there must be an address to the other as other; for example – I will say, at the risk of shocking – God. The act of addressing oneself to the other as other must, of course, mean praying, that is, asking, supplicating, searching out. No matter what, for the pure prayer demands only that the other hear it, receive it, be present to it, be the other as such, a gift, call, and even cause of prayer. This first trait thus characterizes a discourse (an act of language even if prayer is silent) which, as such, is not predicative, theoretical (theo*logical*), or constative. 2. But I will differentiate it from another trait with which it is most often associated, notably by Dionysius and his interpreters, namely, the encomium or the celebration (*hymnein*). That the association of these two traits is essential for Dionysius does not signify that one trait is identical with the other, nor even in general inseparable from the other. Neither the prayer nor the encomium is, of course, an act of constative predication. Both have a performative dimension, the analysis of which would merit long and difficult expositions, notably as to the origin and validation of these performatives. I will hold to one distinction: Prayer in itself, one may say, implies nothing other than the supplicating address to the other, perhaps beyond all supplication and giving, to give the promise of His presence as other, and finally the transcendence of His otherness itself, even without any other determination; the encomium, although it is not a simple attributive speech, nevertheless preserves an irreducible relationship to the attribution. No doubt, as Urs von Balthasar rightly says, "Where God and the divine are concerned, the word ὑμνεῖν almost replaces the word 'to say.'"[1] Almost, in fact, but not entirely; and how can one deny that the encomium qualifies God and *determines* prayer, *determines* the other, Him to whom it addresses itself, refers, invoking Him even as the source of prayer? How can one deny that, in this movement of determination (which is no longer the pure address of the prayer to the other), the appointment of the *trinitary* and hyperessential God distinguishes Dionysius' *Christian* prayer from all other prayer? To reject this doubtless subtle distinction, inadmissible for Dionysius and perhaps for a Christian in general, is to deny the essential quality of prayer to every invocation that is not Christian. As Jean-Luc Marion correctly remarks, the encomium is "neither true nor false, not even contradictory,"[2] although it says something *about* the thearchy, about the Good and the analogy; and if its attributions or namings do not belong to the ordinary signification of truth, but rather to a hypertruth that is ruled by a hyperessentiality, in this it does not merge with the movement of prayer itself, which does not speak *of*, but *to*. Even if this address is immediately determined by the discourse of encomium and if the prayer addresses itself to God by speaking (to Him) of Him, the apostrophe of prayer and the determination of the encomium form a pair, two different structures: "hyperessential and more than divine Trinity, you who preside over the divine wisdom . . ." In a moment I will quote more extensively from this prayer which opens the *Mystical Theology* and prepares the definition of apophatic theologemes. For "it is necessary to start with prayers" (*eukhès aparkhesthai khreôn*; *DN*, ch. 3:680d), Dionysius says. Why? No doubt, to attain union with God; but to speak of this *union*, it is still necessary to speak of *places*, of height, of distance and of proximity. Dionysius proposes to his immediate addressee – or to the one to whom he dedicates his work, Timothy – to examine the name of Good, which expresses divinity, *after* having invoked the Trinity, that principle of Good which transcends all goods. It is necessary to pray in order to *approach* it, "most intimately" – that is, to raise oneself toward it – and receive from it the initiation of its gifts:

It is necessary that we first be lifted up toward it, the source of good, by our prayers, and then, by drawing near to it, that we be initiated into the all-good gifts of what is founded around it. For while it is present to all, not all are present to it. Then, when we invoke it by our most holy prayers with an unpolluted intellect which is suited for the divine union, we shall be present to it. For it is not in a place, so that it would be absent from some beings or have to go from one being to another. Moreover, even the statement that it is "in" all beings falls far too short of its infinity, which is beyond all and encompasses all. (*DN*, ch. 3:680b)

By a series of analogies, Dionysius then explains that, in approaching and elevating ourselves thus, we do not traverse the distance that separates us from a place (since the residence of the Trinity is not localized: it is "everywhere and nowhere"). On the other hand, the Trinity draws us toward it, while it remains immobile, like the height of the sky or the depth of marine bedrock from which we will pull on a rope in order to come to it, and not to draw it toward us:

before everything and especially before a discourse about God, it is necessary to begin with a prayer – not so that the power present both everywhere and nowhere shall come to us but so that by our divine remembrance and invocations we ourselves shall be guided to it and be united with it. (ibid.)

The principle of the Good is beyond Being, but it also transcends the Good (*DN*, ch. 3:680b). God is the Good that transcends the Good and the Being that transcends Being. This "logic" is also that of the "without" which I evoked a moment ago in the quotations from Meister Eckhart, citing Saint Augustine ("God is wise *without* wisdom, good *without* goodness, powerful *without* power") or Saint Bernard ("To love God is a mode *without* a mode"). We could recognize in the negativity without negativity of these utterances – concerning a transcendence which is nothing other (and wholly other) than what it transcends – a principle of multiplication of voices and discourses, of disappropriation and reappropriation of utterances, with the most distant appearing the closest, and vice versa. A predicate can always conceal another predicate, or rather the nakedness of an absence of predicate – as the (sometimes indispensable) veil of a garment can at once dissimulate and reveal the very fact that it dissimulates and renders attractive at the same time. Hence the voice of an utterance can conceal another, which it then appears to quote without quoting it, presenting itself as another form, namely as a quotation of the other. Whence the subtlety, but also the conflicts, the relations of power, even the aporias of a politics of doctrine; I want to say: a politics of initiation or of teaching in general, and of an institutional politics of interpretation. Meister Eckhart, for example (but what an example!) knew something about this. Not to mention the arguments he had to deploy against his inquisitorial judges ("They tax with error everything they don't understand . . ."), the strategy of his sermons put to work a multiplicity of voices and of veils, which he superimposed or removed like skins or garments, thematizing and himself exploring a pseudo-metaphor until reaching that extreme flaying of which one is never sure that it allows one to see the nakedness of God or to hear the voice of Meister Eckhart himself. *Quasi stella matutina*, which furnishes so many pretexts to the Cologne judges, stages the drama of twenty-four masters (*Liber 24 philosophorum* of pseudo-Hermes Trismegistus) who are reunited to speak of God. Eckhart chooses one of their assertions: "God is necessarily above Being [*got etwaz ist, daz von nôt über wesene sîn muoz*]."[3] Speaking thus of what one of his masters says, he *comments* in a voice that no longer permits one to decide that it is not his own. And in the same movement, he cites other masters, Christians or pagans, great or subordinate masters (*kleine meister*). One of them seems to say, "God is neither being nor goodness [*Got enist niht wesen noch güete*]. Goodness clings to being and is not more comprehensive [*breiter*] than being; for if there were no being, there would be no goodness, and being is purer than goodness. God is not good, nor better, nor best. Whoever were to say that God is good, would do Him as great an injustice as if he called the sun black" (ibid., 1:148). (The Bull of condemnation mentions this passage only in an appendix, without concluding that Eckhart truly taught it.) The theory of archetypes that forms the context of this argument attenuates its provocative character: God does not share any of the modes of Being with other beings (divided into ten categories by these masters), but "He is not thereby deprived of any of them [*er entbirt ir ouch keiner*]."

But here is what "a pagan master" says: the soul that loves God "takes Him under the garment of goodness [*nimet in under dem velle der güete*]," but reason or rationality (*vernunfticheit*) raises this garment and grasps God in His nakedness (*in blôz*). Then He is derobed (*entkleidet*), shorn "of goodness, of Being, and of all names" (ibid., 1:152). Eckhart does not contradict the pagan master; nor does he agree with him. He remarks that, unlike the "holy masters," the pagan speaks in accordance with "natural light." Next, in a voice that appears to be his own, he differentiates – I do not dare say that he makes dialectical – the preceding proposition. In the lines that I am preparing to quote, a certain signification of unveiling, of laying bare, of truth as what is beyond the covering garment – appears to orient the entire axiomatics of this apophasis, at the end of ends and after all. Doubtless, here one cannot speak in full rigor of signification and axiomatics, since what orders and rules the apophatic course precisely exceeds the Good or goodness. But there is indeed a rule or a law: it is necessary to go beyond the veil or the garment. Is it arbitrary to still call truth or hyper-truth this unveiling which is perhaps no longer an unveiling of Being? A light, therefore, that is no longer elucidated by Being? I do not believe so. Consider:

> I once said in the school that intellect [*vernünfticheit*] is nobler than will, and yet both belong to this light. Then a master in another school said that will is nobler than intellect, for will takes things as they are in themselves, while the intellect takes things as they are in it. That is true. An eye is nobler in itself than an eye painted on the wall. But I say that intellect is nobler than will. The will apprehends God under the garment [*under dem kleide*] of goodness. The intellect apprehends God naked, as He is divested of goodness and being [*Vernünfticheit nimet got blôz, als er entkleidet ist von güete und von wesene*]. Goodness is a garment [*kleit*] under which God is hidden, and will apprehends God under the garment of goodness. If there were no goodness in God, my will would not want Him. (ibid., 1:152–3)

Light and truth, these are Meister Eckhart's words. *Quasi stella matutina*, that is what it is, and it is also a topology (height and proximity) of our relation to God. Like the adverb *quasi*, we are *beside* the verb that is the truth:

> "As [*als*] a morning star in the midst of the mist." I refer to the little word "quasi," which means "as" [*als*]; in school the children call it an adverb [*ein bîwort*]. This is what I refer to in all my sermons. The most appropriate [*eigenlîcheste*] things that one can say of God are word and truth [*wort und wârheit*]. God called Himself a word [*ein wort*]. St John said: "In the beginning was the Word," and means that beside the word [*wort*], man is an adverb [*bîwort*]. In the same way, the free star [*der vrîe sterne*] Venus, after which Friday [*vrîtac*] is named, has many names . . . Of all the stars, it is always equally near to the sun; it never moves farther from or nearer to it [*niemer verrer noch næher*], and symbolizes [*meinet*] a man who wants to be near God always, and present [*gegenwertic*] to Him, so that nothing can remove him from God, neither happiness, unhappiness, nor any creature . . . The more the soul is raised [*erhaben*] above earthly things, the stronger [*kreftiger*] it is. Even a person who knows nothing but the creatures would never need to think of any sermons, for every creature is full of God and is a book [*buoch*]. (ibid., 1:154– 6)

In its pedagogical necessity and initiatory virtue, the sermon supplements – not so much the Word (*Verbe*), which has no need of it, but – the incapacity of reading in the authentic "book" that we are, as creatures, and the adverbial quality that we must hence be. This supplement of adverbial quality, the sermon, must be accomplished and oriented (as one orients oneself by the morning star) by the prayer or invocation of the trinitary God. This is at once the end and the orientation point of the sermon: "The soul is thus like an 'adverb,' working together with God and finding its beautification in the same self-knowledge that exalts Him. That for all time, may the Father, the Verbum, and the Holy Spirit help us to remain adverbs of this Verbum. Amen" (ibid., 1:158).

This is the end of the Sermon; the prayer does not directly address itself, in the form of apostrophe, to God Himself. In contrast, at the opening and from the first words of the *Mystical Theology*, Dionysius addresses himself directly to You, to God, from now on determined as "hyperessential Trinity" in the prayer that prepares the theologemes of the *via negativa*:

> O Trinity beyond being [*Trias hyperousiè*], beyond divinity [*hyperthèe*], beyond goodness [*hyperagathè*], and guide of Christians in divine wisdom [*theosophias*], direct us to the mystical summits more than unknown and beyond light. There the simple, absolved, and unchanged mysteries of theology lie hidden in the darkness beyond light of the hidden mystical silence, there, in the greatest darkness, that beyond all that is most evident exceedingly illuminates the sightless intellects. There, in the wholly imperceptible and invisible, that beyond all that is most evident fills to overflowing, with the glories beyond all beauty. The intellects who know how to close their eyes [*tous anommatous noas*]. This is my prayer ['*Emoi men oun tauta eutkhtô*]. And you, dear Timothy, be earnest in the exercise of mystical contemplation. (ch. 1:998a)

What happens here?

After having prayed (he writes, we read), he presents his prayer. He quotes it and I have just quoted his quotation. He quotes it in what is properly an *apostrophe* to its addressee, Timothy. The *Mystical Theology* is dedicated to him; in order to initiate him, it must lead him on the paths toward which Dionysius himself has prayed to God to lead him, or more literally to *direct* him in a straight (*ithunon*) line. A ped*agogy* which is also a myst*agogy* and a psych*agogy*: here the gesture of leading or directing the *psyche* of the other passes through apostrophe. The one who asks to be led by God turns for an instant toward another addressee, in order to lead him in turn. He does not simply turn himself away from his first addressee who is *in truth* the first Cause of his prayer and already guides it. It is exactly because he does not turn away from God that he can turn toward Timothy and *pass from one address to the other without changing direction*.

The writing of Dionysius – which we presently believe we are reading or read in view of believing – stands in the space of that *apostrophe* which *turns aside* the discourse in the *same* direction, between the prayer itself, the quotation of the prayer, and the address to the disciple. In other words, it is addressed to the best reader, to the reader who ought to allow himself to be led to become better, to us who presently believe we are reading this text.

Not to us as we are, at present, but as we would have to be, in our souls, if we read this text as it ought to be read, aright, in the proper direction, correctly: according to its prayer and its promise. He also prays – that we read correctly, in accordance with his prayer. None of this would be possible without the possibility of quotation (more generally, of repetition), and of an apostrophe that allows one to speak to several people at once. To more than one other. The prayer, the quotation of the prayer, and the apostrophe, from one you to the other, thus weave the *same* text, however heterogeneous they appear. There is a text because of this repetition.[4] Where, then, does this text have its place? Does it have a place, at present? And why can't one separate the prayer, the quotation of prayer, and the address to the reader?

The identity of *this* place, and hence of *this* text, and of *its* reader, comes from the future of what is promised by the promise. The advent of this future has a provenance, the event of the promise. Contrary to what seemed to happen in the "experience" of the place called *khora*, the apophasis is brought into motion – it is *initiated*, in the sense of initiative and initiation – by the event of a revelation which is also a promise. This apophasis belongs to a history; or rather, it opens up a history and an anthropo–theological dimension. The *hyphen* ("trait *d'union*") unites *the* "new, adjunct writing with that which God himself dictated" (*DN*, ch. 3:681b); it marks the very place of this adjunction. This place itself is assigned by the event of the promise and the revelation of Scripture. It is the place only after what will have taken place – according to the time and history of this future perfect. The place is an event. Under what conditions is one situated in Jerusalem, we asked a moment ago, and where is the place thus named situated? How can one measure the distance that separates us from or draws us closer to it? Here is the answer of Dionysius, who cites Scripture in the *Ecclesiastical Hierarchy*: "Do not distance yourself from Jerusalem, but await the promise of the Father which you have heard from my mouth, and according to which you will be baptised by the Holy Spirit" (512c). The situation of this speech situates a place: he who transmitted the promise (Jesus, "divine founder of our own hierarchy") speaks of Jerusalem as the place that takes place since the event of the promise. But the place that is thus revealed remains the place of waiting, awaiting the realization of the promise. Then it will take place fully. It will be fully a place.

Hence an event prescribes to us the good and accurate apophasis: how to avoid speaking. This prescription is at once a revelation and a teaching of the Holy Scriptures, the architext before all supplementary "adjunction":

with regard to the secret Deity beyond Being, *it is necessary to avoid all speech, that is, every incautious thought [ou tolmeteon eipein, oute men ennoesai]*, beyond what the Holy Scriptures divinely reveal to us [*para ta theoeidôs emin ek tôn ierôn logiôn ekpephasmena*]. For in these sacred texts, the Deity itself manifested that which suited its Goodness. (*DN*, ch. 1:588c; my italics)[5]

This hyperessential goodness is not entirely incommunicable; it can manifest *itself*, but it remains separated by its hyperessentiality. As for those theologians who have "praised" its inaccessibility and penetrated its "secret infinity," they have left no "*trace*" (*ikhnous*; ibid.; my italics).

A secret manifestation, then, if some such thing is possible. Even before commanding the extreme negativity of the apophasis, this manifestation is transmitted to us as a "secret gift" by our inspired masters. We thus learn to decipher symbols, we understand how "the love of God for man envelops the intelligible in the sensible, what is beyond Being in being, gives form and fashion to the unformable and the unfashionable, and through a variety of partial symbols, multiplies and figures the unfigurable and marvelous Simplicity" (*DN*, ch. 1:592b). In brief, we learn to read, to decipher the rhetoric without rhetoric of God – and finally to be silent.

Among all these figures for the unfigurable, there stands the figure of the seal. This is not one figure among others; it figures the figuration of the un-figurable itself; and this discourse on the imprint appears to displace the Platonic typography of the *khora*. The latter gave rise to the inscriptions, to *typoi*, for the copies of the paradigms. Here the figure of the seal, which also seals a promise, is valid for the entire text of the creation. It carries over a Platonic argument, one of the two schemas that I have just tried to distinguish, into another order. God at once permits and does not permit participation in Him. The text of creation exists as the typographic inscription of the nonparticipation in participation:

> as the central point of a circle is shared by all the radii, which constitute the circle, and as the multiple imprints [*ektypomata*] of a single seal [*sphragidos*] share the original which is entirely immanent and identical in each of the imprints, not fragmenting itself in any manner. But the nonparticipation [*amethexia*] of the Deity, the universal cause, yet transcends all these figures [*paradeigmata*]. (*DN*, ch. 2:644ab)

For unlike what happens with the seal, here there is neither contact, community, or synthesis. The subsequent discussion recalls again, while displacing, the necessity for the *khora* to be without form and virginal. Otherwise, it could not suitably lend itself to the writing of the impressions in it:

> One might object that the seal is not complete and identical in all its imprints [*en olois tois ekmageiois*]. I respond that this is not the fault of the seal which transmits itself to each one completely and identically; rather, the otherness

of the participants differentiates between the reproductions of the unique, total and identical model [*arkhetypias*]. (*DN*, ch. 2:644b)

Thus everything will depend on the material or wax (*keros*) which receives the imprints. It must be receptive, soft, flexible, smooth, and virginal, in order that the imprint remain pure, clear, and lasting (*DN*, ch. 2:644b).

If one recalls that the *khora* was also described as a receptacle (*dekhomenon*), one may follow another displacement of this figure, the figure of figures, the place of the other figures. Henceforth the "receptacle" is at once *physical* and *created*. It was neither in Plato's works. Later, Saint Augustine once again assures the mediation, and Meister Eckhart cites him in his sermon *Renouamini spiritu*: "Augustine says that in the superior part of the soul, which is called *mens* or *gemüte*, God created, together with the soul's being, a potential [*craft*] which the masters call a receptacle [*sloz*] or screen [*schrin*] of spiritual forms, or of formal images."[6] The creation of the place, which is also a potential, is the basis for the resemblance of the soul with the Father. But beyond the Trinity, one may say, beyond the multiplicity of images and beyond the created place, the *unmovability without form* – which the *Timaeus* attributed, one may say, to the *khora* – is here found to suit God alone: "when all the images of the soul are pushed aside and it contemplates only the unique One [*das einig ein*], the naked being of the soul encounters the naked being without form [*das blose formlose wesen*] of the divine unity, which is the hyperessential Being resting unmoved in itself [*ein uberwesende wesen, lidende ligende in ime selben*]" (ibid., 3:437–8). This unmovability of the formless is the unique and wondrous source of our movability, of our emotions, of our noblest suffering. Thus we can suffer only God, and nothing other than Him: "Oh! wonder of wonders [*wunder uber wunder*], what noble suffering lies therein, that the being of the soul can suffer nothing else than the solitary and pure unity of God!" (ibid., 3:438).

Thus named, "God is without name [*namloz*]," and "no one can either speak of Him or understand Him." Of this "supereminent Being [*uber swebende wesen*]" which is also a "hyperessential nothingness [*ein uber wesende nitheit*]" (ibid., 3:441–2), it is necessary to avoid speaking. Eckhart allows St Augustine to speak: "what man can say that is most beautiful in respect to God is that he knows how to be silent [*swigen*] on account of the wisdom of the internal [divine] wealth." Eckhart adds: "Because of this, be silent" (ibid., 3:442). Without that you lie and you commit sin. This duty is a duty of love; the apostrophe orders love, but it speaks out of love and implores the aid of God in a prayer: "You must love Him inasmuch as he is a Non-God, a Non-Intellect, a Non-Person, a Non-Image. More than this, inasmuch as He is a pure, clear, limpid one, separated from all duality. And we must eternally sink ourselves in this One, from the Something to the Nothing.

May God help us. Amen" (ibid., 3:448).

This is to speak in order to command not to speak, to say what God is not, that he *is* a non-God. How may one hear the copula of being that articulates this singular speech and this order to be silent? Where does it have its place? Where does it take place? It is the place, the place of this writing, this trace (left in Being) of what is not, and the writing of this place. The place is only a place of passage, and more precisely, a threshold. But a threshold, this time, to give access to what is no longer a place. A subordination, a relativization of the place, and an extraordinary consequence; the place is Being. What finds itself reduced to the condition of a threshold is Being itself, Being as a place. Solely a threshold, but a sacred place, the outer sanctuary (*parvis*) of the temple:

> When we apprehend God in Being, we apprehend Him in his *parvis* [*vorbürge*], for Being is the *parvis* in which He resides [*wonet*]. Where is He then in His temple, in which he shines in His sanctity [*heilic*]? Intellect [*vernünfticheit: rationality*] is the Temple of God.[7]

The soul, which exercises its power in the eye, allows one to see what is not, what is not present; it "works in non-being and follows God who works in non-being." Guided by this *psyche*, the eye thus passes the threshold of Being toward non-being in order to see what does not present itself. Eckhart compares the eye to a sieve. Things must be "passed through the sieve [*gebiutelt*]." This sieve is not one figure among others; it tells the difference between Being and non-being. It discerns this difference, it allows one to see it, but as the eye itself. There is no text, above all no sermon, no possible predication, without the invention of such a filter.

I thus decided *not to speak* of negativity or of apophatic movements in, for example, the Jewish or Islamic traditions. To leave this immense place empty, and above all that which can connect such a name of God with the name of the Place, to remain thus on the threshold – was this not the most consistent possible apophasis? Concerning that about which one cannot speak, isn't it best to remain silent? I let you answer this question. It is always entrusted to the other.

My first paradigm was Greek and the second Christian, without yet ceasing to be Greek. The last will be neither Greek nor Christian. If I were not afraid of trying your patience I would recall that which, in Heidegger's thinking, could resemble the most questioning legacy, both the most audacious and most liberated repetition of the traditions I have just evoked. Here I will have to limit myself to a few landmarks.

One could read *What is Metaphysics?* as a treatise on negativity. It establishes the basis for negative discourse and negation in the experience of the Nothing which itself "nothings" ("*das Nichts selbst nichtet*"). The experience of anguish puts us in relation to a negating (*Nichtung*) which is neither annihilation (*Vernichtung*), nor a negation or a denial (*Verneinung*). It reveals to us the strangeness (*Befremdlichkeit*) of what is (being, *das Seiende*) as the wholly other (*das schlechthin Andere*). It thus opens up the possibility of the question of Being for *Dasein*, the structure of which is characterized precisely by what Heidegger calls transcendence. This transcendence, *Vom Wesen des Grundes* will say, is "properly expressed" (*eigens ausgesprochen*) by the Platonic expression *epekeina tes ousias*. Unable to involve myself, here, in the interpretation of the *agathon* subsequently proposed by Heidegger, I merely wished to mark this passage beyond Being, or rather beyond beingness, and the reinterpretation of negativity that accompanies it. Heidegger specifies immediately that Plato could not elaborate "the original content of the *epekeina tes ousias* as transcendence of *Dasein* [*der ursprüngliche Gehalt des epekeina als Transzendenz des Daseins*]." He makes an analogous gesture with regard to the *khora*: in the *Einführung in die Metaphysik*, a brief parenthesis suggests that Plato fell short of thinking of the place (*Ort*) which, however, signaled to him. In truth, he only prepared (*vorbereitet*) the Cartesian interpretation of place or space as *extensio* (*Ausdehnung*).[8] Elsewhere I try to show what is problematic and reductive about this perspective. Some seventeen years later, the last page of *Was heisst Denken?* mentions *khora* and *khorismos* anew, without any explicit reference to the *Timaeus*. Plato, who is supposed to have given the most determinative *Deutung* for Western thought, situates the *khorismos* – the interval or the separation, the spacing – between beings (*Seiendes*) and Being (*Sein*). But "*e khora heisst der Ort*," "the *khora* means the place." For Plato, beings and Being are thus "placed differently [*verschieden geortet*]." "If Plato takes the *khorismos* into consideration, the difference of place [*die verschiedene Ortung*] between Being and beings, he thus poses the question of the wholly other place [*nach dem ganz anderen Ort*] of Being, by comparison with that of beings." That Plato is afterward suspected of having fallen short of this wholly other place, and that one must lead the diversity (*Verschiedenheit*) of places back to the difference (*Unterschied*) and the fold of a duplicity (*Zwiefalt*) which must be given in advance, without one ever being able to give it "proper attention" – I can follow this process neither at the end of *Was heisst Denken?* nor elsewhere. I merely underscore this movement toward a *wholly other place*, as place of Being or *place of the wholly other*: in and beyond a Platonic or Neoplatonic tradition. But also in and beyond a Christian tradition of which Heidegger – while submerged in it, as in the Greek tradition – never ceased claiming, whether by denial or not, that it could in no case entertain a philosophy. "A Christian philosophy," he often says, "is a squared circle and a misconception [*Missverständnis*]."[9] It is necessary to distinguish between, on the one hand, onto-theology or theiology, and, on the other hand, theology.[10] The former concerns the supreme being, the being *par excellence*, ultimate foundation or *causa sui* in its divinity. The latter is a science of faith or of divine speech, such as it manifests itself in revelation (*Offenbarung*). Heidegger again seems to distinguish between manifestation, the possibility of Being to reveal itself (*Offenbarkeit*), and, on the other hand, the revelation (*Offenbarung*) of the God of theology.[11]

Immense problems are screened behind these distinctions. One may follow, through Heidegger's works, the threads that we have already recognized: revelation, the promise, or the gift (*das Geben*, *die Gabe*, and the *es gibt*, which progressively and profoundly displace the question of Being and its transcendental horizon, time, in *Sein und Zeit*),[12] or yet the *Ereignis* which one sometimes translates, in such a problematic manner, by "event." I will limit myself to the question that my title commands: *How to avoid speaking?* More precisely: How to avoid speaking *of Being?* A question in which I will underscore equally the importance of avoiding and that of Being, as if to grant them equal dignity, a sort of common essentiality, which will not go without consequences. These are the consequences that interest me.

What does the avoidance signify here? In regard to Being or the word "Being," does it always have the mode that we have recognized for it in apophatic theologies? For Heidegger, would these be examples of aberration or of the "squared circle" – namely Christian philosophies or unacknowledged onto-theologies? Does the avoidance belong to the category or to the diagnostic of denial (*Verneinung*), in a sense determined this time by a Freudian problematic ("least of all do I say that")? Or again: with regard to the traditions and texts that I have just evoked, and in particular those of Dionysius and Meister Eckhart,[13] does Heidegger stand in a relationship of avoidance? What abyss would this simple word, *avoidance*, then designate?

(*To say nothing*, once again, of the mysticisms or theologies in the Jewish, Islamic, or other traditions.)

Twice, in two apparently different contexts and senses, Heidegger *explicitly proposed* to avoid (is there denial, in this case?) the word *being*. More exactly, not to *avoid* speaking of Being but to avoid *using* the word *being*. Even more exactly, not to avoid *mentioning* it – as certain speech-act theorists, who distinguish between mention and use, would say – but to avoid using it. Thus he explicitly proposes, not to avoid speaking of Being, nor in some way to avoid mentioning the word *being*, but to refrain from using it normally, one may say, without placing it in quotation marks or under erasure. And in both cases, we may suspect, the stakes are serious – even if they seem to hold to the subtle fragility of a terminological, typographical, or more broadly, "pragmatic" artifice. But in both cases, the *place* is at issue, and this is why I privilege them.

1   First, in *Zur Seinsfrage* (1952), precisely in regard to thinking the essence of modern nihilism, Heidegger reminds Ernst Jünger of the necessity for a topology of Being and of the Nothing. He distinguishes this topology from a simple topography, and he has just proposed a reinterpretation of the seal, of the *typos*, of the Platonic and of the modern typography. It is then that Heidegger proposes to write *Being*, the word *being*, under erasure, an erasure in the form of a crossing out (*kreuzweise Durchstreichung*). The word *being* is not avoided; it remains readable. But this readability announces that the word may solely be read, deciphered; it cannot or must not be pronounced, used normally, one might say, as a speech-act of ordinary language. It is necessary to decipher it under a spatialized typography, spaced or spacing, printing over. Even if this does not avoid the strange word *being*, it should at least prevent and warn against, deviate from, while designating, the normal recourse (if such exists) to it. But Heidegger also warns us against the simply *negative* use of this *Durchstreichung*. This erasure does not, then, have *avoidance* as its essential function. No doubt, Being is not a being, and it reduces to its turns, turnings, historical tropes (*Zuwendungen*); one must therefore avoid representing it (*vorzustellen*) as something, an object that stands *opposite* (*gegenüber*) man and then comes toward him. To avoid this objectifying representation (*Vorstellung*), one will thus write the word *being* under erasure. It is henceforth not heard, but is read in a certain manner. In what manner? If this *Durchstreichung* is neither a sign nor merely a negative sign ("*kein bloss negatives Zeichen*"), this is because it does not efface "Being" beneath conventional and abstract marks. Heidegger understands it as showing (*zeigen*) the four regions (*Gegenden*) of what he here and elsewhere calls the fourfold (*Geviert*): earth and heavens, mortals and the divine. Why does this written cross, according to Heidegger, have nothing of a negative signification? (1) In withdrawing Being from the subject/object relation, it allows Being to be read, both the word and the meaning of Being. (2) Next it "shows" the fourfold (*Geviert*). (3) But above all it *gathers*. This gathering takes place and has its *place* (*Ort*) in the crossing point of the *Durchkreuzung*.[14] The gathering of the *Geviert*, in a place of crossing ("*Versammlung im Ort der Durchkreuzung*"), lends itself to writing and reading in an indivisible *topos*, in the simplicity (*die Einfalt*) of the point, of

this *Ort* whose name appears so difficult to translate. Heidegger tells us elsewhere that this name "originally signifies" "the point of the sword,"[15] that toward which all converges and assembles. This indivisible point always assures the possibility of the *Versammlung*. It gives place to it; it is always the gathering, *das Versammelnde*. "The place gathers toward itself at the greatest height and extremity [*Der Ort versammelt zu sich ins Höchste und Äusserste*]."

Nevertheless, in order to think the negative appearance of this erasure, to gain access to the origin of negativity, of negation, of nihilism, and perhaps also of avoidance, it would thus be necessary to think the place of the Nothing. "What is the place of the Nothing [*der Ort des Nichts*]?" Heidegger has just asked. Now he specifies: the Nothing should also be *written*, that is to say *thought*. Like Being, it should also be written and read under erasure: "*Wie das S̶e̶i̶n̶, so müsste auch das Nichts geschrieben und d.h. gedacht werden.*"

2   Elsewhere, in an apparently different context, Heidegger explains the sense in which he would *avoid* speaking of Being, this time without placing it under erasure. More precisely, the sense in which he would avoid *writing* the word *being*. More precisely still (while remaining in the conditional mode, and this counts for much here), the sense in which "the word 'being' [*das Wort 'Sein'*]" should not take place, occur, happen (*vorkommen*) in his text. It is not a matter of "remaining silent," as one would prefer to do, he says elsewhere,[16] when the "thinking of God" (on the subject of God) is in question. No; the point is, rather, not to allow the word *being* to occur, on the subject of God.

The text is presented as a *transcription*. Responding to students at the University of Zurich in 1951, Heidegger recalls that Being and God are not identical, and that he would always avoid thinking God's essence by means of Being. He makes this more precise in a sentence in which I underscore the words *were*, *ought*, and *write*: "If I *were* yet to *write* a theology, as I am sometimes tempted to do, the word 'being' *ought* not to appear there [take place there, occur, figure, or happen there] [*Wenn ich noch eine Theologie schreiben würde, wozu es mich manchmal reizt, dann dürfte in ihr das Wort 'Sein' nicht vorkommen*]."[17]

How may one analyze the folds of denial in this conditional of writing, in the course of an oral improvisation? Can one recognize the modalities in it without first departing from the foundation and from the thing itself – here, that is, from Being and God? Heidegger speaks in order to say what *would happen if he were to write* one day. But he knows that what he says is already being written. If he were to write a theology, the word *being* would not be under erasure; it wouldn't even appear there. For the moment, speaking and writing on the subject of what he *ought to* or *could* write regarding theology, Heidegger allows the word *being* to appear; he does not use it, but mentions it without erasure when he is indeed speaking of theology, of that which he would be tempted to write. Where does this, then, take place? Does it have place? What would take place?

Heidegger continues, "Faith has no need for the thinking of Being." As he often recalls, Christians ought to allow themselves to be inspired by Luther's lucidity on this subject. Indeed, even if Being is "neither the foundation nor the essence of God [*Grund und Wesen von Gott*]," the experience of God (*die Erfahrung Gottes*) – that is, the experience of revelation – "occurs in the dimension of Being [*in der Dimension des Seins sich ereignet*]." This revelation is not that (*Offenbarung*) of which the religions speak, but the possibility of this revelation, the opening for this manifestation, this *Offenbarkeit* of which I spoke earlier and in which an *Offenbarung* can take place and man can encounter God. Although God is not and need not be thought from Being as His essence or foundation, the *dimension of Being* opens up access to the advent, the experience, the encounter with this God who nevertheless is not. The word *dimension* – which is also difference – here gives a measure while giving place. One could sketch a singular chiasmus. The anguished experience of the Nothing discloses Being. Here, the dimension of Being discloses the experience of God, who is not or whose Being is neither the essence nor the foundation.

How not to think of this? This dimension of disclosure, this place that gives place without being either essence or foundation – would not this step or passage, this threshold that gives access to God, yet be the "parvis" (*vorbürge*) of which Meister Eckhart spoke? "When we apprehend God in Being, we apprehend Him in His outer sanctuary [*parvis*], for Being is the *parvis* in which He resides." Is this a theiological, an onto-theological, tradition? A theological tradition? Would Heidegger adopt it? Would he disown it? Would he deny it?

I do not intend to respond to these questions, nor even to conclude with them. More modestly, in a more hasty but also more programmatic manner, I return to the enigma of avoidance, of negation, or of denial in a scene of writing. Heidegger says (then allows to be written in his name) that if he *were to write* a theology, he would avoid the word *being*; he would avoid writing it and this word would not figure in his text; or rather should not be present in it. What does he mean? That the word would figure in it yet under erasure, appearing there without appearing, quoted but not used? No; it should not figure in it at all. Heidegger well knows that this is not possible, and perhaps it is for this profound reason that he did not write this theology. But didn't he write it? And in it did he avoid writing the word *being*? In fact, since Being is not (a being) and in truth is nothing (that is), what difference is there between writing *Being*, this Being which is not; and writing *God*, this God of whom Heidegger also says that He is not? Indeed, Heidegger does not merely say that God is not a being; he specifies that He "has nothing to do here with Being [*Mit dem Sein, ist hier nichts anzusichten*]." But since he recognizes that God announces Himself to experience in the "dimension of Being," what difference is there between writing a theology and writing on Being, of Being, as Heidegger never ceased doing? Most of all, when he writes the word *being* under and in the place (*Ort*) of the cancellation in the form of a cross? Hasn't Heidegger written what he says he would have liked to write, a theology *without* the word *being*? But didn't he also write what he says should not be written, what he should not have written, namely a theology that is opened, dominated, and invaded by the word *being*?

With and without the word *being*, he wrote a theology with and without God. He did what he said it would be necessary to avoid doing. He said, wrote, and allowed to be written exactly what he said he wanted to avoid. He was not there without leaving a trace of all these folds. He was not there without allowing a trace to appear, a trace that is, perhaps, no longer his own, but that remains as if (*quasiment*) his own. *Not, without, quasi* are three adverbs. *Quasiment*. Fable or fiction, everything happens as if I had wanted to ask, on the threshold of this lecture, what these three adverbs mean and whence they come.

PS. One more word to conclude, and I ask your pardon for it. I am not certain that only rhetoric is at stake. But this also concerns the strange discursive modality, or rather the *step of* (not) *writing* (*pas d'écriture*), Heidegger's pass, impasse, or dodge. What does he do? He says to some students, in short: if I had to write a theology (I have always dreamed of this, but I didn't do it and know that I will never do it), I would not let the word *being* occur (*vorkommen*). It would not have a place, it would not have the right to a place in such a text. I mention this word here but I have never let it occur, it could not figure in all my work, except *in not doing it* – since I always said that Being *is not* (a being, that is) and that it *would have always had to* be written *under erasure*; a rule that I did not in fact always observe, but which I should have respected in principle, starting from the first word, *dès le premier verbe*. Understand me: this is an erasure that would above all have nothing negative about it! And even less of denegation! Etc.

What is thus the discursive modality of this *step of* (not) *writing* and of this abyss of denial? Is it first of all a modality, a simple modality among other possible ones, or rather a quasi-transcendental recourse of writing? We should not forget that we are dealing with an oral declaration, later recorded from memory by Beda Allemann. Heidegger indeed approved this protocol, but while remarking that it did not render present the atmosphere of the discussion, nor would a "complete shorthand report" have done this: no writing could have rendered what had been said *there*.

What was said *there* was addressed to colleagues and students, to disciples, in the very broad sense of this word. Like the address of Dionysius, in his apostrophe to Timothy, this text has a pedagogical or psychological virtue. It remains a text (written or oral; no matter) only in this measure: as repetition or repeatability on an *agogic* path.

But there is never a prayer, not even an apostrophe, in Heidegger's rhetoric. Unlike Dionysius, he never says "you": neither to God nor to a disciple or reader. There is no place, or in any case there is no regularly assigned place, for these "neither true nor false" utterances that prayers are, according to Aristotle. This may be interpreted in at least two ways, which appear contradictory.

1   This absence signifies in effect that theology (in the sense in which Heidegger links it to faith and distinguishes it from theiology and from metaphysical onto-theology) is rigorously excluded from his texts. It is well defined there but excluded, at least in what ought to *direct* it, namely the movement of faith. And in fact, while thinking that solely the truth of Being can open onto the essence of the divinity and to what the word *god* means (one is familiar with the famous passage in the "Letter on Humanism"), Heidegger says no less: "At the interior of thought, nothing could be accomplished that would prepare for or contribute to determining what happens in faith and in grace. If faith summoned me in this manner, I would close down shop. – Of course, interior to the dimension of faith, one yet continues to think; but thinking as such no longer has a task."[18] In short, neither faith nor science, as such, thinks or has thinking as its task.

This absence of prayer, or of apostrophe in general, also confirms the predominance of the theoretical, "constative," even propositional form (in the third-person, indicative present: S is P) in the rhetoric, at least, of a text which yet forcefully questions the determination of truth linked to this theoreticism and to this judicative form.

2   But at the same time, on the contrary, one can read here a sign of respect for prayer. For the formidable questions evoked by the essence of prayer: can or must a prayer allow itself to be mentioned, quoted, and inscribed in a compelling, *agogic* proof? Perhaps it need not be. Perhaps it must not do this. Perhaps, on the contrary, it must do this. Are there criteria external to the event itself to decide whether Dionysius, for example, distorted or rather accomplished the essence of prayer by quoting it, and first of all by writing it for Timothy? Does one have the right to think that, as a pure address, on the edge of silence, alien to every code and to every rite,

hence to every repetition, prayer should never be turned away from its present by a notation or by the movement of an apostrophe, by a multiplication of addresses? That each time it takes place only once and should never be recorded? But perhaps the contrary is the case. Perhaps there would be no prayer, no pure possibility of prayer, without what we glimpse as a menace or as a contamination: writing, the code, repetition, analogy or the – at least apparent – multiplicity of addresses, initiation. If there were a purely pure experience of prayer, would one need religion and affirmative or negative theologies? Would one need a supplement of prayer? But if there were no supplement, if quotation did not bend prayer, if prayer did not bend, if it did not submit to writing, would a theiology be possible? Would a theology be possible?

Abbreviation

DN   *The Divine Names* in Pseudo-Dionysius, *The Complete Works*, trans. Colne Luibheid (New York: Paulist Press, 1987), pp. 47–141.

Notes

1 Quoted by Jean-Luc Marion in *L'Idole et la distance* (Paris: Grasset, 1997), p. 249. Here I refer to this work, and in particular to the chapter "The Distance of the *Requisit* and the Discourse of Encomium: Dionysius." I must admit that I had not read this book at the time of writing this lecture. This book was in fact published in 1977, and its author had amicably sent it to me. Discouraged or irritated by the signs of reductive misunderstanding or injustice concerning me, which I thought I had immediately discerned, I made the mistake of not continuing my reading, thus allowing myself to be diverted by quite a secondary aspect (namely, his relationship to my work); today, after rereading Dionysius and preparing the present lecture, I better perceive the force and the necessity of this work – which does not always signify, on my part, an agreement without reservations. Since the limitations of this publication do not permit me to explain myself, I defer the matter until later. Nevertheless, the few lines in which I distinguish between prayer and encomium, like the references to *Dieu sans l'être*, were subsequently added to the exposition that I had devoted to prayer in the lecture read in Jerusalem. I did this in response and in homage to Jean-Luc Marion, who seems to me to give the impression all too quickly that the passage to the encomium is the passage to prayer itself, or that between these two the passage is immediate, necessary, and in some way analytic. Notably, when he writes: "Dionysius tends to substitute another verb for the *speaking* of predicative language, ὑσμνεῖν, to praise. What does this substitution signify? It no doubt indicates the passage of the discourse to prayer, because 'prayer is a λόγος, but neither true nor false' (Aristotle)" (p. 232). What Aristotle says, as a matter of fact, in the *Peri Hermeneias* (17a), is that

if all *logos* is significant (*semantikos*), only one in which one can distinguish the true and false is *apophantic*, and constitutes an affirmative proposition. And he adds: This does not appertain to all *logos*; "thus prayer [*eukhè*] is a discourse [*logos*], but neither true nor false [*all'outè alethès oute pseudes*]." But would Aristotle have said that the encomium (*hymnein*) is not apophantic? That it is neither true nor false? That it has no relationship to the distinction between the true and the false? One may doubt this. One may even doubt it in the case of Dionysius. For if the encomium or the celebration of God indeed does not have the same rule of predication as every other proposition, even if the "truth" to which it lays claim is the higher truth of a hyperessentiality, it celebrates and names what "is" such as it "is," beyond Being. Even if it is not a predicative affirmation of the current type, the encomium preserves the style and the structure of a predicative affirmation. It says something about someone. This is not the case of the prayer that apostrophizes, addresses itself to the other and remains, in this pure movement, absolutely pre-predicative. Here it does not suffice to underscore the performative character of utterances of prayer and encomium. The performative itself does not always exclude predication. All the passages from the *Divine Names* or the *Mystical Theology*, to which Marion refers in a note (n. 65, p. 249) as "confirmation," involve an encomium or, as M. de Gandillac sometimes translates, a celebration that is not a prayer and that entails a predicative aim, however foreign it may be to "normal" ontological predication. One may even risk the following paradox: sometimes the celebration can go further than the prayer, at least in supplementing it where it cannot "accomplish" itself, namely, as Dionysius says, in the "union" (*DN*, ch. 2:680bcd). Even if the encomium cannot merely bring to light (*ekphainein*) or say, it says and determines – as that which it is – the very fact that it cannot show and know, and to which it cannot unite itself even by prayer. If prayer, at least according to Dionysius, tends toward union with God, the encomium is not prayer; it is at most its supplement. It is what is added to it, when union remains inaccessible or fails to occur, playing the role of substitute, but also determining the referent itself, which is also the cause (the Réquisit, Marion would say) of the prayer. It can incite to prayer, it can also follow it, but it is not identical with it. From many other possible examples, here I recall only the one Marion rightly quotes, underscoring a few words: "We must merely recall that this discourse does not aim to bring to light (εκφαινειν) the hyperessential essence insofar as it is hyperessential (because it remains unspeakable, unknowable, and thus entirely impossible to bring to light, *eluding all union*), but much rather to praise the procession which makes the essences and which comes before all the beings of the [trinitary] thearchy, a principle of essence" (*DN*, ch. 5:816c; cited by Marion on pp. 249–50). This passage may be found on p. 128 of the (often different) translation by Maurice de Gandillac in the *Oeuvres complètes* of Pseudo-Dionysius the Areopagite (Paris: Aubier-Montaigne, 1943). Not to bring to light, not to reveal (*ekphainein*), not to make access to it by a revelation reaching "union": this is not exactly not to speak, not to name, nor even to abstain from attributing (even if this is beyond Being). This is not to avoid speaking. It is even to start to speak in order to determine the addressee of the prayer, an addressee who is also *aitia*, of course, and cause or *requisit* of the prayer, according to a trinitary beyond of Being, a thearchy as principle of essence.

2 Marion, *L'Idole et la distance*, p. 240.

3 *Quasi stella matutina*, in *Meister Eckharts Predigten* (Göttingen, 1924), 1: 142.

4 Repetition appears at once proscribed and prescribed, impossible and necessary, as if it were necessary to avoid the unavoidable. To analyze the law of these paradoxes from the viewpoint of writing (notably in the current sense of the word) or of a pedagogical initiation – which is much more than a "point of view" – it would be necessary to follow very closely such a passage in the *Divine Names*, for example, as that which explains to us why it would be "folly" to "repeat the same truths twice." For example, those of the *Theological Elements* of "our preceptor Hierotheus." If Dionysius undertakes to write other treatises, "and particularly that which one reads here [*kai ten parousian theologian*]," it is only to introduce *supplements* adapted to our forces (expositions, clarifications, distinctions), where Hierotheus had magisterially contented himself with a collective picture of fundamental definitions. Because these supplements do not fill a lack, they repeat without repeating what is already said, virtually. They follow the order given and obey a given order. They transgress no law; on the contrary, "everything happened as if he [Hierotheus] had prescribed that we, and all other preceptors of still inexperienced souls, introduce expositions and distinctions by a reasoning which was adapted to our forces." But the order, the prayer, or the request also come from the reader, from the immediate addressee, Timothy, *as if* he reflected Hierotheus' prescription ("everything happened as if he had prescribed that we . . ."): "And to this task you yourself have often committed us, and have sent back the book of Hierotheus, judging it to be too difficult." From the most difficult to the simplest, the *adjunction* of supplements only compensates for *our* weakness and not for a gap on the side of what there is to read. Even before determining our relationship to the major text of Hierotheus, the first master, this supplementarity will have marked the relationship of Hierotheus' writing to God's writing, or rather, to God's "dictation." And thus the elite or the hierarchy – and analogy – is constituted: "the instructions of his complete and presbyterial thoughts – which might be viewed as *new adjunct writings* in conformity with the writings of those anointed of God – are for those beyond the many. Thus, we will transmit what is divine according to our logos to those who are our equals . . . The eyewitness vision of the intelligible writings and a comprehensive instruction in these require the power of a presbyter, but the knowledge and thorough learning of the reason which bear one to this are adapted to those dedicated and hallowed persons who are inferiors" (*DN*, ch. 3:681bc); my italics [translation modified slightly – KF]). Always in view of a greater sanctification, and thus of aging well, the consideration of age only takes on its sense from this analogy and this teleology.

5 This passage is translated directly from the French version cited by Derrida.

6 *Meister Eckharts Predigten*, 3:437.

7 Ibid., 1:150.

8 Martin Heidegger, *Einführung in die Metaphysik* (Tübingen: Max Niemeyer, 1953), pp. 50–1. In English, see *An Introduction to Metaphysics*, trans. Ralph Manheim (New Haven: Yale University Press, 1959), p. 66.

9 Ibid., p. 6 in the German original and p. 7 in the English translation.

10 Although this distinction is essential and stable, it does not always receive a terminological equivalent as clear as, for example, in Martin Heidegger, *Hegel's Concept of Experience* (New York: Harper and Row, 1970), p. 135: "The science Aristotle has described – the science that observes being as beings – he calls First

Philosophy. But first philosophy does not only contemplate beings in their beingness [*Seiendheit*]; it also contemplates that being which corresponds to beingness in all purity: the supreme being. This being, τὸ Θεῖον, the Divine [*das Göttliche*], is also with a curious ambiguity called 'Being.' First philosophy, as ontology, is also the theology of what truly is. It should more accurately be called theiology. The science of beings as such is in itself onto-theological." See also Heidegger's course on *Schelling* (1936; Tübingen: M. Niemeyer, 1971), pp. 61–2. Insofar as it is distinct from the onto-theological theology, theology had been defined in *Sein und Zeit* (p. 10): a "more originary making explicit" of the being of man in his relation to God, starting from the "meaning of faith." See Heidegger's *Nietzsche* (Pfullingen: Neske, 1961), 2:58–9. In the preceding chapter, "Nihilismus, *nihil* und Nichts," Heidegger defines the essence of nihilism (from which Nietzsche will not have escaped): not to take seriously the question of the Nothing, "the essential non-thinking of the essence of the Nothing [*das wesenhafte Nichtdenken an das Wesen des Nichts*]" (ibid., pp. 53–4).

11 See, in particular, the résumé of a session of the Académie Évangélique, early in December 1953, in Hofgeismar, *Heidegger et la question de Dieu*, trans. Jean Greisch (Paris: Grasset, 1980), p. 335.

12 *Es gibt die Zeit, es gibt das Sein*, says "Zeit und Sein" in 1962. Later printed in Martin Heidegger, *Zur Sache des Denkens* (Tübingen: Max Niemeyer, 1969), pp. 1–25. There is no question of reversing priority or a logical order and saying that the gift precedes Being. But the thinking of the gift opens up the space in which Being and time give themselves and give themselves to thought. Here I cannot enter into these questions, to which in the 1970s I devoted a seminar at the École Normale Supérieure and at Yale University (*"Donner le temps"*), which expressly orient all the texts I have published since about 1972.

13 Heidegger sometimes quotes Meister Eckhart, and frequently in regard to the thinking of the thing. "As *the old master of reading and living*, Meister Eckhart, says, in what is unspoken of their language [i.e., that of things] is God first God" (Martin Heidegger, *Der Feldweg* [Frankfurt am Main: Vittorio Klostermann, 1953], p. 4; my italics). It is always on the subject of the thing that he associates the name of Dionysius (who, to my knowledge, he cites nowhere else), with that of Eckhart: "Meister Eckhart employs the word *dinc* both for God and for the soul . . . Thereby this *master of thought* [my italics] by no means wishes to say that God and the soul are similar to a boulder: a material object; *dinc* is here the cautious and reserved name for something that is in general. Thus Meister Eckhart says, following a passage of Dionysius the Areopagite: *diu minne ist der natur, daz si den menschen wandelt in die dinc, die er minnet* [the nature of love is that it transforms man into the things he loves] . . . Like Meister Eckhart, Kant speaks of things and understands, by this word, something that is. But for Kant, what is becomes an object of representation [*Gegenstand des Vorstellens*]" ("Das Ding," in *Vorträge und Aufsätze* [Pfullingen: Neske, 1954], p. 169). I quote this last phrase because, as we shall see, it is not without relation to the reason for which Heidegger writes the word *being* under erasure. Concerning the concept of *Gemüt* in Heidegger and a tradition that also leads back to Eckhart, among others, see my *De l'Esprit: Heidegger et la question* (Paris: Galilée, 1987), p. 125 and *passim*.

14 By an analogous but no doubt radically different gesture, Jean-Luc Marion inscribes the name of God under a cross in *Dieu sans l'être* (Paris: Fayard, 1982), "crossing G̶o̶d̶

with the cross which reveals Him only in the disappearance, His death and resurrection" (pp. 152–3). This is another thinking of the gift and of the trace, a "theology" which would be "rigorously Christian" by sometimes opposing itself to the most kindred thoughts, those of Heidegger in particular: "these questionings could join together in a topical, apparently modest question: does the name of ~~God~~, who crosses Himself with a cross because He crucifies Himself, arise from Being? We say nothing of 'God' in general, or of thought which takes its starting-point from the divine, hence also from the fourfold; we speak of the ~~God~~ who crosses himself with a cross because He reveals Himself by His being placed on the cross, the ~~God~~ revealed by, in, and as Christ; in other words, the ~~God~~ of rigorously *Christian* theology" (p. 107). By placing a cross on "God" rather than on "Being," Marion proposes to subtract the thinking of the gift, or rather of the *trace* of the gift, because there is also and still at issue a thinking of the *trace*, from the Heideggerian fourfold: "~~God~~ gives. The giving [*donation*], giving one cause to guess how 'it gives,' a donation, provides the only accessible trace of Him who gives. Being/beings, like everything, if it is taken into view as a giving, can therein allow one to guess the trace of another gift. Here solely the model of the gift which one admits is important – appropriation or distance. In the former case, naturally, the agency of ~~God~~ could not intervene, since the giving [*donner*] is included in the fourfold . . . There remains to be glimpsed – if not with Heidegger, at least from his reading and, if necessary, against him – that ~~God~~ does not belong to Being/beings, and even that Being/beings arises from distance" (pp. 153–4). This thinking of the trace is thus also that of a "distance" not reducible to the ontological difference.

15 See, among many other places, the first page of Martin Heidegger, "Die Sprache im Gedicht: Eine Erörterung von Georg Trakls Gedicht," in Martin Heidegger, *Unterwegs zur Sprache* (Pfullingen: Neske, 1959), p. 37. In English, see Martin Heidegger, *On the Way to Language*, trans. Peter D. Hertz (New York: Harper and Row, 1971), p. 159.

16 "Metaphysics is onto-theology. Whoever has experienced theology in its own roots – both the theology of the Christian faith and that of philosophy – today prefers, in the realm of thinking, to *remain silent* [*schweigen*] about God. For the onto-theological character of metaphysics has become questionable [*fragwürdig*] for thought, not on the basis of any atheism, but out of the experience of a thinking that has shown, in onto-theology, the as yet *unthought* unity of the essence of metaphysics." See the bilingual edition of Martin Heidegger's *Identity and Difference*, trans. Joan Stambaugh (New York: Harper and Row, 1969), pp. 54–5 and 121. I have underscored the words *remain silent*.

17 This seminar was translated and presented by F. Fediér and D. Saatdjian in the review *Po&sie* (1980), vol. 13, and the passage I quote was also translated in the same year by Jean Greisch in *Heidegger et la question de Dieu*, p. 334. The German text of the privately circulated edition was quoted, for the passage that interests us, by J.-L. Marion, in *Dieu sans l'être*, p. 93.

18 Report of a session of the Evangelical Academy in Hofgeismar, December 1953, trans. Jean Greisch, in *Heidegger et la question de Dieu*, p. 335.

Translated by Ken Frieden

Luce Irigaray (b. 1930): Introduction

Grace M. Jantzen

Luce Irigaray is a psychoanalyst and philosopher whose work is of enormous importance for many aspects of feminism, not least a feminist philosophy of religion. She was born in Belgium in 1930, and her initial training was in Louvain; she then moved to Paris, and after the student revolts and upheavals of 1968 she became a teaching member of the newly established University of Paris VIII at Vincennes, where she worked closely with the psychoanalyst Lacan. After the publication in 1974 of her book *Speculum of the Other Woman*,[1] which could be described as a feminist rereading of the psychoanalytic and philosophical canon, Lacan had her dismissed from her post. Irigaray continued to write and to lecture in many contexts, worked in close association with the Italian Communist Party, and has had a vast influence especially among feminists, not only on the Continent but also in the English-speaking world. She is currently Director of Research at the Centre National de Recherche Scientifique in Paris.

The article "Equal to Whom?" is a critical review of Elisabeth Schüssler Fiorenza's book *In Memory of Her*,[2] first published in 1983 and translated into French in 1986. It thus forms a useful bridge for English-speaking readers into Irigaray's thought, since many English feminists will be familiar with Schüssler Fiorenza's work; indeed, the idea of a "bridge" assumes great importance in this article. Irigaray begins by considering Schüssler Fiorenza's thesis that the early Jesus movement prominently included many women, whose work and very existence were subsequently written out of the Gospels and early Christian history because of the patriarchal bias of the Greco-Roman world. However, Irigaray then uses her reflections on Schüssler Fiorenza as a launching pad for her own themes on sexual difference and the divine. Before we look at these in more detail, it will be useful to sketch some of the ideas central to Irigaray's work prior to the writing of "Equal to Whom?" – ideas which she takes for granted in this article.

It should hardly be surprising that Luce Irigaray, as a French feminist intellectual, would be heavily influenced by Simone de Beauvoir. However, Irigaray does not simply appropriate Beauvoir's thought, but uses it as a basis for her own thinking, the result of which is in one important respect a complete reversal. Perhaps the most famous line of Beauvoir's *The Second Sex* is her statement, "One is not born woman, but rather becomes a woman."[3] The cultural category "woman" is a social construction of patriarchy; and it is this, not nature, which has rendered women inferior, powerless, and oppressed. Simone de Beauvoir's personal aim and her exhortation to other women is to achieve "transcendence" from nature, to claim equality with men especially in the intellectual and political realms, rather than be stuck in nothing but reproductive activity. But what Irigaray notes (as also does Schüssler Fiorenza) is that such a strategy actually still leaves men as the norm of humanity, to whom women must strive to become equal. It does not open the way for a valuation of *women*. Therefore, although Irigaray of course requires that women should not be discriminated against in law, education, politics, religion, and so on, her aim is not simply to press for equality while leaving the male norm intact, but rather to challenge that norm by insisting on the specificity of sexuality: Women and men are *different*, not simply equal. This emphasis on sexual difference is both the central insight and the source of some troublesome problems in Irigaray's work.[4]

Connected with the theme of sexual difference is Irigaray's account of subjectivity. Here the central influence is psychoanalysis as mediated by Freud and Lacan. One of their most basic insights is that, contrary to the philosophical tradition of Descartes or Locke, human subjectivity is not a simple given. Rather, it is achieved, and achieved at considerable cost. A human being begins life as a mass of conflicting desires: In order to become a unified subject, some of these will have to be repressed, thereby forming the unconscious, which may always threaten to erupt. Moreover, this unification, if it is to effect successful entry into society, will have to take place according to the norms of that society, which in the case of Western modernity are heavily masculine and heterosexual. Thus in Freud's account of the Oedipus stage the young boy under threat of castration represses his desire for his mother and tries to become like his father, eventually taking his father's place in society. The cost of this, however, is a denial of some of his most central longings, especially those for his mother. This denial may be so painful that it results in anger, fear, or hatred toward anyone who reminds him of it; hence the misogyny and homophobia of Western modernity.

Irigaray accepts (with important qualifications) the psychoanalytic doctrine that subjectivity is achieved, not given, and that this achievement is socially and historically constructed. However, in her books *Speculum of the Other Woman* and *This Sex Which is Not One*,[5] she demonstrates that when Freud and Lacan talk about achieving subjectivity, they are talking about *male* subjects. For Freud, the female is defined by a lack: A little girl is a little boy without a penis. Lacan similarly speaks of woman as the "not all"; it is the male for whom subjectivity is possible.[6] For Irigaray, therefore, a twofold question arises: Can women be subjects? And how can women achieve subjectivity *as women*, not becoming "one of the boys" as Simone de Beauvoir wanted to do, but becoming who *we* are in our own right rather than defined in relation to men?

According to Freudian theory modified by Lacan, the achievement of subjectivity (and the repression of unacceptable desires) takes place according to the Law or Name of the Father. This thinly disguised religious formula indicates the authoritative nature of social demand, its patriarchal character, and also its linguistic structure. Indeed the obverse of the boy's repression of his desire for his mother is his entry into the language and civilization and social world of the fathers, which Lacan refers to as "the symbolic." "The symbolic" in French thought designates far more than what are conventionally called symbols; it includes all of language as well as nonlinguistic forms such as music and art. Moreover the symbolic is structured into discourses of incalculable influence; formative among these in the modern West are the discourses of law, science, economics, and religion. But all of these, indeed language itself in the Lacanian view, is always already masculine, its point of entry the Name of the Father.

But then how can a woman speak? And what sort of cataclysm would occur if women did speak? For Irigaray (as for other French psychoanalysts) the question of women speaking is closely tied up with the question of women achieving subjectivity. If becoming a subject means entry into language, and if language is always already masculine, then a woman could achieve subjectivity, if at all, only to the extent that she became masculinized, entered into masculinist structures of rationality and discourse, and did not rock the boat. And of course the discourses of law, religion, and science have served to keep women "in their place," subservient to and within the symbolic order. Irigaray, however, serves notice that things are not that simple. Maybe the reason Freud and Lacan could not discover the answer to their question "what do women want?" the reason they could not admit that women could speak, was because they were not *listening*: They were first defining women into silence and then complaining about it. Irigaray develops a multifaceted strategy of eliciting women's voices, listening for the silences, the lacunae, the sounds from the margins, listening not just to fathers and sons but to mothers and daughters.

Most important in all this, for Irigaray, is the disruption of the symbolic, displacing its masculinist structures by a new imaginary, new ways of conceiving and being which enable women to be subjects *as women*. And since religious discourse has been and continues to be of unparalleled importance in the self-conceptualization of the West, it is the religious symbolic above all which requires to be disrupted. This disruption is what Irigaray is looking for in Schüssler Fiorenza's book; and in the end is somewhat disappointed. But rather than leave the matter there, Irigaray uses her review to suggest how it could be done, how the religious symbolic could be subverted in ways that would enable women to become subjects.

Contrary to much secular feminist thought, Irigaray is clear that religion cannot just be ignored or written off; it has to be transformed. In her essay "Divine Women" she argues that "in order to become," that is, to achieve subjectivity, it is necessary to have a "horizon," an ideal of wholeness to which we aspire.[7] The symbolic of religion, and in particular the idea of God, has provided such a horizon for becoming. However, men have constructed an idea of God which has been destructive of women, and in relation to whom masculinity is exalted and distorted. "Man has sought out a unique *male* God. God has been created out of man's gender . . . He is father, son, spirit. Man has not allowed himself to be defined by another gender: the female. His unique God is assumed to correspond to the human race."[8] But where are women in all this? Although women are often religious, the religions of the West with their male God(s) offer no way for women to achieve *our* subjectivity in relation to a divine horizon. As Irigaray puts it,

> We have no female trinity. But as long as woman lacks a divine made in her image she cannot establish her subjectivity or achieve a goal of her own. She lacks an ideal that would be her goal or path in becoming . . . If she is to become woman, if she is to accomplish her female subjectivity, woman needs a god who is a figure for the perfection of *her* subjectivity.[9]

The masculinist religious symbolic must be disrupted and space made for the female divine. "This God, are we capable of imagining it as a woman? Can we dimly see it as the perfection of our subjectivity?"[10]

It is this agenda which Irigaray brings to her reading of Elisabeth Schüssler Fiorenza's work. She looks for a new account of women subjects in Christendom, and beyond that for a new understanding of the divine horizon, one that will be available to enable women's becoming. But her hopes are only partly fulfilled. Initially she is enthusiastic. Schüssler Fiorenza's hermeneutic of suspicion about the patriarchal bias of early Christian texts leads her to an interpretation "through a hypothesis of blanks, lacunae, overdeterminations, and persistent blindspots": just the sort of tactics Irigaray has used to such effect with the writings of Freud and the Western philosophical tradition. But Irigaray is uneasy about Schüssler Fiorenza's claim that it was the Greco-Roman influence which brought about this silencing of women and that the Jewish roots were more women-friendly. Surely such an opposition between the Greco-Roman and the Judeo-Christian is too simplistic; each of these has multiple strands, some of which are matriarchal and some misogynist.

This historical consideration quickly leads to another: Were women really so central in early Christendom as Schüssler Fiorenza claims? Surely in the Gospels and indeed implicitly in Schüssler Fiorenza's own work, it is after all Jesus who is at the center, not women, even if it can be shown that women were far more significant among his followers than Christendom has acknowledged. Indeed, unless there were this implicit focus on Jesus, unless his words and deeds were taken as crucially significant, it would hardly matter whether there were many women around him or how he treated them. It is only because Jesus is taken as in some sense paradigmatic or central that his attitude to women is normative. Thus, while Irigaray delights in Schüssler Fiorenza's recovery of the hidden women of early Christendom, and sees her book as vastly preferable to neutral/neuter renderings of the Christian message, the question remains: Who is this man Jesus at the center of the Gospels? Is there any way in which a male Jesus can enable women's achievement of subjectivity? Or is this just another rendition of the God-Father limiting the horizon of women's becoming?

It is at this level that Irigaray is ultimately disappointed with Schüssler Fiorenza's book: It does not sufficiently challenge or displace the traditional masculinist religious symbolic. As Irigaray says, "monotheistic religions speak to us of God the Father and God made man; nothing is said of a God the Mother or of God made Woman, or even of God as a couple or couples." Although at a sociological level Schüssler Fiorenza has raised important questions about women in early Christendom, at the level of ontology she remains, even if critically and uneasily, within a monotheistic and trinitarian doctrinal system which affirms both the maleness and the uniqueness of Christ. And as Irigaray says, "sociology quickly bores me when I'm expecting the divine." Perhaps Irigaray does not give Schüssler Fiorenza sufficient credit for her insistence that Scripture and doctrine should be treated as prototype, not archetype, a position which might allow for expansion and change in the directions Irigaray advocates. However that may be, Schüssler Fiorenza herself does not explore the possibilities of a move beyond monotheism and its implicit masculinism; she remains with the Roman Catholic framework.

The excitement of Irigaray's article is that she does not stop with this disappointment, but goes on to make suggestions about how Jesus could indeed be understood in a way that would enable the divine becoming of women. She starts by taking seriously – arguably more seriously than Schüssler Fiorenza does – the doctrine of incarnation, that Jesus was God made flesh. As she points out, the Gospels make much of this: "every stage in the life of Christ is noted and described in the Gospels as an event of the body," from conception and birth to fasting, healing, and wedding festivals, suffering and death. Jesus cannot be reduced to speeches or abstractions. His bodiliness is always central. Now flesh, at any rate human flesh, is always sexually specific, and this is also true of Jesus. He was male. "Why," asks Irigaray, "is his sexual incarnation denied or treated on a human plane alone?"

At first sight that question might appear appallingly misplaced: Has not the maleness of Jesus been used endlessly in the Christian tradition as conclusive proof of the superiority of men, the exclusion of women from the priesthood, the identification of women with the sinfulness of Eve over against the male Christ the second Adam? Irigaray is not denying any of this. Her question rather is getting at something deeper. Maleness is after all only *one* of the sexes; it is only part of humanity, not the whole of it. So if Jesus was male, and was God made flesh, then he was only a *partial* incarnation. He could not be the whole, the unique and only one, since he did not encompass all of humanity. Indeed, so far from seeing the incarnation as an endorsement of Jesus as the unique one, Irigaray argues for "the incarnation of all bodies (men's and women's) as potentially divine; nothing more nor less than each man and each woman being virtually gods." If this is not to be the case, if Jesus is taken as in traditional Christendom as unique, then he "truly does represent the realization of the Patriarchy, the appearance of the father's and the Father's power," and feminists should have nothing to do with defending him. But if he was partial, then his incarnation leaves room for other incarnations, other trinities, other sexualities. The masculinist symbolic is subverted, and the door is open for women to develop a new religious imaginary which will enable our sexuate becoming.

Irigaray suggests that Jesus himself saw his incarnation as a partial one, as he indicated in his promise of the Paraclete. I am not clear whether or not she means this as a sober historical claim (which I suspect would be difficult to substantiate). What is more important is that she sees Jesus as a bridge: a bridge between men and God the Father, but also a bridge in the recognition that incarnation, divine flesh, must also be female, that each of us is (and is to become) divine. Women are not called upon to be equal to men: Are we not rather called upon to be equal to God – God the mother, the daughter, and the sister?

The implications of such a calling reverberate in every corner of theology and throughout the construction of society. Irigaray indicates some of the practical ecclesiastical consequences, such things as the priesting of women and women's celebration of the eucharist. Much more searching, however, is the task here signaled of subverting the masculinist religious symbolic in every theological doctrine and practice, and developing a feminist imaginary of the divine to enable women's becoming. Irigaray has given pointers toward this in "Equal to Whom?" It will need many women and men thinking and working together if we are to develop a religious imaginary respectful of sexual difference; and the result will not be the Christianity we have known.

Notes

1 Luce Irigaray, *Speculum of the Other Woman*, trans. Gillian C. Gill (Ithaca, NY: Cornell University Press, 1985). First published in French in 1974.
2 Elisabeth Schüssler Fiorenza, *In Memory of Her: A Feminist Reconstruction of Christian Origins* (New York: Crossroad, and London: SCM, 1983).
3 Simone de Beauvoir, *The Second Sex*, trans. H. M. Parshley (New York: Knopf, 1954), p. 301.
4 See Tina Chanter, *Ethics of Eros: Irigaray's Rewriting of the Philosophers* (London and New York: Routledge, 1995); Carolyn Burke, Naomi Schor, and Margaret Whitford (eds), *Engaging with Irigaray* (New York: Columbia University Press, 1994).
5 Luce Irigaray, *This Sex Which is Not One*, trans. Catherine Porter (Ithaca, NY: Cornell University Press, 1985). First published in French in 1977.
6 Jacques Lacan, "God and the *Jouissance* of the Woman," in *Feminine Sexuality: Jacques Lacan and the École Freudienne*, ed. Juliet Mitchell and Jacqueline Rose, trans. Jacqueline Rose (London: Macmillan, 1982), pp. 137–48, esp. p. 144.
7 Luce Irigaray, "Divine Women," in her *Sexes and Genealogies*, trans. Gillian C. Gill (New York: Columbia University Press, 1993), pp. 55–72, esp. p. 61. First presented in Venice in 1984.
8 Irigaray, "Divine Women," p. 61.
9 Ibid., p. 63.
10 Ibid.

Selected Bibliography

Burke, Carolyn, Schor, Naomi, and Whitford, Margaret (eds), *Engaging with Irigaray: Feminist Philosophy and Modern European Thought* (New York: Columbia University Press, 1994).
Chanter, Tina, *Ethics of Eros: Irigaray's Rewriting of the Philosophers* (London and New York: Routledge, 1995).
Ward, Graham, "Divinity and Sexuality: Luce Irigaray and Christology," *Modern Theology*, 12/2 (April 1996), pp. 221–37.
Whitford, Margaret, *Luce Irigaray: Philosophy in the Feminine* (London: Routledge, 1991).

Equal to Whom?

I began reading Elisabeth Schüssler Fiorenza's *In Memory of Her* with astonishment and joy. At last something new on Christianity! Being a Christian (male or female) might no longer relate solely to the doctrines we have been taught most if not all the time and up until the present. This new dimension would stem from the fact – one among others if the phrase "among others" can still be used – that from the beginning of the Church, of the Christian community, women were equal disciples, "ministers" in their own right. They were not mere assistants, allowed to participate at designated moments in religious ceremonies, but actual celebrants, notably of the eucharist, just as men and Jesus were.

When I think of all the arguments I have heard against the admission of women to the priesthood, Schüssler Fiorenza's views let in a breath of fresh air and a bit of spirit as well. Aren't these rational yokes precisely what brings about the paralysis of the slightest breath of spirit? As Kazantzakis's St Francis of Assisi put it: The devil must be nowhere more in evidence than in Rome, given the number of religious purges that go on there.

What led Schüssler Fiorenza to this affirmation of the equality among the disciples of Jesus is a feminist critical approach to the establishment and interpretation of fundamental Christian texts and a feminist reconstruction of history. This means that we must interpret what we know of Christian order through a hypothesis of blanks, lacunae, overdeterminations, and persistent blindspots inherent in the patriarchal bias of history. That bias leaves its mark on the discernible historical facts and their practical outcome, as well as on theological truths and imperatives. The bias would be more Greco-Roman than Judeo-Christian. Doubtless Schüssler Fiorenza expresses some reservations concerning such theological expressions, but she speaks of the Jesus movement as "a Jewish movement that is part of Jewish history in the first century" (p. 105). She also writes that "the praxis and vision of Jesus and his movement is best understood as an inner-Jewish renewal movement that presented an alternative option to the dominant [Greco-Roman] patriarchal structures rather than an oppositional formation rejecting the values and praxis of Judaism" (p. 107).

I can find little with which to agree concerning these scissions for different reasons, notably the reduction of several periods in history to a *single* one and the possibility of conjoining and opposing them as a result of this a priori reduction. In reality there is no *one* Judaism and certainly no one Judeo-Christian tradition. As far as Judaism itself is concerned, it is divided into discrete eras, each with its particular characteristics. A rereading of the Old Testament confirms the differences between Genesis and Exodus. Yet this is but a modest indication! Doesn't reducing Judaism to *one* amount to restricting the Israelites to a definition based on their reversals, limited to the horizon of their extinction, rather than affirming their complex history in which is situated, for example, the link between written law and God's disappearance from the field of human perception? According to that interpretation, Jesus would be the God present to the senses of living mortals, the divine made perceptible again through touch, sight, sound, and smell, possibly even taste mediated by smell and the fruits of the earth.[1] An amalgam of the very different epochs of the theophany runs the risk of falling into a state of fascination, a very ambiguous relationship to the Israelite and Christian peoples that is difficult for me to define. Such a reduction risks a progressive closing-off of the pathway to an understanding of those religious phenomena on which neither Jew nor Christian holds the monopoly. Moreover, how can one speak of the Judeo-Christian tradition without drawing extremely fine distinctions since the events in the life of Jesus do not generally carry the same meaning for Jews as they do for Christians? Doesn't this either force the hand of Judaism or else abolish Christianity? Doesn't it minimalize the gap between the divine which can be represented and those aspects of it which cannot? Either a *single* God or none? Doesn't it also overlook the difference in the languages used by these traditions and its impact on meaning, beyond the lack of homogeneity in the use to which these languages are put at various stages in their history? And further, doesn't this ignore the fact that Christianity is in principle not attached to an entire people and much more apolitical than Judaism, etc.?

Besides, what does it mean when Jews and Christians – supposedly less patriarchal or non-patriarchal – are set in opposition to the Greeks and Romans who, in their turn, are viewed as more patriarchal? The Greeks above all, but also the Romans, exhibit a non-patriarchal side to their histories; thus the ages of Aphrodite and the cult of Demeter were neither patriarchal nor simply mythical. They had their own institutions and singular laws, especially as concerned the ownership of property, the transmittal of names . . . and the relationship to the religious.[2] In the beginning divine truth was vouchsafed to women and passed on from mother to daughter. These ages of the divine accompanied the fertility of the earth, its flowers and fruit, and did not dissociate the human and the divine, body and mind, the natural and the spiritual. During those times love was respected in its corporeal manifestations, female fecundity took place both in and outside of marriage, and the public weal was the norm. It is certainly unrealistic to imagine that we could, by an act of determination, bring back the economy of such past eras; but it seems indispensable that we think of them as epochs that do not equate to chaos, to an archaic prehistory of myths and legends. Eras existed when female laws held sway and they possessed their own religions. To proceed to a feminist critical method and reconstruction of history would require close inspection of these women's reigns so as to interpret their qualities and characteristics in order also to come to an understanding of how and why those periods of history were censored by the phallocratic patriarchy, and what is left of them, etc. In any event, this sort of investigation into the nature of gynecocratic ages prohibits the kind of cultural opposition that Elisabeth Schüssler Fiorenza draws between the Judeo-Christian and the Greco-Roman. Such an investigation also calls on us to question our Indo-European legacy, our links to the Orient, our relations to those areas of our civilization where the status of women, and men too for that matter, as divine is conceived of in different terms.

From the same perspective, I would question the female genealogy of Jesus, the importance of women in his life and his mysterious relationship with his father. Is Jesus the equivalent of the most radical entrenchment of the patriarchy, upheld by non-figurative writing? Does he represent an attempt at reconciling the Indo-European and Semitic traditions? Or does he claim to appropriate all such traditions to himself or sum them all up in his person? In Hölderlin's phrase, "Christ is the end." What remains is the unresolved problem of woman's divinity. Being a mother is but one possible mode of woman's service to Jesus; he lacks a wife. Defining her as the Church, as Israel is defined as the bride of Yahweh, is tantamount to saying that Christ is wed to his work alone, which is not the fulfillment of humanity but a model of the patriarchal and the phallocratic. And if Jesus is seen as the totality of Mankind understood generically, then he is both man and woman, a kind of androgyne. Mircea Eliade analyzes the myths of androgyny as Mephistophelean myths. Thus representing Christ, and by extension God, as human totality would confuse him with the Evil One or with an epoch that was in league with him.

But Jesus refuted the notion of himself as this totality when he affirmed that, in order for the spirit to come into the world, he must die. The accepted Church interpretation of Jesus often disregards the fact that he is a bridge. The unanswered question remains: A bridge from whom to whom? From what to what? And what becomes of him when he is locked into patriarchal archetypes with their imperatives of belief and their denegation of all mythology? Since both patriarchy and phallocracy represent myths in action, as do all cultures, doesn't denying this fact lead to a perversion of the spirit and to the cutting off of humanity from its most important realization?

Christian patriarchal order seems indeed nearer to gloomy and repressive reason than to a celebration of the joy of a human incarnation of the divine. Even the happy celebration of the eucharist becomes an obligatory rite under the menace of sin. Nothing could be farther removed from Christ's invitation to share with him the fruits of the earth and to continue with this celebration after he is gone. It is true that Christ attracted the multitude without making demands upon them. Except in the case of those whom he had chosen as his disciples and who had accepted that role? And even from those . . . He demanded that they be available. With that said, those (men and women) who followed him did so of their own volition and not under the onus of a strict discipline. Those men and women who followed him also transgressed the interdictions of their society and culture rather than submit to the existing religious code. Thus Jesus instructed women and pagans, and preached in the open more often than in the temples. In any event, he didn't preach very much, nor did he spend much time poring over sacred texts. However, he did a lot of curing, consoled many, restored both the life of the body and of the spirit, and gave back dignity to those who had lost it, whether they were rich or poor. For Christ isn't just the Lord of the poor as today's preachers rather complacently tell us. He could use strong words to demonstrate his disapproval of the idolatry of the poor: "for you always have the poor with you . . . but me you do not always have." These are the words he offered about a woman who sprinkled perfume over him and whom Jesus' followers reproached for being "wasteful." This is what Schüssler Fiorenza evokes in *In Memory of Her*, sometimes more through her book's title than by virtue of its content. In this instance, Jesus very pointedly chose the woman and not the poor. Did he perhaps single out those (men and women) whom the patriarchy was oppressing?

Having said all that, woman's role in the Gospels really isn't as "central" as Schüssler Fiorenza would have us believe. It is Jesus himself who is at the center, surrounded by women, it's true. But it seems to me naive, demagogical (or maybe a mark of matriarchal acculturation) to say that women were "at the center" of Jesus' life. Yet neither were they excluded from most religious traditions. They took part in public and semi-private relations with Jesus, dinners among friends, festivals and the like. For the most part they were there when he preached and worked miracles; they were present in every aspect of his life: women were privately closer to Jesus than were other pagans. The manner in which women are described in the Bible is more characteristic of the cult of Aphrodite than of that of Dionysus in which, generally speaking, women are exploited by the god.[3] Mary Magdalene is an example of this. I am not surprised that Luke's interpretation in the Gospel should confuse the woman Schüssler Fiorenza quotes at the beginning of her book with Mary Magdalene herself. Her anointment strikes me as a loving one. She loves Jesus, as she attests in public and quite apart from marriage as in the non-Demeterian gynecocratic traditions. But is it a question of "propheticism" or memory? Does free love in its divine form come before or after Jesus?

In the same vein, can it be said that Jesus takes an interest in women because they are disenfranchised or because they are women? The angle of approach is different here, it seems to me. The fact that women turn out to be the poor in patriarchal and phallocratic regimes doesn't mean they got that way naturally as a result of their sex. That said, in women's time the money poor didn't exist. The only ones disenfranchised were those who had neither fruits nor vegetables and, later, grain. Patriarchy and monetary poverty go hand in hand. Gynecocratic cultures succumb to this yoking only where they subsist as part of that patriarchy itself. From this perspective arises the question of Israel's history, fraught with cosmic catastrophes and continual famine through Exodus and Exile, and all the transformations that land has undergone relative to the fruitful earth. What is the significance of men's appropriation of the divine in relation to a respect for the earth, its culture, and world famine?

In this regard, how can we interpret the place of Jesus of Nazareth? His position is complex and contradictory. Attentive to the fruits of the earth to the point of becoming one with them, he nonetheless leads a semi-nomadic life and chooses for his disciples fishers, not gatherers or farmers. One thing is certain: His teachings cannot be reduced to those of one whose generosity toward the little people knows no bounds. Within these parameters, it is short work to classify Christianity as part and parcel of all the rest, a sort of good boy–bad boy socialism depending on the country, region, or culture in question.

Elisabeth Schüssler Fiorenza's position comes close to such a socioeconomic appraisal of the Gospels. I think her interpretation is too reductive when it comes to the question of a possible theology of women's liberation. Women aren't just poor among the poor. As half of the human race, it is their exploitation that makes it possible to exploit others. This exploitation is primarily cultural and only secondarily socioeconomic.

But is Christianity a religion based on a love of the poor and the hope of salvation for the ignorant? While far and away preferable to exploitation and disdain, these qualities of Christianity strike me as but one of its aspects or effects. It is the social outcome of the respect for the incarnation of all bodies (men's and women's) as potentially divine; nothing more nor less than each man and each woman being virtually gods. If Christ's redemption of the world lacks this meaning, then I see no other worthy of such historical loyalty.

However, this message, especially as it concerns women, is most often veiled, obscured, covered over. And while the message is certainly not explicit on all these points, that is no reason to pass over it in silence. There are times in the life of Jesus when his relations with women are quite clear. Thus his public following is made up equally of men and women. Aside from the twelve apostles, Jesus speaks to women just as much as to men, and in numerous instances the Gospels relate his public spiritual exchanges with women. He discusses truth with them and occasionally decides in their favor against the existing social order, particularly on the question of the "gentiles," as Schüssler Fiorenza points out. Certainly original with Christianity is the notion of gentiles (and perhaps it is women who represent their obscure paradigm) having access to the benefits of redemption. Thus Jesus instructs women, but he also listens to them and succumbs to the force of their confidence and faith, understood not as belief but as the power of affirmation, especially in matters of spiritual receptivity and sharing (Schüssler Fiorenza, *Memory*, pp. 140–54).

Contrary to the sociocultural norms of his time, Christ approaches both women and men with the same freedom founded on wisdom rather than on logical reasoning. Read or reread the Gospels and try to find the logic of Jesus' words; he continually contradicts everything he says. Is this indicative of the importance of an age in transition, or is it these contradictions that allow his message to rise above understanding? It's touching but also revolting to hear most priests argue over Christ's contradictions in the language of everyday rationality. The Good News turns to moral platitude or falls into a social bathos bearing little resemblance to the teachings of Jesus, as far as I can see. The irrational in Jesus leads to the liberation of the spirit, not to love, not to nothingness or the spiritual and mystical torture that probably originates in the stifling or paralysis of becoming, particularly along sexual lines.

On this point concerning contradiction, the course of Jesus' life appears close to the teachings of certain Indian sages, the Buddha, for example. They resemble one another on other points as well, including the fact that spiritual becoming and corporeal becoming are inseparable. Every stage in the life of Christ is noted and described in the Gospels as an event of the body: conception, birth, growth, fasting in the desert, immersion in the River Jordan, treks to the mountain or walks along the water's edge, meals, festivals, the laying-on of hands, the draining of physical strength after a healing, transfiguration, trials, suffering, death, resurrection, ascension . . . His life cannot be reduced to speeches given in closed, airless structures, or to repetitive rituals and disincarnation, or to the unsaid, to abstractions of the flesh, or arguing fine distinctions in which the body is lost to lessons in tact. It cannot be reduced to moral injunctions or to debates among clerics

. . . Jesus disliked this. He said so. His words are in the Gospels. He made the point many times. Then why is there so much deafness? Why so many misunderstandings in handing down his story, his memory?

For me the best hypothesis here, the one most in keeping with the accounts of Jesus' life, is that women, who were his witnesses as much as men, were eliminated from all evidence relating to him. The history of the distancing of women from the announcement and sharing of the word and from the practice of the sacraments is patiently and informatively described by Elisabeth Schüssler Fiorenza in *In Memory of Her*. She discusses the first disciples' arguments on the subject and Peter's position in particular. She describes what things were like concerning women's rights and contributions within the missionary communities of Paul's time. She relates how women founded house churches and explains how women and men became the children of God through baptism, while circumcision separated the sexes as far as religion was concerned. And on this point, she recalls that becoming a Christian cannot correspond to racial, family, clan, or national rights, since it comes about as the result of the sacrament of baptism which is made available to all (men and women). And it is baptism that assures individual salvation and access to a religious community. Schüssler Fiorenza distinguishes the theological rights and duties of Christ's male and female disciples from their evolution and transformation following the patriarchalization of the Church. And so on.

Schüssler Fiorenza recounts and explains many things which clarify the status of Christian theology today. I am giving only a very imperfect account of her book. Any cultivated person, but above all any evangelical community, ought to take the time to read *In Memory of Her*. Several hours spent reading her seem far more indispensable than attending some supplemental sermon which, according to the complaints of some clerics, no one (man or woman) understands anyway. It never occurs to these priests, who blame their parishioners for not listening, for their lack of attention and application, that the problem may lie in the image the preacher is projecting. It is true that these ignorant unfortunate Christians (men and women) find themselves in such a muddle of undifferentiated persons, intermediary personal pronouns and possessives, that it's no wonder they fail to know who is who, who is speaking to whom and about whom or what, with all those "ones," those "I" 's uttered in place of you, those "we" 's uttered instead of God, and so forth. Loss of identity is thereby assured, and I refuse to liken it to the communion of saints, if such a thing exists. This subjective dejection that quickly threatens the loss of all spiritual drive, is accompanied today for Christians by the prospect of "martyrdom," the need for a "baptism by blood," rather than by spirit, and announced on the occasion of John the Baptist's feast day.

None of this keeps them from preaching the Gospel in a neutral/neuter fashion on Christmas Day in Notre Dame. Indeed, the whole effect is one of great coherence. That Christmas sermon signed "Paris," based on an evangelical text relating the childhood of Jesus, spoke of nothing else but the neutral incarnation of the word. I'm sure that the most advanced technocracy will have recognized in it the source and tone of its driving force. I'm certain, too, that cultivated (?) Parisians and carefree tourists from all nations can patronize such a God one day a year. But is this about Jesus of Nazareth? And what modern turn of mind necessitates the selection of this particular text and sermon? I see two possibilities: the more or less conscious pressure brought to bear by women's liberation movements and the fear of offending the faithful of other traditions. Actually, at that crowded Christmas afternoon service in Notre Dame, no apparition occurred. There wasn't so much as a trace of the birth of God made man, and no incarnation save the choice of text, the voice of the preacher, and the congregation gathered there. No one and nothing else.

This is obviously scandalous from the point of view of a possible feminine or feminist theology. Women, already made submissive to God the Father and God made man for centuries (sometimes under pain of a martyrdom inflicted by clerical authorities), find themselves by virtue of ecclesiastic decree, through whatever "good will," once again submitted to a neutral God. Up until now they haven't even been freed from motherhood, their only share in the redemption of the world. Out of the question to speak of their divinity as women. But also no images of the divine mother. No more incarnation either. Is this the work of science . . . or . . . ?

Is this how Christians see themselves as adults? Why invite the people to a celebration of the eucharist on Christmas day if not to glorify the felt, the corporeal and fleshly advent of the divine, this coming, all the consequences of which theology seems far from understanding. Was it the calling of theology to turn away or mask the probing mind? Is that the Christian way?

As far as the neuter is concerned, who or what allows us to cancel out the difference between the sexes in a Catholic church today? Is this Paradise with no more men or women? It's a false impression. And may God or gods keep me (us) from its realization! And should most of the clergy refuse to acknowledge the importance of sexuality, it would only be fitting for them to give up on the theology of incarnation. Do you know of any asexual life? Just because the patriarchy takes bets on a life after death and on the neutrality (neuterness) of the logos, doesn't mean that we should, in Christ's name, renounce our respect for life. Such a respect is integral to the witness he bore. Either his time is at an end, and so it's best not to continue exploiting him, even in his death, or else that time has barely come into its own as the result of an effacement of the sexual significance of his message. While other periods in history could afford to avoid that meaning, ours does so at the risk of sinking into absurdity and despair. The pathos of absurdity, so prized by the rich in our culture, leads whole peoples into a sort of profoundly depressing, really almost melancholy, state of unrest and aggression. Haven't they been deprived both of the organizing force of their own societies and of their God(s)? Have they concocted something better for their individual and collective well-being? Money? Apparently the masses are not satisfied with the substitution. A cultivation of the sexual, a spiritualization and divinization of the flesh, remain. Christ is the manifestation of only a part of this: He is God made man. But at least he's flesh and blood, living in the confines of a body and therefore sexual. He openly displays the sexual side of his relations with people. And while we know nothing of his private life, what is there about it that we ought to know? If it is true that certain sacred erotic models remove taboos surrounding sexuality and aid in its cultivation, should public teaching always be accompanied by some revelation of the instructor's private life? What perverseness, what lack of maturity, what childishness makes us want to witness the amorous behavior of those in authority in our society? By means of what narrow interpretation of the flesh do we underestimate instances of chastity as stages along the way to carnal wisdom? Apparently Christ wasn't married. Are we sure that is all we know about it? Why do we want it to be so? Perhaps because we want to avoid the duties that go along with sexual responsibility. Isn't this because we see our relationship to sexuality, and to nature, as the last irreducible reality of our lives as human beings? Of course, this view of nature and sexuality is conditioned upon their realization, not as a destiny or a fault, but as a locus of creation, creation of ourselves as body and flesh.

So is that the reason we ask why Christ's sexuality should have been that of a married man? Isn't marriage, first and foremost, the affair of matriarchs and patriarchs? Isn't it a matter of goods and property rights, names and family privileges, with no necessary connection to the divine? And isn't this so even if matriarchal solutions generally seem closer to the divine than do others as a result of their respect for all life, nature, and truth? Besides, Jesus takes a stand concerning the institution of marriage when he considers the question of divorce and the resurrection of the dead (see pp. 43–4 for Schüssler Fiorenza's comments on Mark 10: 2–9 and 18–27). He does not call upon his followers to marry. Far from suggesting some more or less obscure and perverse chasteness, this lack of allegiance to the institution of marriage may be significant as a resistance to the patriarchal structures set into place at that time. It may also denote a wish to maintain the cult of Aphrodite, to draw one example from our cultural heritage. The cult could potentially be closer to the divine as it allows all (men and women) the possibility of celebrating their love without the need for human social contracts or even a dowry. Along those lines, Mary, Mother of Jesus, might represent Aphrodite, being pregnant outside of marriage and protected as such by the angels and birds of heaven. Other women – Mary Magdalene, the other Mary, etc. – are closer to the aphrodisiac traditions than to others. As for Jesus, he claims to bring the sword, or dissension, to the family (though not among all its members, it's true: The mother–son relationship seems to be spared this, a fact that Schüssler Fiorenza fails to mention (pp. 145–6)). However, their relationship is called into question as concerns Mary's privileged status as Jesus' mother *vis-à-vis* his other women disciples. This is a question which Schüssler Fiorenza does indeed point out (p. 147). We should also recall that "fathers" are not part of Jesus' entourage, of his mixed "family of disciples" (p. 147). This seems cruelly ironic, given that the history of the Church goes counter to this pattern as it ceaselessly (as Nietzsche has it?) covers over the meaning of Jesus' life.

The denegation of Christ's incarnation as a sexual being and the use to which that denial is put in the service of sexual hierarchization and exploitation seem to have blocked an understanding of that sexual nature and confined it to the province of the patricians and Pharisees. This is what I find most compelling in Schüssler Fiorenza's theological-historical argument. But, having said that, I think it's something else that interests me in part, namely the fact that a theology of women's liberation establishes as its priority not equal access to the priesthood, but rather an equal share in the divine. This means that what I see as a manifestation of sexual liberation is God made a couple: man and women and not simply God made man.

Might Christ be the harbinger of this living reality? Why is his sexual incarnation denied or else treated on a human plane alone? To answer these questions, I would call upon the work done by Schüssler Fiorenza in *In Memory of Her* in order to formulate the hypothesis that this denial results from the exclusion of women from preaching the Gospels and from the priesthood. I believe that their lack of an "equal footing" among the disciples and their exclusion from the duties of preaching and the practice of the sacraments weigh heavily on the interpretation of the life of Jesus. At the very least the question has to be asked. Even if it should be necessary to redefine Christ as an exclusively patriarchal figure, it remains important to question why the Christian Church excluded women as ministers, if indeed they were excluded. Actually, this exclusion has been rationalized and has had a profound effect on the way the tradition has been handed down. Moreover, it has probably contributed to the cult of Christ's suffering, which has little to do with the life of Jesus of Nazareth apart from the accident of his passion and death. Jesus' life wasn't a particularly sad one, nor was it filled with drunkenness and debauchery as some would have us believe. His way of life approached wisdom.

That is to say, apart from his relation to the Father? But what does the Father mean to him anyway? And how could he have reconciled such an exclusive loyalty toward that patriarchal paradigm with his oddly liberal attitude toward women? Are we to suspect him of being Machiavellian? Because, after all, it is quite easy to dismiss him as his Father's son or as a member of a male trinity. Yet will that resolve the question of his incarnation? I think not. But I do believe that the question ought to be subjected to women's interpretation and considered a step toward becoming divine (for men and women). Otherwise Jesus truly does represent the realization of the Patriarchy, the appearance of the father's and the Father's power, the phenotype of a genotype glimpsed in the Word, since the father, unlike the mother, propagates outside himself and in a way that remains invisible. Thus, in order to affirm the reign of the father, it became necessary to eliminate the divine phenomenality of the daughter, of the mother–daughter couple, and lock it into the father–Father–son–Son genealogy and the triangle, father–son–Holy Spirit.

If this is the case, what interest can women have in being disciples or priests at all? The important thing is for them to find their own genealogy, the necessary condition for their identity. And saying that Jesus is the son of God–Sophia, as Schüssler Fiorenza has (p. 134), doesn't suffice, or suffices only to confirm the end of gynecocratic genealogy, the son descended from the mother–daughter line. This being the case, it marks the appropriation of the daughter's divine status and of the mother–daughter relationship. This would mean that Jesus entrusts his mother to John and not to a woman at the moment of his death. Thus Jesus would stand for the erection of the system of patriarchal structures at the crossroads of the Greek and Semitic traditions at least. His defense at the hands of some American feminists would be rather comical! It's true that a great many European feminists know little of his life. They hope to be done with these religious traditions without having gauged their impact on the societies in which they live. They often imagine that equality in the workplace and in (neuter?) science will grant them sufficient status as subjects. This strikes me as quite an ingenuous error since they still lack what's needed to define their own sociocultural identity. Many are ready to give up the little they have in order to bring about their neutralization by means of an identification with the generic masculine: they want to be "men" or "man." I wonder if something of this kind isn't secretly at work in Schüssler Fiorenza's book, given the short shrift she gives the divinization of sex in the history of Christianity.

The last chapter of *In Memory of Her* is a call for the overall reconciliation of women: Catholics, Jews, Mormons, black, white, or homosexual, which already take into account a mixture of women's communities. But what is not clearly laid out is the conditions under which these "people of God" can get together. Though an appeal to the *ekklesia* of women is exciting, I am well enough acquainted with women's movements to know that they lack a rallying point. What they lack, at the very least, is the symbol of a divine mother. The so-called "people of God" are a people of men gathered in the name of the father, their father. What women need is a symbolic mother of daughters – woman–mother and lover – and not a mother of sons whose predications are defined by the incest taboo among others. Besides, women cannot make up their own communities removed from choices concerning history. This is why I don't believe that those women who reject the meaning of the incarnation of Christ are ready to come together in the name of sisterhood. And the same is true for those of other religions. In order for women truly to come together, there must be a reinterpretation of the meaning of all religious traditions and an examination of those which leave room for the genealogies of holy women.

Moreover, is it possible to put together the *ekklesia* of women as the "body of Christ"? Is this merely the manifestation of a zealous and pious desire? After all, Christ is not of our sex the way he is part of men's, of the people of men. And it is on selected numbers of them that the privilege of the ministry was conferred. This reality of a human and divine identity is in all likelihood the driving force behind centuries of religious law. Monotheistic religions speak to us of God the Father and God made man; nothing is said of a God the Mother or of God made woman, or even of God as a couple or couples. Not all the transcendental fancies, or ecstasies of every type, not all the quibbling over maternity and the neutrality (neuterness) of God, can succeed in erasing this one reality that determines identities, rights, symbols, and discourse. It is for this reason that I've suggested that the divine incarnation of Jesus Christ is a partial one; a view which, in any event, is consistent with his own. "If I am not gone, the Paraclete cannot come." Why not? What coming of the Paraclete can be involved here, since Jesus is already the result of its work? We do not know the incarnation of the Spirit, but the notion of a Holy Spirit as the pure product of patriarchal culture seems erroneous in view of Jesus' personality. His behavior toward women, in conjunction with his personal qualities, is evocative of a resistance to the patriarchy. Moreover, it is impossible for God to represent three instances of the masculine only as one aspect of the divine. That would be tantamount to ascribing divinity to men and the profane to women. This division, which certain men and women do not hesitate to consider the norm, has not always existed, nor has it always been the same. In the great Oriental traditions, a female trilogy exists alongside the male and, in their movements and their stability, neither one exists without the other.

However, insofar as a respect for the identity and dignity of women is concerned, two bridges must be established or re-established. One is the bridge consisting of the mother–daughter relation; the other is that of feminine identity. It is impossible to ask a woman to be holy, absolved of blame, as long as she is unable to recognize the potential holiness of her own mother. God made man or God the Father are not enough to sanctify the female sex. All those women who have progressed by virtue of the risks and not merely the claims of women's liberation (starting with their own), understand the truth of this statement regardless of the difficulties and suffering it has imposed on them. But these trials are no longer synonymous with a collective pathos. They are born of women's need to be and remain vigilant, careful, and aware, in order to free their bodies and their sensibilities and make them accessible to the intellect and the spirit. It's the path we take "in memory of her" and, if possible, of him. This requires us to let go of those secondary benefits, those attachments and habits, that are correlates of the modus operandi of society as it now exists.

As things stand, how can we ask a priest to absolve us of a sin defined as such by a so-called Christian religion unless he himself is aware of the harm done to a woman who is preached to about God the Father and God made man alone, about a masculine Holy Spirit and about her function as the mother of sons. If today's Catholic religion involves only men and their mother–wives, perhaps it might make better sense to exclude from the churches those other women who cannot find any identity of their own there. Otherwise they ought to be advised that they have to find models for themselves other than those which have been proposed. They ought to be reminded that the Church may provide them with a possible stepping-stone but not with the truth. Without such warnings, welcoming them into the Church exposes their religious openness to constant frustration and a succession of pathological effects that result from it.

Why is it that Catholicism is not in accord with the conduct of Jesus Christ? Why does it provide such a minimal public presence to Mary, Mary Magdalene, Martha, and the others? As for Protestantism, what it allows women in the exercise of pastoral functions is annulled or revoked, at least in part, by the disappearance of anything representing holy women. Patriarchal religions are decidedly cunning! Confronted with the reality of all this, what sense does it make to speak of a woman sinner? Isn't this a designation more appropriate to men, since by definition it is they who practice exclusion and sacrifice and are therefore sinners? This in no way means that women are born saints. What it does signify is that their faults and shortcomings are first of all to be defined in relation to their bodies, their mothers' bodies, and those of their daughter(s). One must first be a subject before being in a position to admit one's sins and seek repentance. In what way are women subjects in our cultures and religions? What words, images, or symbols allow women a social identity other than that of the mother of sons? And even this latter identity isn't freely chosen by women; it falls to them without any decision on their part, unless they kill their baby daughters. For centuries, in the religious communities we call our own, men have stayed pretty much to themselves. They define the systems of representation and exchange by and for themselves. And while women may possibly gain access to these systems, divine identity and divine rite are not accorded them. Should they demand their reinstatement in existing male communities, or does the future hold in store something newer than such "equality," since what does being equal mean as far as religion is concerned? Does it mean being equal to the other disciples, or to God? And how can woman be equal to that other when he is another sex?

In other words, can a claim to equality be acceptable without a fundamental respect for the subjective rights of both sexes, including the right to a divine identity? This would imply nothing more nor less than the remodeling of our culture so as to reconcile the reigns of women with patriarchal history. Only this historical synthesis (often defined as both prehistoric and historic) can reforge sexist hierarchies so as to bring about a cultural marriage between the sexes. All the rest can be tolerated in the interim only as a wish for the equal "redemption" of women and men. But equal means different and, once again not along the lines of the mother–son relation.

During this interim period, a considerable number of women refuse to confine themselves to male–female structures. And even if this withdrawal into same-sex groups doesn't accord with the liveliest and most creative engagement of human culture, those women's groups which have found no other solution to the problem should not be judged too quickly. Most misunderstanding and even provocation take place elsewhere! And isn't the Christian Church today, and for that matter society in general, part of the closed male order? While I do not find myself in agreement with Mary Daly, who often seems to me to lag behind what women might expect by way of a relationship to the divine, I would not be so quick to dismiss her choice of communal sisterhoods as is Elisabeth Schüssler Fiorenza. It may be that Mary Daly and others could do little else in their efforts to save their lives, their truth, and their own way. Personally I prefer to try everything in an effort to preserve the dimension of a sexual mix because that difference seems to me to safeguard those human limitations that allow room for a notion of the divine not defined as the result of a narcissistic and imperialistic inflation of sameness. What's more, both sexes need to form an alliance based on mutual respect; this is still far from happening. Meanwhile this detour through a separation of the sexes is preferable to discouragement, isolation, regression, and servitude. Besides, we still have everything to discover and rediscover about religion among women. So periods during which the sexes remain separate are necessary. Of course these separations cannot be controlled or recognized by men in the way traditional convents were. They must constitute moments of discovery and affirmation of the divine-made-woman (women).

In this regard, it is fitting to recall that in the early days of the Christian Church, communities of women would exclude men in order to pray and to celebrate certain rites dedicated in particular to the mother goddess. These women's communities served as "new families" and furnished "new mothers" to those women who suffered at the hands of their natural mothers (p. 174). Today this task still seems more urgent, more divine, than the one that consists of simply obliging women to have one more child with no concern for their spiritual neglect or salvation.

Nonetheless, there's no question of a "leap" (pp. 24, 26) into another world but of discovering or rediscovering feminine identity by means of concrete instances rather than through "ecstasy." We don't have to become other than what we are. But we do have to mark out a qualitative threshold. For me the mark of that threshold is sexual difference. Within one sex it is usually the quantitative factor that holds sway. What we have to do is avoid the comparative mode through the perception, practice, and expression of our sexuality, our sensitivity, and our spirit by subjectivizing our relation-ships to mother, the universe, other women, and other men. Striking a blow against the mingling of the sexes is not enough to establish an identity. Such an identity risks falling into the trap of internalizing or continuing the internalization of the thing it claims to exclude. All sociological analyses, models, and techniques fail to provide access to such an identity. And this is why *In Memory of Her* disappointed me a little after having pleased me so much. I have to ask the woman who has given us such a work to excuse me. It can be of considerable use to those who hear its message. But sociology quickly bores me when I'm expecting the divine. She describes what already exists without inventing a new subjectivity which I don't believe can be reduced to a neat social effect. This is what certain men (and women) call my "ontological" side, most often without a clue as to what that means. A feminine identity brings ontology into question again, but it can define itself only by going back to that question. And though other social strategies are valuable and useful in part, they lack subjective dimensions for defining the relations to mother, to self, to the world and other living beings, to other subjects (men and women), to existing language and culture. What's at stake here is no stranger to Christianity. Jesus is given a Father and a mother (Mother?). He's the model man–son; he has a vision of the world; he furnishes the parameters of individual, social, and cultural identity. But for women that model is inadequate, because even if, as representative of the life of Jesus, it is not in opposition to them, it does not furnish them certain needed representations of themselves, of their genealogy, and of their relation to the universe or to others. Older religions offer them better examples of mother–daughter relationships, of the divinity of woman in her own sexual body, and of her relation to nature. For me, these form a radical dimension of women's religion which cannot be treated in simple sociological terms. Most societies, at least most societies among men, are organized against nature, in spite of nature or by sacrificing nature, but not by remaining rooted in it and cultivating it. On this score communities of women are urgently needed. Mary Daly is right to be concerned with the cosmic dimensions of culture. And while I haven't read all she has written on the subject, I think it is more useful today to concern oneself with the vegetable than with the animal. This is, in any event, more closely in concert with women's traditions and their solutions for world salvation.

I think that any sermon on the salvation of the soul, on love of the poor, any so-called eucharistic ritual, any evangelical discourse that doesn't concern itself with saving the earth and its natural resources, is perverted. How can certain men and women repeat the words "This is my body, this is my blood" over the fruit of the earth without worrying about how long that earth will remain fruitful? What are these men and women talking about? There is a direct relationship between Jesus' words and the wheat and the fruit of the vine which serve life and are sufficient to it. At the moment of the eucharist, Jesus blesses and shares only what has ripened naturally and nothing that has been sacrificed. In so doing, he is perhaps re-establishing a bridge to those ancient traditions with which he keeps faith. Those traditions are often gynecocratic or matriarchal. Does he appropriate them to himself or act as their mediator? In any case, he respects them and hands them down to us as a legacy, a last sacrament.

Christianity isn't necessarily the religion of a single people. It isn't simply a social religion. It separates Church and State, but it cannot separate Jesus from nature, the divine from the corporeal, or the eucharist from a respect for the earth. Unless, perhaps, *that* Jesus is sacrilegious. I believe it is the majority of his disciples, his male disciples, who are just that.

Translated by Robert L. Mazzola

Notes

1 See Irigaray, "Epître aux derniers chrétiens," in *Amante marine* (p. 175).
2 On this point, see the works of Johan Jacob Bachofen (Swiss philosopher, 1815–87), which are invaluable for the information they provide. However, Bachofen's interpretation of the development of the patriarchy deserves to be questioned.
3 See "Quand naissent les dieux," in *Amante marine* (pp. 129–204).

Works Cited

Irigaray, Luce, *Amante marine, de Friedrich Nietzsche* (Paris: Minuit, 1980).
——"Egales à qui?" *Critique*, 43.480 (1987), pp. 420–37.
——"Femmes divines," *Critique*, 41.454 (1985), pp. 294–308.
——"Les femmes, le sacré, l'argent," *Critique*, 42.467 (1986), pp. 372–83.
Schüssler Fiorenza, Elisabeth, *Bread Not Stone: The Challenge of Feminist Biblical Interpretation* (Boston: Beacon, 1984).
——*En mémoire d'elle*, trans. Marcelline Brun (Paris: Cerf, 1986).
——*In Memory of Her: A Feminist Reconstruction of Christian Origins* (New York: Crossroad, 1983).

Julia Kristeva (b. 1941): Introduction

Pamela Sue Anderson

Kristeva was born in 1941 in Bulgaria. Convent schooling and Communist youth organizations had formative impacts upon her life. In 1966 Kristeva moved to France to do academic research, becoming a doctoral candidate on the Parisian Left Bank. She acquired a research fellowship to work with Roland Barthes during the revolutionary 1960s; her doctoral thesis, *La Révolution du langage poétique*, was published in 1974. Today she is Professor of Linguistics at the University of Paris VII, a psychoanalyst and author of more than a dozen books in psycholinguistics.

Kristeva's grounding in East European Marxism and her education by French Catholic nuns molded her thinking on religion. But her secular education and experience as a foreigner in Paris meant that she also found it logical to turn to psychoanalysis: She sought to understand how the shadow of the child remains with the adult's consciousness as a stranger within. In the 1970s and 1980s her interest grew concerning the child's entry into language in the sense of how this stranger becomes or fails to become part of its linguistic surroundings.[1] Focusing upon the acceptance of the existence of an other by the subjects of psychoanalytic and religious discourses, Kristeva writes *Au commencement était l'amour: psychoanalyse et foi* in 1985.

Here it is necessary to mention Kristeva's unusual expertise in linguistics. For instance, her Bulgarian background included gaining fluency in the Russian language and knowledge of Russian formalism. So, once in Paris, Kristeva offered valuable readings of the Soviet theorist Mikhail Bakhtin, who influenced her own analysis of forms of discourse. In addition, she met the editor Philippe Sollers (whom she married) and other intellectuals on the editorial board of *Tel Quel,* whose publications on the act of writing were influential in subverting Enlightenment philosophy. Not only was she introduced to structuralism, this French scene presented her with the rising stars of poststructuralism. Arriving in 1966 meant that she appeared on the scene the same year as both Jacques Lacan's *Écrit* and Michel Foucault's *Les Mots et les choses.*

Kristeva's involvement with avant-garde writers, especially from 1966 to 1974, ensured her vital role in the new approach to language and subjectivity called psycholinguistics. Instead of looking at the different uses of particular words, language is analyzed as a dynamic structure and a psychic process creating self-identity and gender. Kristeva's ground-breaking *Revolution in Poetic Language* established a new, non-Cartesian account of the speaking subject, introducing the key terms semiotic and symbolic to psycholinguistics.[2] There is also a political optimism in her writing, but this gradually gives way to a pessimism concerning a civilization in crisis.

In 1980, providing background to her study of love, Kristeva analyzed biblical accounts of defilement and the abject. *Powers of Horror* describes the first attempt by the nascent subject to separate itself from its mother. The abject, neither subject nor object, is not a thing but indicates a process. Abjecting the mother, the infant separates itself from a maternal union; this process of abjection creates an initial space for the constitution of identity. But this space will remain empty until the discovery of the father of individual prehistory.[3] In turn, this discovery will give way to a discourse of love, enabling the child to move on to become a speaking subject.

Kristeva's psychoanalytic discourse of love is premised upon a crucial confidence in the analyst. Her recognition of this confidence led to more specific reflections, in 1985, upon the Christian belief in a loving, protective father as essential to entry into a religious discourse.[4] During the 1980s, Kristeva developed an archaeology of love in Western history, traced through the writings of mystics, saints, and theologians. The psychoanalytic discourse of love takes the place occupied by religious discourse. Love reinforces the child's relationship with the father of individual prehistory – a figure which runs through Kristeva's writings on love, as well as those on melancholia.[5]

In the 1990s Kristeva's writings become increasingly negative. On the basis of her experience as a psychoanalyst, she diagnoses the sickness of late twentieth-century civilization: We live in a world without values, filled with hatred. Insisting that our maladies need to be confronted, Kristeva seeks to usher in a therapeutic age which will again find positive values, like those once found in religion. *New Maladies of the Soul* (1995 [1993]) supports the continuing significance of *In the Beginning was Love* (1987 [1985]).

The subtext for the latter is Freud's *The Future of an Illusion.* Kristeva's title combines "In the beginning was the Word . . . the Word was God" (John 1:

1) and "God is love" (1 John 4: 8). "Our God *Logos*" is the key to Freud's psychoanalytic cure; *logos* signifies the "talking cure" in which the word passing between the minds of the analysand and the analyst confronts illusion. But Kristeva pushes beyond Freud's idea of religion as an unshakeable illusion by focusing upon the "transitory, ludic illusions" in a discourse of love. To give illusion its proper therapeutic and epistemological value, the successful analysand must respond to an urge to create illusions while recognizing their true nature.

In the opening chapters of *In the Beginning was Love*, Kristeva argues that psychoanalytic discourse has the potential to replace the reified discourse of faith. The aim is to get behind static linguistic representations, to discover prelinguistic traces of another space of experience. She has already named the receptacle of these traces "the semiotic" from the Greek, *semeion*, for signs; this concept derives from Plato's *Timaeus* where he spoke of the unnameable, unstable receptacle or *chora* which exists prior to the nameable form of the One.[6] The image of the *chora* and its prelinguistic signs specify the status of the unconscious, emotional traces not grasped by the conscious, rational mind. The semiotic stands for something preceding, underlying, and, at times, breaking through language understood as the order of signification. For example, the semiotic is suggested in Augustine's symbolic expression of "sucking the milk [God] givest."

Kristeva's elucidation of the semiotic offers an implicit critique of the God of patriarchy. This builds upon Lacan's theory of the mirror stage in an infant's development, marking the shift from the pre-Oedipal position of love relations with the mother to the Oedipal order of relations. The mirror stage is that transitional period before the child enters both language and culture. Kristeva identifies the essential role played by the infant's identification with its own image and by the nascent self's identification with an imaginary father; this eventually leads to separation from the mother and formation of individual identity. For this formation, the subject must operate within an imaginary stage in which it strives to see itself reflected in its relations to others. Like pre-Oedipal relations, imaginary identifications return in adult life in privileged moments, notably in love relations.

The semiotic contains the pre-Oedipal position of love relations recalled in religious symbolism as signs of the maternal. Kristeva also describes love in psychoanalysis as a transference relation built upon the identificatory structure of narcissism. By introducing the idea of an imaginary father into religious discourse Kristeva proposes a potentially heretical notion: This Freudian father of individual prehistory is part of a religious fantasy, mediating between mother and child. The imaginary father gives the subject an ego-ideal, which makes possible the transition to the symbolic order of language and to acceptance of the other, even to acceptance of the authoritative Other represented by "God the Father Almighty." Kristeva continues to presuppose this mediating figure in recent work.[7]

To conceive of love as a transference relation Kristeva's analysis (in the excerpt reproduced below) builds upon the Catholic creed or "Credo." The two terms, credence and credit, link the religious and economic meanings of faith, implying a confidence in the other as well as an offering to be returned. Kristeva's reinterpretation of the Credo in terms of a psychoanalytic discourse of love sheds light on the possibility of a postmodern God: Insofar as the analysand, as postmodern believer, is forced to accept the existence of an Other, both the creation and critique of the self's protective illusions are made possible.

Preceding her analysis of the creed, Kristeva gives a phenomenology of faith. She tells how faith emerges or fails to emerge in the development of the subject from a child to an adult. In her own experience, the icon of the Virgin mother inspires Kristeva to try to imagine "gentle suffering and mysterious grace." However, the decisive obstacle to this potentially creative imagination was her secular education and consequent repression of any primary identification with a loving agency. Instead Augustine provides her with the example of a semiotic expression of "a continuity or fusion with an Other that is no longer substantial and maternal but symbolic and paternal."

The identification with this Other links the maternal and paternal functions, creating the identity of a subject-in-process. The love of the mother and child oscillates between the image of a mother–infant fusion and the abjection of the mother by the object of desire; such love tends to be too close to constitute an identity by way of identification with a loving other. Augustine expresses the love – *agapè* – of the imaginary father who enables the child to move on, to displace, to signify, to love others outside the mother–infant union. In this way, the third term becomes crucial for transference love.

The psychoanalytic discourse of love recalls the child's imaginary identification with a father who equally represents the mother's desire. But this cannot be achieved if the child remains the mother's sole object of desire. The child must realize that it does not satisfy this desire; the third party can then become its ego-ideal constituting the bridge between the maternal *chora* and the paternal law. Such an ego-ideal bridges narcissistic and Oedipal relations, and eventually bears the burden of what becomes, through social prohibitions, the internalized authority of the symbolic father. The one Almighty God of Christianity represents this authority.

Kristeva demonstrates that Christianity has been unique in tolerating, even encouraging the expression of the normally unspoken, pre-Oedipal pleasure, ego-ideal, and love associated with different aspects of the trinitarian God. With the demise of Christian faith, the psychoanalytic discourse of love between analyst and analysand becomes one of the few ways in which the adult can give expression to its fundamental desires. In the past, belief in a loving and protective God, arising within the semiotic, enabled a recoding of God the Father into the symbolic terms of law. Today religious belief can be, if necessary, replaced with a fundamental trust in a loving analyst and eventual separation. Is this agency of *agapè*, then, the postmodern God?

The Church Fathers debated the relationship between faith (belief)[8] and reason, faith and grace. In contrast, Kristeva analyzes the narrative structure and the linguistic meanings of the Credo, as the foundational text of religious discourse constitutive of Catholic faith. On this basis, faith makes possible a covenant relating the semiotic and the symbolic, as the open emotional traces of the other and the closed rational symbols respectively; faith represents a dynamic relation, fostering creativity and order.

Kristeva prefaces her analysis of Credo, "I believe in one God the Father Almighty . . .," with assertions about etymology and word meanings. The term Credo leading to the Latin form *cred-*, although in the European lexicon, is not clear. The derivation of *dhe*, "to set down," which has several Latin forms, is no more certain. The further etymological problem appears with the Indo-European *kret-*. The general yet not wholly acceptable interpretation of *credo*, *kred-dh-*, and the Vedic *srad-dhati* is "to put one's heart into something." More acceptable are the religious and economic meanings of *credo*. A similar connection exists between credence and credit in the Indo-European vocabulary: *Indra* is the god of assistance; *Sraddha* the goddess of offerings. Although Christians such as Augustine glorify the heart as the seat of faith, in its institutional embodiment Christian faith appears more consistent with the dual Indo-European meanings of faith.

While the religious meaning of faith assumes loving protection, the economic meaning of faith presupposes separation. A characteristic suffering of the believer expresses a double separation between the cosmos and the subject, and between the self and others. The offering of faith, in the sense of credit, bridges such separation. In her words, we must recognize "the separation that underlies faith." In psycholinguistic terms, the real effects of imaginary identifications by the analysand with the loving analyst are paralleled by the believer's identification with Christ's Passion; after an initial identification with love, Christ himself is separated and forsaken yet eventually recognizes the law of the symbolic Father.

With her linguistic insight into classical Chinese, Kristeva finds additional support for the dual meanings of faith. The Chinese, *xin*, "to believe" or "to be worthy of faith," contains the signs for man (*sic*) and speech. *Xin* implies the assertion of belief in a virtuous man who is worthy of confidence, in whose word one can trust. But the Chinese Confucian also looks for something beyond words which offers a harmony of spirit or "a cosmic virtue" (*qi*). *Qi* derives from the void, *xu*, which has power as the space between the believer and nature, the believer and others. In the spoken language, "to believe" is *xin fu*; and *fu* means "to wed." The wedding of personal energy and cosmic law (e.g., the *yin* and *yang* in the Chinese image of marriage) gives meaning to the emptiness of the void at the borderline of body as language and language as body. Access to the materiality of language is conditioned by such semiotic space. Thus religious discourse, read in psycholinguistic terms, affirms the need for the postmodern God to offer primary identifications for Christian believer and non-Christian believer alike. The Christian believer identifies with the Passion of Christ, while even the non-religious subject recognizes a desire to identify with a worthy and loving agency.

Kristeva analyzes the Credo of AD 381 worked out by the Council of Constantinople, but based upon the Nicene Creed of AD 325. Whoever speaks this text confesses his faith in terms of its object: the one trinitarian God. In this credal symbolization the trinitarian God satisfies psychic fantasies, perfectly linking the imaginary, the symbolic, and the real dimensions of Lacanian psycholinguistics. Kristeva offers at least five points supporting the Credo's embodiment of basic human fantasies.

First, the connection with the Almighty Father represents the fundamental desire of every subject. Substantial fusion and symbolic identification with a protective and loving father is both essential to psychic development and source of pleasure. Second, the crucifixion of the God made man recalls a guilt of the son who is put to death. Christ's Passion epitomizes the suffering for guilt (from desire for an incestuous fusion with the parent). Third, the story of Christ's suffering reveals another fundamental depression which conditions all access to language. Immediately prior to language acquisition, every child exhibits a sadness in having to renounce the maternal bliss of immediate gratification: "The child must abandon its mother and be abandoned by her in order to be accepted by the father and begin talking." Fourth, the virgin mother is an image desired by every child; the ideal of virginity suggests that the child can love its mother without fear of rivalry. Yet this ideal of female sexuality has also helped to "infantilize half the human race by hampering its sexual and intellectual passion." Finally, the concept of the three-in-one God, rather than representing dogma to the psychoanalyst, reveals fundamental desires. In moving from the macro-fantasy of faith to the micro-fantasy of the believer or analysand, Kristevan analysis exposes the constitutive sexuality of religious discourse, especially of Christianity. The individual subject's fantasies become manifest in response to specific questions: What about your father's love? What kind of son were you? Or what about your desire for virginity? The answers suggest that desire itself remains a feature of the gendered discourse of the *Credo in Unum Deum*.

Crucial to any Kristevan account of the postmodern God, who would be other than the privileged univocal deity of the modern male subject, is her proposal that a semiotic dimension precedes all linguistic unities, binary oppositions, and symbolic hierarchies. The semiotic as the receptacle of undifferentiated being is premised upon an unrepresentable maternal space shared by the bodies of mother and infant, preceding any stable subjectivity and separate identity. The paradox which has led some to reject this proposal is that the semiotic although prelinguistic can only be articulated linguistically. What has to be proven is that the semiotic as prelinguistic exists and can be recognized as subverting the symbolic order of language in creative poetry and mystic expressions. If it exists, the semiotic space would not be restricted to women. Men and women would have access to a presymbolic experience of both the maternal and paternal functions. After Kristeva, the postmodern God would have to account for both the linguistic formation of our gendered identities and belief in the otherness constitutive of our differences.

Notes

1 See Julia Kristeva, *Revolution in Poetic Language*, trans. Margaret Waller (New York: Columbia University Press, 1984 [1974]); *Powers of Horror: An Essay on Abjection*, trans. Leon Roudiez (New York: Columbia University Press, 1982 [1980]); *Black Sun: Depression and Melancholia*, trans. Leon S. Roudiez (New York: Columbia University Press, 1989 [1987]), esp. pp. 1–47; *Strangers to Ourselves*, trans. Leon S. Roudiez (New York: Columbia University Press, 1991 [1989]).

2 The semiotic and the symbolic are pre-signifying and signifying orders of language. Together they make language a dynamic signifying process. The semiotic contains pre-signifying biological and psychical energies; as such it is distinct from, yet related to the order of signification which is the symbolic. These dimensions imply a model of the human subject-in-process, in which language is not divorced from its prelinguistic source in the body. This model explains how illusions are constituted by language, yet can be confronted by decentering the conscious subject with recognition of an unconscious, semiotic space. See Kristeva, *Revolution in Poetic Language*, pp. 21–30, 68–71.

3 Julia Kristeva, "Freud and Love: Treatment and Its Discontents," in Toril Moi (ed.), *The Kristeva Reader*, trans. Leon S. Roudiez (Oxford: Blackwell, 1986), pp. 244–52.

4 Julia Kristeva, *In the Beginning was Love: Faith and Psychoanalysis*, trans. Arthur Goldhammer (New York: Columbia University Press, 1987 [1985]); also, see Julia Kristeva, *Tales of Love*, trans. Leon S. Roudiez (New York: Columbia University Press, 1987 [1983]). For discussion of Kristeva's account of love as gift, see Philippa Berry, "Kristeva's feminist refiguring of the Gift," *Paragraph*, 18/3 (1995), pp. 223–40.

5 Kristeva, *Black Sun*, pp. 23, 44.

6 Kristeva, *Revolution in Poetic Language*, pp. 24–7; reprinted in *The Kristeva Reader*, trans. Margaret Waller, pp. 92–5.

7 Julia Kristeva, "Reading the Bible," in *New Maladies of the Soul*, trans. Ross Guberman (New York: Columbia University Press, 1995 [1993]), pp. 121–6.

8 A philosophical distinction between faith and belief would not maintain this strict

opposition. Belief as a form of less certain knowledge is open to rational doubt, while only faith stands for the credal formulation to which a believer assents. Insofar as it is locked into a reification of language, faith – unlike belief – blocks the mobility of self-reflective subjectivity.

Selected Bibliography

Berry, Philippa, "Kristeva's feminist refiguring of the gift," *Paragraph*, 18/3 (1995), pp. 223–40.

Chopp, Rebecca, "From Patriarchy into Freedom: A Conversation between American Feminist Theology and French Feminism," in *Transfigurations: Theology and the French Feminists*, ed. C. W. Maggie Kim, Susan M. St Ville, Susan M. Simonaitis (Minneapolis: Fortress Press, 1993), pp. 31–48; reprinted here, pp. 235–48.

Grosz, Elizabeth, *Sexual Subversions: Three French Feminists* (London: Allen and Unwin, 1989).

Kearns, Cleo McNelly, "Kristeva and Feminist Theology," in *Transfigurations*, pp. 49–80.

Kristeva, Julia, *Powers of Horror: An Essay on Abjection*, trans. Leon Roudiez (New York: Columbia University Press, 1982 [1980]).

—— *Revolution in Poetic Language*, trans. Margaret Waller (New York: Columbia University Press, 1984 [1974]).

—— "My Memory's Hyperbole," in *The Female Autograph*, ed. Domna Stanton (Chicago: University of Chicago Press, 1984), pp. 219–37.

—— "Revolution in Poetic Language," "About Chinese Women," "Stabat Mater," and "Freud and Love: Treatment and Its Discontents," in *The Kristeva Reader*, ed. Toril Moi (Oxford: Blackwell, 1986), pp. 89–136, 138–59, 160–86, and 238–71.

—— *Tales of Love*, trans. Leon S. Roudiez (New York: Columbia University Press, 1987 [1983]).

—— *In the Beginning was Love: Faith and Psychoanalysis*, trans. Arthur Goldhammer (New York: Columbia University Press, 1987 [1985]).

—— *Black Sun: Depression and Melancholia*, trans. Leon S. Roudiez (New York: Columbia University Press, 1989 [1987]).

—— *Strangers to Ourselves*, trans. Leon S. Roudiez (New York: Columbia University Press, 1991 [1989]).

—— "In Times Like These, Who Needs Psychoanalysts?" and "Reading the Bible," in *New Maladies of the Soul*, trans. Ross Guberman (New York: Columbia University Press, 1995 [1993]), pp. 27–44 and 115–26.

Lechte, John, *Julia Kristeva* (London: Routledge, 1990).

Oliver, Kelly, *Reading Kristeva: Unraveling the Double-Bind* (Indianapolis: Indiana University Press, 1993).

Wright, Elizabeth, *Feminism and Psychoanalysis: A Critical Dictionary* (Oxford: Blackwell, 1992).

From *In the Beginning was Love*

Credence–Credit

As you know, the history of patristics consists in large part of controversies over the definition of faith. There is discussion of the relative importance of rational certainty versus grace and of the relation among the Father, the Son, and the Holy Spirit. Heresy and dogma derive from these controversies, which I shall not explore here. For the sake of simplicity I shall consider the Credo, the basis of Catholic faith and cornerstone of the Church. But before reading this text, let us attempt a direct, naive phenomenology of faith.

I am not a believer, but I recall having been born into a family of believers who tried, without excessive enthusiasm perhaps, to transmit their faith to me. My unbelief was not, however, a matter of Oedipal rebellion and signal of a rejection of family values. In adolescence, when Dostoyevsky's characters first began to impress me with the violence of their tragic mysticism, I knelt before the icon of the Virgin that sat enthroned above my bed and attempted to gain access to a faith that my secular education did not so much combat as treat ironically or simply ignore. I tried to imagine myself in that enigmatic other world, full of gentle suffering and mysterious grace, revealed to me by Byzantine iconography. When nothing happened, I told myself that faith could not come until I had endured difficult trials. The road to belief was blocked, perhaps, by the lack of hardship in my life. But the vitality, not to say excitability, of my adolescent body came between mournful images of death and everyday reality, and my macabre thoughts soon gave way to erotic daydreams.

Later, in reading about famous mystical experiences, I felt that faith could be described, perhaps rather simplistically, as what can only be called a primary identification with a loving and protective agency. Overcoming the notion of irremediable separation, Western man, using "semiotic" rather than "symbolic" means, re-establishes a continuity or fusion with an Other that is no longer substantial and maternal but symbolic and paternal. St Augustine goes so far as to compare the Christian's faith in God with the infant's relation to its mother's breast. "What am I even at the best but an infant sucking the milk Thou givest, and feeding upon Thee, the food that perisheth not?"[1] What we have here is fusion with a breast that is, to be sure, succoring, nourishing, loving, and protective, but transposed from the mother's body to an invisible agency located in another world. This is quite a wrench from the dependency of early childhood, and it must be said that it is a compromise solution, since the benefits of the new relationship of dependency are entirely of an imaginary order, in the realm of signs. However intelligible or reasonable this dynamic may be (and theology excels at describing it), it appears to be driven, in essence, by infra- or translinguistic psychic processes which behave like primary processes and gratify the individual in his or her narcissistic core. At the dawn of psychic experience Freud saw a primary identification, a "direct and immediate transference" of the nascent ego to the "father of individual prehistory," who, according to Freud, possessed the sexual characteristics and functions of both parents.[2]

This "direct and immediate transference" to a form, a structure, or an agency (rather than a person) helps to bring about primary stabilization of the subject through its enduring character; because it is a gift of the self, it both encourages and hinders the disintegrative and aggressive agitation of the instincts. This is perhaps what Christianity celebrates in divine love. God was the first to love you, God is love: These apothegms reassure the believer of God's permanent generosity and grace. He is given a gift of love without any immediate requirement of merit, although the question of just deserts does eventually arise in the form of a demand for asceticism and self-perfection. This fusion with God, which, to repeat myself, is more semiotic than symbolic, repairs the wounds of Narcissus, which are scarcely hidden by the triumphs and failures of our desires and enmities. Once our narcissistic needs are met, we can find images of our desires in stories recounting the experience of faith: the story of the virgin birth, for instance – that secret dream of every childhood; or that of the torment of the flesh on Golgotha, which mirrors in glory the essential melancholy of the man who aspires to rejoin the body and name of a father from whom he has been irrevocably severed.

In order for faith to be possible, this "semiotic" leap toward the other, this primary identification with the primitive parental poles close to the maternal container, must not be either repressed or displaced in the construction of a knowledge which, by understanding the mechanism of faith, would bury it. Repression can be atheist; atheism is repressive, whereas the experience of psychoanalysis can lead to renunciation of faith with clear understanding. The subsequent loss of a certain kind of pleasure brings the pleasure of another kind of understanding to the subject who has made such a decision; this other kind of understanding is not positive knowledge but strictly private, involving the fundamental dynamics of the psyche.

My adolescent rejection of faith probably had more to do with repression or with my overcoming auto-erotic guilt than with analytic detachment. By contrast, the ordeal of analysis requires, at a minimum, that I (analyst or analysand) accept the existence of an other. As Lacan rightly said, "There is an Other." The treatment of psychosis may suggest to the optimistic analyst that meaning – as well as the subject – is always already there, simply waiting to be established through his interpretation. A certain fideism, or even degraded forms of spiritualism, thereby find their way into psychoanalytic ideology. I hope, however, that through vigilant listening and strict adherence to interpretive logic we can be sure of continuing to see man as divided (both biological organism *and* talking subject, both unconscious *and* conscious), and to understand that man is (tenuously and intermittently) a subject only of the language enunciated by the other – the object, for each member of the group, of his or her desires and hatreds. *Other* in language, otherness in speech, here and now rather than in some "other" world, the analyst listens and speaks, and by so doing makes the other less hellish ("Hell," said Sartre, "is other people"). The result is not to prepare that other for some sort of transcendental existence but rather to open up as yet undefined possibilities in this world.

Credo

"I *believe in* one God the Father Almighty . . ."

Credo: one of the most charged and enigmatic words in the European lexicon. Ernout and Meillet suggest the etymon **kred-oh* (see the Vedic *srad-dhati*, "he believes"), but the derivation leading to the Latin form *cred-* is not clear: the same with **dhe*, "to set down," which gives several Latin forms ending in *-do* (*condo*, "to set down together," *abdo*, "to locate far from," and *sacer dos*, **sakro-dho-ts*, "priest"). The composite **kred-dh* is formally impossible in Indo-European, where **kret-* and **dhe* were independent. The real problems have to do with **kret-*.

Darmesteter was the first to interpret *credo*, *srad-dhati*, **kred-dh-* as "to put one's heart into something." Ernout and Meillet feel that this "relation [with the heart] is a hypothesis for which there is no basis," and Benveniste makes a similar point when he remarks that in Indo-European "heart" can no more be a metaphor for life or spirit than "lung" or "kidney."[3] Mayrhofer, however, feels that the hypothesis is justified: *kred-*, he says, is the composite form of **kerd-*, whereas Ernout and Meillet assume an alternating root, *k'erd-/krd*. Dumézil, who was at one time critical of Darmesteter's interpretation, has withdrawn his objections. According to the dictionary of Monier Williams, the corresponding Vedic word *srat-*, attested only in the composites *srad-dha-*, "to believe," and *srat-kar-*, "to vouch for, give assurance of," is considered in traditional Indian etymology a synonym of *satya-*, "truth." He sees a parallel between *srat-* and the Latin *cor, cordis*, as well as the Greek χαρδια.

Benveniste's comments on the question are important. After reviewing the various etymological interpretations, he argues that from the beginning *credo/srad-dha* had both a *religious* meaning and an *economic* meaning: the word denotes an "act of confidence implying restitution," and "to pledge something on faith in the certainty that it will be returned," religiously and economically. Thus the correspondence between *credence* and *credit* is one of "the oldest in the Indo-European vocabulary." Vedic man deposits his *desire*, his "token," his "magical strength" (more than his heart) with the gods, trusting them and counting on their reward: *Indra* is the god of assistance, *Sraddha* the goddess of offerings. The Vedic religion, it has been said, can be summed up in the three terms faith, gift, and pleasure in giving. Having received the *srad*, god returns it to the believer in the form of his protection; trust in god is based on return, and "faith" implies certainty of remuneration. It is easy to see how the notion could have been secularized to mean "credit" in the financial sense. As for the heart, Christianity would later glorify it as the seat of faith. St Augustine was among the first to use this metaphor, for example, in his exhortation to "read the Holy Scripture with your eyes fixed firmly on your heart."[4]

In its 2000-year history Christianity has known a variety of mystical experiences unique for their psychological subtlety: In extreme cases mystics have gone so far as to reject not only credit-recompense but even the very act of prayer, which they viewed as a selfish request. Nevertheless, in its general tenor and institutional embodiment the Christian faith appears not to be inconsistent with the Indo-European model of belief.

Do the Indo-European languages reflect a type of culture in which the individual suffers dramatically because of his separation from the cosmos and the other? Presumably implicit in such a separation and its attendant suffering is the act of offering – a bridge across the gap – together with the expectation of reward. The human, however, is immersed in the rhythms of the cosmos, which in the Indo-European world dominate the separation that underlies faith.

In reality, it is the biblical God who inaugurates separation at the beginning of creation. He creates a division which is also the mark of His presence: "In the beginning God created the heaven and the earth." *Bereschit*. The source and meaning of Christianity lie in Judaism, which Christians today seem to be rediscovering after years of separation. Psychologically, however, it is Christ's Passion, the "folly on the cross," as St Paul and Pascal called it, that reveals the somber division that is perhaps the paradoxical condition of faith: "Father, Father, why hast thou forsaken me?"

It is because I am separate, forsaken, alone *vis-à-vis* the other that I can psychologically cross the divide that is the condition of my existence and achieve not only ecstasy in completion (*complétude*: reunion with the father, himself a symbolic substitute for the mother) but also eternal life (resurrection) in the imagination. For the Christian believer the completion of faith is real completion, and Christ, with whom the believer is exhorted to identify, expiates in human form the sin of all mankind before achieving glory in resurrection. And yet we observe very real effects of imaginary identifications on the bodies and lives of our nonbelieving patients as well.

This pattern of faith may not be universal, however. The notion of a "gift of the heart" compensated by "divine reward" is apparently of relatively minor importance in Chinese religion, into which it was introduced by Buddhism. In classical Chinese (for example, the *I Ching*), "to believe" and "to be worthy of faith" are expressed by the word *xin*, where the ideogram contains the signs for *man* and *speech*. Does "to believe" therefore mean "to let speech act?" For Confucius *xin* is one of the cardinal virtues: One believes in a man who is worthy of confidence, in whose word one can trust. This moral, social, indeed commercial dimension of *xin* should not be allowed to obscure the fact that, fundamentally, the *xin* man is one who is in harmony with the *qi*, "the spirit" or "cosmic virtue." "If the sovereign is *xin*, he is the incarnation of cosmic virtue."

Thus the Confucians attach paramount value to truthful speech, whether individual, trans-individual, or cosmic. Yet "there are fine but hollow words" and "Heaven says nothing" (Confucius). More radically, Lao Tse denounces words that are beautiful but false: "Credible speech is not beautiful, beautiful speech is not credible." He looks toward the transcendence of speech in something "beyond words," *wu yan*. This leaves the search for harmony with the *qi*. Not that man feels estranged from the cosmic spirit; rather, he is certain of being able to achieve a more complete harmony with it, in particular by various physical and linguistic means, such as calligraphy or *tai ji quan*. Contemplative "faith" as mere psychic experience is here supplanted by the possibility of permanent improvement by psychophysical means, sustained by the optimistic view that we are always part of the *qi*. If we could achieve this mode of being through comprehension alone, we could say that in Chinese tradition the separation of man from nature and of each man from the others is neither strictly localized nor strictly absolute. The *qi* derives from the *void*, which exerts its power as the "space between." But this "void" is not nothingness; in *qi xu*, the sign *xu*, which means "void," contains in stylized forms the ideograms for a "tiger" upon a "hill"; it evokes the breath of *yang* ready to pounce upon the *yin*.

Furthermore, in the Confucian triad heaven–man–earth, heaven and earth cannot fulfill their destiny without man. The Taoist equivalent for this triad is yang–"space between"–yin; thus in the dualities of Chinese religion (Confucianism and Taoism) the parallel to man is the "space between."

Finally, in the spoken language "to believe" is *xin fu*, in which *fu* means "to wed," "to abandon oneself." This evocation of union between the two sexes and, more primitively, of a previous existence within the body of the mother is perhaps appropriate in a view of the world in which man is at one with nature and recommences creation with each of his actions. Here the psychic traces of physical and biological energies are accommodated, cultivated, polished, and harmonized with highly elaborate symbolic constructs; the only thing that seems to be lacking is the "metamorphosis of suffering." That, at least, is what a learned Chinese friend tells me – with regret, or ironic superiority?

Freud's pessimism notwithstanding, his discovery, inspired by and for the benefit of the suffering individual, may well effect that ludic metamorphosis that leads us, at the termination of treatment, to regard language as body and body as language. All plenitude turns out to be inscribed upon a "void" which is simply what remains when the overabundance of meaning, desire, violence, and anguish is drained by means of language. "A tiger leaps upon a mound." Approaching his patients with the aid of a model derived from his own analysis, the therapist is able to apprehend psychic structures unknown to psychiatric nosography. He gives meaning to the "emptiness" of the "borderline" while teaching the patient to cope with the emptiness within self-understanding that is the original source of our anguish and moral pain.

Is psychoanalysis perhaps *also* our "China within?"

Credo in Unum Deum

An early Credo, known as the "Symbol of the Apostles," was in use throughout Western Christendom by the tenth century. The Credo quoted here, based on the Nicene Creed of 325, was worked out by the Council of Constantinople in 381 and has remained in use to the present day.

We believe in one God the Father Almighty, creator of heaven and earth, and of all things visible and invisible:
  And in one Lord Jesus Christ, the only begotten Son of God, begotten of his Father before all worlds, God of God, Light of Light, very God of very God, begotten not made, being of one substance with the Father, by

whom all things were made; who for us men and for our salvation came down from heaven, and was incarnate by the Holy Spirit of the Virgin Mary, and was made man, and was crucified also for us under Pontius Pilate. He suffered and was buried, and the third day he rose again according to the scriptures, and ascended into heaven, and sitteth on the right hand of the Father. And he shall come again to judge both the living and the dead: whose kingdom shall have no end.

And we believe in the Holy Spirit, the Lord and giver of life, who proceedeth from the Father and with the Father and the Son together is worshiped and glorified, who spake by the prophets. And we believe in one catholic and apostolic Church. We acknowledge one baptism for the remission of sins. And we look for the resurrections of the dead and the life of the world to come.

Whoever is speaking in this text does not define his faith except in terms of its object. The God to whom he entrusts his vital speech – his heart – is a trinity. He is first of all the "Father Almighty," the "creator" not only of the person praying but of "all things visible and invisible."

As if to bring himself closer to the person invoking his name, however, this God is also "Lord Jesus Christ, the only begotten Son of God." Begotten by God, he shares his essence, he is "one substance" with the Father; this is amplified by the statement that he is "begotten not made," since no creature can be identical with the Creator. This Son, with whom the person praying is supposed to find it easier to identify, is thus also a "son" (with a small *s*), a "minor" in some sense, yet still a "very God of very God," "Light of Light." Next we have various christological assertions setting forth the history of the Son's time on earth. We are told that he came down from heaven for our salvation, that he made himself a man, becoming flesh by way of virgin birth from the body of a woman, the Virgin Mary. Like the person who invokes his name, this man suffered; he was crucified at a specific moment in history (under Pontius Pilate), he was buried, and on the third day (according to the sacred texts) he was restored to life and ascended to heaven and a place of glory at his Father's side. Ultimately he will return on Judgment Day to judge the living and the dead.

Following this christological excursus we return to the exposition of the trinity. The Holy Spirit is worshiped and glorified jointly with the Son and the Father in whom it "originates." (The Eastern and Western Churches differed on this question, the former denying that the Holy Spirit originates with both the Father *and* the Son.) Like the other two persons of the trinity, the Holy Ghost was mentioned by the prophets. It gives life and serves as mediator: it is "through the Holy Spirit" that the Son was incarnated in the Virgin Mary.

The Credo ends by mentioning the institution that sustains the faith and to which we must also give our hearts. The "catholic and apostolic" Church is the locus of ritual and faith: baptism, confession, remission of sins. Thus from the trinitarian nexus to its "political apparatus" the believer is provided with a structure of support with the help of which he will be able to obtain a reward that no human gift can possibly equal: resurrection and eternal life in the centuries to come.

Does anyone in the West *believe* in all the elements of this admirably logical and unified system? If believers do exist, aren't they a bit like my analysand, many-faceted characters, prepared to accept the Credo in one of their parts or "personalities" while allowing others – the professional personality, the social personality, the erotic personality – to ignore it? Essential as this feature of contemporary religious belief is, it is not the question I wish to discuss here.

As an analyst, I find that the Credo embodies basic fantasies that I encounter every day in the psychic lives of my patients. The almighty father? Patients miss one, want one, or suffer from one. Consubstantiality with the father and symbolic identification with his name? Patients aspire to nothing else, and the process is at once essential to psychic maturation and a source of pleasure (through assumption of the father's power and elevation to the summit of authority). More than any other religion, Christianity has unraveled the symbolic *and* physical importance of the paternal function in human life. Identification with this third party separates the child from its jubilant but destructive physical relationship with its mother and subjects it to another dimension, that of symbolization, where, beyond frustration and absence, language unfolds. Because of its insistence on the paternal function, Christianity shapes the preconscious formulation of the basic fantasies characteristic of male desire.

Thus the substantial, physical, incestuous fusion of men with their fathers both reveals and sublimates homosexuality. The crucifixion of God–made–man reveals to the analyst, always attentive to murderous desires with regard to the father, that the representation of Christ's Passion signifies a guilt that is visited upon on the son, who is himself put to death.

Freud interprets this expiation as an avowal of the Oedipal murder that every human being unconsciously desires. But Christ's Passion brings into play even more primitive layers of the psyche; it thus reveals a fundamental depression (a narcissistic wound or reversed hatred) that conditions access to human language. The sadness of young children just prior to their acquisition of language has often been observed; this is when they must renounce forever the maternal paradise in which every demand is immediately gratified. The child must abandon its mother and be abandoned by her in order to be accepted by the father and begin talking. If it is true that language begins in mourning, inherent in the evolution of subjectivity, the abandonment by the father – the symbolic "other" – triggers a melancholy anguish that can grow to suicidal proportions. "I detest him, but I am he, therefore I must die." Beyond the torment of suicide there is joy, ineffable happiness at finally rejoining the abandoned object.

The "scandal of the cross," the *logos tou stavron* or language of the cross, which some, according to St Paul, would call "foolishness" (I Cor. 1: 18 and 1: 23; Gal. 5: 11) and which is indeed inconceivable for a god as the ancients understood the term, is embodied, I think not only in the psychic and physical suffering that irrigates our lives (*qui irrigue notre existence*) but even more profoundly in the essential alienation that conditions our access to language, in the mourning that accompanies the dawn of psychic life. By the quirks of biology and family life we are all of us melancholy mourners, witnesses to the death that marks our psychic inception.

Christ abandoned, Christ in hell, is of course the sign that God shares the condition of the sinner. But He also tells the story of that necessary melancholy beyond which we humans may just possibly discover the other, now in the form of symbolic interlocutor rather than nutritive breast. In this respect, too, Christianity wins the adhesion of the masses; it supplies images for even the fissures in our secret and fundamental logic. How can we not believe?

A virgin mother? We want our mothers to be virgins, so that we can love them better or allow ourselves to be loved by them without fear of a rival. The unprecedented affirmation of symbolic paternity (carried to the point of insisting on the consubstantiality of father and son) could not have been made without reducing the weight of certain images, which would have made the burden of the father's symbolic authority too heavy to bear; those images have to do with procreative sexuality. By eliminating the mother as well as the father from the primal scene, the believer's imagination protects itself against a fantasy that is too much for any child to bear: that of being supernumerary, excluded from the act of pleasure that is the origin of its existence. Christianity, it must be said, avoids the whole question of procreation and is thus profoundly influenced by the idea of the virgin mother, which Catholicism, particularly in its more exuberant baroque forms, carried to an extreme.

More than one mother has been sustained in narcissistic equilibrium by the fantasy of having a child without the aid of a father; such women are not necessarily paranoid. Yet female hysterics, frequently touched by paranoia as well, relish the not-so-humble role of the virgin mother who is the "daughter of her son," mother of God, queen of the Church, and to top it all off the only human being who does not have to die (even her son must endure the cross). For her life ends according to Orthodox dogma in "dormition" and according to Catholic dogma in "assumption." Such a view of maternity has a strong appeal to man's imagination, as we have seen; it is particularly stimulating to artistic sublimation, as the example of Leonardo proves.[5]

Unfortunately, the proscription of female sexuality helped to infantilize half the human race by hampering its sexual and intellectual expression. Only advances in contraceptive technique have finally made it possible to lift that proscription. Previously, however, women received generous compensation in the form of praise of motherhood and its narcissistic rewards. Hence today, now that so-called artificial pregnancies have given concrete reality to the distinction between sexuality and procreation, femininity and maternity, the image of the virgin mother resonates with the daydreams of modern women with no particular religious vocation simply because there is no secular discourse on the psychology of motherhood.

The Trinity itself, that crown jewel of theological sophistication, evokes, beyond its specific content and by virtue of the very logic of its articulation, the intricate intertwining of the three aspects of psychic life: the symbolic, the imaginary, and the real.

To the analyst, however, the representations on which the Credo is based are fantasies, which reveal fundamental desires or traumas but not dogmas. Analysis subjects these fantasies to X-ray examination. It begins by individualizing: What about *your* father? Was he "almighty" or not? What kind of son were *you*? What about *your* desire for virginity or resurrection? By shifting attention from the "macrofantasy" to the "microfantasy" analysis reveals the underlying sexuality, which prayer circumvents but does not really proscribe; for though the object of desire be transformed, desire itself remains a feature of Christian discourse.

What is the role and significance of the sexualization of psychic life for which psychoanalysis is credited by some and blamed by others?

Translated by Arthur Goldhammer

Notes

1 Saint Augustine, *Confessions*, trans. E. B. Pusey (New York: Dutton, 1951), IV, 1, 1.

2 Sigmund Freud, *The Ego and the Id* (New York: Norton, 1963).

3 Émile Benveniste, *Vocabulaire des institutions indo-européennes* (Paris: Minuit, 1969), 1:175.

4 Saint Augustine, *De doctrina Christiana* IV, 5, 7.

5 Sigmund Freud, *Leonardo da Vinci and a Memory of His Childhood*, trans. Alan Tyson (New York: Norton, 1964).

PART

II

Selected Essays

From Patriarchy into Freedom: A Conversation between American Feminist Theology and French Feminism

Rebecca S. Chopp

I begin my conversation between American feminist theology and French feminism by stating two convictions: first, the need to situate oneself as well as the other in a conversation, and second, the need to establish the framework of the conversation.

By the first conviction, I mean that in any dialogue one needs to be as clear as possible about one's own context, categories, perspectives. Thus I am going to concentrate on American feminist theology and theory. I want to try to understand the historical precedents for feminist theory and feminist theology as forms of cultural politics located within the changes in the lives of American women in this century.[1] These changes, bridging the political and the personal, are the locus for American feminism. American feminist theology needs to be understood in the context of the women's movement, which I define as a broad-based social movement of women who address problems in the cultural and political arenas relating to the needs of women and children.

Second, given my contextualization of American feminist theology, I want to establish a framework for the conversation between American feminist theology and French feminist theory. I will begin by suggesting that feminist theology, placed as it is in the history of pragmatism and American public theology, works for the transformation of political and personal life away from patriarchy into freedom. Given this turn to radical transformation, I want to explore a conversation with French feminism, for I think that French feminism offers us some useful guides for pursuing strategies of diagnosis and transformation. My attempt at a conversation between American feminist theologies and French feminism is going to follow my understanding of American feminist pragmatism, the attempt to use all there is to be used in terms of addressing the problems of the day. I will argue that French feminism is helpful as we address a particular set of problems having to do with the radical transformation of our narratives, our language, and our practices by giving us particular strategies of self-reflexive critique and transformation.

I do not mean that French feminism offers us all the answers or all the strategies that we need, but simply that there is a certain self-reflexivity in French feminism that pragmatically is helpful when we struggle with the terms of our own transformation. For instance, it is now commonly assumed in feminist theory that there is no universal "woman," for the differences among women are many and great. Yet the gender critique of feminism – the basic ordering of practices, values, institutions as marked by man and woman – is central to an analysis of patriarchy, understood as oppressive practices and structures that affect all women, despite, through, and in the midst of their differences. French feminism can help theologians think through the necessity of emancipation from a binary ordering of gender and think toward transformation of a cultural politics of difference.

Feminism, Pragmatism, and Public Theology

In recent years American feminist theorists and American feminist theologians have responded to French theory with cries about the death of the subject. Perhaps most frequently quoted is Nancy Hartsock's provocative question, "Why is it that just at the moment when so many of us who have been silenced begin to demand the right to name ourselves, to act as subjects rather than objects of history, that just then the concept of subjecthood becomes problematic?"[2] Feminist theologians such as Elisabeth Schüssler Fiorenza, Susan Brooks Thistlethwaite, and Mary McClintock Fulkerson have all voiced similar concerns in relation to French poststructuralist thought.[3] As important and necessary as the concern for our subjecthood is, and I take it to be almost irrefutable, it is well worth reflecting on the nature of the American response. What is at stake in this particular response to the French critique of the subject?

It is especially curious since French feminism, in the context of poststructuralism, shares with American feminism the resistance to the universal, autonomous subject of Cartesianism. Whereas American feminism has tended to focus on the critique of foundationalism, French feminism has focused on the critique of humanism, that is, the notion that there is a real or true self buried in the unconscious or secured in an ontology or phenomenology of the subject. And whereas American feminism focuses on the representative functions of language, French feminism concentrates on the performative functions of language. To state the difference perhaps too vividly, American feminism tends to epitomize the phrase "the personal is the political"; French feminism tends to represent another phrase, "the political is the personal." American feminism has focused on economic distribution, social equality, violence against women, and women's rights. French feminism has focused on sexuality, desire, music and aesthetics, and philosophical texts. But if, as I have suggested, American feminist theology is placed within the vast changes in the lives of American women and in the context of the women's movement, we may at least begin to identify the particularity of the American response of privileging the political.

American feminism addresses itself to a variety of questions of American democracy, including the proper utilization of laws, economic practices, and distribution of goods and services for the equal and fair treatment of women as citizens. At the same time, American feminism questions the ongoing interpretation of democratic culture. For democracy is never just a set of laws about equal and fair treatment. Rather it is an ongoing interpretation of itself, an ongoing production of new practices and narratives, of new values and forms of social and personal life that constitute a democracy. If the narrative of the citizen in most democratic theory is tied to male roles in society, what happens when women begin to fill these roles? Or when the rhetoric of democracy is stretched to include not only the rights of the many but responsibilities for the many, and the many now include the vast numbers of children of working mothers?

This is the reason why so many American feminist theorists insist on labelling their work as a form of politics. At one level, the claim is rather incredible – feminist theory includes no sound bites, pleas for office, suggestions for quick political solutions to current national and international problems. But at another level, especially given the history of the role of the pragmatic intellectual in American culture, it makes perfect sense. For as a form of politics, American feminism, at home in the pragmatic tradition, attempts to provide the theoretical analysis, the poetical provocation, and the utopian realism necessary for change in democratic culture. The philosophical tradition of American pragmatism opposed epistemologically-centered philosophy with its spectator view of the human subject; pragmatism understood philosophy as critical reflection on problems of the age. Cornel West in *The American Evasion of Philosophy* maps out this territory, identifying pragmatism as a rich and diverse tradition, characterized by future-oriented thinking and defined as "a cultural commentary or set of interpretations that attempt to explain America to itself at a particular historical moment."[4] West describes philosophy as a wisdom, focused on truth as that which "enhances the flourishing of human progress."[5] Pragmatist philosophy arises out of problems and dysfunctions of a particular situation, and the desire that things can and must be different. Philosophy is the effort to make the future different out of the sufferings, problems, facts of the present. As West says, "These efforts take the forms of critique and praxis, forms that attempt to change what is into a better what can be."[6]

The identification of feminist theology in the US must, first, be placed within this pragmatic tradition of American feminism. As such, feminist theology is a form of politics, addressing problems of the social and personal good, including problems not only of specific legal and economic practices but also cultural and personal practices. American feminist theology is a part of American feminism in general in its pragmatic scope of addressing the needs of the times and anticipating personal and social transformation.

There is another context for American feminist theology, one privileged by its location in the history of American theology. I want to contend that feminist theology takes as its own and remakes the long history of American public theology.[7] The task of demonstrating how feminist theology is a reconstruction of American public theology exceeds the limits of this essay. Nonetheless, it is necessary to identify this history, for not only does it provide a certain theological context, it also aids in clarifying the tasks of feminist theologies.

What is necessary, then, is to construct a model for understanding the theological counterpart to pragmatism, which I will call public theology. Now I can by no means offer an extended argument about the diverse tradition of American theology, so allow me to paint broadly a picture drawn from Sidney Mead.[8] This will not be the only picture, but one, like West's view of pragmatism, that allows us to name a heterogeneous way of doing theology in the American situation. Sidney Mead's reading of American religious history suggests that the particular theological assumptions behind the Constitution, the role of free churches, and the persuasive power of religious morality combined to associate the church with the role of forming, through religious beliefs, the kind of persons and associations necessary for life together in the republic. Mead states, in *The Lively Experiment*:

> The free churches accepted, or had forced upon them the duty and responsibility to define, articulate, disseminate, and inculcate the basic religious beliefs essential for the existence and well-being of society – and of doing this without any coercive power over the citizens at all, that is, armed only with persuasive power.[9]

Public theology fulfilled its duty and responsibility by producing images of, definitions of, and judgments on America, by training citizens in the space of churches (as the place in American society where public and private met), and by forming discourses of morality (we might now say discourses of subjectivity) necessary for life together as well as for individual flourishing.

American public theology begins not in distinguishing Christian tradition from common human experience, but in the movement of Christian practice speaking to the problems, doubts, and desires within the American situation. American public theology has functioned, at times, covertly and overtly to affirm oppressive practices.[10] The ambiguities and distortions of American public theology cannot be ignored. In the midst of claims about freedom, liberty, and justice, American public theology has often become a discourse of oppression. Yet its prophetic spirit, its relation to morality and public judgment, its employment of religious metaphors to criticize the public also allowed for debates within American public theology about its own oppressive practices. Such ambiguities of American public theology must be continually criticized in order to discover ways in which theological discourse can criticize, form, and transform American society. In this theological model, theology functions to criticize the present situation and to anticipate new possibilities, to create communities for public and personal good, and to offer discourses of subjectivity.[11] When feminist theologians attempt to provide new images of being human, to offer new discourses to the public, to criticize the gender division of public and private, they are working out of this rich model of American public theology.

Feminist Theology as Cultural Critique

Related as it is to feminism as a form of pragmatism and to American theology as a form of American public theology, feminist theology constitutes itself as a form of cultural politics around the critique of patriarchy. But precisely as such, it is forced to move beyond the limits of traditional understandings of both pragmatism and public theology. For pragmatism and public theology have been discourses of the dominant culture that attempt to include others into the center of that culture, trying to develop or correct or improve those "others" to ensure successful inclusion. If feminist theology sought only to achieve women's full participation in the public sphere, the confines of pragmatism and public theology would remain secure. But as feminist theology begins to question the very structure, narratives, and ordering of the political, a position of radical transformation occurs. That is, as feminism questions the very nature of the political, pragmatism and public theology become transformed through the critical theory of patriarchy. This critical theory operates through gender analysis, which, according to Joan Scott, arose in feminist theory as a way of getting at "the fundamentally social quality of distinctions based on sex."[12] Gender studies have been helpfully applied in textual studies, in history, in culture, and of course in economics. Indeed, gender studies have become not simply an analysis of how society sees/makes men and women as different, but also how different categories and structures are marked and constituted through a patriarchal ordering of gender division. As Scott maintains, gender is both a "constitutive element in social relations based on perceived differences between the sexes and a primary way of signifying relationships of power."[13] A critical theory of gender construction analyzes not only the division of male and female, but diagnoses the very terms of division itself.

It is the diagnosis of this particular ordering, the seemingly incessant drive to impose an ordering through assigning masculine and feminine categories, where the masculine term is always higher and more valued and the feminine is other and lesser in value, that brings feminism to a position advocating radical transformation in its forms of cultural politics. Feminist theology seeks to critique the binary opposition of values, terms, and practices through gender. Thus it questions the relations of gender terms as descriptive and prescriptive, as interlocking relations of value and power controls. Further, feminist theology seeks to emancipate us from these binary terms and the incessant valuing of one term through the expulsion and devaluation of the other. Feminist theology desires a transformation in which new ways of flourishing, new practices of being human, new discourses of subjectivity are created.

This is, of course, an enormous task. Feminist theologies, and feminist theory in general, must simultaneously address the sufferings of the present age with as much aid as possible and undergo the work of radical transformation. Such a transformation – with the dismantling of the old values, the dominant ways of ordering, the destructive psychic and political constructs of patriarchy, and with the creation of new values, orders, psychic and political constructs of difference – involves a great deal of practical, theoretical work. It is in this dismantling and creating of spaces for transformation that American feminist theology may find French feminism helpful in providing strategies of diagnosis and transformation.

Julia Kristeva and Transformative Discourse

I want to use, in an exemplary way, the work of Julia Kristeva to explore some ways in which French feminism may be helpful to American feminist theology. I choose Kristeva because of her interest in transforming discourses and the transformation of discourses. I understand Kristeva to be centrally concerned not with adaptation or restitution, but with transformation of subjectivity, language, and politics, and with envisioning the possibility of transformation outside the gendered ordering of patriarchy. I think Kristeva provides a space for us, minimally, to ask about the ways in which theology must operate to promote not only the correction of the abuses of patriarchy but also the radical transformation from patriarchy into freedom. In speaking about women in Europe in her essay "Women's Time," Kristeva asks the same type of question that we must struggle with:

> *What can be our place in the symbolic contract?* If the social contract, far from being that of equal men, is based on an essentially sacrificial relationship of separation and articulation of differences which in this way produces communicable meaning, what is our place in this order of sacrifice and/or of language? No longer wishing to be excluded or no longer content with the function which has always been demanded of us (to maintain, arrange and perpetuate this socio-symbolic contract as mothers, wives, nurses, doctors, teachers . . .), how can we reveal our place, first as it is bequeathed to us by tradition, and then as we want to transform it?[14]

This often-quoted and frequently reprinted essay suggests, especially in Kristeva's notion of the third generation of feminism, the immensity of the task before us: the need to question and resist the very ordering of man/woman and thus the formation of not only politics, culture, and language, but even personal identity based on gender division.

Let me use Kristeva's work then as a space to pursue the difficulty and complexity of the transformation from patriarchy into freedom within the context of American feminist theology.[15] At its center, I think this type of transformation is deeply theological, that is I understand this notion of the transformation from sin (equating patriarchy with sin, of course) into freedom to be the movement of the Christian promise. American feminist theology, in my understanding, has as its overarching task the construal of this transformation, and I will address that task in three ways: (1) a critique of the depth texture of patriarchy, (2) the theological possibility of transformation from patriarchy, and (3) theological practices of envisioning personal and social flourishing.

1 A critique of the depth texture of patriarchy

Kristeva, like many of the French thinkers drawing on structuralism and psychoanalysis, suggests that the symbolic order – the ordering of language that gives symbolic meaning – is both the ordering of the subject and the social contract.[16] For Kristeva, the present symbolic order constitutes and is constituted through a binary opposition of gender relations. These relations, according to Kristeva, operate through cultural, linguistic, political, and psychic constructs of power and abjection, meaning and nonmeaning, order and chaos.[17] In the West, these gender relations function through what she calls monotheism, the ordering principle of a symbolic, paternal community that requires men and women to have different relationships to the symbolic. This difference is the condition of relations between men and women.[18]

What Kristeva suggests in her analysis of the symbolic order as "monotheistic" is that there is a certain ordering to the functioning of society, subjectivity, and language that continually constitutes patriarchal relations. Now if this analysis takes the ordering to be ontological, as structured into the very nature of being, then certainly it is neither helpful for change nor useful for interpretation. But if instead this analysis presents the ordering as a heuristic device, a portrait of the general structures of the situation, it serves as a way to draw relationships between needed changes in subjectivity, politics, and language. I want to suggest that something like a notion of the symbolic order or dominant culture is extremely important as a way of rendering explicit how patriarchy is not just isolated acts of injustice but a systematic fault within the present situation, invading our practices of personal narratives, childrearing, linguistic practices, and institutional structures. One of the most important tasks of feminist theology as a continuation and transformation of American public theology is to render judgment upon structures and systems of patriarchy. To do this, theology must be able to portray, at least heuristically, how patriarchy operates through institutions, linguistic practices, forms of subjectivity, and so forth.

Of course, theologians will stumble on the term Kristeva uses to label her depth texture of patriarchy, the term *monotheism*. Though the term has had varied uses in the history of Christian theology, it is generally taken as a critical principle that relativizes all ordering in relation to God.[19] It is tempting to rename Kristeva's concern as "monologism" and to argue that she is using a theological term incorrectly. But it may also be helpful for theologians to pursue monotheism itself as a problematic term in feminism for at least two reasons. First, the monotheism of the Christian God has been tied to the patriarchy of the West, and the critique of it must be traced and analyzed through our historical records and present practices. In what way has patriarchal ordering affected Christian notions of God and vice versa? Second, the logic of monotheism, in Kristeva's understanding, secures the identity of the one through the devaluing and marginalizing of the other. Now monotheism as it has functioned as a religious doctrine has many other uses. But this problematic ordering that is associated with monotheism – the securing of identity through absolutizing of one and the casting out of all others – bears careful scrutiny.

One implication of a depth texture of monotheism in patriarchy for feminist theology is the need for a careful examination of the role of religion and gender in the US. In part, feminist theologians need to insist that theorists pay more attention to the distinctiveness of American history, especially the role played by religion. American feminist theorists have constructed their arguments about private/public in relation to the theories of Jean-Jacques Rousseau, Thomas Hobbes, and John Locke.[20] As influential as these models of liberalism might be, there is another side of the story. To understand fully the models of the American public, it is necessary to understand not only liberalism but also civic republicanism, and to understand particularly the role of churches in American public life, roles both in training of citizens, and also as places of intersection between public and private. Feminist theologians need to call into question American feminist theories that consistently privilege European models of the division of private and public without attention to the particularities of American history, especially since both public and private have been formed in relation to the role of the church as a voluntary association in the United States.

If feminist theology, and feminism in general, needs to pursue a critique of the history of the depth texture of patriarchy – the relation between subjectivity, language, and politics – and the ways in which Christianity has contributed to or resisted this, a great deal of analysis of the present situation must also be done. Why, in this land of democracy and freedom, has half the population consistently been denied self-determination and freedom? What is it about this so-called secular nation that as late as 1982 the Equal Rights Amendment to the Constitution can fail to be ratified? What Kristeva helps us to reflect on is a theological critique of patriarchal ordering, an ordering of the whole and the parts, the ultimate and the penultimate, that consistently and thoroughly places women as less than and other.

2 The theological possibility of transformation from patriarchy into freedom

Is there a way for us to create a space other than patriarchy from which to render this judgment and to work for transformation into freedom? How do we speak of something more and something other than patriarchy without losing the radicality of critique?

Kristeva points us toward thinking of new possibilities for strategies of transformation in her notion of the semiotic modality of language and its function of enlarging the arena of meaning and representing the currently unrepresentable. Kristeva's point of departure from Lacan is her refusal to privilege the symbolic order as the only point of analysis. Kristeva posits that the symbolic order works in relation to the semiotic, the dimension of drives and motility, attesting to "the process that exceeds the subject and his communicative process."[21] Thus Kristeva focuses on language as discourse enunciated by a speaking subject as well as the "conditions of the production of meaning as on the (static) meaning produced."[22] Drawing upon resources in psychoanalysis and linguistics, Kristeva produces a subjectivity that is always heterogeneous and decentered, a subject in process. For Kristeva, the subject in process is a blend of both the symbolic and the semiotic, with the symbolic being constituted through the social contract of meaning, and the semiotic being the transgressive, that which ruptures, irrupts into, and enlarges the symbolic. The signifying practices of art, and increasingly psychoanalysis, open up and transform the signifying subject. For critique, not only as analysis but also as transformation, it is necessary to be able both to enlarge the domain of meaning and to open up the rules of meaning-making. Kristeva does this by refusing to look simply at meaning in a static sense, focusing instead on the process or production of meaning and subjectivity.

I have already explored this point in relation to theological discourse in *The Power to Speak*, in which I use Kristeva's notion of the semiotic to open up theological discourse about God.[23] Feminist theological discourse must resist assertions of eternal division between Word and experience, the ordering of the socio-symbolic contract with its static split of subject and object, and must explore the relation of Word within experience, and experience as always conveying Word, in a manner somewhat parallel to Kristeva's exploration of the semiotic. Word, rather than the paternal law that rules experience, explodes in the semiotic modality to open and transform experience. What Kristeva directs us toward is the recognition that we cannot simply change metaphors or add new experiences to our dominant theological stew and stir, but that we must transform the very terms, patterns, and ordering of how language, culture, politics, and subjectivity work. We can criticize gender opposition and affirm theological practices of difference by opening up the realm of meaning and the rules of meaning-making.

3 Theological practices of envisioning personal and social flourishing

Again, I think Kristeva's work is very suggestive in terms of the procedures of her own work. What Kristeva interrogates is not the symbolic order, the realm of the subject and meaning, but, as she insists, the speaking subject – the subject in process who is always surpassing herself, who speaks in ambiguities, expressing desires and wants she may not consciously recognize.[24] Kristeva continually seeks to uncover the process of the ongoing production of subjectivity. In her early work on the semiotic, she explores the openness of signs and introduces the concept of *negativity* as the process of semiotic generativity that destabilizes the posited unity of the symbolic. In her writings on aesthetics, she is concerned not so much with particular meaning, but with the process of meaning coming to be. As John Lechte has observed, Kristeva views art "less as an object, and more as a process or practice that 'creates' the subject."[25] And with her work on psychoanalysis, she turns to the journey of the soul, to use an Augustinian phrase, to explore how contemporary persons might learn to love. Kristeva argues that it is necessary, at present, to enlarge the imaginary in culture, and that both aesthetics and psychoanalysis must be seen as practices that create new forms of subjectivity, language, and perhaps by extension politics.

Feminist theology can use Kristeva's focus on meaning coming to be to think of itself as practices, not of interpreting meaning already given, but of envisioning personal and social flourishing through new forms of subjectivity, language, and politics. In a sense, this is where French feminism's critique of humanism is very necessary for American feminism as it envisions new forms of freedom utterly without patriarchy.

We might helpfully call this process rhetorical hermeneutics, for feminist theology is best described as productive strategies of critique and transformation seeking, in the tradition of American public theology, to offer persuasive discourses of personal and social flourishing. The concern for hermeneutics in feminist theology rests not in tradition or experience, though these can both be important moments, but in transforming the culture.[26] Feminist theology turns to hermeneutics as a practice, a practice of cultural politics. In much contemporary hermeneutical theory, the real of hermeneutics is the subjective experience of the textual object. When coupled with an assumed position of tradition or with simply the notion of text as encompassing experience, what is being sought is a type of revelation or overwhelming experience from the object side of the subject/object split. In this process, which is referred to as the play of the text and interpreter,[27] the text incorporates our experience or discloses to our experience some originary meaning in the text. Yet, within a feminist rhetorical hermeneutics, the play of text and interpreter cannot be isolated as an autonomous act between a subject and an object. For the play – the play of text, subjectivity, and discourse in interpretation – always already occurs within the practices of cultural politics. Play, from the perspective of a critical theory of gender deconstruction, always involves some form of the politics of culture. For example, when girls play with dolls they are formed in a morality, a subjectivity of relationships; and when boys are given guns and footballs they are formed in a morality of aggression and competition. If we use the metaphor of play we must recall that play is always embodied in social history and, at least in part, is always a form of cultural politics. The practice of hermeneutics in feminist theology brings to the surface the awareness that play is not just letting go, but being formed to a particular form of subjectivity that takes in and assumes as natural, important, or delightful a certain set of norms and values.

But if feminist theology diagnoses the practice of reading through the play of cultural politics, it also functions to open up the process, that is, to engage in play as fantasy, utopia, reconstruction. Feminist theologians need to transform the process of hermeneutics itself through what Kristeva calls poetics, stressing, for instance, not what metaphor conveys, but what metaphor opens up and creates. In this sense, theology, especially a theology in the context of the transformation of public theology, is a constitutive practice forming the process of becoming subjects, individually and collectively. Indeed, several recent works by theologians such as Sharon Welch and Elisabeth Schüssler Fiorenza might be read as moving in the direction of offering new nonpatriarchal discourses of personal and social flourishing for the American culture.[28]

Thus French feminism, at least as represented in the work of Julia Kristeva, offers to American feminist theology some productive strategies of transformation in terms of a critique of the depth texture of patriarchy, some modes of possibility for transformation from patriarchy into freedom, and some new ways of understanding the nature and tasks of theology as practices that envision personal and social flourishing. This is not to suggest there are not other points of contact between French feminism and American feminist theology, including points of conflict and even contradiction. Indeed, this essay should be read as one starting point for the conversation of American feminist theology with French feminism, a starting point that will encourage the serious consideration of the distinctiveness of each feminist project and the differences between American and French feminisms. Yet I hope this essay also makes a point that we who work in feminism dare not forget: Patriarchy is a systematic fault that runs through the small capillaries and the large vessels of power, wreaking its havoc and destruction through institutions, metaphysics, popular narratives, laws, economic practices, and even the representative and performative functions of language. The task we have as feminists in a large sense is the critique of all the specific acts of patriarchy as well as the critique of patriarchy as the dominant form of life, a form which I have suggested we can only speak of in heuristic fashion. To meet the task of moving from patriarchy into freedom, feminism may well need to understand itself as many different approaches working together to create a reality in which difference itself is a way of life that is celebrated.

Notes

1 Ethel Klein, *Gender Politics: From Consciousness to Mass Politics* (Cambridge, MA: Harvard University Press, 1984). Ethel Klein has identified three of these: changes in marriage and divorce practices; the advent of birth control; and the movement of women, across race and class lines, into the workforce. Though Klein concentrates on white middle- and working-class women, these and other changes affect all women in the United States. The shift in the dominant ideology of what it is to be a woman has dramatically changed in the United States, with popular women's magazines now promoting the hegemonic idea of the superwoman instead of that of the suburban housewife.

2 Nancy Hartsock, "Foucault on Power: A Theory for Women?" in *Feminism/Postmodernism*, ed. with introd. by Linda J. Nicholson (New York: Routledge, 1990), p. 163.

3 American feminist theologians are just in the initial stages of responding to French feminism. See Elisabeth Schüssler Fiorenza, "The Politics of Otherness: Biblical Interpretation as a Critical Praxis for Liberation," in *Expanding the View: Gustavo Gutiérrez and the Future of Liberation Theology*, ed. Marc H. Ellis and Otto Maduro (Maryknoll, NY: Orbis, 1990), pp. 140–56.

4 Cornel West, *The American Evasion of Philosophy: A Genealogy of Pragmatism* (Madison: University of Wisconsin Press, 1989), pp. 5.

5 Ibid., p. 230.

6 Ibid.

7 There are some movements toward reconstructing a public theology that need to be noted. First the theologies of both Gordon Kaufman and Francis Schüssler Fiorenza, drawing on pragmatism, can be construed as types of public theology. Second, William Dean's *History Making History: The New Historicism in American Religious Thought* (New York: State University of New York Press, 1988) provides excellent resources for public theology as Dean retrieves the radical empiricism of William James, John Dewey, and the Chicago School in relation to contemporary neopragmatists. Third, Ronald F. Thiemann has recently called for the development of a public theology, *Constructing a Public Theology: The Church in a Pluralistic Culture* (Louisville, KY: Westminster/John Knox Press, 1991).

8 Like the dilemma I faced in a quick survey of pragmatism, it is difficult in a short essay to cite all the sources necessary to make the argument historically for a model of public theology. Again, for the sake of brevity, I will stick primarily to the work of Mead. Sidney Mead, *The Lively Experiment: The Shaping of Christianity in America* (New York: Harper and Row, 1963); *The Nation with the Soul of a Church* (New York: Harper and Row, 1975); and *The Old Religion in the Brave New World: Reflections on the Relation between Christendom and the Republic* (Berkeley and Los Angeles: University of California Press, 1977). I am also drawing upon two anthologies: *The Lively Experiment Continued*, ed. Jerald C. Brauer (Macon, GA: Mercer, 1987), and William R. Hutchison (ed.), *Between the Times: The Travail of the Protestant Establishment in America, 1900–1960*. (Cambridge and New York: Cambridge University Press, 1989).

9 Mead, *The Lively Experiment*, p. 65.

10 For one discussion of the ambiguities of such discourse, see Ronald C. White, Jr., *Liberty and Justice for All: Radical Reform and the Social Gospel*, foreword by James M. McPherson (San Francisco: Harper and Row, 1990).

11 Emerson is a good example of a thinker who argued for a view of individuality that was socially and naturally grounded.

12 Joan W. Scott, "Gender: A Useful Category of Historical Analysis," in *Coming to Terms: Feminism, Theory, Politics*, ed. Elizabeth Weed (New York: Routledge, 1989), p. 82.

13 Ibid., p. 94.

14 Julia Kristeva, "Women's Time," in *The Kristeva Reader*, ed. Toril Moi (New York: Columbia University Press, 1986), p. 199.

15 For important criticisms of Kristeva see Alice Jardine, "Opaque Texts and Transparent Contexts: The Political Difference of Julia Kristeva," and Domna C. Stanton, "Difference on Trial: A Critique of the Maternal Metaphor in Cixous, Irigaray, and

Kristeva," in *The Poetics of Gender*, ed. Nancy K. Miller (New York: Columbia University Press, 1986); Judith Butler, *Gender Trouble: Feminism and the Subversion of Identity* (New York: Routledge, 1990); and Elizabeth Grosz, *Sexual Subversions: Three French Feminists* (Sydney: Allen and Unwin, 1989).

16 Julia Kristeva, *Revolution in Poetic Language*, introd. Leon S. Roudiez, trans. Margaret Waller (New York: Columbia University Press, 1984).

17 One of Kristeva's most interesting notions is that of abjection. See Julia Kristeva, *Powers of Horror: An Essay on Abjection*, trans. Leon S. Roudiez (New York: Columbia University Press, 1982). For the use of this notion in the context of American feminist theory, see Iris Marion Young, *Justice and the Politics of Difference* (Princeton: Princeton University Press, 1990).

18 For her most explicit development of this notion, see Julia Kristeva, "About Chinese Women," in *The Kristeva Reader*, ed. Toril Moi (New York: Columbia University Press, 1986), pp. 138–59.

19 For a different reading of monotheism, see *Monotheism*, ed. Claude Geffre and Jean-Pierre Jossua, trans. Marcus Lefebvre, Concilium series (Edinburgh: T. and T. Clark, 1985).

20 See, for instance, Jean Bethke Elshtain, *Public Man, Private Woman: Women in Social and Political Thought* (Princeton: Princeton University Press, 1981), and Zillah R. Eisenstein, *The Radical Future of Liberal Feminism* (Boston: Northeastern University Press, 1986). These books make invaluable contributions, but we also need work that looks not only at liberal theories and North American feminism but also at North American feminism in the context of North American traditions of liberalism and civic republicanism.

21 Kristeva, *Revolution in Poetic Language*, p. 16.

22 John Lechte, *Julia Kristeva* (New York: Routledge, 1990), p. 100.

23 Rebecca S. Chopp, *The Power to Speak: Feminism, Language, God* (New York: Crossroad, 1986), pp. 10–39.

24 Julia Kristeva, "The System and the Speaking Subject," in *The Kristeva Reader*, pp. 24–33. See also Julia Kristeva, *Tales of Love*, trans. Leon S. Roudiez (New York: Columbia University Press, 1987), and *In the Beginning was Love: Psychoanalysis and Faith*, trans. Arthur Goldhammer, introd. Otto F. Kernberg, MD (New York: Columbia University Press, 1987).

25 John Lechte, "Art, Love and Melancholia," in *Abjection, Melancholia and Love: The Work of Julia Kristeva*, ed. John Fletcher and Andrew Benjamin (New York: Routledge, 1990), p. 24.

26 If hermeneutics is employed in explaining, say, the work of systematic theology in interpreting religious classics, a focus on the tradition will dominate. See David Tracy, *The Analogical Imagination: Christian Theology and the Culture of Pluralism* (New York: Crossroad, 1981).

27 The metaphor of play is an important one for current hermeneutical theories, and one that I think needs a great deal of deconstruction especially in terms of how the deconstructionists use it. See John Caputo, *Radical Hermeneutics: Repetition, Deconstruction and the Hermeneutic Project* (Bloomington: Indiana University Press, 1987).

28 Sharon D. Welch, *A Feminist Ethic of Risk* (Minneapolis: Fortress Press, 1990), and Elisabeth Schüssler Fiorenza, "The Politics of Otherness."

Liturgy and Kenosis, from
Expérience et Absolu

Jean-Yves Lacoste

God and Madness

There is certainly an ascetic moment in all liturgical gestures. Because the liturgy is not a dimension of worldly being, because a human being cannot confront God without first ridding himself of the *a priori* dominion exercised by the world, no one is born the possessor of what is most proper to him; we do not gain access to ourselves without doing violence to the initial conditions of experience or, at best, without dissipating the chiaroscuro in which they cloak the eschatological meaning of selfhood. (And, as we have mentioned, there is no need to question the liturgy to make ascesis intelligible.) But while anyone who refuses to concede to the logic of inherence the immediate right to define him can be required to make the necessary break, asceticism legitimately worries us when it confronts us with gestures that do not derive from any universal requirement. The ascetic will no doubt account for his supererogatory acts by reminding us that they belong to the logic of the vocational being, and that one cannot speak of vocation in a consequent way without also accepting the indivisible singularity of destinies. One may also expect from him the humility of an admission: The most profound break with the worldly order is not the privilege of the person who stands most conspicuously against that order, but can take place in the strictest incognito, in the Kierkegaardian experience of the "Knight of Faith." However, neither reminder nor admission can make the challenge of ascetic excesses meaningless, and they cannot really prevent us from recognizing implications which extend beyond the fate of the individual, or the "unique," and which are important for the entire *disputatio de homine*.

The problem of ascesis is one of literalism, and the problem of interpreting it lies in the suspicions that surround all literalism. From the notion that non-possession defines the human being (and *a fortiori* the human being who confronts the Absolute) more deeply than any relation of appropriation and possession, the ascetic infers that he cannot live a life true to his essence without a literal rejection of property. From the belief that the world is not the human being's final homeland, he may infer that life true to his essence cannot be lived without a literal refusal of all worldly dwelling. Everything may lend itself to his negations. And it is easy to see how, in the hope of a new "land" where the divine generosity will restore a "creation" now obliterated, the ascetic may attempt what we know he cannot completely accomplish – to renounce all participation in the worldly game, or in any case reduce his participation in that game to the barest minimum. It will be objected – and quite justly so – that such renunciation, or attenuation, does not really represent a set of facts that could be guaranteed by the objectivity of conduct. But beyond the rather banal validity of that objection, one point should not escape us: Ascetic excess gives visibility to a transgression that, while it certainly does not exist because of that visibility, does not altogether exist unless it can manifest it. Despite all the strangeness of his gestures, and although those gestures are not universally required of anyone who wants to confront God, in fact the ascetic acts on behalf of all, and as everyone's proxy. The spectacular marginality of the human being who refuses possessions, a place to live, and so on, does no more than express in particularly concrete form the marginality that in any case affects anyone who wishes to subordinate his worldly being to his being-before-God. It may be that the literalism of the ascetic offers a naive interpretation of that subordination. But naivety can be right. And without it, we might perhaps not be aware of exactly what we are doing when we decide to exist face to face with God. Ascetic excess is not significant because it goes beyond what all are strictly bound to do if they want to lead a life that pleases God: It is significant because it pushes to the limit a logic that is already present, even if no more than discreetly implicit, as soon as human beings accept confrontation with the Absolute, and the Absolute alone "suffices" to them. We do not need the excesses of asceticism to make liturgical disappropriation thinkable to us, we do not need them to make it part of our experience. Nevertheless, they provide the best mirror in which to see the final implications of that experience – to see that to exist face to face with God, human beings may dress in clothing closely resembling that of the lunatic.

It is not of course suggested, in using the vocabulary of madness, that the Absolute alienates the individual who consents to radical disappropriation, or that the experience of disappropriation equates to that of the collapse of the ego. And because the French language allows the distinction, one should perhaps speak of the "fool" (*fol*) rather than the "lunatic" (*fou*). The lunatic's madness weighs on him like a turn of fate, while the fool's is an act of freedom. On the one hand, a pure figure of suffering; on the other a choice, or at least consent. These basic truths, which it will serve no purpose to enlarge on here, cannot, however, obscure a profound symbolic solidarity. On the symbolic level, both lunatic and fool bear witness to their wounds. The fool denies his belonging to the world, while the lunatic's insanity prevents him from joining happily in human society, and the denial is not the same thing as the prevention. (For example, the fool may decide to live a life of not belonging to the world with other human beings, while the lunatic is always alone.) However, one can – indeed one should – recognize a true proximity. The fool's extravagance and his conduct exceeding what is required demonstrate an intention to transgress, but the transgressor assumes the features of the mutilated human, poorer than all others, who renounces the claim he might lay to the world without enjoying any right to the final, transfigured realities of the Kingdom. The fool's experience has an eschatological horizon – otherwise we could not account for it – while the lunatic's experience is obviously devoid of such a horizon. But before accounting for it, and in order to explain it better, we should allow ourselves to be disturbed by it, and to do that it will be good to recognize that the fool's madness is just as much a symbolic representation of death as the lunatic's madness. If we set aside for a moment the liturgical justifications he puts forward, the fool is the neighbor of the lunatic – and perhaps they are even indistinguishable, perhaps the fool is just a lunatic by any way of thinking that does not recognize the eschatological implications and (what is more significant for our argument) any way of thinking in which the *eschaton* can be conceived only as human beings' dwelling peaceably in the world. From the vantage point offered (exemplarily) by Hegelian absolute knowledge and the reconciled existence which possesses that knowledge, what reasons for the fool's excesses would we accept? To questions that it is scarcely worth developing here, we shall reply by detecting a note of humor in the fool's conduct.

The Humor of the Fool

Who indeed is better placed than the humorist to provide a critique of experiences which we believe to encompass the whole of the final truth of the ego? No doubt others can do it. We had no need of the fool's experience to spot the aporias in Hegelian eschatology, and it does not come into action until virtually the end of an interpretation of the penultimate realities (or rather at the end of the first attempt at an interpretation). Nonetheless, its intervention is not simply redundant. We do not need the fool to know that while human beings can live at peace with God this side of death, it does not follow that the world's only face after Good Friday is that of the homeland at last vouchsafed. But even when he has no new arguments to impart, the fool reminds us (or, who knows, teaches us) that theories are not refuted only on the theoretical plane, and that each also implies practices which it is important to rebut in a practical way. It is here that the humor shows itself, in the strange face-to-face where the "fool," who formally speaking embodies the "sage" (to use the name given by Kojève to the man who possessed absolute knowledge) no more than a figure in the past of his consciousness, suspects the sage in turn of embodying no more than a fleeting moment in the history of the spirit, and indeed of not embodying that fleeting moment which would attest most reliably to the final state. Certainly the fool does not deny the wisdom of the sage and what constitutes it. Certainly he does not deny that the appropriation of the "saving grace of the Cross" enables us no longer to inhabit the atheistic "world" or the pagan "land" of the beginning, and to bask in the divine proximity. He does not contest the validity of the theological learning that so delights the sage. Lastly, he does not deny that morality, when well understood, has real eschatological implications. But is wisdom, thus defined, and in full awareness of its true grandeur, really an experience with nothing beyond it? That is what the fool's extravagance absolutely refuses to concede; it is just such a further dimension that it is believed to symbolize and anticipate. The fool does not (and above all should not) claim to be the representative of a humanity residing finally within itself, or to propose in contrast to "wisdom" another paradigm which we can follow in imagining a transubstantiation of our present into an absolute future. Disappropriation, and everything associated with it in the ascetic approach, confers no right to achieve the *eschaton*. The fool fines down his relations with the world but does not cease to inhabit the world. He wishes to exist only in the mode of the liturgy, but cannot thereby free himself from the sway of the being-in-fact. However, that does not rob humor of its rights; who knows, perhaps it strengthens them. The "sage" thinks he has the last word, thinks his experience unsurpassable, and inevitably thinks that the fool's experience belongs to an obsolete experiential sphere, outliving itself today in an antiquated way, unaware of the true logic of existence lived in the shade of the reconciling Cross. But because he himself is moved only by the desire for the final proximity of God, and because he knows that humanity can live today at peace with God without that desire being fulfilled, the fool may object in turn that at bottom the sage is satisfied with little, in two ways. On the one hand, he is satisfied with a happiness that bears every sign of being provisional (since speculative knowledge suggests that God is present other than through the Second Coming, since the promises made at Easter – which the sage is either unaware of or misunderstands – remain unfulfilled, etc.), and on the other hand he does not really try to situate in the present all the eschatological meanings that he may perceive. The fool, because he desires the final state (the "angelic" life) more deeply than anyone, but can accede only to a fragile degree of anticipation (which obliges him to whet his humor on his own experience too), is thus able to smile at those who hold that the *eschaton* is already here in the present. And because he knows that human beings cannot desire that God be sufficient to them without translating that desire into excessive conduct, he is able to discern in the sage's experience a certain paradoxical impotence to let the final shine through in advance in the provisional. The sage can always be deaf to the fool's humor and the real threats to his wisdom it expresses. However, that humor can do its work unknown to the target of its protests. It is enough for the moment that *we* are aware of it and that we allow ourselves to learn from it.

Towards a Liturgical Critique of Concepts

Thus the time has come . . . to define the liturgical status of knowledge, and more precisely that of knowledge based on concepts.[1] In Hegelian theory, access to the concept marks the end of the journey of the consciousness. Conceptual knowledge not only judges (and condemns) any appeal to the ambiguous immediacy of the *Gefühl*, but it also clearly and distinctly arrives at a meaning that religious "representations" in fact leave unthought, thus offering itself as untranscendable and the last word. Hegel knows, of course, that the concept is not the only element in the relation of humanity and the Absolute, and that the experience of thought is not the only experience proper to humankind's reconciled existence. But when human beings have – licitly – rendered the homage of their liturgies to the Absolute, and have thus made licit use of "representation" in them, it is to the concept that they are referred, as if to a norm that sets the standard for all experience, in which no case could become a norm that is itself determined by another norm. It is in the mode of the unsurpassable that concepts laying claim to God become manifest to human beings. To possess them, therefore, must engender beatitude.

The reasons provided by the liturgy nevertheless allow us – or rather they oblige us – to reject the theory.

(a) There is certainly no doubting what God prompts us to think or himself decides to think. And if the liturgy comes after the "cognitive time gap" without which we should not know what God's name means, one must readily concede Hegel's point that knowledge implies a certain privilege – and even when the fundamental arguments of Hegelian eschatology are negated in favor of a logic of "last-but-one things," which embraces a logic of "inexperience," knowledge may also enable humankind to live calmly with that inexperience, by letting them interpret it as a particular type of experience. However, when the question of "time gap" arises in this way, we do not assert that one has to work one's way through the entire domain of thought and to think everything thinkable before theological prose can be succeeded by the hymn, the doxology, or the pure and simple presence of the man of God. Indeed, the liturgy takes its place as a matter of urgency. From its first arguments, our thoughts recognize in the *Summum cogitabile* the Person *par excellence*, which it is not enough to speak of, and to which one must speak or before which one must be silent, to hear its silence or its word. God gives us matter for thought, but the first thing he prompts us to think is that the work of the *logos* will be responsible for misunderstandings if it does not enable us to confront God. The liturgy requires knowledge. But knowledge calls for the liturgy. (And perhaps we should also dare say that it would be part of an insidious logic of diversion if that were not the case – an issue that is not absent from the polemic conducted by Kierkegaard against Hegel.)

(b) The hierarchical relation of "concept" and "representation," and their sharp contradistinction, then become singularly problematical. Could the use of "representation" suffice to enable human beings to take possession of what is most essential to them? From Hegel's viewpoint the hypothesis is scandalous and yet it arises emphatically as soon as we seek to justify the (pre-) eschatological meanings that imbue the liturgy. The liturgy attests that peace reigns between God and human beings and reveals in the shadow of death, in the element of the provisional, ways of being that place in parentheses the claims people make through their death. It is not the whole of reconciled existence. Divine forgiveness and the manifestation of God who pardons require conception. Moreover, divine forgiveness must allow reconciliation among human beings. But it is when they receive that forgiveness, and give thanks for it, that human beings first show us a countenance that they are to keep forever – and to receive the forgiveness given, it is certainly not required for them to have acceded to what Hegel calls the concept, nor even to be able to give conceptual reasons (in the ordinary sense of the word) for their joy and their hope. The "kerygma" that authorizes the liturgy, the "gospel" to which the action of grace responds, do not make conceptual elaboration (in the ordinary sense of the term) futile. The narrative testimonies of God's gesture among human beings do not represent the only possible theology. But to the idea of a vesperal, all-enveloping knowledge that reduces them to the rank of mere preliminaries to the fully rational apprehension of the truth, they offer in contrast a morning of knowledge in which obviously not everything thinkable has been thought, but where the essential has been communicated and apprehended. Hegel's contemporary certainly both thinks and prays, after eighteen centuries of Christian history that are also centuries of intellectual history and, one must agree, the source of an authentic deepening of speculative thought. However, he must be conceded one right at all costs, that of being able to confront God without a speculative mastery of what he believes and, *a fortiori*, without being required to achieve an unsurpassable and "absolute" organization of his knowledge. God prompts activity in our thoughts, God indissolubly provokes the gratitude of reconciled humanity. The words human beings use to speak of him do not capture all that he prompts us to think. The image blends into the concept, the story into the argument. However, they achieve all that can be expected from them if they provide us, in the absence of a knowledge that cannot be transcended, with the means to offer praise that knows exactly to whom it is directed. There is nothing to prevent anyone who so wishes, even after the necessary critique of Hegel's eschatology, from wanting to maintain the distinction between "representation" and "concept." On one condition, therefore: to know that possession of the "concept" is not really necessary for human beings confronting God as their ally, to lead the existence most worthy of him.

(c) Thus one should be clearly aware of an aporia which culminates in Hegel after haunting the whole history of philosophy and which unbalances the Hegelian structure all the more markedly because it is also a theological structure: his inability to let us imagine the experience of the child, and those resembling children, other than as an embryonic experience. In the terms that Hegel shares with the whole metaphysical tradition of the West, childhood can be defined only as a lack. The full exercise of reason is denied to the child. The wisdom (in the ordinary sense of the term) that the philosopher seeks is not accessible to the child. Inasmuch as human beings are only truly human when they make a show of "wisdom" and "reason," the child is thus only the beginning of the human subject: It has no interest for itself, but only for what (perhaps) it will become. And one does not need a highly developed sense of inference to realize that where (in Hegel) the possession of conceptually unsurpassable knowledge governs the advent of human beings at last equal to themselves, neither the child's experience nor that of child-like people can have any eschatological significance whatsoever. The prayers of children and those like them – "simple" people – nevertheless falsify this theory. Today the field of praise and of the action of grace is open, even to those who cannot now or never will be able to possess "absolute knowledge" or, more broadly, strictly conceptual knowledge. The child and the "simple" person are no doubt not fully aware of what they are doing when they pray. They do not realize that by praying they put their belonging to the world in question. They are not aware of the subversive power of their acts. But because they know enough to confront a God whose benevolence they know, it must be said that they have the power to perform gestures that have a final value and to insinuate into the provisional (no doubt without their knowledge) truly eschatological modes of being. The child and the "simple" person (the "collier" . . .) do not refuse when God puts thoughts in our minds and theirs. They will probably have the humility to believe the "sages" more learned than they are in things divine. However, we cannot posit a liturgical organization of the *disputatio de homine* without requiring the sage to show a much more far-reaching humility: In fact, he has to acknowledge that his wisdom does not possess the necessary conditions for completely human existence (to the extent that it can be lived in the time that leads us to death), and that it is therefore a superfluity.

The Minimal Human Being

We can thus grasp the extent of a disparity. The reasons that protect the fool's excesses and authorize his irony are strong. However, they cannot prevent the fool from making us anxious nor nullify the theoretical weight of that anxiety. What names should be given to human beings, and how should we conceptualize their humanity? There is no lack of replies to that question, and they can be set out, without contradicting each other, in the specialized vocabulary of the various philosophical traditions. Human beings are the animals to which it befalls to have a world. They are the reasonable animals, entrusted with the double task of the hermeneutic – to perceive the sense – and the apophantic – to spell out the meaning. They are political animals, capable of placing the "co-being" that *a priori* defines them in the setting of a city where the greatest possible freedom and justice reign. They are the technicians who take the destiny of objects in hand. They are the artists – the "poets" – whose works offer us, to believe the Philosopher, the greatest possible presence of Being. They are the liturgists empowered in the world to confront God. And we could say more, and give further explanations, without the fool having serious objections to the concepts – in the plural – that record the plurality of experiences through which humanity articulates its identity. But in the absence of theoretical objections (we cannot picture human beings who could be sufficiently defined only by their participation in the liturgical game), there is nevertheless an objection that is acutely evident in the very practice of the fool.

One of the properties of the concept of the liturgy is that it subordinates the worldly being to the being-before-God, and there is no need for the fool's testimony to defend and illustrate the concept. After all, the liturgical act of subversion is accomplished in the most perfect discretion each time human beings attempt to pray, and thus proves a note in their humanity, no doubt the last note, one that also allows the *a priori* conditions of experience and the relation they may have with diversion to be questioned, and in any case a note that abrogates nothing in the human things we do when we are not praying.

Now if it is not such an abrogation that the fool undertakes, he certainly bears the responsibility for his critical stance or, if one wishes, his multiple distancing. The fool does not seek the abolition of the logos, the very notion of which would be absurd – but he affirms to us that to give praise is worthier of human beings than the loftiest exercise of rationality. He does not deny that the demands of ethics are tied to political duties – but it is in the guise of a servant that he performs those duties, standing on the fringes of the city rather than taking a seat in its assemblies. He does not deny that "poetry" is an essential possibility for us and that it enables us to leave traces of our passage in the world – but his masterwork is the liturgy, which is no more a *poiesis* than it is a *praxis*, and for which leaving traces in the world is not an essential function. Among the categories in which humanity is commonly perceived, he does not reject the pertinence of those that either do not explicitly mention or do not mention at all the liturgical dimension of being; nevertheless, it is only in the most tenuous possible way that experience touches on those categories.

Thus it is in the guise of the *minimal* human being[2] that the fool confronts us, in the guise of a "neighbor" whom we should perhaps, in the true sense of the words, hesitate to recognize as a "fellow being." The disparity certainly does not detract from the "fundamental" or the "essential." Beneath the divergence in conduct, the fool's humanity is – obviously – beyond doubt for us. No formal question of ontology of the person arises here. However, the questions start to come very quickly if one remembers that the fool provides us here with a basis, not for conceiving a possible attitude of *homo religiosus* as he confronts transcendence (he could provide it, but that is another subject), but for interpreting reconciled existence. The paradox is therefore that between the fulfilled and the unfulfilled, in the time that the words of reconciliation pronounced on Good Friday and the words of promise offered at Easter enable us to live, they who hold to those words, insofar as they care radically for the Absolute, are bound to undergo a marked diminution to the essential (in which the essential itself may seem to us to be mutilated). This diminution is surely not a requirement. Because ethics has a liturgical status, and ethical requirements are inseparable from political duties, the logic of the penultimate cannot be applied exclusively as a logic of noninterest in the life of the city. Because history has perhaps been fulfilled since the days when God spoke his last words, but has certainly not been completed, no one can judge the anachronistic conjugality. And because the reconciliation of God and humankind is also the reconciliation of God with the cosmos, the liturgical relation of humanity and God cannot annul the links of knowledge, mastery, or transfiguration that humankind maintains with the cosmos. *Nevertheless, it remains licit for reconciled human beings to find joy in the peace given to them, and in the peace that should reign among them, and nowhere else.* Yet the fool who finds that joy disturbs us because his conduct is iconoclastic. The concepts that frame our thoughts of a human being's humanity form paradigms, images of being human, but here these images are broken. The fool is less than the philosopher, less than the scholar, less than the politician. He effaces himself behind them, and it is no surprise that his name is not mentioned when we try to imagine the unsurpassably human person. But in effacing himself, he leaves us with a problem. What if minimal human beings, reduced liturgically to the essential and almost less than the essential, were to derive from themselves and from the Absolute a richer experience than that of the philosopher or the scholar? What if they were able to arrive at the truth of their being and carry their (pre-eschatological) aptitudes for experience to the limit? To answer these questions, we must first, in reiterative mode, set out the perplexities that disappropriation introduces into the *disputatio de homine*. The pre-eschatological destitution to which the fool's experience attests will be assigned its hermeneutic place. That assignment will enable us to close the debate engaged with all theories of religious emotion. It will then be possible to link dispossession and beatitude in the hermeneutics of an experience that we consider to be fundamental.

Human Beings in their Place (Resumption)

The elegance of choice may fascinate, but it cannot force acquiescence: Poverty and "holy madness" manifest a real secret of being human, yet that secret leaves us in the enigmatic interim where we seem to lose any ability to take the measure of what we are. We cannot give an account of the liturgy without eschatological reference; transgression and subversion of the initial state are the watchwords here, because the *a priori* conditions of experience mean that it remains ambiguous. However, one could not refer to the ultimate without confessing that (for once) the trivial evidence is right, and that the *eschaton* is available to us, in whatever mode. We can certainly fall back on the *a priori*, but that would be to set aside the part of history in which we have enabled ourselves to pronounce God's name (or God has enabled us to pronounce his name) and of existing face to face with him. And we can also suppose that today the final state has such a grip on us that our present no longer hangs on any future – but that would be to forget that humankind reconciled to the Absolute has still received promises, and exists in the element of the unfulfilled. It is too late for the transcendental to be sufficient to define us, and too soon to suggest an equation of the real and the eschatological: The present (our present, the present lived against a horizon of the divine manifestation) is conceived in the category of the last-but-one. But while it is reasonably simple to form a concept of the penultimate, an aporia seems to arise when we point out that the logic of reconciled existence is in fact a logic of negation. The penultimate is not the provisional, and it is not the final state. It does not, of course, break all links with the provisional (only death can annul the laws of the material being), and the logic of finality is already at work (the Absolute grants its peace irrevocably, and can "reign" this side of death). From the interpretation of the "night" to that of the excesses of the fool, however, the path we have travelled has taught us to detect first in the pre-eschatological interim the combined conditions for some extenuation of the worldly being and an incontestable critique of eschatological anticipation. To refuse to exist in a mode of appropriation does not authorize the seizure of belongings that will not pass beyond this world. We do not achieve the *eschaton* for the sole reason that we want to reduce as far as possible the part we play in the world's game. The fool's excesses show him to be not a transfigured human being, but a minimal human being. And if his experience is not to be disqualified, if we are to admit that in fact it encompasses the greatest possible proximity of (mortal) human and God, we must therefore say that it is without measure: not that it is measured (and found wanting) against a presence without reservations in the world, and measured against the immediate achievement of the *eschaton*, but that it rejects these two measures. Yet are other means of measuring the nature of being human or – if you will – other hermeneutic points, available to us? There is one reply, and no doubt only one: We shall say of the fool that symbolically he inhabits Good Friday.

Anthropologia Crucis

A change of stance would then be necessary. We can ask the fool to justify his excessive conduct – and to some extent this is just what we have done. Where the lunatic's madness is a burden of fate, we can readily discern in the fool's madness the features of the plan, human nature's decree on the meaning and truth of humanity. The lunatic's experience is suffering, while the fool's experience was first understood as belonging to the category of a decision; the fool showed himself to us as one who removes the mask each of us wears so that our true human face can be seen. But we cannot mention the Cross without questioning whether the fool's experience should be thus understood right to the end, and without also discerning in it – the words find their place here through necessity – the blinding reality of a passion. The fool shatters our images of being human, and on the face of it this breakage is his work, and his triumph over ways of being that are inessential and/or linked with re-creation. However, this reading trips up over experiences in which we cannot perceive the application of a design, and in which only the Absolute can account for, if they should be accounted for, humankind's deviations. We can choose poverty, or the dispossession of will or desire. We can commit, to borrow the hyperbole of an eros, the conceptual solecism of positing that God alone is sufficient in order to draw the conclusion that he alone is necessary. But how can we use the language of choice, when the fool is presented in the guise of Bernadette Soubirous browsing the grass in front of the grotto where she had her visions, or of Jean-Joseph Surin sharing all the sufferings of the lunatic, or again of the Byzantine *salos* or the Russian *yurodivi*, where we feel that they do not play the part of the lunatic among human beings without also being associated with their pathology? No doubt dissimulation, and any possibility of irony cloaked by that dissimulation, cannot be ruled out. Philip Neri is clad by day in buffoon's clothing and spends his nights in contemplation and praise. The *salos* and the *yurodivi* simulate immorality (that is probably the most recurrent trait in their experience), the better to criticize all moralism.[3] However, we shall refuse to allow ourselves to be reassured. Even if he is miming (but how can one simulate madness without risk?), the fool represents a frightening otherness. Humility is not enough to supply the reasons for his humiliation. And that is why, if we want to refuse to see him merely as evidence of an incoherence and collapse of meaning, we cannot avoid giving the burden of interpreting his experience to the historic Good Friday, under the conceptual code of the Passion.

The entire architecture of the question of being human is necessarily affected. The question is commonly raised – with every appearance of constraint – in a mirroring mode. The subjective genitive is identically the objective genitive: To pose the question is to bring oneself into question, and to reply just for oneself. Thus knowledge is fulfilled as reflection. And even if one cannot speculate on the nature of being human without allying prescription to description, and if he who speculates has no need to claim, in order to validate his speculation and his replies, that he is the public incarnation of the wholly human person, the mirror-like structure is not thereby challenged; it is merely a matter of pointing out that what the mirror reflects back to me is not only, or first, my indivisible particularity, and that in fact the image shows the face of every human being. Yet any mirror effect is annulled here, as soon as the image stops providing the tempo and the keys for its interpretation, but confronts us with a pure and simple enigma. We can certainly recognize the fool's humanity, just as we recognize that of the lunatic or any human being, without requiring that the Cross be the hermeneutic point of his or her poverty. Our aptitude for experience embraces the possibility of a confrontation with the nonsensical, a pure ordeal of the negative. Insanity, or what looks like insanity, does not kill human beings (even if it must be seen as a heavily loaded symbol of death), and perhaps requires us to assert still more categorically the fundamental solidarity that binds us to the extra-vagrant, to those who seem to exclude themselves from human society. That being duly conceded, however, the categorical nature of the affirmation will never permit us the alchemy that might transmute non-sense into meaning. And it is this that authorizes us to say that the only possible imputation of meaning comes here from elsewhere, and that what we see in the fool's humiliated humanity, assuming that it has a place in the logic (and is not a teratology) of experience, is in fact an image of the humiliated humanity of God himself. Thus we can be more specific as to the fool's name: He is the *fool in Christ*, he whose destiny becomes intelligible only in the light of another destiny, that of the crucified one in whom and by whom God restores peace between humankind and himself.

Religious Experience – The Last Critique

We can thus agree: The refusal to let the relation of human beings and God be formed on an experiential plane, and more particularly to allow "experience" to develop in the privileged element of feeling, here gains strong *a posteriori* legitimation. A christological theory of experience – that is, a theory in which the secrets of the liturgy are unveiled at the ultimate moment, beyond any phenomenological data that claim to apply always, everywhere, and to everyone, or in any case to apply wherever the Absolute is known as the subject and promise of a relation, in the singular meeting of God and humankind in Jesus of Nazareth – would not limit its purpose to interpreting the darkness of Good Friday and the dereliction of the crucified Christ. Human beings can enjoy the divine proximity in their lifetime before death, and there is no shortage of texts that could be invoked here as christological confirmations. But is that proximity attested and demonstrated only in enjoyment? That proposition has been denied, and we can deny it still more peremptorily here. In fact the Cross, in the paroxysmic mode, is the place of inexperience. The existence of God is affirmed there, for one does not speak ("My God, my God, why hast thou forsaken me?") to one who does not exist. Moreover, God is not absent from the Cross: just as the humanity of Jesus of Nazareth is the humanity of *God*, so the death of Jesus is *his* death, *his* Passion, and not a human drama for which he might show a distant compassion. However, on Good Friday the christological relation of humankind and God ceases to be governed by consciousness – and we advise against the pious but virtually senseless interpretation which attempts to preserve unstated proprieties by supposing that the crucified Christ, in the midst of the sufferings of his agony, still enjoys from the peak of his soul the beatifying vision of God.[4] God can be the all-nearest (and there is no closer proximity than that to which christology bears witness) even when he is absent to our senses. Human beings can confront God, exist *coram Deo*, without demanding that God grant them the fruition of his presence. The affective experience of consciousness therefore abandons all right to verify or falsify the relation of humankind and God.

The hermeneutic of religious emotions thus comes up against what it finds unthinkable. Certainly it does not see itself as disqualified. The emotions of the religious man do not reveal only the ascendancy of the "earth" over consciousness; and if the divine can be contaminated (experientially) by the sacred, the reticence prompted by the *a priori* risk of that contamination should not make the affective so suspect that it must be inescapably ruled by ambiguity. But since we are prohibited from concealing that the relation of humankind and God can also take the form of an *experimentum crucis*, we must begin by referring to the excess of inexperience over experience, to the point of negation of experience pure and simple. The desire ("anxiety") for the *eschaton* is innate in human beings, even if it has to be deciphered like a palimpsest, and this desire can be assuaged in advance within the limits of the worldly being. Nevertheless, frustrating it weighs more heavily, because it brings us back from the totally unwarranted, from what we cannot really fit into an organic and necessary development of experience (the sacred is immemorially accessible to us, but God touches the experience of consciousness only through grace), to the point where without presumption we can speak the language of universality. It would surely be taking things too far to interpret "spiritual life" so tragically that its most commonplace experiences (accidie, aridity, the "night") seem to be clear and distinct participations in the experience of the crucified Christ. But it is not in the least excessive to suggest that the experience of the crucified Christ, the epitome of the minimal human being, shows at close range the gap that separates the penultimate from the ultimate, and thus can in the end interpret the most everyday aspects of "spiritual life." The crucified one is the bearer of reconciliation, and he is also the first to be reconciled. Moreover, the fool matters to us only inasmuch as he is a fool in Christ: not the (anachronistic) witness to a battle with the angel in which numinous forces reduce the human condition to incoherence, but, paradoxically, to an alliance and a peace. His destiny is pre-eschatological and has no other significance than this. The notion of an *anthropologia crucis* then tells us that, for the human reconciled with the Absolute, Good Friday is not primarily a past incident in the restitution of the origin, but remains the secret of a present held at a distance from the absolute future just as it stands at a distance from the initial state. We may thus learn from the fool and his like, as we learn from the crucified Christ, that it is the lot of reconciled human nature to exist face to face with a God whose paternal countenance is not hidden from him, *coram Deo*, and that all affective confirmation is strictly speaking inessential here.

Perfect Joy

There is more that can and must be said. A well-known apothegm, heard by Brother Leonard from Francis of Assisi, puts it well.

> I return from Perugia, and I arrive here in deepest night. It is wintry weather, muddy and so cold that icicles of frozen chilly water form on the edges of my tunic and keep banging against my legs, and blood spurts from the wounds. And I come to the gate all mud and cold and ice, and after I have knocked and called for a long time a brother comes and asks: Who is it? And I reply: Brother Francis. And he says: Go away; this is no decent hour to be out and about; you shall not come in [. . .] And I stand again before the gate and I say: For the love of God, take me in this night. And he replies: I will not do it [. . .] I tell you that if I keep my patience and am not shaken, there lies the true joy and the true virtue and the salvation of the soul, *Dico tibi quod si patientiam habuero et non fuero motus, quod in hoc est vera laetitia et vera virtus et salus animae.*[5]

Here there is mention of humiliation and mention of joy; patience authorizes the first to engender the second. Could the Cross and the experiences lived in its shadow therefore permit us to recast the terms in which the question of happiness, or of beatitude, is usually raised? To the logic of multiple negation and disappropriation which we have allowed to unfold, it would be easy to object that it is a logic of misfortune: either a nihilist logic (Nietzsche), or an outdated logic of unreconciled existence (Hegel). Yet this double objection fails against affirmations stronger than any negation or tension. The humiliated human being (the pauper, the fool, etc.) does not of course possess the final reality of his being, because the *eschaton* cannot be achieved this side of death. The reasons why humiliation can be borne with patience, and why this patience is a source of real joy, are nevertheless eschatological reasons which break the circle surrounding the being-towards-death. The only concept we can use to imagine a homeland worthy of the human condition is that of the Kingdom of God, and God can certainly reign over humans in the world this side of death. We have said, of the human being who confronts God liturgically, that he or she then exists as a function of his or her own absolute future and in a certain sense places death in parentheses. Of those for whom only the Cross gives meaning to experience, but for whom the origin of joy is humiliation, we may then say that they are able to interpret Good Friday in the light of the event of Easter, and that their joy is an advance response to the fulfillment of the promises made at Easter. Joy certainly does not annul what springs from the effects of patience; and it will always be irresponsible to invoke the final transfiguration of all things while forgetting that he who is risen is the crucified one, that he bears in his glory the stigmata of his Passion, and that all knowledge of our present is gained through meditation on Good Friday. However, an experience of Good Friday that is already transfused with the exultation of Easter is possible. We shall not expect a last word from it, because this last word cannot be spoken as long as the world and the earth – and death – hold dominion over us. On the other hand, we shall indeed receive a penultimate word.

It is too soon for the question of being human to be organized purely and simply as an *anthropologia gloriae*, and too late for world and earth to possess the conditions of all happiness. The paradoxical joy that is born of humiliation is perhaps, then, the *fundamental tonality* of pre-eschatological experience. The reconciled human being, despite Hegel, is still at a distance from his absolute future. And despite Nietzsche, disappropriated and humiliated human beings are not reduced to nothing, and do not reduce themselves to nothing, but live today from the future fulfillment of God's promises. Humanity engages in what is most proper when it chooses to confront God. The argument can now be sharpened: thus one can say that a person most precisely describes himself or herself when he or she accepts an existence in the image of a God who has taken humiliation upon himself – when a *kenotic* existence is accepted.

Translated by David H. Thompson

Notes

1 [Editorial note: Lacoste now develops his discussion of the fool with reference to Hegel's investigation into the nature and teleology of knowledge. For Hegel, knowing is accumulative and evolutionary. The mind participates in an ongoing dialectic of reason wherein the thesis is negated by an antithesis which then gives way to a new synthesis (which, in turn, is a new thesis). If this is the process of intelligence, the psychology of such intelligence requires a movement from representations of the world (which constitute one's consciousness) to concepts which grasp the organizing principles, the truth, of the representations (which constitutes one's self-consciousness). Representations are intuitions of the world on the way to becoming thoughts (concepts). To be fully human, to be adult and intelligent, requires being able to conceptualize, or reason about, what is given of one's experience of the world in representations. So the fool needs to become a sage. Lacoste criticizes this Hegelian logic.]

2 The phrase is taken from D. Ritschl, *Zur Logik der Theologie* (Munich, 1984), pp. 215–17. For Ritschl it designates, in a christological context close to our own line of reasoning, the reduction of man only to the concerns of God and his neighbor. However, the *reductio ad essentiam* is achieved in Ritschl's work without the ascetic negations – thus no one could suspect the essential of being less than the essential.

3 On "holy madness," cf. J. Saward, *Perfect Fools* (Oxford, 1980) and I. Goraïnoff, *Les fols en Christ dans la tradition orthodoxe* (Paris, 1983), though the second of these works is weakened by its totally uncritical use of hagiographic material.

4 This is the argument of Thomas Aquinas: *ST* IIIa, q. 46 a.8.

5 Francis of Assisi, *Writings, SC* 285, pp. 118–20.

Postmodern Critical Augustinianism: A Short *Summa* in Forty-two Responses to Unasked Questions

John Milbank

1   The end of modernity, which is not accomplished, yet continues to arrive, means the end of a single system of truth based on universal reason, which tells us what reality is like.

2   With this ending, there ends also the modern predicament of theology. It no longer has to measure up to accepted secular standards of scientific truth or normative rationality. Nor, concomitantly, to a fixed notion of the knowing subject, which was usually the modern, as opposed to the premodern, way of securing universal reason. This caused problems for theology, because an approach grounded in subjective aspiration can only precariously affirm objective values and divine transcendence.

3   In postmodernity there are infinitely many possible versions of truth, inseparable from particular narratives. Objects and subjects are, as they are narrated in a story. Outside a plot, which has its own unique, unfounded reasons, one cannot conceive how objects and subjects would be, nor even that they would be at all. If subjects and objects only are, through the complex relations of a narrative, then neither objects are privileged, as in premodernity, nor subjects, as in modernity. Instead, what matters are structural relations, which constantly shift; the word "subject" now indicates a point of potent

"intensity" which can rearrange given structural patterns.

4   The priority given to structural relations allows theology to make a kind of half-turn back to premodernity. One can no longer commence with modern inwardness: This is only marked negatively as "intensity" or potential, and the things that can truly be spoken about are once again external. However, this externality is no longer, as for premodernity, an organized spatial realm of substances, genera, and species, but rather a world of temporary relational networks, always being redistributed, with greater and greater "freedom," as one passes from mineral to vegetable to animal to cultural animal. So the point is not to "represent" this externality, but just to join in its occurrence; not to know, but to intervene, originate.

5   Externality is therefore a kind of process. One cannot look at this process as a whole, but one can try to imagine what it means, its significance. All cultures, all "religion," in effect see their temporal processes as microcosms of the whole process. Of course, postmodernism denies the point of doing this, except as a game. Yet to understand one's own proffered words or actions as just arbitrary, itself implies a speculation on the arbitrariness of the process in general: its universal production of the merely contingent. Christian theology, by contrast to nihilistic postmodernism, yet with equal validity, imagines temporal process as, in its very temporality, reflecting eternity; as the possibility of a historical progress into God, and as something recuperable within memory whose ultimate point is the allowing of forgiveness and reconciliation. This speculation is utterly unfounded, is inseparable from a narrative practice of remembering, and yet, in postmodern terms, it is just as valid or invalid as claims about supposedly universal human needs, desires, or modes of interaction. Modernity dictated that a sensible theology would start from "below"; postmodernity implies that conceptions of the "below" – of human subjectivity and relationship – are only constituted within the narrative that simultaneously postulates the "above." Once the epistemological approach from the subject is shown to be as foundationalist as premodern metaphysics, the latter makes a strange kind of return: but as a necessary "fiction" concerning the unseen relation of time to eternity, not as a record of "observation" of this relationship.

6   Postmodern theology does not, therefore, begin with an account of the subject, for this is not neutrally available. By the same token, it is not seriously challenged by modernist discourses claiming to narrate a universally fundamental genesis of the subject in individual lives or in human history: Freudianism, Marxism, sociology. On the other hand, it faces a new and perhaps more severe challenge from the implications of a more thoroughgoing perspectival histori-

cism which is what intellectual postmodernism is really all about. If Christianity is just one of many possible perspectives, then why believe any of them? Is not each perspective a strategy of power, every discourse but the means to assert that discourse? Postmodernism seems to imply nihilism, albeit of a "positive" kind, embracing contingency and arbitrariness as the real natural good.

7   Whatever its response may be to nihilism, postmodern theology can only proceed by explicating Christian practice. The Christian God can no longer be thought of as a God first seen, but rather as a God first prayed to, first imagined, first inspiring certain actions, first put into words, and always already thought about, objectified, even if this objectification is recognized as inevitably inadequate. This practice which includes images of, talk about, addresses to, actions toward "God," can in no way be justified, nor be shown to be more rational, nor yet, outside its own discourse, as more desirable, than nihilism.

8   But is this really all that can be said? That Christianity is just "on a level" with other practices, other discourses? Not quite. First, it may be argued that Christianity can become "internally" postmodern in a way that may not be possible for every religion or ideology. I mean by this that it is possible to construe Christianity as suspicious of notions of fixed "essences" in its approach to human beings, to nature, to community and to God, even if it has never fully escaped the grasp of a "totalizing" metaphysics. Through its belief in creation from nothing it admits temporality, the priority of becoming and unexpected emergence. A reality suspended between nothing and infinity is a reality of flux, a reality without substance, composed only of relational differences and ceaseless alterations (Augustine, *De Musica*). Like nihilism, Christianity can, should, embrace the differential flux.

9   Yet here arises the second point regarding whether Christianity is just "on a level." For nihilism, the flux is a medium of perpetual conflict, a pagan *agon* where the most powerful rhetoric will temporarily triumph, only to succumb to an apparently or effectively more powerful discourse in the future. Because there are no fixed categorical areas for different discourses/practices, they ceaselessly overlap and contest for influence. Lyotard and others rightly do not envisage a peaceful coexistence of a plurality of discourses alongside each other, without mutual interference. The best that can be hoped for is some mitigation of the severity of conflict, a set of formal rules of engagement such as is provided by the market or bureaucracy – forms which can survive many changes in the actual content of "truth." For this reason, postmodern nihilism remains in continuity with liberalism and the Enlightenment. Christianity, however, unlike many other discourses, pursued from the outset a universalism which tried to subsume rather than merely abolish difference: Christians could

remain in their many different cities, languages, and cultures, yet still belong to one eternal city ruled by Christ, in whom all "humanity" was fulfilled. In this way it appears as a "precursor" of enlightenment, and any claim of outright Christian opposition to enlightenment is bound to be an oversimplification. But the liberty, equality, and fraternity latent as values in Christianity do not imply mere mutual tolerance, far less any resignation to a regulated conflict. On the contrary, Christianity is peculiar, because while it is open to difference – to a series of infinitely new additions, insights, progressions toward God, it also strives to make of all these differential additions a harmony, "in the body of Christ," and claims that if the reality of God is properly attended to, there can be such a harmony. And the idea of a consistently beautiful, continuously differential, and open series, is of course the idea of "music." In music there must be continuous endings and displacements, yet this is no necessary violence, because only in the recall of what has been displaced does the created product consist. Violence would rather mean an unnecessarily jarring note, a note wrong because "out of place," or else the premature ending of a development. Perhaps this is partly why, in *De Musica*, Augustine – who realized that creation *ex nihilo* implied the nonrecognition of ontological violence, or of positive evil – put forward a "musical" ontology. Christianity, therefore, is not just in the same position as all other discourses *vis-à-vis* postmodernity; it can, I want to claim, think difference, yet it perhaps uniquely tries to deny that this necessarily (rather than contingently, in a fallen world) entails conflict.

10   Explication of Christian practice, the task of theology, tries to pinpoint the peculiarity, the difference, of this practice by "making it strange," finding a new language for this difference less tainted with the overfamiliarity of too many Christian words which tend to obscure Christian singularity. The idea that this practice is essentially "music" would be an example of this "making strange." And as a second example, this music implies "community" in a very particular sense. For Christianity, true community means the freedom of people and groups to be different, not just to be functions of a fixed consensus, yet at the same time it totally refuses *indifference*; a peaceful, united secure community implies *absolute* consensus, and yet, where difference is acknowledged, this is no agreement in an idea, or something once and for all achieved, but a consensus that is only in and through the interrelations of community itself, and a consensus that moves and "changes": *a concentus musicus*. Christianity (and not even Judaism, which postpones universality to the *eschaton*, a final chord) uniquely has this idea of community: this is what "Church" should be all about (Lash).

11   Unless it reflects upon the singularity of Christian norms of community,

theology has really nothing to think about. For Christian practice, like every practice, is all external, a matter of signs and actions interpellating "persons." The tradition already insisted that "God" is only spoken about with reference to certain historical happenings and memories; a postmodern emphasis will add that God is never seen, never looked at. The response to God is response to the pressure of the unknown, and if Christians ask "What is God like?" then they can only point to our "response" to God in the formation of community. The community is what God is like, and he is even more like the ideal, the goal of community implicit in its practices. Hence he is also unlike the community, and it is this inexpressible reality that the community continues to try to respond to.

12 If God can only be given some content through community, then speaking of God is not just a matter of words, but also of images and bodily actions. These all articulate "God."

13 The community as substantive peace, as musical difference, is actually performed, ideally imagined, and in both these aspects, contemplated.

14 Augustine already put the idea of the peaceful community at the center of his theology; thought of God, of revelation from God, was for him inseparable from the thought of heaven, of words and "musical laws" coming down from heaven. The heavenly city meant for Augustine a substantial peace; but this peace could also be imperfectly present in the fallen world, in the sequences of time, and time redeemed through memory.

15 One way to try to secure peace is to draw boundaries around "the same," and exclude "the other"; to promote some practices and disallow alternatives. Most polities, and most religions, characteristically do this. But the Church has misunderstood itself when it does likewise. For the point of the supersession of the law is that nothing really positive is excluded – no difference whatsoever – but only the negative, that which denies and takes away from Being: in other words, the violent. It is true, however, that Christians perceive a violence that might not normally be recognized, namely any stunting of a person's capacity to love and conceive of the divine beauty; this inhibition is seen as having its soul in arbitrariness. But there is no real exclusion here; Christianity should not draw boundaries, and the Church is that paradox: a nomad city.

16 The religions and polities that exclude, characteristically seek to identify one thing that must be removed; a scapegoat, which can become in some ambiguous fashion "sacred," because of the efficacious effect of its expulsion, bearing away all that is undesirable, together with all the guilt of the community.

At the same time, the relationship of the community to the transcendently divine often demands further acts of distinction in the form of "sacrifice." The divine demands an offering, the violent separation, by fire or knife, of spirit from body, a purging off, to send up to heaven. Originally these were human sacrifices, then later commuted, symbolic ones, but still, frequently, in addition, the lives of those fallen in holy wars, or else the sacrifice of a pure ascetic spirit that has become indifferent to disturbing emotions.

17   Instead of multiple difference, there is dualism here; the banished, the purged off, over against the included, the subsumed. The law of this dualism implies an ever-renewed conflict both within and without the city-gates. This is the *traditional* mode of violence, whose existence must certainly be noted, though it is different in kind to modern/postmodern regulated and "indifferent" conflict. Of course, legal monotheism, and Christianity when it has failed to escape this mode, remains half-trapped by this dualism. Whereas a Christianity true to itself should oppose all modes of violence: the premodern violence of law, the modern violence of norms of subjective "rights," the postmodern violence of total lack of norms. Yet the rejection of dualistic violence grows throughout the Bible: Monotheism and creation out of nothing eschew the idea of a "chaotic" realm over against the divine, in eternal conflict with it. And the Jewish idea of law aspires to the idea of a law at one with life, with Being. But there is still some exclusion of the positive, some attempt to secure in a code the harmony of Being, and no complete recognition that perfect, divine rule is beyond all coercion. In a sense, this is a failure to have a perfect monotheism, and exhibits residues of dualism; in another sense monotheism alone is inadequate, as it cannot think of God as primarily the openness of love to the other.

18   Where there is a positing of a sacred over against a chaotic other, then the supremacy of the sacred can always be deconstructed, for it appears that there is something more ultimate that includes both the sacred and chaos, that governs the passage between them. Is not this passage itself chaotic? Hence there is a hidden connection between premodern pagan dualism and postmodern dualism. The latter's self-proclaimed paganism is a kind of deconstructed paganism, for the real pagans were always hoping to subordinate the admitted conflictual diversity of the gods to a harmonious order; an open celebration of the finality of the *agon* was only latent. But Christianity, which is not dualistic in this fashion, and already admits the flux of difference, is therefore outside the reach of deconstruction (in precisely Derrida's sense).

19   If premodern religions and postmodern nihilism are secretly akin; indeed, different moments of a "dialectic" (postmodernism claims to refuse

dialectic, but this is the instance of its failure to do so; it is right to make the effort), then, by contrast, one can trace in the Bible the slow emergence of opposition to the common factor of violence in all human norms. For it gradually takes the part of the scapegoat, and starts to place a ban on revenge against those who first violently excluded their brethren (the protection of Cain by God). The Hebrews were originally nomads, and chance and prophecy constantly recalled them to their nomad status (Girard).

20   In the course of this nomadic history, sacrifice is also commuted. Finally, in Christianity, God is thought of as asking only for the offering of our free will, in a return of love to him. This is no longer in any sense a self-destruction or self-division, but rather a self-fulfillment, an offering that is at the same time our reception of the fullness of Being. It is receiving God: "deification."

21   In a world dominated by evil and violence, self-offering, to God and others, inevitably involves suffering. This is why there is suffering at the heart of Christ's perfect self-offering to God.

22   This is not, of course, the offering of a blood sacrifice to God. Before the cross comes the preaching of the kingdom. The kingdom is really offered by Christ to humanity, and the cross is the result of a rejection of this offer. However, this very rejection tends to suggest the "original" character of human sin; to sin, theology has speculated, is to refuse the love of God, and so to render oneself incapable of recognizing God, by substituting the goals of human pride in his place. The putting to death of God shows what evil is: its nihilistic pointlessness, its incomprehensibility (Schwäger).

23   This speculation continues: Evil cannot fully see itself as evil; therefore only the uncontaminated good, God himself, can fully suffer evil – not in eternity, which is beyond suffering, but in the human creation, hence the necessity for the *Deus Homo*. Such a speculation is an important part of Christianity, a theoretical component which a postmodern approach can recognize as actually "taking off" from the narrative sources, as *not* fully grounded in them, and yet as validated merely by the profundity of the picture of God which results, merely by the pleasing shape of the conceits which it generates. However, at the same time a postmodern approach must do more justice to the narrative, practical, social level than in the past. For if Jesus' perfect suffering belonged to his "interiority," then how can it make any difference to us, how would we know about it? Much past theology has seemed to suggest that there is a change, consequent upon the atonement, in the divine attitude toward us, a change to which we are just "extrinsically" related, and

which is just "positively" revealed to us. However, if the perfect character of Jesus' suffering is recognized by us, then this can only mean that it is more present "on the outside," in his deeds and words, and even in the words used by others which compose the record of Christ; for it is only the recorded, interpreted Christ who saves us, and this mediation does not conceal some more original, "self-present" Christ – that would be a mere asocial phantom. The speculation about atonement is grounded in a narrative relation to which we must constantly return: The Church considers that in all its actions it can learn to suffer truly (and thereby perceive our previous original sin of unperceived egotism) from the story of Jesus, so that its plot can be fulfilled universally. Does this practical situation imply the finality of Jesus, his identity with the divine word? The more subtle reply is, not quite, for practice cannot claim to "know" the finality of what it treats as final. Even a theoretical, speculative discourse conceived as having a "second order," "regulative" function is finally excessive (in a positive sense), and makes its own peculiar contribution to the content of Christianity, thereby insinuating itself back into first-order discourse from which it is only relatively distinguished (as all speech both orders and regulates, and regulates only in giving new orders). Thus, in the New Testament itself, speculative considerations about the atonement are celebrated in poetic, devotional terms. Already the metaphors and mythical "metanarratives" implying incarnation and atonement are "somewhat in excess"; they not only secure the first-order level of "historical" narrative recitation, they also go speculatively beyond this to suggest a particular "mythical" picture of God as becoming incarnate, suffering in our stead. Nothing justifies this speculation except itself, and the way it then enriches the stories told, and redoubles the perceived significance of Christian practices.

24   For the traditional speculation, God cannot endure the contradiction of sin; creation must offer itself back to God; evil prevents it from doing so; therefore God must offer creation back to God, through the incarnation of the *Logos*, who includes all things. Yet for early Christianity, it is clear that God suffers a contradiction until all make for themselves the offering already made by Christ. The "incarnation" has no meaning, therefore, except as "the beginning," the foundation of the Church, a new sort of community of charity and forgiveness, as a space for the possibility of this offering. For Augustine, it is the *Church* that is the adequate sacrifice to God; in other words the realization of perfect community. The centrality of incarnation and the cross in no way contradicts the truth that the central aspect of salvation is the creation of perfect community.

25   Christianity is primarily about this hope for community. But it offers more than hope: It also remembers perfect community as once instantiated by

the shores of Lake Galilee; this is a memory compounded only of words and images. But there should be no pathos here, and Christianity has too often been sunk in this pathos. It is not that we have a few fragments of memory in lieu of the "real presence" of the resurrected Christ, but that these fragments are the real saving presence; they provide us – within the whole network of tradition within which they belong – with a new *language* of community. The Christian claim is that the narratives about Christ show what love – a difficult and demanding practice requiring more subtlety, style, and correct idiom than mere "well-meaning" – is. That here is the *Logos*, the lost harmonic pattern of genuine human life, which can now be reappropriated.

26   What are we to make of the fact that a "resurrection" forms a part of this memory? Resurrection is no proof of divinity, nor a kind of vindication of Jesus' mission. And no very good "evidence" survives, only the record of some strongly insisted–upon personal testimonies. What we have is the memory of community, of "ordinary" conversation, of eating and drinking, continuing beyond death. Without this element, there could not really be a memory of a moment of "perfect" community, for this is normally inhibited by the forces of nature as we know them, and by death especially.

27   To remember the resurrection, to hope for the universal resurrection, is a "political" act: for it is the ultimate refusal of all denials of community. The return of all the dead in reconciliation; the innocent, the guilty, the oppressed and the oppressors, is looked for (Peukert).

28   The resurrection is about the persistence of the ordinary, and the doctrine of the Incarnation locates God in the ordinary, even if this is an ordinariness "transfigured." Although this doctrine is a radical speculation that was only gradually articulated, it is also a rebuke to attempts to formulate metaphysically the divine perfection; one can make groping attempts, but finally God's perfection is most like this particular life, historically obscure, almost lost to view.

29   God is most to be found in this life recognizably like our own, yet also recognized as uniquely "other," because we take it as judging all other lives.

30   The doctrine of the Incarnation – of Jesus' "identity" with the divine *Logos* – secures this practical relation of the Church to Jesus, yet also goes beyond and reinforces it in the way suggested above. Its real validation is in allowing us to imagine a peaceful, totally charitable God, who cannot force us, and yet cannot let us go. Also, by returning us to the narrative, by tying us to contingency, it suggests that divine goodness is no generalized intention, but

always takes a very particular "form," that it is inseparable from aesthetic harmony.

31   Yet in the memory of Christ we are given the language of salvation, and not formulas for how to use this language. For the universal offering to be made, the Church must creatively construct her own response to Christ. This is why there is a work of the Spirit that can be distinguished from that of Christ, even though this response itself is ideally and infinitely fulfilled within the Godhead.

32   For if evil is truly overcome in the perfect harmony of Christ's life in community with his followers, and in the language of this community which we remember, this still does not mean that here we possess a *gnosis*, in the sense of a given formulaic wisdom that we must just recite or magically invoke. Instead, this language allows us to *escape* from the dominating effects of human discourses which totally subsume all differences, new occurrences, under existing categories. Atonement means that the flux is permitted to flow again, that the *Logos* only really speaks with its real intent in the ever-different articulation of our responses. The Holy Spirit is associated with this diversity of answers. But they all form the continuous unity of the body of Christ.

33   The doctrine of the Trinity is a statement of faith that God is, "in himself," as he has been imagined by us to relate to human history. Here we imagine him to speak once as a word that unifies all other words, and as continuously achieving that final unification of all other words by articulating a manifold response to the one word. So God involves not just the first difference of expressive articulation of content (inseparable from content), but also the second difference of interpretation of expression (inseparable from expression, making expression always already conversation). Without this second difference, we would be tempted to think that the expression just carried us back to a preformed content, or else that God was but a single *ratio*, which would be little better than seeing him as but a single person. With this second difference, one truly has a moment of response to expression in God, which goes beyond, is "excessive" in relation to the expression. Hence the love that subsists between Father and Son is communicated as a further difference that always escapes, or, as Stanislas Breton puts it, "an *infinite* relation" (Derrida and Labarrière).

34   God as Trinity is therefore himself community, and even a "community in process," infinitely realized, beyond any conceivable opposition between "perfect act" and "perfect potential." A trinitarian ontology can therefore be a differential ontology surpassing the Aristotelian *actus purus*.

35   "In the image of the Trinity" means that "human beings" are moments of particularly intense and adaptive "recollection" within the temporal process, although such recollection is constitutive of the temporal process itself. For a present moment "is" in its repetitive holding of the past, yet in this "remembering" it escapes at one level the temporal continuum and arrives as a "meaning" which has a free capacity for adaptation and expansion (Augustine, *Confessions*; Deleuze).

36   The human mind does not "correspond" to reality, but arises within a process which gives rise to "effects of meaning." It is a particularly intense network of such effects. Our bodily energies and drives (for Augustine in *Civitas Dei* the *ingenium* which images the power of the divine Father) are made "present" and articulate (so alone constituted and sustained) through the happening of linguistic "meaning," which is also the event of a "truth" which cannot "correspond." For Augustine this second moment is the cultural training of the artist's *ingenium*; it is also that active memory by which we constantly learn through repeating our individual and collective biographies. Knowledge "surfaces" as the process of learning, which is true if divinely "illumined" – it is not a knowledge of an object outside that process (God being this process, in its infinite plenitude).

37   The mind is only illumined by the divine *Logos*, if also our "preceding" energies, and our "emergent" desires, correspond to the Father and the Spirit respectively. We know what we want to know, and although all desiring is an "informed" desiring, desire shapes truth beyond the imminent implications of any logical order, so rendering the Christian *Logos* a continuous product as well as a process of "art." Moreover, if all that "is" is good and true, then no positive reality can be false as a "mistake," or as "noncorrespondence," but only false as deficient presence, embodying the shortfall of an inadequate desire. Now desire, not Greek "knowledge," mediates to us reality.

38   All desire is good so long as it is a restless desire (a more-desiring desire) which is moved by infinite lack, the pull of the "goal." Such desire is nonviolent for it could only be content with the unrestricted openness, nonpossessiveness and self-offering of resurrected bodies. Yet this is not the cold "detachment" (both in relation to creatures and away from creatures) of a "disinterested" *agape* sundered from *eros*. This would imply that finite reality, as for Neoplatonism, by always lacking, always being unworthy of erotic attachment, must always be evil. For Augustine, Christianity goes beyond this by conjoining to "the goal" also "the way," which means a constant historical determining that desire is well-ordered, not just through its deference to infinite fruition, but also by a particular selective pattern of finite use. The *appropriate* preferences of *eros*, the

"right harmonies" within a musical sequence, alone ensure that this sequence "progresses" toward the infinite goal. For every new act, every new word, may be either enabling or inhibiting, and although inhibition is mere negation, this can only be registered by the "fine judgment" which recognizes an aesthetic distortion (*De Trinitate*).

39   "The way" is not theoretically known but must be constituted through judgment in the repeated construction and recognition of "examples," which cannot be literally copied if they are to be genuinely "repeated." The first example, Christ, by being first, inevitably defines the way, because this way is considered to be a single way (if not single we are back in agonistics: This is the only reason its singularity matters). Because Christ is remembered as a *founder*, whose character is by definition not representable in terms of prior cultural orders, it is inevitable that his character will *entirely coincide* in its representation with the new categories of the new ecclesial society. Hence as founder, Christ is also the total realized collective character of the Church which is yet to come, and will itself include all cosmic reality. It follows that the *topos* Christ-founder surprisingly bears in itself the elements of a "high" christology. The correspondence of Christ to God, or the identity of the entire "pattern" of his life (which is what *persona* really implies, not any substantive "element") with the *Logos*, only makes sense within the broader context of the correspond-ence of the ecclesial "way" to God. For the "pattern" of Jesus' life is only provisionally and canonically complete; as the "context" for the new society it cannot "belong" to an "individual" and this is why one should hold onto, but reinterpret, the Chalcedonian insight that Jesus possessed no human *hypostasis*. For the "patterns" or "coherencies" of our lives never belong to us, are not "completed" at our deaths, and can be repeated, or even more fully realized, by others: This is supremely true of a pattern that is taken to be canonically normative, as eschatologically coinciding with the identities of all of us, as omni-repeatable and so as "divine."

40   Furthermore, "the way" is not defined solely as such a repetition. Were this the case, then we would be remaining within the logic of parts and wholes which characterized Greek thinking about both the individual and society, and tended to exile individual awareness and expression to the asocial realm of *theoria*. By contrast, as Augustine saw, the primacy (or equal primacy) of desire implies that "individuality" arises only through the constant rupturing and "externalization" of the subject. To contemplate is now to desire the other, to enter further into relation both with God and with human beings and angels. And the way is a community, not just christological supplementation, but from the outset the inclusion of interpretative response in the relations of Mary, of John the Baptist, and the disciples to Christ. This is why there is a historical

happening of Christ not *just* as the image of the Father, but also as the relation to the father, which as invisible, and indeed only "imagined" in language, can only be made present as the inner-relatedness of the Church, including its "initial" relation to Jesus in his own relatedness to the traditional imagining of a Father-God. Desire exceeds even the Christian *Logos*, and yet fulfills it and therefore does not after all exceed it (according to the logic of "substantive relations"), because the *usus* of the cultural product, understood "aesthetically" as a work of art, is not exhausted even by a sympathetic judgmental attentiveness to its "perfect" specificity. Desire, through reapplication, both respects this perfection and undoes it through joining the work to the continuous musical series. Hence the way is Christ, but equally the Church. And both are "real" as the cultural happening of "meaning"; "liberal versus conservative" debates about the historicity of the resurrection etc. will have no place in a postmodern theology.

41 "The way," which is redemptive, is only the proper occurrence of creation. This is why Augustine is right to think that the "economic" trinitarian series of Paternal voice–Christ–Ecclesia discloses to us a trinitarian ontology which allows us to describe the universal happening of humanity in and through time. In this account of participation in the Trinity (presented as "trinitarian vestiges" in the soul) the historical mediation of the Trinity is upheld by Augustine *more* than by others, precisely because he makes this process the metahistorical context for all historical reality, and so wisely and necessarily obscures its singularity: it is not just one revelatory event within an order that is quite otherwise (*De Trinitate*).

42 Creation is always found as a given, but developing "order." As the gift of God, creation also belongs to God, it is within God (together with the infinity of all articulations that there may be) as the *Logos*. But existing harmonies, existing "extensions" of time and space, constantly give rise to new "intentions," to movements of the Spirit to further creative expression, new temporal unraveling of creation *ex nihilo*, in which human beings most consciously participate. Yet even this movement, the vehicle of human autonomy, is fully from God, is nothing *in addition* to the divine act-potential, and not equivocally different in relation to him. The latter conception would be "pagan," "gnostic," "Cabbalistic," whereas it is God himself who is differentiation, ensuring that this process is "music," not the ceaseless rupture and self-destruction of a differentiation poised "univocally" (Deleuze) between an "indifferent" transcendence and an anarchic finitude. The trust that in our linguistic and figurative creations we can constantly recognize, when it arises, the aesthetically "right" addition, which is, in its specific content, a criterion of self-validation, is now the mode of recognition of a transcendental/

277

ontological possibility of "participation" (Kant). And so translates for us, "faith in the triune God."

Acknowledgment

I am grateful to my colleague Dr Richard Roberts for suggesting the description "Postmodern Critical Augustinianism" for my theological project.

Bibliography

Augustine, *The City of God, De Trinitate, Confessions, De Musica.*

Balthasar, Hans Urs von, *The Glory of the Lord: A Theological Aesthetics. Vol. I, Seeing the Form,* trans. E. Leiva-Merikakis (Edinburgh: T. and T. Clark, 1982).

Deleuze, Gilles, *Logique du Sens* (Paris: Minuit, 1969).

——*Différence et Répétition* (Paris: Presses Universitaires de France, 1972).

——(with Felix Guattari). *A Thousand Plateaus,* trans. Brian Massumi (London: Athlone Press, 1988).

Derrida, Jacques, *Of Grammatology,* trans. G. G. Spivak (Baltimore, MD: Johns Hopkins University Press, 1982).

Derrida, Jacques, and Labarrière, Pierre-Jean, *Altérités* (Paris: Osins, 1986).

Girard, René, *Of Things Hidden Since the Foundation of the World,* trans. Stephen Bann and Michael Metteer (London: Athlone Press, 1987).

Kant, Immanuel, *Critique of Judgement,* trans. Werner S. Pluhar (Indianapolis: Hackett, 1987).

Kierkegaard, Søren, *Repetition,* trans. H. V. and E. H. Hong (Princeton, NJ: Princeton University Press, 1983).

——*Philosophical Fragments,* trans. H. V. and E. H. Hong (Princeton, NJ: Princeton University Press, 1985).

Lash, Nicholas, *Easter in Ordinary* (London: SCM, 1989).

Lyotard, Jean-François, *The Postmodern Condition,* trans. Geoff Bennington and Brian Massumi (Manchester: Manchester University Press, 1984).

——*The Differend: Phrases in Dispute,* trans. Georges van den Abbeele (Manchester: Manchester University Press, 1988).

Milbank, John, *Theology and Social Theory: Beyond Secular Reason* (Oxford: Blackwell, 1990).

Peukert, Helmut, *Science, Action and Fundamental Theology* (Cambridge, MA: MIT Press, 1986).

Schwäger, Raymund, *Der Wunderbare Tausch: Zur Geschichte und Deutung der Erlosungslehre* (Munich: Kosel, 1986).

Metaphysics and
Phenomenology: A Summary
for Theologians

Jean-Luc Marion

I

The question of God cannot be said to begin with metaphysics. But it seems – or at least it might once have appeared – that the question of God began to be closed from the moment when metaphysics was reaching its conclusion and started to disappear. This has all happened during the century which is now ending, as though the question of God could not avoid joining in the fate of metaphysics, for better or worse. All this has also happened as though, in order to keep the question of God open, thus enabling us to render it a "reasonable service" (Romans 12: 1), it was absolutely necessary to keep to the strictly metaphysical interpretation of all philosophy.

But would it not be possible, and should we not therefore also, in a contrary way, pose a quite different preliminary question: Is philosophy equivalent to metaphysics? To remain rational when posing questions about God, must we necessarily and exclusively follow the paths which lead to "the God of philosophers and savants," since this route would of necessity start from the conclusions of metaphysics? Reversing the question in this way may cause surprise and disquiet, or, on the contrary, appear to dodge the radical nature of the philosophical situation of our century. Yet this line of enquiry seems inevitable, in that only a reversal of this kind still leaves truly open the possibility of fairly considering at least three questions, which I will raise, without claiming to answer them explicitly in this essay: (a) Is it not the case that metaphysics, at least in terms of its historic role, reached its positive conclusion with Hegel and its negative with Nietzsche? (b) Has not the task of philosophy been to take us beyond these conclusions, through the whole of this century, by assuming nonmetaphysical forms, the most potent (though not the only one) of which remains phenomenology? (c) Does speculative Christian theology as understood in its exemplars – and in this context I am of course thinking primarily of St Thomas Aquinas – belong to metaphysics in the strict sense, or has it been a response to the specific conceptual demands of the Revelation which gave rise to it?

We will therefore examine first the metaphysical form of philosophy and what it achieves through thinking about God – then the phenomenological form of philosophy and the possibility which it concedes to God.

II

The mere mention of the concept of the "end of metaphysics" arouses controversy. This could probably be avoided by taking care to agree on a precise and verifiable definition of "metaphysics" itself. And this is all the more true since historically it could be defined in a way that was almost universally accepted. In fact, the concept of metaphysics appeared relatively late but with a clear definition. One of the first people to accept it (which is not to imply that he made it his own, since he only uses it to comment on Aristotle, and elsewhere with caution) was St Thomas Aquinas. He precisely fixed its theoretical scope: *metaphysica* "simul determinat de ente in communi et de ente primo quod est a materia separatum" ("simultaneously distinguishes the general being and the prime being, separate from matter").[1] In spite of conclusive modifications to the acceptance, among other things, of being in general as an objective concept of being, we find this dual definition sanctioned by Suarez from the very beginning of his *Disputationes Metaphysicae*, a work which itself assigns once and for all to modern philosophy the concept and the word "metaphysics": "Abstrahit haec scientia a sensibilibus, seu materialibus rebus . . . et res divinas et materia separatas et communionem rationem entis, quae absque materia existere possunt, contemplatur" ("This science makes abstract palpable or material things . . . and it contemplates on the one hand things that are divine and separated from matter, and on the other common reason of being, which can [both] exist without matter.")[2] This duality in one and the same science, dealing at the same time with "essences" (*les étants par excellence*) and with "being in general," will lead, with the "metaphysics of the schools" (*Schulmetaphysik*) of the seventeenth and eighteenth centuries, to the canonical schema of "metaphysics" divided into *metaphysica generalis (sive ontologia)* and *metaphysica specialis (theologia rationalis, psychologia rationalis,*

Jean-Luc Marion

cosmologia rationalis).³ Kant's critique is situated entirely within this arrangement, since the triple refutation of special metaphysics in the "transcendental
dialectic" of the *Critique of Pure Reason* rests, as is often forgotten, on the
rejection – in the "Analytics of principles" – of the "vainglorious name of
ontology."⁴ In a rigorous history of ideas, metaphysics is defined thus: the
system of philosophy from Suarez to Kant, as a single science concerned both
with what is universal in "common being" (*l'étant commun*) and in "essence"
(or "essences"). This textually derived datum seems difficult to challenge.

But there remains the task of interpreting it. The historically narrow
acceptance of "metaphysics" is the natural consequence of its strict definition:
But, for that very reason, can we confirm that notion conceptually? Can we read
into it more than a scholarly, not to say pedagogical nomenclature, one which
has no genuinely speculative range, and, which in any case is incapable of taking
us to the heart of the question of metaphysics? This doubt would be a serious
threat if we did not have at our disposal a conceptual elaboration of that popular
notion of "metaphysics" – the one which Heidegger gives in the section of
Identität und Differenz entitled "the onto-theological construction of metaphysics." From this crucial text we will here only retain a single thesis. Indeed, the
chief difficulty in metaphysical science stems from the problematic character
of its unity: How can one and the same science (*una et eadem*) at the same time
(*simul*) deal with common being (thus of no being in particular) and with
essence (thus with a supremely particular being)? True, in both cases we have
an abstraction, but one which is taken from two contrary interpretations: in
one case, an abstraction with regard to all real being, therefore an abstraction
only based on reason, and in the other, an abstraction in view of being that is
all the more concrete for being unaffected by any materiality, thus a real
abstraction.

Now, Heidegger goes beyond this superficial but traditional contradiction,
by proposing that we take the relationship between the two functions of the
same "metaphysics" to be that of two intersecting and reciprocal "groundings"
(*Gründungen*): "Being (*das Sein*) shows itself in the unconcealing overwhelming
as that which allows whatever arrives to lie before us, as the grounding in the
manifold ways in which beings are brought before us. Beings as such, the arrival
that keeps itself concealed in unconcealedness, is what is grounded; so grounded
and so generated, it in turn grounds in its own way, that is, it effects, it causes.
The perdurance of that which grounds and that which is grounded as such not
only holds the two apart, it holds them facing each other."⁵ The internal unity
of "metaphysics," which prevents it from breaking up into two alien sciences,
derives from the fact that between the science of being in general and that of
essence there is exerted the influence, in modes which are intrinsically
reconciled, of the single establishment of the "ground" (*fondement*). The
common Being grounds beings and even essences; in return essence grounds,

281

in the mode of causality, the common Being: "Being grounds beings, and beings, as what *is* most of all, account for Being."[6]

In and beyond the scholarly notion of metaphysics, the onto-theological construction thus produces the ultimate concept of "metaphysics" by recognizing its unity in the overlapping resolution of the ground (through being as such) with the ground in the mode of causality (through what *is* most of all, *das Seiendste*). We admit that we have at our disposal no other strict determination of "metaphysics," that is to say, one which is historically confirmed and which works conceptually. It is because the definition remains precise that it makes the possibility of "metaphysics" thinkable, as well as its impossibility – and indeed it may possibly enable us to understand the changeover which goes beyond it and takes it up in a higher aspect.

III

The definition which renders "metaphysics" intelligible also enables us to imagine that it might become impossible. The delimiting of the possible necessarily implies these two postulates, giving equal status to each. The overlapping grounding of onto-theology offers a working hypothesis for the historian of philosophy – and, in my view, the most powerful one. It also enables us to understand why we have been able to talk of the "end of metaphysics." Nietzsche's critique of philosophy, as a Platonism to be overturned and subverted, in fact fits in perfectly with the Heideggerian hypothesis. First it is the critique of the concept of being in general, consigned to the ranks of those "notions on the highest plane, that is to say the most general, the most empty, the last vapours of dissipated reality."[7] Here he is challenging the legitimacy of a general abstraction of matter and of sensory things, and with that the basis for the traditional possibility of a science of "being in general" (*metaphysica generalis*). As a corollary, Nietzsche denies that any essence, operating from an immaterial parallel world, exercises a function of "grounding" (and in his problematics, of "vengeance") upon being in general: neither as a logical principle, nor as a universal ground, nor as a "moral God," is the least *causa sui* any longer admissible: Why should being as such, that is to say a material being, require that another being should constitute its possibility, as its ground? Why should that which is require further grounding – instead of answering for itself alone? In this way we find doubt cast on the original function of the science of essence (*metaphysica specialis*). This double disqualification becomes one in the single and final identification of becoming (common being, *metaphysica generalis*) with Being (essence, *metaphysica specialis*): "To place the seal of Being upon becoming – that is the pinnacle of speculation!"[8] Nothing can ground, since nothing requires or necessitates a grounding.

Metaphysics no longer provides a reason for Being, nor does Being have a place in metaphysics. Nietzsche thus confirms negatively the Heideggerian definition of "metaphysics" as the onto-theological system of the mutual or overlapping grounding between essence and existence (*l'étant commun*).

What can we conclude from this? First, the obvious thing: The most pertinent definition of "metaphysics," historically and conceptually, is one which enables us to question it: It is a fact that the notion of the ground, precisely because it can envisage being in its totality, can equally be disclaimed *qua* ground. For, if the ground is metaphysically necessary due to its universal capacity to answer the question, "Why a being rather than nothing?" it is open to the nihilistic refutation in the question, "Why a reason rather than nothing?" The ground assures the legitimacy of metaphysics, but not its own legitimacy. Now, the obviousness of the question "Why?" can – and probably must – always become blurred when confronted by the violence of the question which asks in return "Why ask 'why'?" And if metaphysics is indeed defined as thinking about a universal grounding, it cannot but collapse, when the obvious necessity of there being a grounding of being turns out to be thrown into question. This limitation of "metaphysics" is all the stronger since, first, it is a direct consequence of its definition, upheld but turned against itself; and secondly because it requires only a mere suspicion ("Why ask 'Why'?") and not a proof to invalidate metaphysics. The "end of metaphysics" is in no way an optional opinion. It is a matter of rational fact. Whether we accept it or not, it dominates us absolutely, as an overwhelming event. The very fact that one can deny it, and that, in order to do so, one must argue against it and therefore recognize it, is sufficient confirmation.[9] We are dealing with a fact, a fact that is in a way neutral, admitting and influencing without distinction all theoretical options. Besides, refusal to accept the fact of the "end of metaphysics" seems all the less defensible since it is a transitive concept. Its transitivity can be expressed as follows: in the same way that the onto-theological definition of metaphysics directly implies at least the possibility of the "end of metaphysics," the "end of metaphysics" directly implies the "end of the end of metaphysics."[10] There is no paradox here: From the moment when "metaphysics" admits a precise concept, historically verifiable and theoretically operative, it follows that it can be subject to criticism within its boundaries, but it can also offer, thanks to these same boundaries, the possible horizon of its transcendence. On the other hand, for as long as metaphysics has lacked this concept, the question of the philosophy to come, that is to say today's philosophy, has also remained closed, beyond its critical period. The "end" (*Ende*), Heidegger suggested, remains fundamentally a "place" (*Ort*). If the concept of "metaphysics" fixes its boundaries, this same end generates an undisturbed finality for philosophy. The transitivity of "metaphysics" does not lead solely to its "end," but also to its transcendence – ultimately more than a metaphysics, it is a meta-metaphysics.

At the point we have reached again, the "end of metaphysics" still operates in the most visible way on a privileged point – essence. Indeed, if the notion of grounding no longer enables us to legitimize in general the concept of "metaphysics," it follows in particular that the assimilation of God into the function of final ground becomes (or may become) illegitimate. This identification runs through the whole history of philosophy and of its metaphysical aspect: but it always interprets this ground from the standpoint of effectivity or actuality: τη οὐσία ὢν ἐνέργεια in the words of Aristotle, "purus actus non habens aliquid de potentialitatae" for St Thomas Aquinas, *causa sui* according to Descartes, "sufficient reason of the universe" in Leibniz.[11] Thus, metaphysics takes the word "God" to mean essence operating as and through its effects (*efficience*), in such a way that, in *metaphysica specialis*, it can thus assure a ground for all being in common. The "end of metaphysics" brings about the "death" of this "God." But against the aggressive or despairing trivialities which take over this theoretic event, it is also necessary to measure its precise importance. We must in no way deny the importance of this definition of the divine through the effects of its ground, nor must we underestimate its theoretical fertility. We have honestly to ask a simple question: Do the effects of the ground make it possible truly to conceive of that through which God is God, even in philosophy? For do even the "God of the philosophers and savants," the *causa sui*, "sufficient reason," *actus purus* or ἐνέργεια offer a name divine enough to make God appear? At the very least is it impossible today to admit even the possibility of such a suspicion? Now, it is no more than this possibility which is enough for us to recognize "the death of God" in the "end of philosophy." For God is one whose divinity ought never possibly to be absent. If it is absent, be it ever so imperceptibly, we are no longer talking of God – but of "God," who is stigmatized as an idol by those inverted commas.

IV

If the "death of God" in philosophy belongs essentially to the "end of metaphysics," and if the latter follows essentially from the concept of "metaphysics," then the transcendence of onto-theology becomes the condition for going beyond the naming, in philosophy, of "God" as the effective ground.

It remains for us to decide whether philosophy can withdraw itself from its metaphysical aspect, and thus from its metaphysical destiny. Certainly, Heidegger postulated a strict equivalence between "metaphysics" and "philosophy," to the benefit of "thought." But, beyond the fact that he himself claimed, in certain decisive periods, even after 1927, "metaphysics" as that in which thought should play a part, his first step away from "metaphysics," *Sein und*

Zeit, remains strictly philosophical. How is he able to do this? By taking phenomenology to be the method of ontology (in an acceptance radically renewed by the ontological difference). In this way, he only restricted himself to repeating Husserl's gesture by positing, with his *Ideen* in 1913, the equivalence between phenomenology and phenomenological philosophy. Despite the hesitations of the two great phenomenologists, we cannot really speak of an ambiguous or undecided relationship between phenomenology and metaphysics. One can simply concede that the radical innovation which phenomenology achieved in (and for) philosophy has perhaps not yet, in its most decisive sense, been fully measured. It is therefore necessary to sketch this in, albeit with broad strokes.

Phenomenology starts from a tautological principle, the "principle of non-presupposition," formulated as early as 1900, at the beginning of the second volume of *Logische Untersuchungen* (*Logical Investigations*): "strict exclusion of all statements which could not be realized phenomenologically from beginning to end."[12] The tautology is certainly a real one, yet is not without meaning: Phenomenology is present when, and only when, a statement shows us a phenomenon – anything which does not appear, in one way or another, cannot be taken into account. To understand is ultimately to see. To speak of something in order to make it visible – speaking to see. Otherwise speech has no meaning. But how do we see? How does the statement make itself visible and assume the status of a phenomenon? To this second question Husserl was to reply more explicitly at the beginning of *Ideen* (1913), positing the "principle of principles," which states: "that all primarily donative intuition is a source of the right to knowledge, that everything which presents itself to us in 'primary intuition' (that is to say in its corporeal effects) must be accepted as exactly what it purports to be."[13] For something to be realized as a phenomenon means that it offers itself in unreserved effectivity, which we call "corporeal, *leibhaft*"; for a statement to appear as a phenomenon comes to the same thing as its taking bodily form; the phenomenon gives flesh to a discourse. How does the statement make this flesh of phenomenality its own? By intuition (Husserl uses *Anschauung* or "*Intuition*" interchangeably). One intuition is enough, whatever it may be, for the phenomenon, the flesh of the discourse to become present; indeed, intuition exercises an incontestable right of possession and an ultimate cognition, since only another intuition can contradict the first intuition, such that in the last instance one is always left with an intuition. Of all the acts of cognition, the most corporeal is that achieved by intuition.

The flesh of discourse appears to the flesh of the mind – the phenomenon to the intuition. Phenomenology calls this encounter a "donation": the intuition gives the phenomenon; the phenomenon renders itself through intuition. Doubtless this donation can always examine itself, authenticate itself or not, admit its limits – but it can never see itself challenged or rejected, unless by the authority of another intuitive donation – which confers the universal validity of the "principle of principles."

The scope of this principle, often underestimated, cannot be pondered on too much. (a) The "principle of principles," deploying intuition as the ultimate instance of donation, pushes it beyond the Kantian prohibition: The sensible intuition is joined by the intuition of essences and the intuition of the categories. (b) Since intuition gives fleshly form, the Kantian caesura between the "phenomenon" (uniquely sensible) and the thing-in-itself must disappear: This is achieved by intentionality. (c) As intuition alone donates, the *I*, even the transcendental and constituting *I*, must remain held by and therefore within an intuition: "The primary impression" precedes consciousness in time, even inasmuch as the latter remains pure, and imposes on it a factualness which is in no way derivative, but primary. (d) These doctrinal decisions, as determinant as they may be (and none of the later phenomenologists has cast doubt on them), must never be allowed to distract our attention from that of which they are all the product: The "principle of principles" posits that in the principle (of philosophy and initially of experience) there is nothing but intuition; now, in its capacity as donor of every phenomenon and above all as initiator of phenomenality in general, intuition operates primarily *a priori* as a primary *a posteriori*. Hence this essential paradox: In phenomenology, the sole legitimate *a priori* becomes the *a posteriori* itself. The term "principle of principles" must not mislead us: the principle here is that there is no principle at all, at least not if we understand by "principle" that which precedes "that from which begins . . ."[14] Alternatively, we will say that that which takes the place of principle, i.e. intuition in its role as donation, always precedes the consciousness which we have of it retrospectively. The duplication of the "principle" shown by the "principle of principles" must on no account be understood as the statement of another principle (after those of identity or of sufficient reason), more essentially *a priori* than those preceding it, but, in the manner of a superlative – like the (non-)principle which supersedes all anterior principles, in that it states that in the principle there is no *a priori* (transcendental) principle, but there is an intuitive *a posteriori*: The donation precedes everything and always does so. Thus phenomenology goes unambiguously beyond metaphysics to the strict extent that it rids itself of any *a priori* principle, in order to admit the donation which is primary in as far as it is *a posteriori* for the person receiving it. Phenomenology goes beyond metaphysics insofar as it renounces the transcendental project, to allow an ultimately radical empiricism to unfold[15] – ultimately radical, because it no longer limits itself to sensible intuition, but admits all intuition that is primarily donative.

This reversal of the *a priori* principle to the profit of the *a posteriori* immediately brings with it two determinant theses, about *ontologia* and about the ground respectively. The first flows directly from the donation: the appearance of phenomena takes place without recourse to Being (*l'être*), at least not necessarily in the first instance. Indeed the appearance can be of any intuition whatsoever, due to its "giving itself" and its corporeal presence; these three terms are sufficient to define the perfect phenomenality of a phenomenon, without however in any way having recourse to Being (*l'être*), to being (*l'étant*), still less to an "objective concept of being."

It is legitimate to ask whether every phenomenon, in as far as it appears, does not do without Being, at least in an initial stage – a phenomenon without Being. Therefore phenomenology could free itself absolutely, not only from all *metaphysica generalis (ontologia)*,[16] but also from the question of Being (*Seinsfrage*).[17] The replacement of metaphysical and ontological concepts by phenomenology is marked by some clearly identifiable transpositions. Let us list the principal ones. (a) Affectivity is henceforth replaced by possibility, in the sense where Heidegger – "More than effectivity, possibility arises" – reverses Aristotle's basic thesis that "the act (ἐνέργεια) is thus first in relation to the potentiality (δύναμις) according to the genesis and the time," as much as according to the οὐσία.[18] (b) Certainty as a privileged mode of the truth is replaced by donation: That which the *ego* defines according to the limits of what it sees (*certus, cernere*), is succeeded by the fact of the donation of the phenomenon, through itself, according to its own demands. (c) The οὐσία, as a privileged meaning of being (*l'étant*), thus possessor of its own distinct estate (following the original – landowning – meaning of the Greek term), is replaced by the datum of Being, which from the outset defines every being as a being-as-given (*étant-donné*). The being-as-given designates being (*l'étant*) in such a way that, for it, its Being (*son être*) is not at first equivalent to possessing its own resources (*fonds, οὐσία*), but to being received in the Being, to receive the Being, or rather to accept the gift of Being (*recevoir d'être*). In all these cases it would be necessary to attribute generally to each being-as-given the status of a "beyond the state of being" (*statut d'un au-delà de l'étantité*) (ἐπέκεινα της οὐσία), which Plato reserves exclusively for the ἰδέα τοῦ Ἀγαθοῦ.[19] General metaphysics, like *ontologia*, ought therefore to give way to a general phenomenology of the donation of every being-as-given, whose *Seinsfrage* could possibly constitute a simple region or a particular case. The replacement of metaphysics (here of general metaphysics) by phenomenology goes to the point of radicality.

V

We thus arrive at the second of the theses which follow from the "principle of principles." It concerns *metaphysica specialis* in its more particularly theological function. We have accepted, following Heidegger but also according to the facts of the history of philosophy, that in metaphysics, "God" essentially has the function of the ultimate ground, the "last Reason," the *causa sui*. We no longer need here to discuss whether this is an appropriate interpretation of the divine function, nor even whether it offers with the ground a sufficiently divine aspect of God among a problematic new choice of names for the divinity. We simply have to ask whether the connection between "God" and all the other beings, or – which comes to the same thing – with being in general, can be understood and realized as a ground, or, following an efficient causality, from the point where the "principle of all principles" has overdetermined the fact and the effect of Being through the most original intuitive donation, in such a way that being in effect (and therefore in need of a founding cause) is replaced by being-as-given (being in its capacity as given). If intuition, of itself and to itself alone, offers not only the fact of the given, but especially its "source of right," why should this phenomenon still require from a cause its entitlement to be (*le bon droit de son fait*) – a cause which would interpret the phenomenon as an effect? Besides, should the donation consider itself as starting from the effect, or, conversely, should the effect be received as an (attenuated) aspect of the donation? In its precise function as a given, the phenomenon does not have a "why?" either, and therefore does not demand one. In phenomenology, the ground does not find itself so much criticized or refuted (as is still the case, essentially in Nietzsche, who probably never really reaches his "third metamorphosis"),[20] as stricken with theoretical uselessness. "God" could no longer be thought of as the ground of being, from the moment when the primary donation delivers (hands over, gives) him as a being-as-given, and therefore delivers (liberates) him from any requirement to be a ground. As one result, no longer being conceivable *ad extra* under the aspect of ground, "God" could no longer either be conceived of *ad intra* under the aspect of the *causa sui*. Thus the replacement of the *metaphysica generalis* of a being as a grounded effect by the phenomenological donation of the being-as-given inevitably carries with it the replacement of the *metaphysica specialis* of the grounding, by the phenomenological "source of right" granted to the being-as-given.

The denunciation, virulent rather than well-argued, of a possible transposition of special metaphysics into phenomenology, or else of a theological hijacking of phenomenology, betrays chiefly, all things considered, a rather positivist drift in the approach of the phenomenological method itself. But it also conveys, without thematizing it, a basic misinterpretation of phenomenology, for to stigmatize a return of special metaphysics in the form of phenomenology supposes that this is phenomenologically possible; yet, by definition, it proves itself impossible, where the requirement of the ground is no longer principally brought to bear. Someone will perhaps reply that this transposition well and truly takes place, thus proving that certain people claiming to be phenomenologists no longer deserve the title – which is precisely what the objector wanted to demonstrate. But this reasoning in its turn is open to several objections. First it implies that an essential and often eminent part of that which has always been accepted as coming under the heading of phenomenological method has not ceased to betray it; it remains for me to demonstrate this conceptually and in detail: an immense and difficult task. But this enterprise would quickly become dogmatic, since it presupposes not only that there is a single phenomenological method, which precedes all doctrines, but also that it has not evolved since Husserl's idealistic and constituent moment, between 1913 and 1929, up to the present day. None of these points is self-evident, the less so since it is an essential of phenomenology that the _a posteriori_ makes it possible and therefore that no forbidden _a priori_ predetermines it. If any one philosophy indulges in transparent method and naked thought, it is phenomenology. It has won for itself, in the face of metaphysics, the right to make its own use of the "return to things themselves!" – to which one might add the gloss "It is forbidden to forbid!"[21] The sole criterion in phenomenology derives from the fact – from phenomena that an analysis manages to exhibit, from what it makes visible. That which shows itself justifies itself by this fact alone.

But if a re-establishing of _metaphysica specialis_ seems like a pure methodological impossibility, that does not, however, imply that phenomenology takes no heed of _that which metaphysica specialis_ used to deal with in the metaphysical register. Could not the replacement already noted of _metaphysica generalis_ by phenomenology also be repeated, in connection with that which _metaphysica specialis_ dealt with in the onto-theological mode? Putting this question is not directed to a restoration for its own sake – the absurdity of that has just been stressed – but to a handing-over: returning to things themselves, and possibly to the same things, in order to reveal them no longer according to the aspect of the ground, but according to that of the donation, no longer – as it happens – according to the effects (being as effect, _causa sui_), but according to the being-as-given (_ens in quantum datum_). For the three beings which were privileged by _metaphysica specialis_, that is to say the world (_cosmologia rationalis_), the finite spirit (_psychologia rationalis_), and "God" (_theologia rationalis_), deserve, in their capacity as "thing itself," to be tested as to the possibility (or impossibility) of their appearance as phenomena, and therefore of the intuition which might (or might not) class them as given. In no case could this requirement be challenged, since it results directly from the phenomenological reduction – the suspension of all transcendence, precisely in order to measure what is thus found to be given in immanence. Besides, the phenomenological takeover of _that which_ was the concern of _metaphysica specialis_ already has a long history going back to Husserl. Some results have to be accepted today as established knowledge. Let us first consider the world.

The early Husserl in fact relieved the classic metaphysical aporia (Descartes,

Kant) of the necessity, or indeed the impossibility of demonstrating the existence of the external "world." The intentionality (later Heidegger's *In-der-Welt-Sein*) directly ecstasizes consciousness in the world, without the screen of representation; it (intentionality) always finds the world already given, because, more essentially, it gives itself in the first instance to the world. The constitutional relationship of consciousness to objects will exploit intentionality to the point of putting it at risk, but the later Husserl was to take a firm hold of the noesis–noema relationship under the control of the "principle of correlation." The question of the world thus disappears finally from the horizon of objectivation, to enter that of the being-as-given – the being-as-given in totality. Secondly, we turn to the finite spirit: The obsession with the Cartesian *ego* still holds back Husserl and even Heidegger from abandoning its interpretation, if not always theoretical, at least always constituent, unless it be by "anticipatory resolution." There followed from that the subordination of ethics to theory, or the disappearance of ethics. The lasting service performed by E. Levinas is that of having, in an extraordinary Copernican revolution, established that ontology, even if fundamental, could not attain the ground, because this ground was not governed by theoretical philosophy, but by ethics. Thus not only did ethics become the *philosophia prima* – which, only to itself, would remain a development of metaphysics – but it shifted the center of the *ego* toward the always already open, offered, and destitute face of other people, and therefore toward the being-as-given of others. The *ego* no longer provides a foundation through (self-)representation; it always reveals itself already preceded by the being-as-given of others, whose contra-intentionality it submits to, unobjectively. In line with this, the passing of the *ego* to that which I call "the interlocuted" does not offer any difficulty: It is sufficient to apply the reversed intentionality to other beings-as-given. According to the rules of donation, the *ego* thus attains a secondarity which is nevertheless more phenomenal than any representative primacy. To the *ego* others appear to be the nearest being-as-given.

There remains the question of "God," which, for obvious reasons, has always been the one least broached by phenomenology. These obvious reasons are derived from the reservations, different but convergent, of Husserl and Heidegger. Husserl noted precisely (and without returning to it, even in his late writings), that the assumption of any kind of "God" came under the heading of reduction, that "God," transcendent in every sense, would therefore not appear.[22] But if the function of ground is thus presupposed, does this not then indicate that Husserl was thinking of the "God" of metaphysics? When Heidegger gives God the seal of the *causa sui*,[23] he is doing no more than still explicitly dealing with the "God" of metaphysics. Can phenomenology go no further than these denials[24] or these warnings? There are some who would restrict the answer to these questions to a choice between philosophical silence and unreasoning faith. We know that most of the time the sole purpose of this alternative is to resort to serene silence at the expense of reason. But, aside from revealed theology, there is no reason to prevent reason, in this case philosophy in its phenomenological guise, from pushing reason to its limit, that is to say, as far as itself, without accepting any other limits but those of phenomenality. The question then becomes: What phenomenal face can the "God of philosophers and savants" assume – if he ever assumes one? More precisely, what phenomenon could claim to offer a luminous shadow of this "God," such as to correspond to the replacement of being by the being-as-given? Must we not, almost inevitably, respond to the being-as-given with a donor, even a donor-being (*étant-donateur*)?

And in this case, how do we distinguish this donor-being from a grounding being[25] or *causa sui* and how then do we avoid, in this long operation, condemning a simple restoration of the most metaphysical *theologia rationalis*?

This objection, lucid as it might be, is only convincing if one fails to recognize two arguments. (a) In the hypothesis in which a donor does correspond to the given, it would only be equivalent to a (metaphysical) ground if it itself retained a status of being and if the donation made of the being-as-given by the donor remained contained within the horizon of causality, understood as effect (*efficience*). Now neither of these assumptions can be taken as read. On the contrary, it is possible that the donation might only arise once it has gone radically beyond causality, in a mode whose own rationality it does not suspect. It is possible that the donation obeys demands which are infinitely more complex and powerful than the resources of efficient causality. Besides, even in the history of metaphysics, the sudden appearance of efficient causality in "God's" sphere of influence marks the decline rather than the consecration of *theologia rationalis* – Leibniz, as lucid as he was impotent, bore witness to this. The objection thus betrays the fact that it depends much more on metaphysics than on the thesis which it contests, since the objection cannot prevent itself from understanding the thesis prematurely from the outset in an exaggerated mode of metaphysics, that is, as an effect. (b) A second argument nevertheless renders these precautions useless. For the response to the being-as-given does not take on the aspect of the donor, but that of the being-as-given *par excellence*. If the world can be defined as that which appears as the being-as-given in totality, if, for me, other people can designate that which appears as the closest being-as-given, then "God" defines himself as the being-as-given – *par excellence* and *not* as the donor-being. This supremacy denotes neither sufficiency nor efficient causality nor primacy, but the fact that he (God) gives himself and allows a giving that is being, more than any other being-as-given. In short, with "God", we are dealing with the being-as-given *par excellence*, the being who is completely given (*l'étant-abandonné*).

The phenomenological aspect of "God" as the being-as-given *par excellence* can be outlined by following the guiding thread of the donation in its simple form. (a) The term "given *par excellence*" implies that "God" is given without restriction, without reservation, without restraint. "God" does not give himself partially according to one outline or another, as a created object which, however, only offers to the intentional gaze the appropriate face of his sensible visibility, leaving to appresentation the duty of giving back that which does not give itself – but God gives himself absolutely, with every aspect offered, with no outline withheld, in the way that a Cubist painter explodes the dimensions of objects, so that all their appearances are juxtaposed, despite the constraints of perspective. "God" reveals himself given unreservedly, with nothing withheld. His obviousness unfolds in the atonal tonality of dazzlement. It follows that "God" disseminates himself – that which he spreads still remains himself, in the sense perhaps that the modes in which the Spinozan *substantia* is expressed still remain this *substantia* itself. The donation *par excellence* implies an ecstasy outside itself, in which the self remains all the more itself for being in ecstasy. Now that the *causa sui* can only fold *efficience* back on itself, the donation that "God" achieves cannot remain equal to itself (donation as action) except by becoming ecstatic in that which it gives (donation as gift). If, as Malebranche maintains, the "God" of metaphysics only acts for himself, then the "God" of phenomenology, in precisely the opposite way, acts only to the extent that he does not remain (in) himself.

(b) This donation *par excellence* carries with it another consequence: the absolute mode of the presence which saturates each and every horizon, with a dazzling obviousness. Now, such a presence without limit (without horizon), which alone precisely matches the donation without reserve, cannot present itself as an object, which of necessity has limits. It follows that it occupies no space, captures no attention, attracts no gaze. "God" in his very dazzlingness shines by his absence. His obviousness creates a void – it empties the saturated horizons of everything that is visible and definable. The absence or the unknowability of "God" does not contradict his donation, but on the contrary attests to the supremacy of this donation. "God" becomes invisible not *in spite of* his donation, but *by virtue of* this donation. One would have to show a very low respect, even a downright militant rejection of transcendence, to be scandalized by his invisibility. If we saw him, as we see a worldly being, then we would already have ceased to be dealing with "God." (c) The donation *par excellence* can thus turn directly into being a donation by abandonment. The being-as-given, with absolutely nothing withheld, exerts a phenomenality such that, due to its intrinsic invisibility, it can never see itself granted the status of phenomenon. The phenomenon *par excellence* runs the risk, through its very excellence, of not appearing – of remaining in abandonment. Indeed, most other phenomena become available to the eye which sees, defines, and manipulates them. Here, by contrast, a radical non-availability makes their abandonment inevitable. And we verify this each time we see the donation misunderstood, on the pretext that, since it is given without repossession or retreat, it abandons itself to the point of disappearing as an object that is possessable, manipulable, discernible. The donation *par excellence* in fact risks seeming to disappear (by default) precisely because it gives itself unreservedly (by excess). And every day we see for ourselves this strange but inevitable paradox.

VI

Of course, the aspect of "God" in phenomenology which I have just outlined, even if it is definitely opposed to the metaphysical aspect of a "God" *causa sui*, is nevertheless still traceable to "the God of philosophers and savants," and in no way to "the God of Abraham, Isaac and Jacob." But one could still object that this aspect is scarcely distinguishable from the latter: The being-as-given *par excellence* in fact bears the characteristics of a precise type of manifestation – that of the saturated phenomenon, or more precisely, of the saturated phenomenon of the revelationary type (*le phénomène saturé du type de la révélation*).[26] May we not here fear a confusion between phenomenology and revealed theology? It appears that this confusion can be avoided by two clear distinctions. (a) Phenomenology can, of itself, only identify the saturated phenomenon of the being-as-given *par excellence* as a possibility; not only a possibility as opposed to effectivity, but above all a possibility of the donation itself. The characteristics of the being-as-given imply that it gives itself without forethought, without measure, without analogy, without repetition – in short, it remains unavailable. Its phenomenological analysis therefore has no bearing except on its representation, its "essence," and not directly on its being-as-given. The intuitive accomplishment of this being-as-given demands, more than phenomenological analysis, the real experience of its donation – which brings us back to revealed theology. Between phenomenology and theology the frontier passes between revelation as possibility and revelation as historicity. Between these domains there is no possible danger of confusion.[27] (b) It is certainly true that phenomenology can describe and construct the being-as-given, and even the being-as-given *par excellence*; but it is probably not for it to have access to the donation identified in and with an aspect face; or rather, even if it can, where necessary, make from the aspect one of its themes, it cannot and ought not claim to understand it as the aspect of charity; when the being-as-given swings round to become charity (the being loved or loving, the lover in the strict sense), phenomenology gives way to revealed theology, exactly as, so Pascal would say, the second order yields to the third. Here again, no confusion can creep in.

It is very clear that these theses cannot be developed here in a fully adequate way. However, they will be enough to indicate which new path phenomenology is marking out, beyond the metaphysics from which it has taken over, toward philosophy – and without returning to *metaphysica specialis*. And on this path, rational thought about God, which philosophy cannot forget without losing its own dignity, or even its mere possibility, at least finds a certain coherence.

Notes

1 *In Generatione et Correptione, Proemium*, n. 2, ed. R. Spiazzi (Rome, 1952), p. 316.
2 *Disputationes Metaphysicae*, I, *Proemium*, O.o., ed. Berton (Paris, 1856–78), vol. 25, p. 2.
3 On the history of this doctrine, see, in addition the recent work by J.-F. Courtine, *Suarez et le système de la métaphysique* (Paris, 1990, esp. Part V), and those by E. Vollrath, "Die Gliederung der Metaphysik in eine *Metaphysica generalis* und eine *Metaphysica specialis*," *Zeitschrift für philosophische Forschung*, XVI/2 (1962), A. Zimmermann, *Ontologie oder Metaphysik? Die Diskussion über dem Gegenstand der Metaphysik* (Cologne, 1965).
4 Such is the scope of the celebrated declaration, whose radicality and complexity is often underestimated: "and the vainglorious name of an ontology, which claims to give an *a priori* knowledge of things in general (*überhaupt = in communi*) in a systematic doctrine (for example the causality principle), must give way to that more modest name, of a simple analytic of pure understanding" (*Critique of Pure Reason*, A247/B304; see also A845/B873). We would still wish to know, of course, whether *ontologia*, in its historically accepted sense (from Goclenius to Clauberg) has ever claimed to achieve anything more or other than a "simple analytic of pure understanding," since it has never laid claim to "being" as its subject, but only to the *cogitabile* (see the documents collected by J.-F. Courtine, *Suarez*, pp. 246–93, 422ff.). Have we ever taken seriously the hypothesis that "ontology," taken in its historical sense, might ever have dared to come to terms with "being" as such? Should this fact not throw doubt on the immediate possibility of a science of being *qua* being, which was not first a science of "being as something thinkable," and thus a submission of the *ens in quantum ens* to description? Is it not astonishing that the very term *ontologia* should have remained unknown to Aristotle and the medieval thinkers, and should have been introduced only by the moderns, in a situation explicitly claimed as Cartesian? (Clauberg, *Metaphysica de ente, quae rectius Ontosophia* . . . (Amsterdam, 1664), especially at 5 note c, taken up again in the *Opera omnia Philosophica* . . . (Amsterdam, 1691, and Hildesheim, 1968), vol. I, p. 283).
5 Heidegger, *Identität und Differenz* (Pfullingen, 1957), pp. 60–1; *Identity and Difference*, trans. Joan Stambaugh (New York and London: Harper and Row, 1969).
6 Heidegger, *Identität und Differenz*, p. 62 (English translation).
7 Nietzsche, *Götzendämmerung* (Twilight of the Idols), " 'Reason' in philosophy," no. 4.
8 Nietzsche, *Wille zur Macht* (*The Will to Power*), no. 617 = *Nachgelassene Fragmente* (Herbst 1885 bis Herbst 1887), 7 [54], *Nietzsche Werke*, ed. G. Colli and M. Montinari, VIII, i (Berlin and New York, 1974), p. 320.
9 There are several ways of refusing to accept the "end of metaphysics." One might be to postulate that "metaphysics" remains identical to itself, without any real history; but

then one would be forced to take up the presuppositions of nihilism without accepting them (as did Blondel with Schopenhauer and the philosophy of will); or to produce non-historically a philosophy which has never been propounded (as did Maritain interpolating an "intuition of Being" in the texts of St Thomas to meet the needs of contemporary existentialism; as also did Cohen and Natorp for the "return to Kant" without the "thing in itself"); or, more positively, to have to reinstate an author in the face of a unanimous tradition which claims him by distorting him (as Gilson did for St Thomas). On the other hand, it could be a matter of "transcendences" of metaphysics which, without knowing (or wishing to know) it, reproduce its most classic theses and aporia, as did Carnap and the first logical positivism rediscovering the difficulties of empiricism.

10 See my essay "The end of metaphysics," *Laval théologique et philosophique*, 1986/1.
11 Respectively *Of the Soul*, ed. G. P. Goold, Loeb Classical Library (London: Heinemann, 1975), III, 5, 430a 18; *Summa Theologiae* (London: Eyre and Spottiswoode, 1964), I2, q 3, a 2; *Les Objections et les réponses*, in *Oeuvres philosophiques* (Paris: Garnier Frères, 1967), vol. 2, p. 565; *Principles of Nature and of Grace*, in L. E. Loemker, *G. W. Leibniz: Philosophical Papers and Letters* (Dordrecht: Reidel, 1969), pp. 636–42.
12 *Logische Untersuchungen* (Tübingen: Max Niemeyer, 1968), vol. II, p. 19.
13 *Ideen I*, ed. Walter Biemel, vol. III of *Husserliana: Edmund Husserl, Gesammelte Werke* (The Hague: Martinus Nijhoff, 1950), p. 62.
14 Aristotle, *Metaphysics*, ed. T. E. Page, Loeb Classical Library (London: Heinemann, 1933), Δ, 1, 1012b34.
15 I gladly repeat a formulation which E. Levinas only puts forward with reservations: "phenomenology is only a radical mode of experience," *Le temps et l'autre* (Paris: Fata Morgana, 1979).
16 We therefore should not even talk of "general metaphysics" in the works of Husserl (and still less of *metaphysica specialis*, whether real or apparently threatening), contrary to what D. Janicaud writes in *Le tournant théologique de la phénoménologie française* (Paris: Combas, 1991), p. 43; rather we should apply generally the conclusion in my analysis of Husserl's "I without Being," *Réduction et donation. Recherches sur Husserl, Heidegger et la phénoménologie* (Paris: Presses Universitaires de France, 1989), p. 240, and thus radically confirm *Dieu sans l'être* (Paris: Fayard, 1982; 2nd edn, 1991).
17 See also *Réduction et donation*, pp. 240ff.
18 Respectively Heidegger, *Sein und Zeit*, 7th edn (Tübingen: Max Niemeyer, 1953), no. 7, p. 38, and Aristotle, *Metaphysics* θ 8, 1050, a 2–3.
19 Plato, *Republic*, VII, 509 b9. It is clear that I am following a line of research opened up by E. Levinas (*Totalité et Infini. Essai sur l'extériorité* [The Hague: Martinus Nijhoff, 1961], and especially *Autrement qu'être ou au-delà de l'essence* [The Hague: Martinus Nijhoff, 1974]). But it seems to me that this thesis can be generally applied to any intuitive donation, and therefore, according to Husserl, to all phenomenality without exception.
20 Nietzsche, *Thus Spake Zarathustra*, trans. R. J. Hollingdale (Harmondsworth: Penguin Books) I, 1. For a justification of this allusive judgment, see my study *L'Idole et la distance* (Paris: Grasset, 1987) (1) and 1991 (3), sections 4–7.
21 This formulation could incidentally also serve as an approximate translation of "Prinzip der Voraussetzungslosigkeit." On the subject of this debate, see D. Janicaud, *Le tournant théologique, passim*, and the clarification by J.-L. Chrétien, *L'Appel et la réponse* (Paris, 1992), pp. 9ff., and by M. Henry in *Phenomenology and theology* (Paris, 1992), pp. 129ff.,

as well as the balanced commentary by J. Colette, "Phénoménologie et métaphysique," *Critique* 548–9 (Jan. 1993), pp. 56–7. On the question of phenomenological method I have adopted this comment by D. Franck: "Such a method goes beyond the strict framework of descriptive phenomenology, while at the same time relying on it. But was that not already the case with Husserl's analyses of time, of other people, or of the body, and is phenomenology not characterized, as it goes from one turning point to the next, by the fact that it does not cease to deviate from itself and that all these deviations end in some way by being part of it?" ("Le corps de la différence," *Philosophie*, no. 34 (April 1992), p. 86). It would be wise for us to stick to the simple admission by Janicaud himself: "As for the spirit of Husserlian 'philosophy,' no one is its guardian" (p. 36), except, of course, for Husserl's own writings.

22 Husserl, *Ideen* I, section 56. Incidentally, Husserl here explicitly evokes "God" under the aspect and in the function of a (*fondement*) (*Grund*), p. 139.

23 Heidegger, *Identität und Differenz*, pp. 51 and 64.

24 J. Derrida, "Comment ne pas parler. Dénégations," in *Psyché* (Paris, 1987), pp. 535ff. But here *dénégation* (denial) has nothing to do with dogmatic negation, it leaves open the status of prayer and, in a paradoxical manner, supports the play of "divine names." At least, in principle denial should do that, despite Derrida's tendency to reduce denial to a simple affirmation requiring to be denied.

25 F. Laurelle suggests that I could scarcely avoid this conclusion, in his remarks, which are by the way both pertinent and constructive, in "L'appel et le phénomène," *Revue de Métaphysique et de Morale*, 1989/1, pp. 27–41.

26 See my essay "Le phénomène saturé," in *Phénoménologie et théologie*, ed. J.-F. Courtine (Paris, 1992), esp. p. 127.

27 This distinction has been very finely drawn by J. Derrida, in a text devoted to Patocka, but especially to "Christian logic": "It needs to conceive of the possibility of such an event [the revelation], but not the event itself. A major difference, which makes such a discourse possible without reference to religion as established dogmatics, and enables us to propose a thinking genealogy of the possibility and the essence of the religious which is not an article of faith . . . The difference here is subtle and unstable. It demands fine and watchful analyses. Under different headings, and in different directions, the discourses of Levinas and Marion, perhaps also of Ricoeur, share this situation with that of Patocka"; that is, to offer a "non-dogmatic doublet of dogma . . ., in any (conceptual) case which 'repeats' without religion the possibility of religion" ("Giving death"), in *L'éthique du don. Jacques Derrida et la pensée du don*, ed. J.-M. Rabaté and M. Wetzel (Paris, 1992), pp. 52ff. My only disagreement relates to the identification of this "doublet" indiscriminately with "philosophy, metaphysics" for, when we have to conceive of a possibility, especially such a radical one, of impossibility itself, only phenomenology is suitable – and certainly not metaphysics, the thinking about effectivity *par excellence*.

Translated by Angus McGeoch

Asyndeton: Syntax and Insanity.
A Study of the Revision of
The Nicene Creed

Catherine Pickstock

Let not the wise man glory in his wisdom, neither let the mighty man glory in his might,
let not the rich man glory in his riches: But let him that glorieth glory in this, that
he understandeth and knoweth me, that I am the Lord which exercise loving kindness,
judgment, and righteousness in the earth: for in these things I delight, saith the Lord.

(Jeremiah 9: 23–24)

Once we are dead, the nightmare of death can no longer assail us. The unspoken objective of modernity is to relinquish death by means of death, which is to say, to abolish time. The infinite accumulation of simulacra is the stockpiling of dead value, the neutralization of life, and where there is no life, there death can have no dominion. Ever since the Baroque anxiety of mutability, modern existence has sought to mobilize every resource in the hypertrophy of *eros* and the attenuation of *thanatos*, and the purpose of my essay is to delineate one important example of the way in which language has been pressed into the service of this secular cause, this process of spatialization which has occurred on every level of modern Western culture.

Asyndeton, syntax characterized by the absence of explicit conjunctions, has been employed by the Anglican liturgical revisers responsible for the compilation of *The Alternative Service Book* 1980 (ASB henceforth) to replace the former use of hypotactic (subordinated) and paratactic (explicitly coordinated) syntax of *The Book of Common Prayer* 1549 (BCP henceforth). This has occurred throughout the liturgical rites of the ASB, and indeed, across all denominations, including the Episcopal BCP of 1979, the Roman Missal, and British Reformed liturgies. In this essay, I shall consider the implications of the use of asyndeton in the Rite A Nicene Creed of the ASB, which is the text ratified by the International Consultation on English Texts. The same Credal text, with slight differences,[1] is included in Rites 1 and 2 of the Episcopal BCP.[2] It will be seen, more generally, that the changes effected in favour of transparency have been far from innocent, and more important, that contemporary language forms – and asyndeton is by no means an isolated example – have so incorporated a secular and spatial semantic as to render them radically incompatible with the temporality of sacral doxology.

The syntactic usurpation of parataxis and hypotaxis by asyndeton was effected in accordance with the revisers' general principle of transparency, whereby archaic or opaque morphological, syntactic, and lexical forms are replaced, "updated," by the forms of contemporary usage. The triumph of asyndeton accords with modern literary practices (from the Romantics onwards) which favor the seeming spontaneity and authorial delitescence of aggregative syntax as against the rational processes of hypotaxis. It is a commonly held belief that the simple structures of asyndeton are more readily apprehensible, especially in the linear context of oral liturgical recitation. However, there is no psychological evidence to support this, and since meaning resides not in things themselves, but in the connections between things (that is to say, in conjunctions), asyndeton can be seen not as the syntax of simplicity and clarity, but rather, that of opacity and disorientation. Asyndetic units are placed in juxtaposition (confrontation) with each other, with no explicit thematic, logical, (or theological) relation. In the case of the Nicene Creed, it can be seen that the usurpation of complex syntax by asyndeton, together with other changes executed in favor of transparency, have serious implications for the doctrinal content of the liturgical text as a whole. The effects of these changes point to a general failure to take account of the intimate link between linguistic form and its content, resulting in a textualization of once verbal and conceptual deeds.

I shall examine three main concerns: first, the representation in the Nicene Creed of the Trinitarian doctrine of three-in-one; secondly, the representation of a sacral temporal order, and the importance of this with respect to the Creed's position in the service of Holy Communion; and thirdly, the liturgical collusion with secular modernity, as expressed in the shift from the model of open-ended doxological desire as excess, to desire framed by the capitalist logic of lack, semelfactive acquisition, and consumption. The first section comprises a brief syntactic analysis, and the second two sections extend the results of this analysis to establish modes of syntax as philosophical and theological categories.

1 The Trinity

In the BCP Nicene Creed there is no explicit elucidation of the doctrine of three-in-one, and the word "Trinity" is not used. Instead, this doctrine, irreducible to any verbal explication, is performed syntactically. This is true also of the original Greek text, and relates to the Credal function as a catechetical performative utterance.[3] A synactic enunciation of the text performs not only the boundaries of belief, and the communal boundary of the participants who ratify its contents by virtue of their utterance of it, but also the Trinitarian doctrine itself. The Creed fulfills its ancient catechetical function not as an exposition apart from faith, but as a performative act of faith, summarizing the narrative of salvation, and assimilating the events of history within the aegis of the Trinity. When we say the Creed, we "confess" our faith, which is to say, we acknowledge, and even more, we praise. The Credal enactment of doctrinal and cognitive boundaries is deeply embedded in worship, and locates its genesis in doxology.[4]

The doctrine of three-in-one is performed by means of a combination of two syntactic extremes, coordination and subordination. This results in a textual organization best described as organic. On the most basic level of the text, the Creed is divided into three sections (two paragraphs) of continuous prose, each concerned with a respective Trinitarian hypostasis. These sections are by no means discrete or atomic, but are continuous with the whole by means of their organic syntax. First, each successive clause develops from its immediate precursor in a linear fashion. For example, "And of all things visible and invisible" modifies the preceding clause which supplies the base of its ellipsis, "Maker." This preceding clause is in turn a modification of its own immediate precursor, "the Father Almighty," and so on. This movement of linear modification is balanced by more complex anaphoric modification, whereby a clause reaches further back for its semantic satisfaction. So while, "*By whom* all things were made," which occurs in the second section (concerning the second person of the Trinity), refers to the previous clause, "Being of one substance with *the Father*," this preceding clause refers back to the opening of the first section (pertaining to the first person of the Trinity), which is to say, to God as "Maker of heaven and earth." The relative pronoun in "*who* for us men, and for our salvation" bypasses its precursive clause (which pertains to the Father), and refers once again to the opening clause of the second section, "And in *one Lord Jesu Christ*." These are just a few instances of the complex, embedded syntax, but they are sufficient to express the zig-zagging of anaphoric references, entwining these two persons of the Trinity in organic, hypotactic, and paratactic relation. Each clause engages in a reaching back to the opening clause, "I Believe in one God," which straddles the entire text in unimpeded lineage. Each clause finds in this opening clause its semantic consummation, at the same time as it proceeds paratactically onward to the succeeding clause.

Anaphora provokes a recalling of a previous instant of the text, and, in the context of oral performance, engages the participant in a complex activity, simultaneously anticipatory and anamnetic. In recollecting a fragment, one has simultaneously a consciousness of the remainder of the whole, as well as anterior parts, in such a way that each consequent appearing (upon familiarity) will be regarded as an inevitable result of its antecedent and of the text as a whole. Upon such a model, no clause stands in isolation. The final line can trace its continuous lineage to the first line, and is contingent upon the entire text for its meaning. The figural dynamic instigated by the anaphora is balanced with the linear movement of free modifiers and paratactic coordination ("and . . . and . . . and") which abounds, and functions to carry forward the narrative of Christ, neutralizing any disjunctive effects of full stops, or other punctuation marks.[5] It is significant that there are only seven full stops in twenty-one lines of prose, and each is diffused by an "and" (to be sure, there are no fewer than twenty coordinating conjunctions in all), with three exceptions, where discontinuity can be understood as motivated by rhetorical effect.[6]

The second section, pertaining to the Son, does not lexically repeat the "I believe," but refers anaphorically to the opening clause (indeed, the first eighteen lines of text depend upon the opening "I believe" as the main verb), so setting it within the same frame: we cannot utter "I believe in one Lord Jesu Christ" except by means of belief in God "the Father Almighty," and belief in one or belief in the other is belief in one and the same thing. The third section, concerning the Holy Ghost, is structured almost entirely by means of embedded and aggregative "-who" clauses, each referring back to the third object of belief, the Holy Ghost, which itself recalls the earlier assertions of belief. All three persons of the Trinity, as well as the Church and its rites, and the anticipation of the life of the world to come, are bound into the same act of belief. The complex layers of subordination mean that it is impossible to isolate a single portion of the text without in some sense summoning the entire Creed.

Hypotaxis functions in the Creed to perform the hypostatic union, while the coordinating conjunctions express the co-equality of the three hypostases which constitute the single and simple *ousia*. Any "rational" (hypotactic) expression of logical relation at the points between the three Credal sections would risk a subordinationist interpretation of Trinitarian relations. Nonetheless, parataxis alone would not be adequate, for the persons of the Trinity are neither added on to one another, nor are they discrete in the way that paratactic units of syntax might suggest. By combining the two syntactic extremes, rallying the entire syntactic resource, the Creed is able to enact in its form the complex simplicity of the structure of the Trinity. The organic syntax prevents the necessary linearity of the text (in orality, each line is uttered at the expense of its precursor, and disappears as soon as it comes into existence) from being annihilative: It hypotactically connects the beginning with the end, and that end is to be found in the beginning, so that no instant of time is lost without simultaneously being saved.

The replacement of organic syntax by asyndeton in the ASB Nicene Creed inevitably results in some change to the felicity of this Trinitarian performance. The ASB version is characterized not by Trinitarian relation, but by fragmentation and discontinuity, syntactically, lexically, and typographically. The text is organized not as continuous prose, but into "lines" (thirty-five in all), positioned beneath one another, and divided into five paragraphs. It converts six sentences into thirteen, twenty coordinating conjunctions into nine, and five subordinating conjunctions into one. The first paragraph, pertaining to the first person of the Trinity, occupies an enclosed sentence, terminated by an undiffused full stop, which is to say that the second paragraph, pertaining to the Son, omits the coordinating conjunction. Similarly, a new sentence is begun in order to relate the events of salvation history, beginning with Christ's descent from heaven. There are no conjunctions to unite this descent with the activity of the Holy Spirit in the incarnation. The two events, descent and incarnation, are portrayed implicitly as two distinct stories with the same protagonist. Because of the discontinuous syntax, the phrase "for our sake," occurring twice, cannot pervade the whole narrative, but refers only to Christ's descent and his crucifixion. The other actions, incarnation, suffering, burial, his rising again, stand alone, unincorporated into the same salvific plan, listed, as it were, by chance. A paragraph is installed between the section on the Holy Spirit and that of the Church. Jasper and Bradshaw[7] provide no explanation for this. The paragraphic lacuna is spurious, for not only does it conform with the general semantics of rupture,[8] but it is anathema to disjoin the work of the Holy Spirit from that of the Church. The final complex sentence of the 1549 version links together the Holy Spirit, the Church, the rite of baptism, the resurrection, and the life of the world to come. Although this is (implicitly) the work of the whole Trinity, it is the Holy Spirit's sphere of activity to effect salvation through the Church and the sacraments.

Thus, in an act motivated by syntactic simplification, the revisers unwittingly engaged in an act of Trinitarian complication.[9] The five parallel but enclosed sections convey parallel but disjunct hypostases, and a Church and rites which subsist in parallel but discrete realms. The only cohesion obtained for the persons of the Trinity, and the events of salvation history, is conventional, relying upon our pre-established knowledge, and upon the implicature of temporal iconicity[10] whereby one infers the unified chronicity of the fabula (events abstracted from their textual arrangement) from the sequential position of events in the text. But it is not temporal or chronological unification which is the significance of the Credal performance, but rather thematic unity.

Asyndeton is unable to convey any such logical relations between things, thus affording a diminution of the catechetical and performative functions of the Creed. It also proposes a significant epistemological assumption: that is, by eliminating a syntactic performance of Trinitarian relations, the Creed presents these relations, and the events of salvation history, as in some sense "given," obtainable, scrutable, but, significantly, *other* from the Credal text. Precisely because the text does not verbally perform the relations, it places them within the category of objects, external to the attitude of worship, available to verbal representation. The text, therefore, points from itself, not in a self-effacing way toward God, but in the manner of a merely functional index, toward objects of knowledge, *located* elsewhere, which can then be semelfactively consumed by a willing individual. The paradox is that by committing oneself actively to performance, one renders oneself open to the surprise of that which arrives, whereas by positing a given fact which is passively to be registered, one disguises, by means of a false humility, the claim to mastery over objects and therefore their secret derivation from the knowing subject, concealed in any act of transparent empirical representation. Performativity in liturgy operates not according to the self-present subject's full command of the action, but rather according to his submission to a *narrative* mode of knowledge (to use Lyotard's term), in which that which he knows and does is subordinate to that which passes through him, beyond his analytic grasp. The deserting of performance for a constative mode in the ASB indicates a casting of the language of doxology in the idiom of *scientific* knowledge.[11]

2 The Representation of Time

The complex syntax of the 1549 Creed is paramount in the assertion of a sacral temporal order, both on the level of the Credal text in isolation, and also with regard to its part within the service of Holy Communion. The syntactic contribution to this representation of time is closely linked with the use of tense.

The Creed makes use of two tenses, present and aorist (preterite), and these two tenses are to be associated with two different (but, as I shall show, not incompatible) temporal planes, that is, the sacral and the inhabited respectively. The present tense is used in the performative verbs "I believe," "I acknowledge," and "I look," as well as to describe the ontological attributes of the Trinitarian persons, for example, the Holy Ghost "proceed*eth*" in the present, and the Son is described by means of the present participle, as "*being* of one substance." The present tense has no specified temporal boundaries, thereby being pertinent not only for reference to the local or punctual present moment, but also for the extended and generic present.[12] The aorist, used to narrate the events of salvation history and, in the third section, with reference to the Holy

Ghost who "*spake* by the prophets," is the prototypical tense of narration because of its perfective (accomplished) aspect which cognitively packages the web of experience into synthetic units amenable to linear representation, that is, to placement along a time line.[13]

The linearity of the aorist does not run counter to the sacrality of the present tense but enables the aorist to perform the sacral reentry of the past into the interstices of the present. Because of its retrospective intelligibility, the aoristic narrative voice obtains from its apparent distance from the past events which it narrates an authority and detachment which enables those events to speak for themselves. Narration involves a prospective movement along the frontier of the past events, experienced, as it were, from their inception. Although the temporal organization of aoristic narrative is prospective, the perspective on the events is retrospective, thus engaging the reader in an act which is both anamnetic and expectant. Prospectivity surfaces in the cognitive space in which experience is mapped onto language. It is only when we tell a story that we retrace forward what we have already traced backward. The process of narrating the past in language reopens the space of contingency that once belonged to the past when it was present.

The two tenses, present and aorist, can be aligned with the two syntactic orders, figural (hypotactic) and linear (paratactic). These two orders are essential in the depiction of the Trinity as a consummation of the idea of a divine presence which is not opposite to temporal existence. They are akin to Augustine's notion of the Trinitarian *distentio* of memory, understanding, and desire, as espoused in *De Trinitate*.[14] The prospective movements of paratactic and aoristic narrative enact anticipatory desire, while the positive, figural use of time affirmed by the anaphoric motions of hypotaxis enact an anamnesis. According to Augustine, the return of the image to its archetype is a process through time, rather than a semelfactive accomplishment or an event requiring the abolition of lived time. The three spiritual properties in which he discerns the Trinitarian image of God pertain to the essential temporality of the human condition, and especially of human thought. There can be no purely present thought, for all cognitive classifications take place within time, are committed to memory, and must involve desire. Understanding can only take place in the context of something both known (remembered) and something searched for (desired), in such a way that all thought is involved in an interplay between the trace of memory and the lure of desire. In drawing a comparison between the psychological trinity and God, Augustine establishes an analogy between temporal existence and the generation and procession of the second and third persons of the Trinity. In this respect, he shows that God *is like* conscious existence, that even within God there is something akin to memory and desire. But this does not mean that God is either loss or lack, but rather that he is an excess, a searching and overflowing, a losing and recalling, an endless giving and fulfillment. The paratactic and aoristic elements of the Creed enact the assumption into God of temporality, that is to say, retrospection and the anticipatory nature of desire. But this Credal desire is not a negative lack, but a temporalized nothingness which intends its own consummation, an intending which invokes and gives rise to a temporal future. This desire "knows" what is being longed for – it is the tacit knowledge of anticipation. Upon the Christian model, desire does not lack its object. The act of desiring is simultaneously that of attainment.

The asyndetic ASB Creed performs a humiliation of sacral time, for asyndeton reifies disjunction and clausal isolation. Each clause is a new beginning and a new departure, uttered necessarily at the expense of, rather than by means of, its textual inheritance. This invokes a violent temporal order, for asyndeton is the syntax of the moment, the reiterated presence of absence, in which each instant is instantly surpassed, and each utterance is its own annihilation, the point where the clause declares its own impossibility, and is bound to fall silent. The asyndetic clause is the constitutive moment of abolition, dissolving in its own time, drawing its own exterior edge, the line of its own dissolution.

Asyndeton has been favored by modernity for its elimination of the authoritative presence of the writer. Because it dispenses with all conjunctions, it is associated with free thought and subjectivity. However, it is subject to a different kind of tyranny, that of temporal ordering reduced to a sequence of discrete present moments.[15] The aggregative passage of self-annihilating clauses is not diffused on other (lexical) levels of the text.[16]

While on one hand, asyndeton invokes a violent temporal order, it also seeks to harness this expeditious flight in such a way that it imitates the modern capitalist dynamic of mass production, negative or "identical" repetition, and an assimilation of time into a vacuum of stasis. The simpler the juxtaposition and the briefer the asyndetic units as components of a sequence, the closer the text is brought to the genre of catalogue or list. Like the units of information found in a telephone directory or library catalogue, the list appears to occupy space in a timeless domain. So, on the one hand, asyndeton is a subversive form, for it juxtaposes disconnected elements without any realization of rational (causal, purposive, conditional, or complex temporal) relations within conventionally diachronic narrative structures. But on the other, it is a strangely restricted form, apparently cataloging events in the form of an ordered list, and into chronological time. But whether asyndeton is natural to, or imposed upon, a narrative (and in the Rite A Creed, the latter is the case, for the revisers have *removed* connective and rational conjunctions in order to attain asyndetic prose), asyndeton contributes a static component which is highly undesirable in the Credal text, as I shall explain.

According to Gérard Genette's classifications of narrative,[17] one can see the

Creed as an example of "accelerated narrative." The "speed" of a narrative refers to the relation between a temporal dimension and a spatial dimension – that is, the relation between duration of fabula and length of text. The Institution Narrative, as it occurs in the Eucharistic Prayer, is the opposite, a decelerated narrative, covering a short period of time (two parallel utterances occurring during the Last Supper) in great detail, occupying approximately thirteen lines (Rite A). The pace of the Creed is much accelerated, and necessitates a more massive presence of ellipsis,[18] sweeping down from eternity, and documenting in brevity the procession of salvation history in thirty-five lines (Rite A). The Creed is what Genette would classify as a narrative "summary,"[19] a narration in a few paragraphs of several days, months, or years of existence, without details of actions or speech,[20] whereas the Institution Narrative constitutes a "scene"[21] where the contrast in tempo reflects also a contrast of mode, from nondramatic to dramatic narrative, the detailed actions coinciding with the most intense and highly charged moment of the liturgical narrative. The larger narrative strokes of the Credal summary can be seen to occupy a preparatory space in the movement of the overall liturgical text, and as the participants approach the actions of the Eucharistic event, the actions spread out, becoming more detailed as they are experienced at closer range, this deceleration effecting an attenuation of inhabited time and charging the increased intensity of the proceedings.

The important narrative distinction between the Creed and the Institution Narrative cannot be sustained by the contemporary usurpation of complex syntax by asyndeton, for mere acceleration of the Credal tempo will not heighten the distinction: It is not a matter of speed of time, but quality of time, and as we have seen, Credal asyndeton is unable to convey sacrality. On the contrary, the use of asyndeton reduces the differentiation, for it is necessary that the distinction is made syntactically, and, as we shall see, the Institution Narrative, and particularly Christ's words, are asyndetic (though in a different way from the Rite A Creed, as I shall show). The asyndetic Creed dissolves into its own stuttering, enacting the indistinct and chaotic disappearance of the secular quotidian moment which is marked precisely by its lack of creed. The use of asyndeton here gives rise to a paradox, for it is at once a static bulk of immobile density, unable to flow by virtue of the absence of connections, and a jagged dance of clashing forms, contributing a disarray, and inducing the reader to abandon the passive role as recipient, or the synactic role as participant, to engage in an individual re-establishment of order, reading the text neither doxologically nor engaging in doctrinal performance, but rather, in order to make sense of the random juxtaposition of elements. The lack of rational connection in the Creed presents the elements of salvation history and the relation between the Trinitarian persons as models of imbalance and incompletion. And liturgical participation becomes not a matter of devotional recitation, but the experience of a need to control. The Credal text instructs the reader not in matters of faith, but in modes of apprehension.

Unlike hypotaxis, which involves a processing of events, events in asyndeton are, supposedly, just rendered, enabling the reader to come to his or her own decision. However, asyndeton is itself an imposition, for it imposes the tyranny of mundane time, the leveling of difference within unmediable peculiarity, the yoking of the disparate without explanation, and, in the case of the Creed, the deliberate disjunction of what was originally connected. It is the syntax of infinite possibility, because not bound, and yet it is the most confined, bound fast at the infinite (indefinite) crossroads, realizing the incarceration of emancipation. Its error is to suppose that "freedom" is uncontingency. In its state of freedom from laws, asyndeton discovers too late that it cannot move, that it cannot effect anything outside itself. And in this state of incarcerated emancipation, untied yet static, it can only fold a thousand times in upon itself. It is purified but made powerless by its punctuation. Every clausal embarkation is, potentially, the last. The asyndetic text is one governed by hiatus and lacuna, distance, and short-circuiting, a sum which never succeeds in bringing its various parts together to form a whole. It is the violent yoking of asymmetrical sections, paths that suddenly come to an end, unfinished, hermetically sealed, vessels that cannot communicate, in which there are fissures between things that are contiguous, jigsaw pieces from any or many different puzzles, forcibly made to interlock in a certain place where they may or may not belong. The irony is that the powerlessness of this privatized autonomy is mimicked in the very text which exists to provide a means of escape from the spiral of secular hubris.

3 Capitalism and Desire as Lack

And so it is that with the diminution of the performative component of the utterance of synactic belief, the removal of the doxological function, and the elimination of the enactment of the Trinitarian relations by means of complex syntax, the surface of the page, with its new typographical play, short lines arranged beneath one another, surrounded by large white spaces, is the primary, or only, locus of action. The performative component of worship, once situated in the verbal actions of the worshipers, is now fixed as a textualized display which issues proliferating, mystifying, and unhierarchical effects. The result is that there is no differentiation in narrative perspective, no suspense.

While the committee responsible for the compilation of the ASB favored the apparent monosyllabic clarity of asyndeton, on another level, asyndeton can be seen as accommodating characteristics of disorientation and opacity, embodying the contemporary, secular sentiment of uprootedness and flux. In the plastic arts, Imagism, Fauvism, Expressionism, Futurism, Cubism, and Dadaism share the same tendency to fragment their presentation, while deliberately subverting aesthetic givens. It is no accident that each of these movements found literary as well as plastic expression. The erasure of hierarchy which occurs in asyndetic form facilitates a display of difference (a juxtaposition of the disparate), but such difference succeeds only in a leveling of differences to "the same" by virtue of its absolute, unmediable peculiarity. And it is in this respect that the enclosed units of the Creed, placed in unmediated juxtaposition, come close to the effects of a list. On one hand, the elements of the Creed, on the macro level of the text, show a radical juxtaposition of disparate elements, yoked together as if to assert their equal weight, maintaining semantic and semiotic coherence, producing uniform incongruity. But on the other hand, the micro level of the text, the yoking of diverse activities without locating them rationally, spatially, or temporally (except with respect to inhabited time, by iconic implication, and certainly not affording a context within sacral time), is a joining in false concord of materials so essentially different as to defy repeatedly our efforts to control or order them. Such attempted harnessing of difference, and radical dislocation of events from their overall part in history, and from their divine purpose, effects only a semantic drainage, a lexical diminution, and a diabolical elimination of purpose altogether.

As I have mentioned, since the Romantics, parataxis (and especially its radical form, asyndeton) began to surface in the works of Stein, Joyce, Céline, and Pound (all of whom were basically conservative, writing by means of disorder to depict the same), during a period of political upheaval, cultural shift, technological revolution, secularization, and the invention of modern methods of communication which necessitated a reappraisal of the traditional concepts of space and time along new, secular models. The increase in use of asyndeton may be seen as an ambiguous manifestation, superficially supportive of change (in its promiscuous yoking of opposites), but deeply anxious about the loss of stability, as seen in its list-like assembly of chaotic, unrelated elements. It was a power-filled manifestation of insecurity and weakness to which the angst-filled writer resorted. Whatever the motivation of the liturgical use of asyndeton in the Creed, by placing the emphasis upon difference rather than upon coherence, the revisers held up a mirror to the present secular reality. Such a reality sees only discontinuity and violence, and does not perceive a universe in which every tiny detail is permeated with divine presence and purpose.

The asyndetic structure of the Rite A Creed engages in a leveling of clauses, in such a way that each is unidimensional and self-sufficient. It is not part of a greater movement, but is internal to itself. Any clause could be removed, effecting neither the autonomy nor codependence of any other clause. The asyndetic clause derives its value from itself alone, and is not contingent upon any other member of this fragmented and atomic textual society.

Since meaning resides in the connections between things, readers of asyndetic texts have much more work to do in supplying what is absent. The several elements of salvation history are related as isolated units, devoid of syntactic or lexical indication of their purpose, or connection with the text as a whole. The third paragraph (Christ's ascension, and his promise to return) relates events so unexplained and unincorporated that their inclusion seems erroneous, and makes a scientific epistemological assumption, as I mentioned at the end of the first section. This would-be "accelerated" narrative is not one that is continuous, but one that stops and starts with every clause. It effects a reification of singular verbal units, a list of semelfactive actions, the arbitrary disjunctive components of a catalogue.

The earlier combination of hypotaxis and parataxis in the Creed represented a stressing of proper coordination and subordination, a liturgical expression of the seamless continuity between the components of the Christian whole. The vehicle of the revolutionary device of asyndeton asserts a universe of the secular incomplete, the overfull, and the aborted. It is the syntax of discontinuous juxtaposition of unmediated difference, the catalogic contour against, and constitutive of, the void, representing the dissolution of thought, the syntax of insanity, where words are hurled against a fundamental absence of language. And while, on the one hand, asyndeton, in its proximity to the form of the list, can be seen as a powerfully ordering device, yet it conveys *confrontational* juxtaposition, resulting in the sense of abyss and control by force. The product of a century marked by disruption, asyndeton is a device which enables authors to mimic and control chaos. But in the liturgical context of the Creed, which exists to fulfill catechetical, synactic, and doxological functions within the sacred *polis* marked by its arena of delineated belief, cohesion, kinetic and kenotic eventfulness, asyndeton offers only a drama of waiting as its major action, and frustration as its major effect. It issues antidramatic drama, and uses the liturgical stage as a pretext for action which undermines the possibility of acts.

As a crucial component of this antidrama, asyndeton introduces into the Credal text a notion of desire as lack, and a lack which is not balanced by any representation of desire as excess. The model of asyndeton presupposes a dreamed-of object lurking behind every real object, which the reader must discern and supply – as if to say, "there is an object that desire feels the lack of; hence the [textual] world does not contain each and every object that exists; there is at least one object missing, the one that desire feels the lack of; hence, there exists some other place that contains the key to desire (missing in this [textual] world)."[22] Gilles Deleuze and Félix Guattari show this lack to reside at the heart of capitalist economy whereby desire is equated rigorously with lack, deliberately organizing wants and needs amid an abundance of production, making all of desire teeter and fall victim to the great fear of not having one's needs satisfied.[23] The reader of an asyndetic text is required to act out an individualist endeavor of self-orientation, to acknowledge absence, and to attempt to supply what is missing. This lack does not inspire interpersonal and synactic *eros*, but rather encourages an inward-turn, a search to supply isolated nutrients of cognition, rather than a kinetic drawing of the reader onward through the text as a whole. Asyndeton places absence in high relief, lack becomes its virtue; It proclaims the reader's necessary presence. The reader is discovered, not as a doxological participant whose individuality is effaced in the liturgical context, but as reified by means of the need to fill in the lacunae which disclose the fissures of such a "lined" experience. This kind of desire, seen in the light of Jacques Lacan's critique of psychoanalysis, is paradoxical, for it is both a longing to dissolve the individual subject (that obstructs the pleasurable route to the archetypal fetal reunion, apparently the final *telos* of all desire as lack), and yet also constitutes the contemporary evidence of that pleasure's irrecoverability, and the secular impossibility of the dissolution of the enterprise individual. It is significant that in the 1549 Creed, the text departs from the original Greek by making use of the first person singular pronoun in "I believe." At this moment of doxological intensity, in the synactic utterance of "I," there occurs a self-abasement, an elimination of individual disparity. This occurs, paradoxically, precisely at the moment when the locuters acknowledge most explicitly their individuality, in the "I." This is the "I" under erasure, a non-I, unlike that of the ASB which, returning to the Greek plural pronoun, makes explicit the plurality of the locuters. It is an irony that in the 1549 Creed it is the participants who are leveled to equality in the context of their doxological expression, and yet in the ASB leveling is an activity which occurs only in the text, that is, in the lack of clausal differentiation, endlessly convertible, exchangeable, indistinct, and yet, precisely, unmediably "different."

The use of asyndeton in the Creed engages the reader in a new relationship with God, placing humanity in a position of apparent power, a relationship which is not doxological, but rather one which is informed by suspension, frustration, and the desire to control, for the syntax hovers in a perpetual friction of absence and demand, a friction which is unable to find release, given the absence of pacific hypotactic excess.

The capitalist promise of "production" is just that, a promise, but a promise based on the vast and undefined chaos of the quotidian tongue where no promise can be a certainty, its performative felicity being impeded by the absence of synaxis. The supply of produce, the consummation of desire, is illusory, tied as it is to the asyndetic model of "lack." Units of asyndeton are enclosed by their exclusion, captives of their own departure, of no use to the greater whole. They are suspended at the point of passage, poised at the interior of the exterior, for although there is lexis (linguistic units of fact), there is forever stasis, for the lexis is starved of the kinesis of conjunction, and the necessary meaning which makes sense of facts. Asyndeton is the seed and the death of things, the Garden of Adonis, the syntax of dehydration, for it reduces itself to nothing at the same moment that it parades itself as something – it is that nothing which is secular existence itself. It is turned inward toward itself in a continuous irony, the equivocation of endlessly reversible, unresolvable (except by death) short circuits. The only possible, but transient, resolution is the movement to the next clause, a procession of violence, whereby this movement can only be achieved at the expense of the past, that is, the clausal precursor. Disarmed in advance of the binding (conjunctive) muscle of life and ribs of movement, and yet in the guise of the tamed, comprehensible form of short, finite sentences, the asyndetic clause *seems* available to yield to its onlooker its discrete promised tableau of new information, but it is already empty. What the reader unmasks is never more than a mask of assembled, Sirius-burned letters. Asyndeton may be seen in the light of Deleuze and Guattari's "logic of desire" which shows that desire modeled upon lack is doomed from the outset to fall short of its object because it obliges us to choose between production (or process) and acquisition, or the stilling of the process.[24] It suppresses the fact that a process can constitute its own attainment, which is the case with desire as excess. As if to mimic the logic of desire, such texts produce a sense of production, and leave us with a textual acquisition, but also, an incomplete procedure, which is to say, a mask, delivered only after the reader has engaged in a self-aggrandizing reading conducted in the light of the text's writing and unwriting of itself.

This is not to say that asyndeton is universally to be eschewed as "naughty" syntax. There are two types of asyndetic expression, which I shall call *monitored* and *mysterious* respectively. In the mysterious words spoken by Christ at the Last Supper as represented in the BCP of 1549 (an amalgam of scriptural sources), Christ speaks in complex syntax, but it is differentiated from the narrative which surrounds it, in the immediately preceding passage, "who, in the same night . . .," which is a straightforward, linear narrative in the aorist, like the narrative which interrupts Christ's words, "Likewise, after supper . . ." Although Christ makes use of two subordinating conjunctions ("*which* is given for you," and "*which* is shed for you"), which provide purposive information with respect to his actions, as well as a temporal adverbial, "as oft as," and a causal coordinating conjunction, "*for* this is my blood," these instances of orientation and connection do not diffuse the overall asyndetic mystery. For there is asyndeton on the internal level of each of his two parallel utterances:

(i)   [Take], [eat]; [this is my body which is given for you]: [do this in remembrance of me] . . .

(ii) [Drink ye all of this]; [for this is my blood of the new testament, which is shed for you and for many of the remission of sins.] [Do this, as oft as you shall drink it, in remembrance of me.]

There is also an asyndetic structure with respect to the juxtaposition of the two utterances themselves, for no explanation is provided as to their connection, except as to manner of execution, "Likewise," and temporal location, both the implicature of iconicity, derived from the order in which the utterances occur, and also lexically, provided by the temporal adverbials, "after supper," and "and when he had given thanks." The Rite A version of the Institution Narrative has a simplified syntax, for the causal coordination "*for* this is my blood" has been removed. Furthermore, as in the case of the Creed, the ASB has converted the continuous prose of the 1549 version into "lines" of isolated utterance, thus effecting a visual, typographic, asyndetic self-enclosure, as well.

The combination of both hypotaxis and parataxis in the 1549 Institution Narrative serves a purpose, for it facilitates an important differentiation between human (narrative) and Christic (direct) speech. How, then, can it be that Christ makes use of asyndeton, to which I have attributed a nihilistic drift, at the Last Supper? The answer lies in the matter of modes of rationality. Premodern language reflected a sacral universe in which all elements formed a constitutive part of the greater whole, and in which one element recalled another. Its fundamentally hypotactic structure allowed itself to be subverted by an order which was beyond its own reason, because, although it was hierarchically embedded, it did not preclude difference or change. It followed a narrative openness by which its task of perpetual eucharist was never ended. As I shall show, Christ's use of asyndeton at the Last Supper is a reminder in every liturgical performance that human reason is incomplete, and that the work of praise is never finished. By contrast, contemporary language claims to be open, unprocessed, and rendered spontaneously, but in fact, it operates according to a closed system which exalts unmediable difference to such an extent that there can be no difference. Such an exaltation means that in the liturgical text no distinction is made between human rationality and the wisdom of God.

Christ is often represented as a madman. The insanity of the Cross, the non-sense of sacrifice, was a wisdom which drowned in the "rationality" of the world, and revealed there its non-sense. By the asyndetic silence which binds his anamnetic utterances at the Last Supper, his speech opens a void, an arena of emptiness (fuller than fullness) which no words can "explain," for it is a mystery that can only be performed, received, and then repeated. These lacunae provoke a breach between human "rationality" and divine wisdom, where only God (beyond all contraries) can discern the "reason" in non-sense. And so it is the world which becomes culpable in relation to language, compelled to order itself by these strange linguistic tableaux, compelled by Christ's unfathomable words to perform a task of inadequate recognition and reparation, the task of restoring "reason." And in the light of these words, such a task can only be performed by means of an acknowledgment of that reasonable reason which emerges precisely from unreason and must, in the end, dissolve into that unreason, for that unreason is superior by far to our "reason." While humanity had once measured its own sanity by means of its announcement of clausal subordination and relation, and had measured madness by its refusal to accommodate such hierarchies, in the Institution Narrative the world is made to abase itself before this madness.

But how then should one relate this Christic asyndeton to the asyndeton of modernity and the Rite A Creed? First, the latter eliminates the distinction between the deliberately and necessarily self-humiliating "rational" syntax of the earlier version, and the asyndetic words of Christ later to come. Secondly, the modernist asyndeton of Rite A is very different in type from that used by Christ at the Last Supper. The Rite A Credal asyndeton is retained and maintained: it is carefully ordered according to the hidden convention (implicature) of iconicity. Its list-like structure shows it to emerge from a struggling toward order. But its order is only chronological order, that is, the order of mundane, annihilative time. And so, with each assertion of timely order, the asyndetic clause must submit to ultimate disorder. It traverses, in unmediable variations, the surface upon which they meet, the typographic spatial surface which both binds and separates these variations, like the figures painted on the Grecian urn, a plenitude of emptiness which culminates in the void, the human "reason" suspended between the oneiric and the erroneous, the syntax of despair. Such monitored, fixed, closed "order" is the illusory reason of humanity, more imposing and authoritative for its seeming spontaneity than the revealed and visible attempts at ordering rendered by means of hypotaxis and parataxis.

Christ's asyndetic utterances at the Last Supper pertain to no such implication of verisimilitude. There is no chronology in his utterances, except that of their speaking. His asyndeton is not monitored by chronology, but leaps beyond such controlled arbitrariness into the region of eternal truth, exploding in gestures, paradigms, and words, the distinction between order and disorder, reason and unreason. His locutions are universals, uttered in the generic present tense which issues no temporal boundaries, each a tableau on its own, and yet everywhere pertinent. The repeated command to repeat, "Do this in remembrance of me," is a present imperative, a recall that is anticipated, a detour not by the past but by the future, when after is before, and before is afterwards, whereby isolating a homogeneous movement of time becomes a delicate task, and disturbs our reassuring ideas about retrospection and anticipation. Christ's naming of the bread and the cup as body and blood is achronic, and affords the tableaux a climactic rather than a chronological identity, in accordance with its being a "scenic" rather than "summary" narrative, to use Genette's terminology. Christ's actions of breaking the bread and lifting the cup are connected neither temporally (for in scenic narrative, time is attenuated), nor logically, but climactically. Christic asyndeton, uttered in the space of his presence, is perfectly clear and natural, like the language of dream, expressed in speech of impeccable linguistic coherence. But it is only on "waking," that is, going out from the sacred polis (where even the impossible is possible) at the moment when the coherent universe appears to give up its place to another (whose logic is "different") that that which was limpid and logical loses its transparency. Christ's universal truths are open and forever searching their unbounded application. They do not refer to semelfactive events located on a narrative thread. The confinement of the asyndetic Christic tableaux, surrounded by the differentiated speech of humanity, is a confinement which, by means of its lack of chronological monitoring and closure, glorifies the climactic, dislocationary difference of Christ.

By situating our narrative of things into the explicitly and humanly "rational" form of hypotaxis, and Christ's dicta in ineffable asyndeton, we discern this Christophanic difference. This is a liturgical expression of the relationship between the worshiper and God, and human use, and simultaneous derision, of earthly rationale in the face of the incomprehensible wisdom of God which inhabits the silent lacunae of Christ's asyndeton. And so, by making use of our mechanisms of "reason," as in the 1549 Creed, that is, in our delineation of what we "understand" of the Trinity and of salvation history, we engage in a necessary humiliation of our false reasoning and abase ourselves before the eternal truth which remains inscrutable: the insane figure of God incarnate is the wisdom which cannot be understood by empirical or "logical" investigation, Christ made man, but seen by men as a madman. And so, the "generation unbelieving" (Mark 9: 19) is to us as Christ was to that generation: "but we proclaim [*kèrussomen*: proclaim, announce, extol, invoke, preach, teach publicly, that is, we utter as our creed] the crucified Christ, who was to the Jews an offence [*skandalon*] and to the Gentiles a folly [*mōrian*: absurdity, madness], but to those whom God has called, both Jews and Greeks, is Christ the power of God and the wisdom of God. For the folly of God is wiser than man's wisdom, and the weakness of God is stronger than man's strength" (1 Corinthians 1: 23–25). God submitted to the most lowly of human forms, the fool, and so brought shame to the wise, and chose the weakest frame to shame the strong. And so by being, in his asyndetic emptiness, fuller than plenitude, He nullified the false fullness of "reason." Divine absence is yet more apparent than earthly presence, for in God there can be no such distinction between presence and absence. Saint Paul writes, "It is because of him that you are in Christ Jesus, who has become for us wisdom from God, that is, our righteousness, sanctification, and redemption. Therefore, as it is written, 'Let him who boasts boast in the Lord' " (1 Cor. 1: 30–31).

The instances of absence in the asyndetic Creed are imposed and deficient, a lack sustained by deliberate removal of cohesive markers, a coercive absence.

Upon such a model, desire emerges as the result of denial. There is no ultimate *telos* to this desire, no object posited as the goal of this lack, except a false direction: for the enclosed clauses can look only to themselves, and the reader, in reading, can only, likewise, look to himself. The asyndetic absence issuing from Christ's words, however, is modeled on a different structure, for God is the object of all desire, depicted in the vanishing points between Christ's mysterious anamnetic utterances, the infinite object which can never be "reached" for it is forever more, and yet is attained by means of every reaching. The object of desire is inaccessible in the ordinary sense of something uniquely graspable. The desire with which we fill the gaps is a desire which can never fully fill, but which is not without direction, and is forever filling. It is in this asyndeton, where connections are not withheld, but are inscrutable, in the gaps which we fill with our desire, that, and by means of the act of desiring, we gain knowledge of the infinite object of our desire. The Christophanic asyndeton is characterized by an absence which is not imposed, is not a negation of what was once apparent, but rather is a real absence, and occurs, for the One beyond all contraries, precisely at the instant of real presence.

The enforced negation of the asyndetic Creed sets up a mercantilist dynamic which places desire on the side of acquisition, causing the reader to look upon the clausal lacunae as a lack, the lack of an object, making all of desire fall victim to the great fear of not having one's needs satisfied, of supplying that which is mundanely absent, of fixing, territorializing, textualizing, monitoring, and controlling (the very structure that claimed freedom and spontaneity as its probity). Such monitored, time-bound syntax displaces the real desire, which lacks nothing, which does not lack its object, which is forever filling, and is not a semelfactive acquisition to end all acquisitions. Such desire, the present, ardent, eternal, and adored plenitude, opens up in the unspeakable speech of Christophanic asyndeton. But in the ASB, this perpetual filling–overflowing is repressed, for that unlocatable, emancipatory desire (*jouissance*) is capable of calling into question the established order of society which chooses to operate according to the logic of lack.

Something like desire can be discerned in God, that is, in the Trinity, and it is not a desire determined by denial or lack, but by excess and searching. Desire of this kind is not at odds with the social harmony, but it is explosive, for there is no limit to its excess and its reach: 'no society can tolerate a position of real desire without its structures of exploitation, servitude, and hierarchy being compromised.'[25] It is therefore of vital importance for a society to repress desire, and even to find something more efficient than repression, so that repression, hierarchy, exploitation, and servitude, that is to say, denial, are themselves desired.

The asyndetic Creed leaves the traditional Credal functions of performative enactment of Trinitarian relations, catechetical explanation, doxology, synaxis of participants, and representation of a sacral temporal order, unfulfilled. Lurking behind these failures is a more sinister appropriation of secular mercantilism. Because of its enforced absence (its imposed asyndeton), a dynamic of desire as lack is called into play. False lacunae are created which fragment the narrative of salvation history, eliminating its continuity and purpose. These false gaps merely engender the notion that there is a ready-made precise content which fulfills and deletes a need, along a ruthlessly linear plane. The accumulation of asyndetic clauses repeats this need–acquisition model, one clause after another, constantly inducing new desires, repackaged, for your desire as lack, each one parading as the commodity to end all desires. But there is no product, no real object of desire, except discrete items which expire the instant they are consumed, only to be succeeded again. The syntactic form of the liturgy is itself purveying those elements in modernity which are themselves substitutes for the order of genuine divine desire. Liturgists have, then, become accomplices to the hegemony of "Capital," impeding the route to the divine, and holding up a mirror which both mimics and perpetuates the secular (dis)order.

Notes

1 These differences are as follows: the Episcopal text comprises three paragraphs, and not five; it opens with the first person singular pronoun "I" instead of plural "We"; the Greek preposition *ék* is translated as "of" instead of "from" (see note 8 below).

2 *The Book of Common Prayer According to the Use of the Episcopal Church* (New York: The Church Hymnal Corporation, 1979), pp. 326 and 358.

3 Frances Young, *The Making of the Creeds* (London: SCM Press, 1991), pp. 3ff.

4 The Credal confession of faith is a natural successor to the summary passages of proclamation and acclamation of God and his saving action found in the Jewish scriptures, for example, Deuteronomy 5: 4, 26: 5.

5 For example, the colon separating the first and second sections is to be understood as a rhetorical pause rather than a marker of logical relations (see Manfred Görlach, *Introduction to Early Modern English* (Cambridge University Press, 1991), p. 58). It is immediately succeeded by a coordinating conjunction, which neutralizes any disjunction caused by the hiatus. The Father is thus connected (coordinated) with the Son by means of a colonic reaching, and a coordinative affirmation (welcoming).

6 Lines 10, 19, and the end, denoting points which require cognitive pause or to allow time for an accompanying gesture.

7 R. C. D. Jasper and Paul F. Bradshaw, *A Companion to the Alternative Service Book* (London: SPCK, 1986).

8 The semantics of rupture can be seen, for example, in the ASB translation of the Greek preposition *ék* as "from" rather than "of." Jasper and Bradshaw (ibid.) assert that this is a "clearer and more literal translation" (p. 198). However, if "from" were the desired

relation, the Greek preposition would have been *ápo*. "From" is a preposition of deictic departure, of procession away. The 1549 translation of *ék* as genitive "of" conveys not so much the notion of possession as that of *genus*, both "out of" and "including," the same and yet different, continuing the theme of sonship and begetting which characterizes this section. Although one must speak of Trinitarian "persons" in order to speak at all about the Trinity, this speaking must remain no more than a mode of affirming. Father, Son, and Holy Ghost are not in any sense atomic, but indwell one another: each is infinite, eternal, perfect, and so on, but there are not three infinities, three eternities, and three perfections. They are distinct neither in substance nor accident, but in *relation*, as Augustine suggests, as begetting, being begotten, and proceeding. The persons are belonging to, or precisely *of* one another, coinherent, in simple, yet complex, unity.

9 On the level of lexis, the complication of divine attributes can be seen in the ASB's division of originally compound epithets (e.g., "Father Almighty," "one Lord Jesus Christ") into separate attributes ("the Father, the Almighty," "one Lord, Jesus Christ").

10 Roman Jakobson, "Quest for the Essence of Language" (1965) in *Language of Literature*, ed. Krystyna Pomorska and Stephen Rudy (Cambridge, MA: Harvard University Press, 1987), pp. 418–27.

11 Jean-François Lyotard, *The Postmodern Condition: A Report on Knowledge*, trans. Geoff Bennington and Brian Massumi (Manchester University Press, 1984), esp. pp. 18–27 (and *passim*), [originally published in France as *La condition postmoderne: rapport sur le savoir* (Paris: Minuit, 1979)].

12 Bernard Comrie, *Tense* (Cambridge University Press, 1985), p. 36.

13 Suzanne Fleischman, *Tense and Narrativity* (London: Routledge and Kegan Paul, 1990), pp. 24ff., 252–61.

14 Saint Augustine, *De Trinitate* (AD 400–416), in *Patrologia Latina*, trans. Marcus Dods (Paris: J. P. Migne), vol. VIII, pp. 819–1098.

15 For example, our understanding of the asyndetic "I came; I saw; I conquered" is reliant upon the chronological verisimilitude between fabula and story.

16 A humiliation of sacral time can be seen in various lexical alterations. For example, the passive construction "is seated" replaces the present active "sitteth," effecting a diminution of temporal boundaries, describing a condition of seatedness as a local peculiarity, characterizing only the mundane present moment (the passive construction is also dubious in that it portrays Christ as the recipient of an unnamed external agency, conveying an Arian notion of Trinitarian relations). Similarly, the Holy Spirit's intervention into historical time is committed into the perfect tense. Unlike the aorist "spake" (or "spoke"), the perfect is the tense of subjective recollection, reducing the distance between the narrator and the narrated events. Its reduced and undetached temporal structure mean that this tense is seldom, if ever, used in formal narrative – see Fleischman, *Tense and Narrativity*, pp. 29ff., 252.

17 Gérard Genette, *Narrative Discourse*, trans. Jane E. Lewin (Oxford: Blackwell, 1980), p. 87.

18 Ibid., pp. 92–3.

19 Ibid., p. 95.

20 Ibid., pp. 95–7.

21 Ibid., p. 109.

22 Clément Rosset, *Logique du pire* (Paris: Presses Universitaires de France, 1970), p. 37 (my additions in square parentheses).

23 Giles Deleuze and Félix Guattari, *Anti-Oedipus, Capitalism and Schizophrenia* (London: Athlone Press, 1984), pp. 28 and *passim*.

24 Gérard Genette, *Narrative Discourse*, p. 87.

25 Ibid., p. 32.

New Jerusalem, Old Athens
From *The Broken Middle*

Gillian Rose

Would that they would forsake Me but observe My Torah (*Palestinian Talmud*, "Haggigah" 1: 7)[1]

Dina *de-malkhuta dina* "the law of the kingdom is valid law"[2] (Shmuel – third-century *amora*)

Between these two affirmations of two bodies of law – the revealed law and the law of the nations – Judaism has wrestled with the antinomianism they jointly imply: for adherence to the law of the nations could impugn the allegiance to *halacha* – even if only by spiritualizing it for the sake of a general social ethic. The relation between these two kinds of law has been raised in Rabbinic sources as the idea of "natural law" – law common to uncommanded and commanded man – but natural law is invariably rejected as contrary to the system of *halacha*. The implicit issue of the relation of *halacha* as specific law to the law of the nations, the idea of a "natural law" common to peoples with different positive laws, has, therefore, not been pursued in the way it was developed by Cicero and subsequently Roman law, or, in the early modern period, between Christian polities – *De Jure Naturali et Gentium*, etc. The idea of "natural morality" has been more liberally entertained, since, historically, it is far weaker and, focusing on the individual, it contains no implicit or explicit comparison between *halacha* and non-*halachic* law.[3] The issue of "natural morality" is frequently raised as a preliminary and provisional discourse on the way to discussion internal to the corpus of revealed and oral law, or, as Maimonides expounds it, the written law and its interpretation – the commandment or oral law – both revealed to Moses on Sinai.[4] What is striking about recent formulations and disputes over the relation of ethics and *halacha* is how, within this explicitly intra-normative and intra-Judaic concern, the modern tension between freedom and unfreedom is discernibly at stake, yet there is no evidence of the modern metaphysic of nature and freedom on which this problematic is otherwise invariably assumed to depend.

The contrast between the different formulations of the initial question concerning the relation of ethics and *halacha* indicates the difference in the underlying ideas of the form and content of law. Underlying these divergencies in modern Judaic self-understanding, evident in the conceiving of law and ethics, lies the context within which the question of ethics and *halacha* is posed – modern legality and morality – which is itself transposed into divergent self-reflections, evident in the jurisprudence dirempted between sociology and philosophy.

Aharon Lichtenstein, in a now famous article, first published in 1975, asks "Does Jewish Tradition Recognize an Ethic Independent of Halacha?"; while Eugene Borowitz questions "The Authority of the Ethical Impulse in 'Halakhah.'"[5] Two intrinsically different modes of address are posed here. On the basis of Weber's distinctions, it appears that Lichtenstein questions the ethical legitimation of *halacha qua* traditional authority, while Borowitz questions the ethical legitimation of *halacha qua* legal-rational authority. *Prima facie*, Lichtenstein asks whether *halacha* is *equitable* by inquiring into the *status* of equity within *halacha*, while Borowitz asks whether *halacha* is *egalitarian* by inquiring into the *flexibility* of *halacha*. Lichtenstein focuses on the ethical potential "within" *halacha*, while Borowitz focuses on the ethical potential "of" *halacha*. Yet, paradoxically, it is Lichtenstein who demonstrates the flexibility of *halacha*, while it is Borowitz who demands that ethics be as "categorical" (unconditioned) as *halacha*, and not a secondary kind of imperative, "its own way," the position he attributes to Lichtenstein, and it is Borowitz who inquires into the *status* of women.

Lichtenstein considers several preliminary definitions of ethics: *lex naturalis*, *derekh eretz*, natural morality. Although the Rabbis were opposed to natural law thinking, Lichtenstein concludes that all rationalizing of *halacha* presupposes natural morality. The contemporary concern is whether *halacha* – either *din*, specific statute, or the whole of Judaism as an ethical system – needs an additional ethical supplement. To avoid the simple equation of law with morality, which would imply that no instance of uncertainty concerning "what ought I to do" need arise, Lichtenstein proceeds to consider *lifnim mishurat hadin*. It was transformed by Nahmanides from the negative, condemnatory judgment that destruction befell those who, within the limits of Torah, yet failed to act "beyond the line of the law," into the suprapositive counsel of perfection: "Ye shall be holy" and act beyond the line, i.e. the strict demands of the law. This morality of aspiration is supralegal but not optional. Lichtenstein scours the traditional sources to bring out the range of connotations of this unique idea of "supralegality," from an actionable, rigorous obligation to supreme idealism. *Lifnim mishurat hadin* is gradually delineated as a situational or contextual morality. By contrast with a formal ethic which is categorical and fixed, *lifnim mishurat hadin* balances universal and local factors in any specific case instead of assimilating each case to the average of the category or class under which, strictly speaking, it falls. Overall, this discussion supports Lichtenstein's defence of *halacha* as multiplanar and not deductive. The penumbral regions of *mitzvot* or *din*, specific or strict statute, are continually complemented and never completed with *lifnim mishurat hadin*.

It is with the noncategorical status of this equitable element that Borowitz takes issue. He argues that the supralegality of *lifnim mishurat hadin*, presented by Lichtenstein as "imperative in its own way," amounts to no more than a vague species of command and is all of a piece with Judaism generally which manages to be both highly ethical as a whole, yet qualifies the ethical by leaving it unqualified. He agrees that there are varying levels of authority within Rabbinic Judaism but argues that the ethical impulse is so restricted or denied that it can provide no remedy for issues such as the status of women. The much vaunted flexibility of *halacha* is sacrificed when such an issue arises, even though a solution is crucial to its continuing legitimation and future survival. Instead the cumbersome resistance of Rabbinic Judaism proves its formal, outmoded reliance on human rather than divine authority which it shares with other fallible social institutions.

Borowitz is right to raise the changing status/role of women as a crucial test for *halacha*, according to which the category of "woman" has always been explicit. But the remedy he proposes is bizarre: that ethics "ought to come as a categorical or unmediated imperative,"[6] even though he has argued against Schwarzschild's Cohenian fusing of legality and morality[7] and accuses contemporary Rabbinic Judaism both of excessive formality[8] and of excessive tampering with the imperative quality of the Torah's ethical behests.[9]

Instead of searching for a conception that would render both ethics *and* law more flexible, or questioning the conditions which drive them apart and rigidify them, Borowitz imports the Kantian categorical ethic back into Judaism; the same ethic which has itself been fundamentally questioned by modernity, and which displays the qualities of absoluteness, unconditionality, formality, and imperativeness which he otherwise deplores in the idea of law. This way of enlarging the idea of *halacha* with an ethics imperative in an unquestionable sense coincides with the very mode of *halachic* judgment rejected by Lichtenstein. Furthermore, Lichtenstein does not subordinate ethics to law as "imperative in its own way." He sets out the universal and local jurisprudence at stake throughout the sources in a variety of carefully related expositions.

Neither Lichtenstein (on substantial grounds) nor Borowitz (on formal grounds) are able to remedy, say, the changing "status" of women because they will not confront directly the modern problematic of freedom and unfreedom which their disagreement nevertheless implies. Judaism, with its substantial legislation of women, in the Talmudic tractates of the Third Division, *Nashim*, "Women," cannot dissemble its assumptions and impositions. This does, indeed, constitute a significant difference from modern positing of formal legal equality which veils and perpetuates substantial ethical inequality.

The apparent coincidence of the modern question of the legal status of women with the Talmudic *Seder* on "Women" leads, however, to an invalid comparison, for the form of law in each case offers no *tertium quid*. There is no contextual equivalent in *halacha* for modern, formal, civil law, within which the comparison between form and actuality can arise out of the observable inversion of meaning in configuration. So when Steven Schwarzschild argues, without reference to the dispute over ethics and *halacha*, that the priority of practical reason in post-Kantian philosophy shows that Judaism is qualified to lead the way in the convergence of philosophy and Judaism,[10] he overlooks the drawback evident in the dispute over ethics and *halacha*, that Judaism recognizes no formal law, while post-Kantian philosophy has inherited the diremption presupposed in Kant's priority of practical reason, of the categorical imperative, between inner morality and outer legality, which nevertheless would be imported back into Judaic self-definition by Borowitz. In short, he avoids the question as to whether there is anything on which to converge, or whether, rather, Judaism and philosophy converge on a middle broken between ethics and law.

The dispute reveals more than any idealization of Judaic jurisprudence will concede: that exclusive emphasis on subjective freedom insists on remaining ignorant of the inversion of intention, while exclusive defence of legal procedure as self-perficient casuistry insists on remaining ignorant of inversion of form in configuration. Once again, within *halachic* Judaism, as within philosophical presentation of Judaism from Rosenzweig to Levinas, there is *no comprehension to complement commandment*: no recognition of freedom and unfreedom. And there is also the further irony that the unresolvable, intra-normative diremption of Judaism between ethics and *halacha* should become the model, the aspiration for new political theologies winged between singularity and holiness, that would mend their broken middles at the furthest remove from the conflict of the laws.

New Jerusalem, Old Athens: The Holy Middle

This rediscovery of Judaism *at the end of the end of philosophy*, at the *tertium quid*, the middle of ethics, occurs at the deepest difficulty of both philosophy and Judaism, where they are equally cast into crisis over the conceiving of law and ethics, ethics and *halacha*. This convergence on ethics turns out to be a mutual aspiration *without* a third, a middle, on which to converge. Yet the converging proceeds apace in the form of holy middle, loveful polity – beyond nature and freedom, freedom and unfreedom – but also without law and therefore without grace. This converging by philosophy and Judaism corrupts. For, in spite of the inversion of their previous meliorist intentions into contrary configuration, they introduce no reflection on that repetition; but, claiming such unconstrued inversion to be the "totalized" and "totalizing" domination of Western metaphysics, and its cognates, they would enthrone the equally "total" expiation of holy jurisprudence, refusing any recognition of their own implication in the *rearticulation* of domination.

There are two kinds of proclaimed "end" to philosophy: the end of "metaphysics" from Kant to Nietzsche, Rosenzweig and Heidegger, which may well found a *new thinking*; and the end of "philosophy" from Hegel and Marx to Lukács and Adorno, which raises the question of the *realization* of philosophy. By "the end of" the end of philosophy, I mean the discovery in the long debate between Judaism and philosophy – understood in relation to the Greek quest for the beginning – principles, causes – of the missing middle, the *tertium quid* – ethics, which finds itself always within the imperative, the commandment, and hence always already begun.

If Heidegger celebrates "The End of Philosophy,"[11] Levinas celebrates the end of the end of philosophy as ethics, presented in philosophical as well as in Judaic form – *lectures talmudiques*. Yet this is a distinction with much less difference than Levinas claims. For Levinas' "overcoming" of ontology depends on characterizing ontology as the non-ethical other; while Heidegger's ethical impulse depends on the characterization of Western metaphysics, his other, as "onto-theology." To be sure, Levinas denies the ethics in the "other" of his authorship, while Heidegger makes no claims for the ethics in his authorship. Yet *Ereignis*, "the Event of appropriation," presented as playing and interplaying of the fourfold dimensions of time – "pure space and ecstatic time" – or as the four-beinged "round dance of appropriating" by "earth and sky, divinities and mortals,"[12] this ethical paganism, shares with its "Judaic" counterpart of responsibility, initially domesticated and subsequently traumatized, the reintroduction of Revelation into philosophy, the incursion of unique alterity, divine singularity. Furthermore, they share this reintroduction of Revelation *without raising the question of realization*; and hence without critique of the metaphysics of nature and freedom which would make the specific history of modern freedom and unfreedom reconstructable. The current Heidegger controversy therefore remains far too close to its quarry.[13] For the production of holy middles, where Revelation is opposed to a totalized history of "Western metaphysics" – "metaphysics" unified, thereby, since the Greeks – continues to be licensed by the inventions of his late thinking. We are ourselves the test-case which we would project back to 1933–4: called by postmodern theology to the Kingdom – pagan, Judaic, Christian – beyond "Western" metaphysics, we are blandished away from the very modern anxiety of polity: the opposition between morality and legality. Instead of heeding the anxiety of beginning in the equivocation of the ethical, we respond to new repetition in the feast – the promise of unending angelic conviviality – new but ancient political theology.

Taylor's postmodern "a/theology" and Milbank's postmodern *Beyond Secular Reason* offer Christian New Jerusalem for old Athens.[14] These authorships provide evidence of that prodigious, omniscient, "contemporary," "Western" intellectuality that would crown postmodern theology or a/theology: "queen of the sciences." Each self-declaredly "postmodern," their work is comprehensive while decrying comprehension: It disrespects and breaks down further the already lowered barriers between philosophy and literary criticism in the one case, between philosophy and social theory in the other, which are then gathered up and completed as postmodern a/theology or theology. Thereby is vindicated an old prognostication: that if we fail to teach theology – we will usurp it. Or, to cite the very words of John Henry Newman himself in 1852, *The Idea of a University*: "supposing Theology be not taught, its province will not simply be neglected, but will be actually usurped by other sciences . . ."[15]

In spite of their shared scope and fervent ambition for postmodern a/theology or theology – what do these two bodies of thought have in common? Nothing – where sources, style, tone and method are apparent. Working closely with Nietzsche and Derrida on that "shifty middle ground *between* Hegel and Kierkegaard,"[16] Taylor inserts Heidegger and recent French thought into the terrain: while Milbank's argument covers the development of secular politics to classic sociology from Malebranche to Durkheim and Weber, from Hegel and Marx to Catholic Liberation Theology, classical philosophy, and mediaeval theology, all also oriented, however, by recent French thought, as *trivium* to its ultimate ecclesiology. Stylistically, they are even more diverse: Taylor offers a montage of text and illustration, accruing grammatical, phonetic, and graphological juxtapositions and complications, learnt, it would seem, from *Finnegans Wake*; Milbank offers a treatise, four books in one, with sober, sustained argumentation, paced temporally and spatially from beginning to end. In tone, Taylor is masked ironic, transgressive and extravagant; Milbank is straight, logical – in spite of his ontology of narration – severe, authoritative, and original. Yet, we are explicitly offered by the one, a deconstruction of theology; by the other, a deconstruction of classical and modern secularity; by the one, a deconstructive a/theology; by the other, "Difference of Virtue, Virtue of Difference."

In *Erring*, Taylor deconstructs "Death of God," "Disappearance of Self," "End of History," "Closure of the Book," which are translated into deconstructive a/theology in four paratactic "moves": "Writing of God," "Markings," "Mazing Grace," "Erring Scripture," to culminate in Dionysian "joy in . . .

suffering";[17] "The 'Yes' of anguished joy breaks the power of the law and fissures the 'Notshall' of history,"[18] while "The unending erring in scripture is the eternal play of the divine milieu," for, in play, "which is interplay," "the entire foundation of the economy of domination crumbles."[19] In *Altarity*, the middle ground between Hegel and Kierkegaard is no longer occupied by Nietzsche but by Heidegger and recent French thinkers. Yet the whole is framed by Hegel as "Conception" and Kierkegaard as "Transgression," titles of the opening and concluding chapters. Hegel is expounded as the identity of difference and identity, Kierkegaard as the Abrahamic transgression of the ethical from *Fear and Trembling*, and every other author is locked into this opposition between knowledge and faith which Taylor nevertheless knows Kierkegaard invented for his pseudonym, Johannes *de silentio*. No transgression occurs, for Abraham's arm is stayed by an angel, but the work concludes by affirming the opposition between "the Law" and "the Call of the Other," an erring in time, where *Erring* offers a nomadicism in space.

In *Theology and Social Theory: Beyond Secular Reason*, Milbank demonstrates, by a genetic-archaeological reconstruction, that "secular discourse" is constituted by its opposition to orthodox Christianity as "pagan" theology or antitheology in disguise.[20] In four "sub-treatises" the complicity of secular reason with an "ontology of violence" is rehearsed: first, in eighteenth-century politics and political economy; second, in all nineteenth-century sociology which, including Weber, is presented as a "Positivist Church"; third, in Hegel and in Marx, whose impulse toward the nonsecular is said to be indecently recruited for secular science; this equivocation, evident to Milbank, is itself, with indecent alacrity, recruited to "a 'gnostic' plot about a historically necessary fall and reconstruction of being, with a gain achieved through violence undergone."[21] These two treatises conclude with attempts to terminate the dialogue between theology and sociology and between theology and liberation respectively. Fourthly and finally, at the threshold to the last great treatise, Milbank disentangles his self-declared nihilistic voice from his Greek-medieval voice to complete nihilism with Christian logos and virtue which "recognizes no original violence."[22] Not the difference of nihilism nor the virtue of the Greeks; not liberal, of course, but equally "Against 'Church and State' "[23] – that is, without natural rights and without natural law – transcendental difference" is "encoded" as a "harmonic peace" beyond the circumscribing power of any totalizing reason.[24] Without violence or arbitrariness, and yet with difference, non-totalization and indeterminacy, and without representation, the Augustinian "other City" is "advocated" as "the continuation of ecclesial practice": it is "the imagination in action of a peaceful, reconciled social order, beyond even the violence of legality."[25] The active imagination of "the *sociality* of harmonious difference"[26] (emphasis in original) sketches the peaceful donation of "the heavenly city" where "beyond the possibility of alteration" "the angels and saints abide . . . in a fellowship [whose] virtue is not the virtue of resistance and domination, but simply of remaining in a state of self-forgetting conviviality."[27] Between this heavenly city and the sinful city, founded on the murder of Abel, of the *saeculum*, "the interval between fall and final return of Christ,"[28] God sends a salvation city, the "City of God on pilgrimage through this world" which does not exclude anyone but "provides a genuine peace by its memory of all the victims, its equal concern for all its citizens and its self-exposed offering of reconciliation to enemies,"[29] "its salvation . . . 'liberation' from political, economic and psychic *dominium*."[30]

This explication of pilgrimage and inclusivity effectively destroys the idea of a city: Its task of salvation deprives it of site; while its inclusive appeal deprives it of limit or boundary that would mark it off from any other city and their different laws: "the city of God is in fact 'a paradox, a nomad city' (one might say)."[31] The otherwise always indicted features of gnostic demiurgic soteriology in this messenger city, and the precondition of violence committed by sinful cities in this "peace coterminous with all Being whatsoever" should be noted in this "encoded narrative."

The new Jerusalems have emerged: postmodern a/theology as nomadic ecstasy – Dionysian joy; postmodern theology as nomadic ecclesial eschatology – harmonious peace; both breaking the frame in their antinomianism, and both reinstating the frame in their dependence on law transgressed – joy that "breaks the power of law";[32] or law subdued – peace that is "beyond even the violence of legality."[33] Taylor with joy but without sociality; Milbank with sociality and glimpses of angelic conviviality; both converge on the acknowledgment of difference, but in so doing reinstate the *age-old* oppositions between law and grace, knowledge and faith, while intentionally but, it will turn out, only apparently, working without the *modern* duality of nature and freedom.

This replacing of old Athens by new Jerusalem consigns the opposition between nature and freedom to one of any number of arbitrary, binary, metaphysical conceits – instead of recognizing it as index and indicator of freedom and unfreedom – and then proceeds to complete such "deconstruction" in holiness. This founding and consecrating of holy cities inadvertently clarifies what that discarded opposition made it possible to reflect upon; reflection which is disqualified by its disappearance. Furthermore, those two Christian holy cities – Protestant (Taylor), Catholic (Milbank) – arise on the same foundations – antinomian and ahistorical – as the Davidic cities of Leo Strauss and Levinas.

These authorships – Strauss and Levinas – also embrace the paradox in presenting Judaic theologico-political prophecy or ethics *in philosophical terms* as the end of the end of philosophy. They also claim for Judaism the solution of the theologico-political or the ethical problem without the opposition between nature and freedom: Strauss presents Judaism *contra* nature; Levinas, *contra* freedom. Consequently, both represent Judaism or Jewish history eschatologically: for Strauss, in *Philosophy and Law*, however, "the prophet is the founder of the [ideal] Platonic state,"[34] and while the "era that believes in Revelation / is *fulfilled*," this is not because of the belief but because what is revealed is "a simple binding Law, a divine Law, a Law with the power of right."[35]

These philosophical presentations of Judaism which have made Judaism accessible and available for rediscovery at the end of the end of philosophy – *die Ironie der Ironie*, for the religion historically denigrated as superseded – are, nevertheless, *deeply* misleading. They misrepresent the rationalism or knowledge against which they define themselves; they misrepresent Judaism; and they misrepresent the history and modernity in which they are implicated. Strauss misrepresents Greek rationalism and ignores the connection between the birth and development of philosophy and earlier strata of pre-Olympian Greek religion.[36] If philosophy begins "in wonder" then it is not a response to what is wonderful, but to what is awe-ful: it begins too, even apotropaically, in fear and trembling.[37] Preserving all cognition for philosophy while insisting that Judaism is always already commanded, they avoid any recognition of the struggle between universality and aporia, from Kantian judgment to Hegelian speculative experience, of the predicament of universal and local jurisprudence which characterizes modern philosophy as much as modern Judaism.

Moreover, they both misrepresent Judaism. The "Talmudic argument" rehearses a rationalism which is constantly exploring its own limits – the oral law a never-ending commentary on the written law, according to which knowledge and responsibility are renegotiated under the historically and politically changing conditions of both. Yet Strauss and Levinas present Judaism as unchanging and without a history; internal and external, as commentary, as law, as community. Strauss gives priority to medieval Judaism, while Levinas' decision that modernity compels him to give priority not to "the relation of ethics and halacha" "but rather [to] the passage from the non-ethical to the ethical," arguing that the latter "is truly the necessary of our time" when all authority and morality is "called into question," draws attention systematically away, as demonstrated above, from the mainstream debate within modern Judaism over ethics and *halacha*, from which he nevertheless takes his terms, and which, far from being specific to Judaism, shows the mutual difficulty shared by Jewish and non-Jewish thinkers in the conceiving of law and ethics. It is this evasion which permits postmodern political theology to allude to a Judaism, taken from Rosenzweig, Buber, or Levinas, as an open jurisprudence, a holy sociology, instead of confronting the configuring of conceiving of law and ethics in the shared context of modern legality and morality.

These four kinds of holy cities – pagan (Heidegger), Davidic (Levinas), nomadic Protestant (Taylor), nomadic Catholic (Milbank) – consecrated in the shifting sands of ahistoricism and antinomianism, may be compared in the terms made explicit by the last two as *postmodern political theologies*. First, they are "political theologies" because they present a solution to the political problem: for Taylor, economies of domination will crumble;[38] for Milbank, salvation "must mean 'liberation' from political, economic, and psychic *dominium*, and therefore from all structures belonging to the *saeculum*."[39] Second, they are "postmodern" because their politics and their theology are explicitly developed without the prevalent, guiding, modern contraries of nature and freedom, critiqued as the tension of freedom and unfreedom; not therefore re-presentable, they can only be presented as "holiness": for Taylor, "the coincidence of opposites extends the divine milieu"; while for Milbank, ecclesial practice extends to the divine.[40] Significantly, both lay claim to the middle: Taylor joins "the eternal play of the divine milieu" while Milbank distinguishes his ontology from Levinas' by denying that "mediation is necessarily violent."[41] So third, then, the agon of postmodernisms: within the holy play, the holy city, holy nomads – beyond nature and law, freedom and unfreedom – they resonate with and claim to do justice to the unequivocal middle. But where is this middle? Neither ecstatic affirmation vaunting its "totally loving the world," nor eschatological peace vaunting its continuity with untarnished ecclesial practice, display any middle.[42] There are no institutions – *dominium* – in either: Taylor offers no exteriority; Milbank offers no interiority. Without command and without revelation, Taylor's ecstatic affirmation remains exiled in an interior castle; whereas, with Milbank's Latinity of "sociality" and "charity," how could "peace" bequeathed as "harmonious" arise, without acknowledging the *polis* intruding into such vague sociality, without acknowledging eros and agape intruding into such tamed "charity"? In both cases, without anxiety, how could we recognize the equivocal middle? In fact we have here middle *mended* as "holiness" – without that examination of the *broken* middle which would show how these holy nomads arise out of and reinforce the unfreedom they prefer not to know.

This rediscovery of the holy city, pagan, nomadic, Judaic, these mended middles over broken middle, at the end of the end of philosophy, may be witnessed as the postmodern convergent aspiration which, in effect, disqualifies the third, the middle, on which they would converge. This very converging corrupts – for in figuring and consecrating its city, this holiness will itself be reconfigured by the resource and articulation of modern domination, knowable to these postmodern ministers only as mute and monolithic sedimentation.

Postmodernism is submodern: these holy middles of round-dance, ecstatic divine milieu, irenic other city, holy community – face to face or *halachic* – bear the marks of their unexplored precondition: the diremption between the moral discourse of rights and the systematic actuality of power, within and between modern states; and therefore they will destroy what they would propagate, for once substance is presented, even if it is not "represented," however continuous with practice, it becomes procedural, formal, and its meaning will be configured and corrupted within the prevailing diremptions of morality and legality, autonomy and heteronomy, civil society and state. Mended middles betray their broken middle: antinomian yet dependent on renounced law; holy yet having renounced "ideals"; yearning for nomadic freedom, yet having renounced nature and freedom. This thinking concurs in representing its tradition – reason and institutions – as monolithic domination, as "totalitarian," while overlooking the *pre*dominance of form – abstract legal form – as the unfreedom *and* freedom of modern states, thereby falling into the trap, not of positing another "totalitarian" ideal, but of presenting a holy middle which arises out of and will be reconfigured in the all-pervasive broken middle.

This holiness corrupts because it would sling us between ecstasy and eschatology, between a promise of touching our ownmost singularity and the irenic holy city, precisely without any disturbing middle. But this "sensual holiness" arises out of and falls back into *a triune structure* in which we suffer and act as singular, individual and universal; or, as *particular*, as represented in institutions of the *middle*, and as the *state* – where we are singular, individual, and universal *in each position*. These institutions of the middle represent and configure the relation between particular and the state: They stage the agon between the three in one, one in three of singular, individual, universal; they represent the middle, broken between morality and legality, autonomy and heteronomy, cognition and norm, activity and passivity. Yet they stand and move between the individual and the state. It has become easy to describe trade unions, local government, civil service, the learned professions: the arts, law, education, the universities, architecture and medicine as "powers." And then renouncing knowledge as power, too, to demand total expiation for domination, without investigation into the dynamics of configuration, of the triune relation which is our predicament – and which, either resolutely or unwittingly, we fix in some form, or with which we struggle, to know, and still to misknow and yet to grow ... Because the middle is broken – because these institutions are systematically flawed – does not mean they should be eliminated or mended.

The holy middle corrupts because it colludes in the elimination of this broken middle – drawing attention away from the reconfiguration of singular, individual and universal at stake. Away from the ways in which under the promise of enhanced autonomy – whether for individuals or for communities – the middle is being radically undermined in a process of *Gleichschaltung* which, unlike the Nazi version, is quite compatible with the proclamation and actuality of civil society, with the proclamation and actuality of plurality, with the proclamation and actuality of postmodernity.

This public person, so formed by the union of all other persons, formerly took the name of *city*, and now takes that of *Republic* or *body politic*; it is called by its members *State* when passive, *Sovereign* when active, and *Power* when compared with others like itself.[43]

Before we orient our theology, let us reconsider this passage in relation to the city and philosophy. Neither politics nor reason unify or "totalize": they arise out of diremption – out of the diversity of peoples who come together under the aporetic law of the city, and who know that their law is different from the law of other cities – what Rousseau called "power," and which we now call "nation." Philosophy issues, too, out of this diremption and its provisional overcoming in the culture of an era – without "disowning" that "edifice," it (philosophy) steps away to inspect its limitations, especially when the diremptions fixated in the edifice have lost their living connections.[44] We should be renewing our thinking on the invention and production of edifices, that is, cities, apparently civilized within yet dominating without – not sublimating those equivocations into holy cities. For the modern city intensifies these perennial diremptions in its inner oppositions between morality and legality, society and state, and the outer opposition, so often now inner, between sovereignty and what Rousseau called "power," and which we call "nations and nationalism"; and which recurs, compacted and edified, in Levinas as "war," as the spatial and temporal nomad in Taylor, as the nomadic city which "remembers all the victims" in Milbank.

Look again at the labyrinth on Taylor's book, setting off this spatial and temporal nomadicism: on the cover of *Erring* we look down on a maze, and are placed not in joyous disempowerment but in panoptic dominion, notwithstanding that in the text, the maze is celebrated as "the horizontality of a pure surface," and we are said to be situated "in the midst of a labyrinth from which there is no exit."[45] Toward the end of *Beyond Secular Reason*, we are told that the nomad city means that "space is revolutionized" and no longer defensible.[46] It is worth looking more closely at these festive vulnerabilities. Taylor has put a unicursal maze on his cover – which offers no choice of route – as opposed to a multicursal maze – with choice of route. In either case, it is the beginning and the end which give authority to the way, and meaning to being lost – especially to any conceivable relishing of being lost. If the beginning and the end are abolished so that all is (divine) middle – *Mitte ist überall* – joyful erring would not be achieved nor would pure virtue "without resistance"; one would be left helpless in the total domination of the maze, every point equally beginning and end. This is to encounter not pure freedom but pure power and to become its perfect victim.

Violence lurks in the labyrinth. The "imagination in action" of holiness elevates what it would exclude as its Other: so that violence migrates into the nonlegitimate authority of the labyrinth, into the unmitigated penance for "all the victims" enacted by the city of salvation. This husbanded violence becomes explicit when Taylor moves to "reframe" postmodernisms.[47] He summons the paintings of Anselm Kiefer[48] as witness and presentation of "the Disaster," the central imagery of which is the pure surface of the desert and no longer of the labyrinth. Yet this pure surface, companion to the pitiless, shadowless glare of the sun, is spoilt in the texture of the canvases, with their straw detritus submerging ancient photographic shards. Alleviated enough to pass from pure silence – which would not be repetition in lamentation for new Zion, but unfigured trauma, indistinguishable from the absolute figure of the pure superficies of the labyrinth – from the shadowless surface to the shadow of spirit – figured enough to signal event, the ruined desert is still not configured enough to represent.

"Death Event"[49] is posited to rename epochality, or "Death City" to rename modernity; "origin" of new ontological political theologies which replace any comprehension of death's declension. *The Writing of the Disaster* (Blanchot), extended to the Painting of the Disaster (Kiefer, on Taylor's reading), the Filming of the Disaster (Andrey Tarkovsky's *Ivan's Childhood*),[50] and the Theology and Sociology of the Disaster (Metz, Fackenheim, Bauman) present old Athens, ancient *and* modern, as the city of death. But, by making death the meaning of the city, they return the polis to the firmament – but to stars torn out: dès-astres,[51] to cosmic disorder, to the cosmo-polis, the "world" of depredation and devastation. Presupposing this ontological disorder of the appropriation of being (*das Ereignis*), they invariably proceed to found a new city – New Jerusalem. This twin sacrality of overburdened polities – cosmic and holy – recreates the unknowing tumult of spirit out of which such authorship is nourished, without that agon of authorship which would fail toward anxiety of beginning, equivocation of the ethical, and toward apprehension, in its three senses of know, fear, arrest, of the diremption of ethics and law, configured in the middle, broken but locatable – in history, in polity, in institutions, in *dominium*. Instead, the ontology and sociology of the city of death prefers fondly to imagine its holy end of history – love and the state undirempted – in the new community.

> It is necessary that God unveil His face; it is necessary that justice and power be rejoined. There must be just institutions on this earth.[52]

Social Utopianism

The alternating of *imperium* and ecclesiology, already evident in modernist Liberation and Holocaust theology and sociology, and yielding the pattern of much postmodern intellectuality, follows from the disqualification of critique and of equivocation, so that all power is either completely bad or completely good – total domination or holy community.

This idea of the "autonomous community" haunts the temporal as well as the divine state. Formerly figured as the collective interest of all, as the state as such, "the community" now seems to leave the predicament of the boundary to the larger or smaller, unspecified, political entity, so as to guard its benignity and magnanimity – its loveful cohesion: the European "community," the "community" charge, the Jewish "community," ethnic "community," "community" architecture, etc. This currency of "community" avoids any immediate implication of state, nation, sovereignty, representation – of power and its legitimation – yet it insinuates and ingratiates the idea of the perfectly enhanced individual and collective life. Having lost all sureness of political discrimination, we no longer know where power resides – in all institutions, in the theoretical comprehension and critique of them, in ourselves, ontically or reflexively; even less, when it is legitimate, when illegitimate, when nonlegitimate; least of all, how it is articulated and reconfigured.

Yet the more the middle is eroded, the more its illusion proliferates. Irreducibly singular and potentially universal, but never holy, the individual is the site of the agon between the particularity of civil society, the precarious legitimation or nonlegitimate authority of the middle, and the moral allegory of the state. With no "reality," we have as "individuals" only a perpetually embattled and changing actuality.

The arguments for postmodern architecture, and for community architecture, aim to redress the faults and limitations of modernism in architecture, understood as totalizing domination, by restoring the middle, whether the "human" – color, scale, diversity, and play – of postmodernism; or the "public realm" or "civic space" of community architecture. Both captivated by the premodern, postmodern architecture plunders it with gleeful pastiche, community architecture plunders it with brutal sincerity, for fixed styles or immediate vernaculars. Yet these attempts to restore the middle have the effect of undermining it. For, once again, they involve the projection of social utopianism on to architectural practice; the projection of a holy, a princely, middle which will again be reconfigured by the broken middle it seeks to heal. The more the illusory independence of the individual and "the community" is figured in a middle – architecture – the more vulnerable that *topos* will become to the animus of social dystopia; while the reconfiguration of individual and state proceeds apace without recognition in its imbricated legal space.

Even the neo-modernist "New Architecture"[53] of Foster, Rogers, and Stirling, especially of their unexecuted plans, shares the declared ambition of postmodern and community architecture to re-create the public realm, to restore the commonwealth in a way which implies a classical, substantial idea of social virtue, while acknowledging the declaimed "plurality" and "diversity" of modern life. They share this ethical impulse with the now discredited Modern Movement and the principles of the international style. In the famous statement by Hitchcock and Johnson, in 1922, the style, defined as the "frame of potential growth," is distinguished by three principles – volume or enclosed space, not mass or solidity; regularity, not axial symmetry or balance; and the infamous proscription of applied decoration or ornament, and the emphasis on the intrinsic elegance of materials, technical projection, and fine proportions.[54] These principles, considered anti-aesthetic, were "sanctioned" in structure and design by their affinity to Gothic and classical precedent, and by modern living, "the proletarian superman of the future,"[55] an ominous phrase, to which Le Corbusier will add "superwoman." The "loss of ornament" is admitted to be ambiguous, and to refer to incidental, applied ornament which is replaced by surface itself as ornament. Such building is "sociological": the hierarchy of functions is evident – with the universal given priority over the particular, and style over local tradition.[56]

In more metaphysical vein, the theoretical writings of Mies van der Rohe and of Le Corbusier display a comparable philosophical reflection on reinventing architecture by combining classical virtue with modern will-to-power, in both cases drawing, explicitly or implicitly, on Aquinas and Nietzsche, to produce a new architectural ethic. Reading Nietzsche's emphasis on the remorseless discipline of "giving form" as convergent with the Thomist emphasis on the analogy between God and the world and intra-convertibility of the beautiful and the good, Mies argues for a "super-rational" architecture in self-conscious answer and opposition to the examination of modern cultural alienation which he knew in the writings of Simmel and Guardini.[57] From Francesco Dal Co's presenting of Mies' "Notes," it appears that he considered it the responsibility of the architect to find a *tertium quid* between non-form and excess of form, both disturbing features of modern life.[58]

Le Corbusier, by contrast, declaims and enacts a Zarathustrian neo-Thomism in his book *The Decorative Art of Today* (1925), seeking to educate by pointed paradox which restores the question of meaning to the reader.[59] Proclaiming the "elimination of the equivocal," the text unravels the equivocality in this idea of elimination in view of the "inexplicability of cause" yet "explanation of the concatenation" which underpins an ethics that would provoke activity, the provisional assumption of "mastery," yet cherish the awareness of mystery.[60] Thanking St Thomas for a rational faith – equally sense of touch and truth – Le Corbusier's declarative persona would insinuate "productive morality," which, as it were, opposes the *ressentiment* against time, "the cult of the souvenir,"[61] and, like Zarathustra, would set up new law tables:

If some Solon imposed these two laws on our enthusiasm:

THE LAW OF RIPOLIN
A COAT OF WHITEWASH

We would perform a moral act: *to love purity –* !

We would improve our condition: *to have the power of judgement . . .*

Everything is shown as it is . . . you will be *master of yourself.*[62]

"Whitewash" can mean to clean and clarify, but it can also mean to suppress, to hide the truth; and this equivocation emerges when premodern "whitewash," geared to a culture, is driven out by the culture of cities, and is prescribed to restore the criterion of rule, illustrated revealingly by the "three black heads" of a tribesman and his two sons "against a white background," captioned "fit to govern, to dominate."[63] The book concludes with the reiteration of the command "to eliminate the equivocal," the call to activity, backed now by this inapplicable, equivocal history – the modern citizen called to activity and to mastery.[64]

These quintessential delineations of architectural modernism based on active excellence, on virtue, display an ethical impulse disturbingly analogous to that underlying neomodernist, postmodernist, and community architecture. Mies van der Rohe and Le Corbusier aimed to solve the political problem in metaphysical terms, producing social utopianism by reproducing the illusion of architectural independence. They deliberately but unselfconsciously posited holy middle over broken middle. Yet no systematic exploration of the discrepancy between these evident ethical intentions or meanings and the resultant built form or architectural configuration has been sustained. Instead, new architecture remains caught in the same discrepant illusion of meaning convergent with configuration, and will know no reason for the inevitable repetition of their alienation.

While Gustav Landauer defined every historical event as "an ever-renewed deliverance from a topia (existing order) by a utopia, which arises out of it,"[65] this anarchist perspective, if reconstructed, inadvertently implies a general law: that one day's utopia will become the following day's dystopia. For architecture, this means that it – architecture – can never be what it is to be: called to create place, "topia," it always also creates no-place: "*u-topos.*" Whether ideal place, utopia, or its inversion, dys-topia, architecture deals in the illusion and disillusion attendant on its responsibility for conceiving and executing an independent rational order, a responsibility which has only been enlarged when it comes to mean not only building or built form but its relation to immediate context and environment – the creation of "place" as much as sculpture and function in space. Architecture is the form of this illusion of rational independence, and the most synaesthetic, most exposed bearer of social u-topianism. It must mend the middle – heal the split between civil law and the state, yet it is itself also the middle, and stands for, represents the middle: the built form of institutions, such as, house, school, market, corporation; and of local administration, such as, hospital, police station. Architectural form configures our cognitive activity and normative passivity, distinguishable and indistinguishable from cognitive passivity and normative activity. This omnipresent form of nonlegitimate domination – some architecture, not all – has been moved into a position where it requires legitimation, and yet, this dangerous politicization has been deflected yet again by aestheticization. The princely middle elevated ostensibly to assuage the ravages of modernism ensures that the range of argument about architecture remains "utopian."

Karl Mannheim separated "ideology" from "utopia": interested and unobjective, "ideology" seeks to stabilize dominant interests, while "utopia" is a directive for action – it seeks to transform society by exaggerating existing elements which inherently tend to negate it.[66] Mannheim conceded the difficulty of applying this distinction in practice, for the very interest it is meant to clarify may itself determine judgment.[67] But it is also true that change may stabilize pre-existing dominance, and stability may serve utopian interests. Yet the distinction conceptualizes the negations out of which utopia in general and, *a fortiori*, architectural utopia, arise – of posited totality and of static actuality. In positing the theoretical separation of the ideological from the utopian impulse, the distinction may conceptualize the peculiar burden of architectural autonomy, its social utopianism, bearing the rational ideal aloft, while at the same time isolated from ideological reconfiguration which may be legitimized, *ex silentio*, without aesthetic or representation, in un-assuming legal and social identifications.

> Religion remains the ideal, unsecular consciousness of its members because it is the ideal form of the *stage of human development* which has been reached in this state.[68]

In Marx's account of ideology, which Mannheim was attempting to neutralize, the utopian element is itself an indicator of the configuration of domination. In a Christian state, prior to the political emancipation of religion, the state itself, in order to fulfill its religious pretensions, must either become "the bailiff of the Catholic Church," i.e. become powerless; or, true to the Holy Spirit of the Scriptures, be dissolved as a state, i.e. give up its power.[69] Whether toward Church or toward sect, the "Christian" state as such has no future. Once religion is relegated to civil society, individuals become religious as an expression of their true but separated life – an imaginary communal sovereignty, now lived as the warring sovereignties of civil society.[70] Utopia – imagined or built – moves into the broken middle and indicates the changed relation of the individual to herself.

> Political emancipation is at the same time the *dissolution* of the old society on which there rested the power of the sovereign, the political system [*Staatswesen*] as estranged from the people. The political revolution is the revolution of civil society. What was the character of the old society? It can be characterized in one word: *feudalism*. The old civil society had a *directly political* character, i.e. the elements of civil life such as property, family, and the mode and manner of work were elevated in the form of seignory, estate and guild to the level of elements of political life. In this form they defined the relationship of the single individual to the *state as a whole*, i.e. his *political* relationship, his relationship of separation and exclusion from the other components of society. For the feudal organization of the life of the people did not elevate property or labour to the level of social elements but rather completed their *separation* from the state as a whole and constituted them as *separate* societies within society. But the functions and conditions of life in civil society were still political, even though political in the feudal sense, i.e. they excluded the individual from the state as a whole, they transformed the *particular* relationship of his guild to the whole state into his own general relationship to the life of the people, just as they transformed his specific civil activity and situation into his general activity and situation. As a consequence of this organization, the unity of the state, together with the consciousness, the will and the activity of the unity of the state, the universal political power, likewise inevitably appears as the *special* concern of a ruler and his servants, separated from the people.
>
> The political revolution which overthrew this rule and turned the affairs of the state into the affairs of the people, which constituted the political state as a concern of the whole people, i.e. as a real state, inevitably destroyed all the estates, corporations, guilds and privileges which expressed the separation of the people from its community. The political revolution thereby *abolished* the *political character of civil society*. It shattered civil society into its simple components – on the one hand *individuals* and on the other the *material* and *spiritual elements* which constitute the vital content and civil situation of these individuals. It unleashed the political spirit which had, as it were, been dissolved, dissected and dispersed in the various cul-de-sacs of feudal society; it gathered together this spirit from its state of dispersion, liberated it from the adulteration of civil life and constituted it as the sphere of the community, the *universal* concern of the people ideally independent of those *particular* elements of civil life. A person's *particular* activity and situation in life sank to the level of a purely individual significance. They no longer constitute the relationship of the individual to the state as a whole. Public affairs as such became the universal affair of each individual and the political function his universal function.[71]

The breaking of the middle is exposed here in its main configuration: the fact and fiction of the "individual" who emerges split – naturalized as "egoism" and allegorized as "ethical." For "the perfection of the idealism of the state was at the same time the perfection of the materialism of civil society."[72] On the one hand, political community is generally reduced to the means for the commerce of civil society yet, on the other, civil freedom will be abandoned should it conflict with political life.[73] In feudalism, statuses, privileges, guilds, formed the middle of legal estate, and determined individuals as their particulars, as *members* of the middle, which, corporatively, faced the separated state; with the dissolution of this feudal middle, the "individual" emerges with two separate lives: merely particular existence outside any middle, and yet bearer of the universalist aspirations, of citizenship, enjoyed by each – enjoying, that is, the arbitrary fate of civil society, and "active" in the increasingly imaginary state.

When all *dominium* or law is simply equated and indicted as "total," the very diversity of its articulation disappears so that critique is disqualified. For there are many conceivable combinations of the "autonomy" of civil society and the "autonomy" of the state, and what would otherwise appear only as a change in quantity or as an inverse ratio – an increase in one balanced by a decrease in the other, e.g. more freedom of civil society, less state control – may be in effect a reconfiguration, which matches the "increase" in individual "autonomy" with increase in powers of the police state. Attention to the agon of the middle where individuals confront themselves and each other as particular and as universal yields the dynamics always at stake in any comprehension of diremption – the articulation and reconfiguration of activity and passivity, norm and cognition, morality and heteronomy.

Community architecture bears all the marks of ecclesiology – it seeks to reclaim and abolish the middle. The kingdom of God is presented here more uninhibitedly than in any other new political theology.

This unequivocal chart appears in a book called *Community Architecture: How People are Creating Their Own Environment,*[74] the cover of which has an image of Prince Charles, shoulder-to-shoulder with a casually dressed architect whose emphatic *élan* of arm and hand and pursed lip contrasts with the Prince's corrugated forehead and incredulous, gaping mouth. These two gesticulating figures appear free-standing against a background montage of framed photos – "ordinary" women discussing over a table covered with architectural plans, and three laboring lads in what looks like an "ordinary" backyard.

The differences here charted between "conventional" and community architecture fall into simple oppositions, respectively, between passive versus active user; imperious versus companionable expert; manipulation of people versus manipulation of the system; large versus small scale; wealthy versus decaying location; single versus plural functions; international style versus the regional and vernacular; cold technology versus convivial technology; static versus flexible product; profit, financial and political, versus quality of life; hieratic versus demotic operation; and, finally, totalitarian ideology versus pragmatic mutuality.

To the community is implicitly imputed the ideal speech situation of a small-scale democratic society, with no clash of particular and general will. Yet, like the idea of an emergent church, this collectivity is imagined in opposition to the political and social totality – it is regional as opposed to national – and projects the predicament of sovereignty and representation onto the presupposed environing body politic. "Community" is opposed to *imperium* as a type of noncoercive social cohesion maintained not only without politics but without sociology – without addressing the question of how its authority is legitimized. For that is achieved by the opposing terms on which the idea of the community relies: the charismatic appeal of the Prince is smuggled in iconologically to distinguish the community from the type of legal-rational domination exemplified by impersonality, bureaucracy, technology. The personality of the Prince stands in for the middle which is also personified as the architect: legitimizing charisma rubs its contraposto regal shoulder with its intermediary, the newly humbled expert. Attention is thereby deflected from the inevitable reproduction of all those oppositions charted *within* any "community" which presupposes the separation between civil society and the state at its base – appearing here as the opposition between the "needs" of "people" and the imperatives of the middle, "architecture," conceived, however, as continuous with the interests of the bureaucratic, technological, autonomous state.

While the longed-for community is fixed and allegorized in the Prince, monarch-to-be serving apprentice as the genie of every locality, "the evils" of both civil society *and* dirempted polity are merged in the figure of "the architect," who takes on the separated life of each "citizen" – as a particularity, vulnerable and remorseless, and as aspirant universality, frail and self-fearing. The dirempted middle is further eroded as its princely illusion proliferates, for the ethical root of the collectivity – its potentiality – is further torn out from civil egoism by a conceptualization and iconization which reclaims an ethical immediacy for "the people" and yet projects its egoism, its dirempted particularity and universality, on to its Other, "the architect." This is to avoid any anxiety of beginning – any reconsideration of our general initiation into both sides of the equivocation, and thus to preclude any transformation or education. Instead it is the architect who is to learn, not "the people." Such imaginary liberation from "total" domination amounts to legitimation of a new architectural utopianism – where the celebration of the regal middle takes place at the wake of the disenfranchised "people."[75]

The two new kinds of political theology – the theological "imagination in action" and the architectural imagination "in practice" – would resist "domination" by solidarity in irenic community, whether configured in the mind of God or the mortar of man. They succeed, however, in legitimizing new absolute sovereignties, which reinforce the diremption left unknown but reconfigured at its source. This political theology aspires to overcome law and its charted oppositions without the labour to recognize its own formation and implication in persisting diremption. Legality, whether in theology or architecture, understood to be violent *per se*, reappears as violent in holy or royal authority.

Against the tradition from Pavel to Kant which opposes law to grace and knowledge to faith, this work has shown that the modern congregation of the disciplines – from philosophy to architecture – *loses faith* when it renounces concept, learning, and law. Each discipline claims its "other" from concept and law – by "passivity beyond passivity," as "victims" or as "locality" – and then these pluralities demand to be unified and statically affirmed as "community." These forced reconciliations of diremption in the "new" forms of civil immediacy and holy mediation sanctify specific violence as they seek to surpass violence in general.

The more the middle is dirempted the more it becomes sacred in ways that configure its further diremption.

Notes

1 Cited in J. D. Bleich, "Is There an Ethic Beyond Halacha," in N. M. Samuelson (ed.), *Studies in Jewish Philosophy* (Lanham: University Press of America, 1987), p. 542.
2 For a recent discussion, see M. Washofsky, "Halakhah and political theory: a study in Jewish legal response to modernity," *Modern Judaism*, 93 (Oct. 1989), p. 293.
3 A. Lichtenstein, 'Does Jewish Tradition Recognize an Ethic Independent of Halacha?," from M. Fox (ed.), *Modern Jewish Ethics* (Athens: Ohio University Press), pp. 103–6.
4 See Maimonides' "Introduction to Mishneh Torah," in I. Twersky (ed.), *A Maimonides Reader* (New York: Behrman House, 1972), p. 35.
5 Lichtenstein, "Jewish Tradition," pp. 102–23; Borowitz, in Samuelson (ed.), *Studies in Jewish Philosophy*, pp. 489–505.
6 Borowitz, "The Authority of the Ethical Impulse," p. 500.
7 Ibid., p. 495.
8 Ibid., p. 503.
9 Ibid., p. 502.
10 "Authority and Reason contra Gadamer," in *Studies in Jewish Philosophy*, pp. 161–90; "Modern Jewish Philosophy," in A. A. Cohen and P. Mendes-Flohr (eds), *Contemporary Jewish Religious Thought* (New York: Free Press), pp. 629–34.
11 "The End of Philosophy and the Task of Thinking," *On Time and Being*, trans. Joan Stambaugh (New York: Harper and Row, 1977), pp. 55–78.
12 "Time and Being," pp. 15–22, tr. pp. 15, 19, 21, and "The End of Philosophy," p. 66.

On Time and Being: "The Thing," *Poetry, Language, Thought*, trans. A. Hofstadter (New York: Harper and Row, 1977), pp. 172, 173, tr. pp. 179, 180. See Rose, *Dialectic of Nihilism* (Oxford: Blackwell, 1984), pp. 72–84.

13 See, *inter alia*, *Die Heidegger Kontroverse*, ed. Jürg Altwegg (Frankfurt am Main: Athenäum, 1988). For elaboration, see Rose, "Diremption of Spirit: on Derrida's *De l'esprit*," in *Judaism and Modernity* (Oxford: Blackwell, 1993).

14 Mark C. Taylor, *Erring: A Postmodern A/theology* (Chicago: University of Chicago Press, 1984; *Altarity* (Chicago: University of Chicago Press, 1987); John Milbank, *Theology and Social Theory: Beyond Secular Reason* (Oxford: Blackwell, 1990).

15 Newman, *The Idea of a University 1852*, ed. M. J. Snaglic (Notre Dame, IN: University of Notre Dame Press, 1982).

16 Taylor, *Erring*, p. 99.

17 Ibid., p. 182.

18 Ibid., p. 169.

19 Ibid., p. 134.

20 *Theology and Social Theory*, p. 3.

21 Ibid., p. 4.

22 Ibid., p. 5.

23 Ibid., pp. 406f.

24 Ibid., pp. 6, 5–6.

25 Ibid., p. 6.

26 Ibid., p. 5.

27 Ibid., p. 391.

28 Ibid., pp. 391–2.

29 Ibid., p. 392, first set of inverted commas in original.

30 Ibid., p. 391.

31 Ibid., p. 392.

32 Taylor, *Erring*, p. 169.

33 Milbank, *Beyond Secular Reason*, p. 6.

34 Leo Strauss, *Philosophy and Law; Essays towards the Understanding of Maimonides and his Predecessors*, trans. F. Baumann (Philadelphia: Jewish Publications Society, 1987), p. 105.

35 Ibid., pp. 110, 106.

36 See, for example, F. M. Cornford, *From Religion to Philosophy* (1912, reprint, Brighton: Harvester, 1980), ch. IV, pp. 124–53.

37 J. Harrison, *Prolegomena to the Study of Greek Religion* (1903, reprint, London: Merlin, 1980), ch. 1, pp. 1–31.

38 *Erring*, p. 134.

39 *Beyond Secular Reason*, p. 391.

40 *Erring*, p. 169; *Beyond Secular Reason*, p. 6.

41 *Erring*, p. 134; *Beyond Secular Reason*, p. 306.

42 *Erring*, p. 169; *Beyond Secular Reason*, pp. 6, 433–4.

43 Rousseau, *The Social Contract*, trans. G. D. H. Cole (London: Dent, 1973), p. 14, tr. p. 175.

44 See Hegel, *The Difference between Fichte's and Schelling's System of Philosophy*, known as the *Differenzschrift*, trans. H. S. Harris and Walter Cerf (Albany: State University of New York Press, 1977), pp. 12–13, tr. pp. 89–90.

45 Taylor, *Erring*, p. 168.

46 Milbank, *Beyond Secular Reason*, p. 392.

47 See Taylor, "Reframing Postmodernisms," in *Shadow of Spirit*, ed. Berry and Wernick (London: Routledge, 1992), pp. 11–29.

48 Compare Mark Rosenthal, *Anselm Kiefer* (Chicago: Prestel, 1987), especially "On Being German and an Artist: 1974–1980," pp. 32–75, and pp. 89–104.

49 See Edith Wyschogrod, *Spirit in Ashes: Hegel, Heidegger, and Man-Made Mass Death* (New Haven: Yale University Press, 1985).

50 See Andrey Tarkovsky's argument in *Sculpting in Time, Reflections on the Cinema*, trans. Kathy, Hunter-Blair (London: Bodley Head, 1986), especially ch. 1, "The Beginning," pp. 15–35.

51 See Maurice Blanchot, *The Writing of the Disaster*, trans. Ann Smock (Lincoln: University of Nebraska Press, 1982), e.g. pp. 2, 55.

52 Levinas, "To Love the Torah More Than God," p. 193, trans. H. A. Stephenson and R. I. Sugarman, *Judaism*, 28/2 (1979), p. 220.

53 See Deyan Sudjic, *New Architecture: Foster, Rogers, Stirling* (London: Royal Academy, 1986).

54 H.-R. Hitchcock and P. Johnson, *The International Style* (New York: Norton, 1966), p. 20.

55 Ibid., p. 93.

56 Ibid.

57 Francesco Dal Co, "Excellence: The Culture of Mies as Seen in his Notes and Books," in *Mies Reconsidered*, ed. J. Zukowsky (Art Institute of Chicago, 1986), pp. 72, 76, 78, 80.

58 Ibid., p. 81.

59 *The Decorative Art of Today*, trans. J. I. Durnett (London: Architectural Press, 1987), pp. xxi–xxvi.

60 Ibid., pp. xxvi, 175, 180–1.

61 Ibid., pp. 167, 189.

62 Ibid., p. 188.

63 Ibid., p. 190.

64 Ibid., p. 192.

65 Karl Mannheim, *Ideology and Utopia*, trans. L. Wirth and E. Shils (London: Routledge and Kegan Paul, 1966), p. 178.

66 Ibid., p. 36

67 Ibid., pp. 176–7.

68 Marx, "On the Jewish Question," *Early Writings*, trans. R. Livingstone and G. Benton (Harmondsworth: Penguin Books, 1977), p. 225.

69 Ibid., pp. 1, 224–5.

70 Ibid., pp. 225–6.

71 Ibid., pp. 196–7, tr. pp. 232–3, emphasis in original.

72 Ibid., p. 197, tr. p. 233.

73 Ibid., p. 195, tr. p. 231.

74 Wates and Knevitt, *Community Architecture: How People are Creating their own Environment* (London: Penguin Books, 1987), pp. 24–5.

75 For further discussion, see Rose, "Architecture to Philosophy – The Postmodern Complicity," *Theory, Culture and Society*, 5 (1988), pp. 357–71.

Saintliness and Some Aporias of Postmodernism
From *Saints and Postmodernism*

Edith Wyschogrod

Postmodernism's appeal to context, to social epistemology, contextualizes commonsense arguments endorsing altruistic action. It highlights the extreme situations of the twentieth century that bring into high relief the contrast between the radical altruism of those who place themselves totally at the disposal of the Other, become hostage to the Other, and those who respond with tepid benevolence or, worse yet, contribute to harming others.

At this point, after the long route of analyzing saintly life in postmodern terms has been traveled, three charges leveled against postmodernism can be weighed. The first is postmodernism's attack on the lawful, the second its assault on the past, and the third its unmaking of the subject or self. Critics of postmodernism argue that in unburdening itself of nomological structure it has thrown away morality, that in shedding the past it has created a historical vacuum upon which totalitarianism can supervene, and that in attacking the self or subject it has opened the possibility of an abuse of the Other because there is in *sensu strictu* no Other and no self to be held responsible. Is postmodernism not an expression of moral decadence rather than a solution to the problem of decline?

Consider postmodernism's antinomianism, an attack on the lawful. For some postmodernists thought is the captive of a politics that shapes it so that thought qua thought is discredited when its embedding politics is rejected. This case is stated in an extreme form by Deleuze and Guattari: "Thought as such is already in conformity with a model that it borrows from the State apparatus, and which defines for it goals and paths, conduits, channels, organs, an entire *organon*" (*TP*, p. 374). Behind this critique is the historical example of the radical injustice of National Socialism and what Deleuze and Guattari believe to be elements of Fascism that infiltrate many contemporary states. "From thought to *l'univers concentrationnaire*" appears to be the political motto of those who see in the old metaphysics an urgent need for a new politics.

Less radical is the notion that thought qua thought is "legitimated" but separated from morality, and the latter cordoned off as undesirable. Thus Sloterdijk writes:

> Under a sign of the critique of cynical Reason, enlightenment can gain a new lease on life and remain true to its most intimate project: the transformation of being through consciousness. To continue enlightenment means to be prepared for the fact that everything that in consciousness is mere morality will lose out against the unavoidable amoralism of the real. (*CCR*, p. 82)

Both types of antinomianism, that of Deleuze and Guattari and that of Sloterdijk, are manifestations of the will to ecstasy, both texts the work of postmodernism in its empirical ecstatic form. The will to joy, the "transformation of being through consciousness," is, for Sloterdijk and Deleuze and Guattari, the "telos" of metaphysics. Joy is to be enhanced by contributions from the arsenal of modernism so that the machinic is harnessed to the flesh. Such ecstasy is expressed, for example, in the new worldwide culture of music – rock, new wave, and their successors – in which the body as a whole is both sensorium and medium for aesthetic expression. I argued that Deleuze and Guattari's antinomianism derives from an account of desiring production that conceals a metaphysical monism beneath the differential and pluralistic character of their version of the real. I shall not go over this ground again except to notice that the single-minded quest for ecstasy by way of a hidden monism is bound up with the coercive seam in the otherwise an-archic postmodernism of Deleuze and Guattari.

The character of Sloterdijk's antinomianism is the result not only of a broken metaphysics but also of a broken politics in that two quite different and opposing political wills are the starting point of his work. On the one hand, there is the postmodern expression of the will to joy derived from Nietzsche; on the other, there is as the work's immediate backdrop, the historical experience of a National Socialism that Sloterdijk unequivocally rejects. His use of Nietzsche stemming from the first consideration is modified by the second. "It was perhaps Nietzsche's theoretical recklessness that allowed him to believe that philosophy can exhaust itself in provocative diagnoses without . . . thinking seriously about therapy" (*CCR*, p. 206).

Yet is there not a danger in the fact that postmodernism draws upon the immediate past? And once "morality" has been repudiated and eclecticism enjoined as a principle of selection, does not a strange contiguity and juxtaposition of elements become likely? Sloterdijk's repudiation of National Socialism is strongly voiced in his work. It is hard to imagine a more forceful expression of revulsion than his endorsement of Adorno's remark: " 'All culture after Auschwitz, including the penetrating critique of it, is garbage' " (*CCR*, p. 287). Yet there is a quasi-unconscious deployment of a Fascist detritus that fissures this critical discourse.[1] For example, in the context of a discussion of Hitler's SS as Death's Head (*Todtenkopf*) units, he writes:

> Fascism is the vitalism of the dead . . . embodied in [Western culture] in vampire figures that, for lack of their own life force, emerge as the living dead among the not yet extinguished to suck their energy into themselves. Once the latter are sucked dry they too become vampires. Once they become devitalized they crave the vitality of others. (*CCR*, p. 286)

Is the contagion of vampirism spread to its victims so that all become vampires? Does Sloterdijk know that vampirism was attributed to Jews and does he intentionally reverse this discourse by attributing it to the SS? If so, how can one explain the contagion that allows the attribution of the "disease" to its victims? Who are the victims? People in general, the German populace that accepted Nazism, the victims of the SS? The ambiguities of Sloterdijk's discourse persist within the ambit of his broader quest for ecstasy.

Ecstatic postmodernism's ambiguities arise in part from its failure to go deep enough and in part from its wresting from the ruins a metaphysics that will allow for the return of an all-encompassing unity not, of course, without first paying homage to topographical difference (Deleuze) or the "kynical" absurd (Sloterdijk). It is noteworthy that there is no mention, critical or otherwise, in Sloterdijk's work of the discourse of alterity beginning with the dialogical philosophies of Buber, Rosenstock-Huessy, and Marcel or of the recent analysis of this tradition by Michael Theunissen.[2] Suffice it to say that ambiguity pervades the discourse of postmodern ecstatics insofar as alterity remains an absent absence.

Julia Kristeva's work is especially disquieting in this regard. Repelled by National Socialist discourse, she is nevertheless led by the ecstatic empirical thrust of her thought to bring this discourse into the closest contiguity with the language of ecstasy or *jouissance* in a way that ultimately renders their discrimination nearly impossible. The compelling reasons she believes exist for this doubleness come to the fore in the course of her analysis.

Rejecting the inside/outside and self/other dichotomy, Kristeva develops a phenomenology of the abject, a new psychological type that experiences itself as the discarded refuse, the trash, of the psyche. Neither an object – objects provide a locus for the establishment of homologous meanings – nor an other

– others flee signification altogether – Kristeva's abject is a liminal being. "What is abject [neither object in the strict sense nor other], the jettisoned object, is radically excluded and draws me towards the place where meaning collapses" (*PH*, p. 2).[3] Thus, for example, the infant who rejects its food as separating it from its desire for the parents identifies with the loathed object, spits it out, and in ejecting the food ejects itself (*PH*, p. 3). It will, Kristeva contends, continue to see itself as something loathsome because the ego and the superego have driven it away. Hounded into exile, as it were, "from its place of banishment, the abject does not cease challenging its master. Without a sign it beseeches a discharge, a convulsion, a crying out" (*PH*, p. 2). It is not difficult to interpret saintly anorexia described by Weinstein and Bell as a version of saintly abjection. The saint can be viewed as an abject loathsome to herself/ himself but taken up into the compensatory love of God. This interpretation would reduce the role of alterity, the appeal of the other's destitution in saintly life, to an endless quest for overcoming abjection.

Kristeva argues that in abjection a certain uncanniness appears which comes to acquire independent existence but whose origin is forgotten. "[I]t harries me as something radically separate, loathsome. Not me, not that. But not nothing either. A weight of meaninglessness about which there is nothing insignificant and which crushes me. On the edge of non-existence and hallucination" (*PH*, p. 2). Compounded of Kierkegaard's dread as well as Freud's and Heidegger's *Unheimlichkeit*, Kristeva's uncanniness nevertheless differs from the uncanniness of all of them in that the abject's lack is allowed no subsistence. Thus, in her interpretation of Freud's famous case of little Hans, no sooner does the child recognize the phallic lack of his mother and perhaps himself than it is replaced with the horse, "a hieroglyph having the logic of metaphor and hallucination" (*PH*, p. 35). Little Hans creates, in the manner of the abject, what is absent. The principle of hieroglyphic substitution opens the possibility for "the subject of abjection" to develop a language of her/his own and, as such, to be "eminently productive of culture. Its symptom is the rejection and reconstruction of languages" (*PH*, p. 45).

Abjection challenges theories of the unconscious that are sustained by negation. The abject, unable to locate herself/himself, unsituated, self-exiled, becomes a "deject." Like Deleuze's nomad, Kristeva's abject asks not "'Who am I?'" but "'Where am I?'" and, like the schizorevolutionary, is "a deviser of territories" (*PH*, p. 8). To be sure, for Kristeva it is "a space that is never *one*, nor *homogeneous* nor *totalizable*" (*PH*, p. 8), a place of exclusion upon which the abject/deject will live her or his *jouissance*. Despite this affirmation of difference, Kristeva has strayed onto the pleasure plateaus of Deleuze and Guattari, onto the territory of a body without organs, a body without alterity which, on the one hand, is declared to be nontotalizable but, on the other, is the hypostatic pleroma of *jouissance*.

This homogeneity is attested in her treatment of the Other, that Other who no longer has a grip on the stray: The abject/deject is an *Auswurf* (my term), a castaway, that enters "an abominable real . . . through jouissance" (*PH*, p. 9). The *jouissance* of abjection is without alterity, the ecstasy that comes from a repeated iteration of self-loathing. Like the other empirical ecstatics, Kristeva's is a broken discourse, one in which the plenum becomes not a nihil but the abject's sick and sickening plane of *jouissance*. The abject, repugnant to others and having no "clean and proper" self, replaces the desired Other with internal fluids such as urine or blood (*PH*, p. 53). An older phenomenology of qualities – Sartre's analysis of the sticky, for example – is now applied to the abject's plane of ecstasy.[4]

Kristeva relates this analysis of psychological abjection to the history of religions, which she interprets as a nexus of collective expressions of abjection, paganism or Greek religion, Judaism and Christianity, each with its own means of purifying the abject (*PH*, p. 17). Mark C. Taylor observes that her analysis "recalls Hegel's tripartite interpretation of religion."[5] Unlike Hegel, however, the dialectical relation of Western religious patterns in Kristeva does not culminate in their resolution:

> Advancing from the Greek, through the Jewish, to the Christian, the sacred is transformed from exteriority to interiority. While the Greek suffers the sacred from without and the Jew encounters it in and through willful transgression, the Christian experiences the sacred as an outside that is inside, forever faulting his identity.[6]

For Kristeva, arguing against Hegel, the tension between Greek and Jew is not reconciled in Christianity.

The Hegelianism that is rejected in the irreconcilability of religious oppositions reenters through the backdoor in Kristeva's understanding of the historical route taken by abjection. Thus, she maintains, the move from a naive and unmediated paganism, matrilinear in character, is succeeded by biblical Judaism's fear of a matrilineal power that could threaten the paternal Law and its distribution of the categories of pure and impure (*PH*, p. 91). What is extruded, the maternal, does not disappear but builds a victimizing and persecuting machine by ascribing sanctity to a people and segregating it from the nations of the world (*PH*, p. 112). The theme of exclusion is further elaborated in the Christian conception of sin and retribution in which the righteous are cordoned off from the sinners and the whole played out as a scenario of eternal bliss and eternal punishment. This, in turn, leads to the "final" stage of Kristeva's dialectic: "the catharsis par excellence called art" that purifies and is "destined to survive the historical forms of religion" (*PH*, p. 17). Sin, Kristeva claims, is transcended when, as Nietzsche revealed, it becomes integral to the beautiful (*PH*, p. 122).

Although Kristeva's discourse breaks with Hegel on the matter of the dialectical sublation of the religious moments, she replicates Hegel's ordering of Western religions. In his analysis of Hegel's early theological writings, Mark C. Taylor shows that, for Hegel, Old Testament religion is not merely dialectically overcome but despised as representing the nadir of Spirit. Hegel declares: "'How were [the Jews] to recognize divinity in a man, poor things that they were, possessing only a consciousness of their misery, of the depth of their slavery, of their opposition to the divine?'"[7] Yet, for Kristeva, because abjection is subversive, there is a certain *pli* or fold in her analysis that distinguishes it from the early Hegel's description of Judaism as the religion of stones and fecal matter.[8] Despite this difference, Kristeva writes:

> In opposition to Apollonian . . . Greek corporeality, flesh here signifies according to two modalities: on the one hand close to Hebraic flesh (*basar*), it points to the body as eager drive confronted with the law's harshness; on the other it points to a subdued body, a body that is pneumatic since it is spiritual, completely submersed into divine speech in order to become beauty and love. (*PH*, p. 124)

Biblical monotheism, argues Kristeva, is to be exorcised by a Christianity that is the penultimate stage before the *jouissance* of aesthetic quietism.

There is in this account a forgetting of postmodernism's perspectivalism. Kristeva fails to notice that the Exodus, for example, may have been interpreted by classical Christianity through the symbolics of prefigurement, but it is an epic of freedom for Jews and, to a considerable extent, has become so for Afro-Americans against the ground of a quite different metaphysics.

The matter is even more complex because Kristeva goes on to declare that it is one of Christianity's insights that both "perversion and beauty" belong to the same libidinal economy. It would seem that, for Kristeva, the multiple modes of expressing abjection are determined not by moral concerns when these concerns are proscriptive but, as in the case of Genet, through the transformation into beauty: "[S]in is the requisite of the Beautiful. . . . the Law of the Other becomes reconciled with Satan" (*PH*, p. 122). It is the *aestheticization* of the Law that is, for Kristeva, therapeutic both at a psychological and at a metaphysical level rather than the surrender of nomological discourse to the discourse of the Other. The joker or wild card (Derrida), the simulacrum (Deleuze and Guattari) that might be invoked as tropes for the saint as quick-change artist of social and personal transformation could be borrowed by Kristeva to describe the being that belongs to the Other. But the implication to be drawn from Kristeva's account of the Other is that the Other is a floating signifier to be transformed into beauty. Her discussion of the abject is a double discourse: An explanation of abjection in its many forms but also a subtle endorsement of it through a certain break in the discourse of abjection.

This manifests itself in a particularly puzzling way in her extended analysis of Céline.

Céline's anti-semitism, and Kristeva's treatment of it, is an exceedingly complex matter, and my remarks will bear only on its relevance for the problematics of saintly life. There is, on the one hand, Kristeva's exposure of Céline the "Fascist ideologue" who rages against Jewish monotheism and displaces this by Fascist mystic positivity. And yet Kristeva, through an almost invisible conceptual slippage, avers: "It is impossible not to hear the liberating truth of [Céline's] call to rhythm and joy, beyond the crippling constraints of a society ruled by monotheistic symbolism and its political and legal repercussions" (*PH*, p. 179). To be sure, "the liberating truth" is bound up with "the deadliest of fantasies" (*PH*, p. 174), as Céline's pamphlets show. Yet she asks:

> Do not all attempts . . . at escaping from the Judaeo-Christian compound . . . to return to what it has repressed, converge on the same anti-Semitic Célinean fantasy? [T]his is because . . . the writings of the chosen people have selected a place, in the most determined manner, on that untenable crest of manness seen as symbolic fact – which constitutes abjection. (*PH*, p. 180)

The entire discourse of the chapter "Ours to Jew or Die" is written with an abhorrence of Fascism that is at the same time a lure, a willing subjection to its seductive power not only to disclose it but to speak the transgressive and unspeakable discourse with pleasure through the mouth of another.

Yet it could be argued there is a concept of saintly existence that shows itself in Kristeva's work apart from her analysis of abjection. Lacan, she insists, connects saintliness to the psychoanalyst (*PH*, p. 27), the witness to abjection, to its decoding, and to its cathartic explosion in the patient. If this is the case, the further question must be asked, "Who is the analyst?" Not the psychoanalyst but the writer of genius is the "master" analyst, who reaches the point where writing transcends itself: "the sublime point at which the abject collapses in a burst of beauty that overwhelms us – and that 'cancels our existence' (Céline)" (*PH*, p. 210). It is the writer, Céline, who appropriates the discourse of abjection in its most violent form and who transforms it into beauty.[9]

It is not inapposite in the context of Kristeva's transcendence of abjection through its aestheticization to recall Kierkegaard's admonition to "reason from existence not towards existence, whether moving in the palpable realm of fact or in the realm of thought" (*PH*, p. 31). The consequences for existence of this aestheticization cannot be ignored for the Other since abject/deject is not only "a hieroglyph" marked by the sign of negation but a flesh and blood existent for whom this negation is nihilation.[10] To bestow a shadowy existence on the Other is to exert the power of negation.

Kristeva's docetism, her failure to treat the Other as a creature of flesh and blood, leads indirectly to a certain general inattentiveness to the distribution of discourse, to the question, "Says who?" the liberating question of postmodernism posed compellingly by Foucault and Sloterdijk among others. She explicates the abjection of paganism, Judaism, and Christianity and the abjection described in Céline's Fascist idiolect but forgets that men and women who wield or lack power, who kill or are killed, are both the objects of these discourses and their controllers. In the context of contemporary history, to be an abject of another, not least of all an abject in the writing of Céline, is to be implicated not in a speculative but in an actual chain of death.

The preference for a joy beyond pleasure, for an ecstaticism that is different from solicitude, shows itself elsewhere in Kristeva's work, in her preference for the madonnas of Giovanni Bellini over those of Leonardo Da Vinci on the grounds that, in the distanced look of Bellini's Virgin, "unlike the solicitude in Leonardo's paintings, [there is] ineffable jouissance" (*DL*, p. 347).[11] The face of the Virgin is averted, the gaze is "never center[ed] in the baby."[12] It seems that there is in Bellini's madonnas "a shattering, a loss of identity, a sweet jubilation where she is not."[13]

Ecstaticism does not require temporal difference and deferral but a reinstatement of that very present that postmodernism has rejected. Yet, in repudiating both classical and modern metaphysics to which they attribute a logic of presence, Deleuze, Kristeva, and other French postmodernists posit difference *en principe*. This conflict can come to the surface in the work of Peter Sloterdijk, for example, because, by refusing to totally reject the intellectual aims of the Enlightenment, he is less embarrassed by signs of the logic of presence in his work than are most postmodernists. Thus in the last sentence of the *Critique of Cynical Reason* he concludes: "[C]ourage can suddenly make itself felt as a euphoric clarity or a seriousness that is wonderfully tranquil within itself. It awakens the present within us. In the present, all at once, awareness climbs to the heights of being . . . No history makes you old" (p. 547). To gain the pleromatic fullness of ecstasy requires a present that forgets history for the reasons discussed earlier, because who in the century of man-made mass death could attain ecstasy without amnesia?

The Problem of Saintly Individuation

The discourse of postmodernity is a language of desire, its economy a libidinal economy, its ethic often bound up with a conatus toward satisfaction. In considering postmodern "metaphysics," differential forces, quanta of power or desire, are stipulated but there is considerable variation in the way these forces have been interpreted by postmodern thinkers. Desire may be described in terms of difference and yet may function as a hypostatic plane of libidinal satisfaction, not seamless yet without alterity. I have argued that the reverse Platonism of Deleuze attempts to maintain difference while sublating the Other. Where lack or negation appears to be mandated, phantasmatic being is made to take its place in order to maintain the differential character of discourse. But if postmodernism is to be differential, then alterity must be thought of in terms of lack, absence, and negation. On the other hand, it could be asked, is alterity nothing but negation and lack, a nonplace from which a certain speech, the speech of the Other, issues? And, depending on the answer, how does lack bear on the altruism of saints?

The question for saintly life is not only "Can there be difference without lack?" but also "How is the object of saintly life and action to be described in terms of lack?" Must there not be a positivity bound up with living for the Other? And if differential postmodernism, in contrast to pleromatic post-modernism, allows the nonconceptualizable Other to be the object of saintly work, must there not also be a "subject" of saintly life? If saint and Other are segregated by the radical character of alterity itself, how can the saint come into relation with the Other?

For there to be a saint who initiates action, who relieves suffering, who experiences compassion, there must in some sense be singular beings who are saints. Yet both ecstatic and differential postmodernisms are fairly well agreed that an account of the subject as an originary consciousness fails to grasp the "infrastructures" that fissure metaphysical conceptions of consciousness. The conditions for saintly life as something singular must be stipulated and the kind of ideality deconstructive analysis undermines must be detached from the term *singularity* by bringing to light the difficulties connected with individuation.

Much of the critical work has already been done in the examination of reference and exemplarity. It remains only to suggest how positive singularity can avoid the logocentric implications so penetratingly exposed by postmodernist critics. To distinguish naively construed individuality from saintly singularity, it is convenient to apply the term *particularity* to the received notion and the term *singularity* to saintly existence.

The concept of particularity is bound up with the problem of reference. To see this, it may be useful to retraverse some old ground. I argued that, for recent analytic and phenomenological philosophies of language, the question of how propositions represent the world poses difficulties resolved only at the price both of neutralizing the world's otherness and of introducing mediating notions that explain and stipulate the connections between language and the world. Phenomenological philosophy posits a consciousness that provides access to phenomena whereas analytic philosophies of language specify conditions of intralinguistic coherence. What is to count as a particular is established within the constitutive frameworks of consciousness on the one hand and propositional truth conditions on the other.

For phenomenology, particulars are constituted as such by a consciousness that is intentional. They acquire signification through their relation to a generic universal, an essence, an *eidos*, a form of unity constituted by a consciousness that bestows meaning on them by creating assemblages, a unity that conjoins both material and ideal objects. Particulars are what is presided over by the eidos.[14] Because the eidos is something purely conceptual, it extends over an infinity of possible particulars which "fall under it as its 'particular exemplifications.'"[15] For Quine's linguistic philosophy, particulars conform to the pattern established in his famous dictum: "To be is to be the value of a variable." One meaning that can be ascribed to particulars then is that they are whatever can be substituted for a variable in a proposition. Like Husserl, Quine envisions particulars as multiplying ad infinitum, a problem that arises when one thinks of counterfactuals or unrealized particulars, those that did not and could not come into being. Both Quine and Husserl have a horror of the infinite – of the runaway flow of particulars – and so have recourse to universals.[16] For both Husserl and Quine, particulars derive their meaning from the constructs that regiment them and are homogeneous with one another with respect to the properties stipulated by the ordering construct. Particulars are monadic in a double sense: first, as part of what is heuristically united by the construct, for example, the relation of the eidos of red to the assemblage of red objects brought together by it (Husserl), and second, as freestanding wholes themselves – at least when they are time-tied particulars – in the sense of being numerically distinct from one another (Quine).

On either view of particularity, saints could be interpreted as particulars, as living specimens of the virtues of compassion, generosity, and courage. The notions of exemplarity they presuppose have already been subjected to extended criticism. In the present context, it suffices only to notice that, were the relation between universal and particular, however liberally construed, to determine the character of saintly acts, saintly behavior could be thought of as a series of acts, if not homogeneous, at least commensurable with one another, regimented by the essence of saintliness, and saints themselves could be thought of as members of an ideal social whole: a tribe, a militia, or a club.

How is saintly singularity to be described if we are not to fall back into some premodern or modern notion of particularity? How is the Other to be construed if we are not to resort to the notion of a larger whole characterized by suffering and privation? How then is the singularity of the Other to be preserved if it can be preserved? Can the Other simply be without further elaboration the One who I am not?

"Negativity Is Not Transcendence"

I have repeatedly stressed the extirpation of lack in ecstatic postmodernism.[17] The reason for this insistence is *not to show that the Other is what I am not*, for this only reinstates the Other as another myself, as the obverse of my fullness and positivity. Such a relationship is one in which I am interchangeable with the Other so that the arena of social transactions is flattened out into a single terrain of homogeneous parts. When this situation is pushed to the extreme, as it is in Blanchot's novel *Aminadab*, as Levinas shows, it becomes absurd:

> Between the persons circulating in the strange house where the action takes place, where there is no work to pursue, where they only abide — that is, exist — this social relationship becomes total reciprocity. These beings are not interchangeable but reciprocal, or rather they are interchangeable because they are reciprocal. And then the relationship with the Other becomes impossible.[18]

If neither I nor the Other is *constituted* as lack, the Other *manifests* negativity as a destitution that is "parasitic" upon lack. For the saint, need is expressed in the Other's very existence as well as in concrete manifestations of suffering through war or natural catastrophe, through poverty, illness, or psychic injury. Every Other is different from a "self" that is seen as a hollowed-out interiority (Levinas), excessive expenditure (Bataille), desiring production (Deleuze), or a textual marginality, the result of spatial deflection and temporal delay (Derrida). The negativity of destitution is not a secondary "phenomenon" of lack but something primordial, the always already riven character of suffering, and displays itself as such to the saint. This mode of negation is to be distinguished from the negation that belongs within the totality of a system such as the negation of labor that overcomes the resistance of material being and is dependent upon anterior material existence. Nothing whatsoever precedes the destitution of the Other.

If the Other manifests herself/himself through destitution yet does not gain identity through being an alter ego or what I am not, is there some alternative way in which the Other is distinguishable and which will, at the same time, display the Other's singularity? This brings to the fore the question of the Other's positivity, her/his *supra-ontological* or *me-ontic* being in that the Other is always already the object of a desire that exceeds any expectation of fulfillment. The saintly desire for the Other is excessive and wild. In traditional Christian theological language, the saint desires not only the welfare of the Other, the cessation of another's suffering, but also the Other's beatitude; not only to sit at the right hand of God oneself but to desire the elevation of the Other.

Recall too that saintly struggle on behalf of the Other is a wrestling with time, the mode of temporalization I called earlier "the time that is left." If saintly action is to be effective, suffering must cease before the saint's life and the life of the Other come to an end, in Jewish and Christian hagiographic language, the time of earthly life when change is still possible before the fixity of eternal life begins. The problem of an ever-diminishing time span bears directly on saintly singularity in that this singularity is definable in part as the complex of occurrences that come to pass between the beginning and the end of the saint's activity. The time of a saintly life as expressed in hagiographic narrative is the time-before-it-is-too-late that is, as Kierkegaard claims, lived forward but remembered backward. Each telling of the saint's story, so long as the tradition in which the narrative is embedded remains vital, is an ever-renewed soliciting of the narrative's addressees. To those situated within this tradition, hagiography hammers home its own mode of temporalization, the time-before-it-is-too-late.

Nowhere is this time scheme more forcefully interpreted than in Kierkegaard's tale of the subjection of choice to the compression of time. Imagine, he declares, that a child is offered the alternative of buying a book or a toy. The choice is open so long as the child is still deliberating, but once he selects the toy and the money is spent he cannot go back to the beginning before the choice was made and buy the book. Similarly the knight errant who throws his destiny in on the side of one army over another and then loses cannot turn around and offer his services to the winner. The victor can only say, " 'My friend, you are now my prisoner; there was indeed a time when you could have chosen differently, but now everything is changed.' "[19] The saintly future is the time-that-is-left in which to alleviate suffering before it is too late.

To return to the problem of singularity, the suffering of the Other is, *from the standpoint of the saint*, always greater than the intention that strives to relieve it. The singularity of the Other speaks from the non-place of the difference between the saint's desire and the Other's own suffering so that the Other's singularity is always an excess, more than can be encompassed by saintly intention. What is absolutely Other gives itself to the saint as this excess. The Other, then, as seen by the saint, is the one whose suffering exceeds any saintly effort at amelioration. This is neither a factual description, since saintly effort is often effective, nor an expression of psychological pessimism, which could only paralyze action, but rather a depiction of the infrastructure of saintly experience.

This is a crucial point missed in the theoretical accounts of altruism considered earlier. Rescher believes that moderate benevolence is an adequate response to the need of others whereas Urmson considers a more extreme saintly response desirable. For both, the need of the Other is inherently satiable. To put it otherwise, when need dries up, altruism is no longer required so that it must be generated afresh with each new situation. A postmodern reading attributes to the Other an unceasing impingement upon saintly existence.

Saintly singularity *as seen from the standpoint of the saint's "flock" and addressees* takes as its starting point the visible manifestations of saintly desire for the Other, the saint's acts of generosity and compassion. From this perspective, saintly singularity is desire released from the bonds of a unifying consciousness, a desire that is unconstrained and excessive yet guided by the suffering of the Other. Despite the pain of saintly existence, the addressees of saintly discourse (if not always the saint) see the Other not as a weight or burden but as light, to borrow the oxymoron of Kundera, with the unbearable lightness of being.[20] In actuality, no saint can always carry such generosity through to the end.

I have also maintained that postmodern saintliness is not premodern saintliness, because inscribed in postmodern saintly life is the weight of recent history. Hagiography, when written in the idiolect of the postmodern saint, bears the trace of the rational and egalitarian suppositions of the Enlightenment as well as the force of the Kantian moral law and the criticisms and appropriations of it in utilitarian and pragmatic ethics. If liberal theories of justice (Rawls), phenomenological ethics (Scheler), and contemporary Kantianism (Gewirth) referred to in this study fail to persuade, it will not do to return nostalgically and uncritically to an older ethos. Nostalgia is amnesia, a wiping out of both the sea-changes brought about by recent history and the sins of older communities such as slavery in ancient Greece and the persecution of Jews, Moslems, and heretics by medieval Christianity. This backward thrust is an example of what I called earlier the myth of the tabula rasa and leads to impossible dreams such as Alasdair MacIntyre's hope for the restoration of a monastic ethic or a return to an Aristotelian version of the good life as one governed by the classical virtues.

The postmodern saintly life as a new path in ethics is not a proposal to revert to an older hagiographic discourse, least of all to hide behind its metaphysical presuppositions. It is instead a plea for boldness and risk, for an effort to develop a new altruism in an age grown cynical and hardened to catastrophe: war, genocide, the threat of worldwide ecological collapse, sporadic and unpredictable eruptions of urban violence, the use of torture, the emergence of new diseases. In an epoch grown weary not only of its calamities but of its ecstasies, of its collective political fantasies that destroyed millions of lives, and of its chemically induced stupors and joys, the postmodern saint shows the traces of these disasters. Just as postmodern art forswears the aesthetic purity of modernism, just as postmodern philosophers are only now beginning to forge the instruments for bringing vastly different philosophical languages into discursive contiguity, postmodern saints derive their modes of action from their immediate modernist predecessors as well as from traditional hagiography.

Borrowing the compassionate strands of the world's religious traditions, the absurdist gestures of recent modernist art and literature, and modern technologies, saints try to fashion lives of compassion and generosity. They may remain uncanonized, for postmodernism does not encourage institutional canonization, but this does not mean that they need to go unrecognized or unappreciated. The names of saints, revealed under the "rotten sun" (Bataille) of postmodern existence, are written *sous rature*, under erasure (Derrida), and show as faint traces of alterity (Levinas) beneath the catena of altruistic actions that constitute postmodern hagiography.

Abbreviations

CCR   *Critique of Cynical Reason*, trans. Michael Eldred (London: Verso, 1988).
DL   *Desire in Language*.
PF   *Philosophical Fragments*, trans. Howard V. Hong and Edna H. Hong (Princeton, NJ: Princeton University Press, 1985).
PH   *Powers of Horror: An Essay in Abjection*.
TI   *Totality and Infinity*, trans. A. Hingis (The Hague: Martinus Nijhoff, 1978).
TP   *A Thousand Plateaus: Capitalism and Schizophrenia*, trans. Brian Massumi (London: Athlone Press, 1988).

Notes

1 The indiscriminate juxtaposition and appropriation of historical elements has been seen as a danger even in postmodern architecture. Thus Charles Jencks in *What Is Postmodernism?*, p. 20, writes that postmodern architect Leon Krier's plan for the reconstruction of Washington, DC, has been unfairly compared with the urban planning of Albert Speer under National Socialism. This characterization misses the "irreducibly plural reality" of Krier's work.

2 Michael Theunissen, *The Other: Studies in the Social Ontology of Husserl, Heidegger, Sartre, and Buber*, trans. Christopher Macann (Cambridge, MA: MIT Press, 1984), situates the notion of alterity as a critical focus in the history of phenomenological and dialogical philosophy.

3 Mary Douglas in *Purity and Danger: An Analysis of Concepts of Pollution and Taboo* (Harmondsworth: Penguin, 1970) addresses the problem of liminality in terms of the fear aroused by borderline forms of life in nonliterate societies.

4 Jean-Paul Sartre, *Being and Nothingness: An Essay on Phenomenological Ontology*, trans. Hazel Barnes (New York: Philosophical Library, 1956), pp. 600–15, analyzes such qualities as the soft, the sticky, the slimy as revelations of being.

5 Mark C. Taylor, *Altarity* (Chicago, University of Chicago Press, 1987), p. 167.

6 Ibid., pp. 167f.

7 Cited in Mark C. Taylor, *Altarity*, p. 9.

8 Ibid.

9 On violence as productive of beauty see Yukio Mishima, *Sun and Steel*, trans. John Bester (Tokyo: Kodansha International, 1970). "To combine action and art is to combine the flower that wilts and the flower that lasts forever" (p. 50).

10 That the body becomes a hieroglyph can be seen in Kafka's "The Penal Colony," trans. Willa and Edwin Muir, in Kafka, *The Complete Stories*, ed. Nahum Glatzer (New York: Schocken Books, 1976). The Harrow inscribes into the flesh of the condemned man a script "that cannot be deciphered with the eyes" but is deciphered, as it were, with his wounds (p. 150).

11 Julia Kristeva, *Desire in Language: A Semiotic Approach to Literature and Art*, trans. Thomas Gora et al. (New York: Columbia University Press, 1980), p. 247.

12 Ibid.

13 Ibid.

14 Edmund Husserl, *Experience and Judgment: Investigations in a Genealogy of Logic*, trans. James S. Churchill and Karl Ameriks (London: Routledge and Kegan Paul, 1973), p. 350.

15 Ibid.

16 Willard van Orman Quine, "Meaning and Translation," in J. A. Fodor and J. J. Katz, *Structure of Language* (Englefield Cliffs, NJ: Prentice-Hall, 1968), p. 462.

17 The title of this section is found in Levinas, *TI*, p. 40. Levinas denies the primordiality of negativity because, for him, negativity requires a being that is prior to it. Thus negativity has its place in the world of totality, for example, in connection with work that transforms the world that sustains it, but "metaphysics does not coincide with negativity" (*TI*, pp. 40–1).

18 Emmanuel Levinas, *Time and the Other*, trans. Richard A. Cohen (Pittsburgh: Duquesne University Press, 1987), p. 83.

19 Kierkegaard, *Philosophical Fragments*, p. 20 n.

20 Milan Kundera, *The Unbearable Lightness of Being* (New York: Harper and Row, 1987).

Index

CPSIA information can be obtained
at www.ICGtesting.com
Printed in the USA
JSHW061935040822
28915JS00005B/108